Fictions of Consent

RaceB4Race

RACEB4RACE: CRITICAL RACE STUDIES OF THE PREMODERN

Series editors
Geraldine Heng
Ayanna Thompson

A complete list of books in the series is available from the publisher.

Fictions of Consent

Slavery, Servitude, and Free Service
in Early Modern England

Urvashi Chakravarty

PENN

UNIVERSITY OF PENNSYLVANIA PRESS

PHILADELPHIA

Copyright © 2022 University of Pennsylvania Press

All rights reserved. Except for brief quotations used for purposes of review or scholarly citation, none of this book may be reproduced in any form by any means without written permission from the publisher.

Published by
University of Pennsylvania Press
Philadelphia, Pennsylvania 19104-4112
www.upenn.edu/pennpress

Printed in the United States of America on acid-free paper
10 9 8 7 6 5 4 3 2 1

A catalogue record for this book is available
from the Library of Congress.
ISBN 978-0-8122-5365-8

*For Jake and Phineas
And in loving memory of Koli*

CONTENTS

Note on Transcription	ix
Introduction. "Too Pure an Air for Slaves to Breath In": Slavery "Before" Slaves in Early Modern England	1
Chapter 1. Marking Service: Livery, Liberty, and Legal Fictions in Early Modern England	14
Chapter 2. "Leaue to Liue More at Libertie": Race, Slavery, and Pedagogy in the Early Modern Schoolroom	45
Chapter 3. "Am I Not Consanguineous?": The Foreign *Famulus* and the Early Modern Household	89
Chapter 4. Faithful Covenant Servants and Inbred Enemies: Indenture and Natality in *Paradise Lost*	131
Chapter 5. "Of a Bondslaue I Made Thee My Free Man": Servitude, Manumission, and the *Macula Servitutis* in *The Tempest* and Its Early American Afterlife	171
Epilogue. Fictions of Consent in the Atlantic World	198
Notes	213
Bibliography	261
Index	277
Acknowledgments	289

NOTE ON TRANSCRIPTION

Throughout the text, quotations for the most part retain their original spelling—including *i/j*, *u/v*, and *ff* for 'F'—as well as their original punctuation and capitalization. However, *vv* has been modernized to *w*, double hyphens have been changed to single, and long *s* is rendered as short *s*. In addition, I have italicized early modern titles throughout, and have given title words originally rendered entirely in capital letters with an initial capital. On occasion, I have standardized an early modern title's punctuation and capitalization in my in-text discussion for ease of reading; on those occasions, the bibliographic apparatus reflects the original title. I have also expanded contractions and fossil thorns, using square brackets for print expansions and italics for manuscript expansions. Textual insertions are marked with carets in transcription.

Fictions of Consent

INTRODUCTION

"Too Pure an Air for Slaves to Breath In"

Slavery "Before" Slaves in Early Modern England

In John Lilburne's Star Chamber case of 1638, a legal query arose around the perhaps excessive use of corporal punishment. But the problem was less the violence itself than what it registered about its recipient: that he was a slave. "Whipping," it was averred, "was painful and shameful, *Flagellation* for Slaves." The marking of English bodies in bondage, however, created a legal and intellectual dilemma, for, the record continues, "In the Eleventh of *Elizabeth*, one *Cartwright* brought a Slave from *Russia*, and would scourge him, for which he was questioned; and it was resolved, That *England* was too pure an Air for Slaves to breath in."[1] This arresting assertion would come to encapsulate a truism about slavery in England: that it could not exist.

Fictions of Consent is, nonetheless, a book about slavery in early modern England. The phrase "too pure an Air for Slaves to breath in" may be familiar to us as a summary of England's attitude to bondage. Yet it derives from a seventeenth-century Star Chamber case that cites a sixteenth-century decision of which no legal record has yet been found, in reference not to enslavement but to corporal punishment.[2] This truism, that is to say, is mediated, nostalgic, and unreliable—much like the persistent belief (and, sometimes, a strategic investment) in an early modern England innocent of slavery. The exceptionalism of English freedom was celebrated in the late sixteenth century by William Harrison, who famously insisted that "As for slaues and bondmen we haue none," for "such is the priuilege of our countrie . . . that if anie come hither from other realms, so soone as they set foot on land they become so free of condition as their masters, whereby all note of seruile bondage is vtterlie remooued from them."[3] And as recently as 2018, HM Treasury in the United Kingdom sent out a Twitter message that "Millions of you helped end the slave trade through your taxes," reminding taxpayers that they had contributed to the cost of emancipation and celebrating the fact that, as the Treasury put it, "In 1833, Britain used £20 million, 40 percent of its national budget, to buy freedom for all slaves in the Empire. The amount of money borrowed for the Slavery Abolition Act was so large that it wasn't paid off until 2015. Which means that living British citizens helped pay to end the slave trade."[4] The Treasury's message glorified the end of the slave trade even as it crucially overlooked the fact that payments were made to enslavers, not those whom they enslaved—and that the descendants of enslaved people may themselves have been paying the bill for abolition. Although it was swiftly deleted, this message illustrates the kinds of national fictions around slavery that have persisted in the past centuries. It is the roots of these fictions that this book examines, and the ways in which early modern English iterations of service and servitude laid the conceptual and rhetorical groundwork for such pervasive and lasting narrative and ideological strategies around slavery.

In the pages that follow, I explore literary and cultural representations of the kinds of servitude that informed and circumscribed the service that sixteenth- and seventeenth-century English men and women performed, and the ways in which that service in turn anticipated and allowed the forms of indenture and bondage that settled and strengthened in the New World.[5] If to talk about slavery in early modern England might appear an oxymoronic proposition, in light of the legacy of Cartwright's case, this book argues that we must understand the service that was universally enacted in terms of the slavery that nobody was supposed to embody. Thus, we come to recognize bondage not as an alien or alienable phenomenon, but as a quintessentially and fundamentally English condition and concern. Even before the development of a transatlantic trade in slaves, slavery, I suggest, informed the languages, literatures, and learned conduct of English men, women, and children. And as I shall discuss, it also framed their reception of "blackamoors" in classical and contemporary texts. My aim here is not only to demonstrate, in conversation with scholars such as Michael Guasco, that slavery was vital to England.[6] Rather, it is to argue that slavery *was* English, and moreover that service was fundamental to its conception, as the long ideological history of slavery was rooted in a set of everyday relations and sites of service—the household, the family, the schoolroom—that simultaneously, and paradoxically, seemed to refuse the possibility of servitude yet honed the fictions that underwrote and authorized bondage.

Slavery and bondage were of course not only commonplace in the early modern world; they constituted it. And early modern English audiences and readers would almost certainly have encountered discussions of slavery outside England's borders. They may have read the daring tales of kidnap, bondage, and escape that characterized captivity narratives, or responded to the petitions for the redemption of captured English travelers and sailors taken prisoner in Algiers or Barbary; they had perhaps witnessed processions of redeemed captives and enjoyed representations of slaves (ancient and early modern) on the Renaissance stage, even as they remembered the notorious cases of schoolboys, such as Thomas Clifton, who were kidnapped and impressed into playing companies; most unsettlingly, they may have known of the sixteenth-century slaving voyages of Francis Drake and John Hawkins, among others, and perhaps would eventually subscribe to the joint stock companies which, later in the seventeenth century, invited "Native Subjects" to become "Sharers" in order to finance the procurement of *"Negroes"* to "furnish his Majesties *American Plantations.*"[7] But English readers and audiences did not only confront slavery in the form of returned English captives or migrant servants; they also performed, ventriloquized, and vivified both classical and contemporary slaves as memories, specters, alternates, and intimates in the slave plays that English schoolboys read and enacted as part of their grammar school education. These plays—principally comedies by Terence and Plautus—were as ubiquitous as they were significant for their depictions of wily slaves, faithful freedmen, and errant sons learning to become citizens of Rome. But they also staged the kinds of slaves, and the forms of bondage, that would come to inform not only the characters and plots of early modern plays, but the ways in which concepts of slavery and manumission were conceived, fictionalized, and disseminated.

It is therefore this book's contention that the schoolroom, rather than the sea or the shore or the slave market, was the primary contact zone for slavery. Slavery was not a foreign phenomenon but intimately familiar, seeded in the spaces which were both quotidian and quintessentially English, for slavery, crucially, lay at the heart of the humanist curriculum.[8] The place where schoolboys must be acculturated to the conduct of elite civic participation, the grammar school classroom, was also the first point of contact for the schoolboys' encounter with figures who, convention and commonplace asserted, did not exist in England.

In a country which had "too pure an Air for Slaves to breath in," to be a slave was a legal impossibility. But to be a slave was also to malinger in a civic no-man's-land. In early modern England, everyone was (at least technically) a servant—up to and including the monarch, who was God's servant. In this service structure which characterized England and that incorporated every English man and woman, slavery was not an extreme or onerous version of service but rather its obverse, a sign that one was excluded from a civic community molded around the enactment of a service that was explicitly articulated as volitional. It is now a commonplace to remark that early modern England was a service society, that every man and woman understood his or her position in a social and political economy that was organized by the strictures, possibilities, and discourses of service. Yet an equally powerful early modern rhetoric insisted that this widespread—and effectively compulsory—service be understood not as coerced but rather as willing, volitional, consensual; as, paradoxically, "free." Rooted in the assurance which the *Book of Common Prayer* offered its readers, that God's "seruice is perfecte fredome," service must not only be performed freely; it *was* liberty.[9] An even longer philological heritage reinforced this sense: the most common term for a Roman slave was *servus*, a word which etymologically signaled not the slave's bondage but rather his deliverance from death to the saving grace of servitude.

Thus, if the fiction that England could not legally compass slavery proved a peculiarly persistent one, the only condition that authorized bondage was—ironically—masterlessness. Indeed, the first year of Edward VI's reign saw the passage of a statute which promised a ruthless but effective solution to the persistent social problem of vagrancy in early modern England. Since masterless men represented a long-standing social and economic problem, the 1547 Vagrancy Act authorized a definitive and draconian response: slavery. Under the provisions of this Act, vagabonds or "masterless men" could now be taken, legally and explicitly, into bondage. The statute is striking as much for its clear elaboration of the judicial mechanisms deployed in adjudicating a "loiterer's" bondage—two witnesses, two Justices of the Peace—as for the brutality thereby authorized, which included beating, branding, and near-starvation:[10]

> whosoeuer ... shal, eythrr like a seruing ma[n] wanting a Master, or like a begger, or after anye suche other sorte, bee lurking in any house, or houses, or loytering, or idly wander by [th]e hyghwaies side, or in streetes, in cities, towns, or vyllages, not applying the[m]selfe to some honest, and allowed arte, scyence, seruice, or labour, and so do continue by the space of three dayes, or more together, and not offer themselues to labour with any that wil take them, according to their faculty: & if no man, otherwise wil take them, do not offer themselues to woorke for meate and drinke, or after they be so taken to woorke, for

the space agreed betwixt them & their master, doe leaue their woorke out of conuenient time, or run away: that then euery suche person shall be taken for a vagabonde, and that it shalbe lawful to euerie such master offring such idle person seruice, and labour, and that beinge by him refused, or who hath agreed wyth suche idle persone, and from whom within the space agreed of seruice, the said loyterer hath run[n]e away, or departed before the end of the couenaunt betwene them, and to any other person espying the same, to bringe or cause to be brought the sayde person so lyuing idly, and loiteringly, to two of the next Justices of the peace there resiaunt, or abiding, who hearinge the proofe of the idle lyuynge of the said person by the saide space lyuing idly, as is aforesayd, approued to them by two honest witnesses, or confession of the partye, shall immediatly cause the saide loiterer to be marked with an hoat Iron in the breast, the marke of V. and adiudge the saide persone lyuynge so idly to suche presentour, to be his slaue.[11]

The Act specifically targets those "loytering . . . idly"; it is the masterless man who refuses work who, by a deliberative judicial process, will be branded and "adiuge[d]" a "slaue." Bound for a period of two years, the "saide slaue" occupies a position of true abjection; the master is entitled to feed his slave only "bread and water, or small drinke, and such refuse of meate as he shal thinke meete" and "cause the said slaue to woorke by beatinge, cheyning, or otherwise, in suche woorke and labour (how vile soeuer it be) as he shall put him vnto." The Act is clear about the status and vendibility of the slave, confirming that "any Master . . . may lett, set forth, sell, bequeath, or geue the seruice & labor of such slaues or seruantes . . . to any person or persons . . . after such lyke sort and maner, as he may doe of *any other his moueable goodes or cattels*" (emphasis added).[12] Even as the slave is relegated to "cattel" [chattel], the Act warns that should the slave "runne awaye, departe, or absente him from his said master by the space of xiiii. daies together, withoute licence" the consequences are even more severe: two Justices of the Peace may "cause such slaue, or loyterer to bee marked on the forehead, or the balle of the cheeke with an hoate Iron, with the signe of an S that he may be knowen for a loyterer, and a runne awaye"; a "seconde runninge awaye" may result in being "condempned to suffer paines of deathe, as other felons ought to doe."[13] Although the "loiterer's" slavery is in effect for "only" a period of two years, the punishment that awaits the runaway is a permanent somatic marker: an "S" for "slave," branded on the most visible part of the body, the face. The temporal limits to the slave's bondage might conceptually anticipate the chronological constraints on practices of indentured servitude in the seventeenth-century Atlantic world, yet the branding of the body in default with an immutable somatic marker portends the legibility and the permanence of a later racialized slavery.[14] But the Vagrancy Act also explicitly constructs a framework of consent: the idle vagabonds must "offer themselues to labour," delaying no more than three days, and persist in that work in order to remain free. When the alternative, however, is slavery, starvation, branding, and death, the consent enacted under these circumstances appears as little more than a fiction: if the servant does not consent, slavery must ensue.

Although the Vagrancy Act itself was repealed after two years, this book explores the persistent and pervasive fictions of consent that also organized different forms of early modern service and labor more broadly. I use the word "fiction" deliberately, to gesture to two related but distinct meanings of the term in early modern England and today. John Bullokar's *An English Expositor* (1616) glosses "fiction" as "A feined deuice, a lye," while Robert Cawdrey, in *A Table Alphabeticall* (1604), bluntly defines it as "a lie, or tale fained."[15] Yet other lexicographers appear to adopt a gentler understanding of the term. Thus, in *A Dictionarie French and English* (1593), Claudius Hollyband suggests that it is "a thing fayned, an imagination," while Edward Phillips, in *The New World of English Words* (1658), defines it as "a feigning, or inventing."[16] By using the term, therefore, this monograph emphasizes the ways in which such a "fiction" gestures on the one hand to an act of imagining, and on the other to deliberate mendacity, an attempt to authorize particular forms of servitude through categorical obfuscation. So cynically marshaled in the 1547 Vagrancy Act, these fictions of consent around early modern service, I argue, would come to authorize later forms of Atlantic bondage and slavery.

In early modern English contexts, this book proposes, such fictions of consent underpinned a range of practices which conscripted their participants into forms of service insistently framed as free: liveried patronage, household service, apprenticeship, grammar education, indentured servitude. But these fictions of consent, as I will demonstrate, also colluded with the strategies of race-making, blood, and family to secure their very real effects—and it was in so doing that they laid the foundations for the ideologies of Atlantic slavery. What I hope this book will show, therefore, is not only that slavery was an essentially English phenomenon, but that the conceptual strategies which constructed and sustained it were articulated and accrued in a range of everyday locations: crafted in the crucible of early modern literary and cultural texts, performed and ratified in pedagogical contexts, conveyed on the page and the stage, and rehearsed in legal documents as well as popular writing, private correspondence, and public discourse. Thus, the fictions of consent this book explores are polyvalent and palimpsestic, inscribed by a number of hands rather than a singular agential force. It is not only their apparent creators—the magistrate, the jurist, the patron, the master, the playwright, or the dramatic character—who determine their dissemination and dispersal, but also their seeming mediators and inheritors: family servants, contracted apprentices, playgoing audiences, indentured servants. Across this book, forms of state authority, authorial imagining, and audience absorption intertwine in recording, receiving, and ratifying the fictions of consent that could—and would—underwrite slavery.

There is, of course, another powerful kind of fiction at work, in early modern England as today: the fiction of race. To state that race is a fiction is not to suggest that its effects are illusory.[17] Rather, it is to underscore that the operations of race are as strategic and deliberate as its consequences are deeply felt. As a function of power, designed both to signify and to justify subjection, race-making colludes with other kinds of fictions to articulate its "strategic essentialisms."[18] Imtiaz Habib points out that "the first recorded use of the word 'blackamore' (blak e More) to signify an African ('born in Barbary') occurs in 1547"—the same year as the Vagrancy Act.[19] A watershed moment in the history of early modern blackness thus suggestively coincides with a striking edict authorizing early modern slavery. I invoke this association not to conflate blackness with slavery, nor to attempt to "determine" the provenance of racialized slavery. Rather, the suggestive temporal confluence here, I propose, posits the *collusion* of early modern fictions of consent, such as those evident in the 1547 Vagrancy Act, with the fictions of race. As I will show in this book, whether it is in addressing the (il)logics of livery as a legible signifier of servitude, reimagining the racial register of Roman slaves in the grammar schoolroom, or situating the household servant within the frameworks of both family and slavery, early modern fictions of consent were coextensive with, and constitutive of, fictions of race. As the coarticulation of service and servitude was increasingly limned by the logics of family, race, and blood, it anticipated the racial and rhetorical strategies of Atlantic slavery—and simultaneously secured its futures.

Although the last two decades have witnessed increasing critical interest in early modern service, the fact that few scholars have explored the contingencies and implications of the 1547 Vagrancy Act as fully as might be warranted gestures to a larger scholarly as well as popular lacuna around early modern slavery.[20] This gap may seem to reflect the legal lacuna around slavery in early modern England, an omission that—as has been pointed out in relation to the 1587 case of the Portuguese physician Hector Nunes, who discovered that he had no redress under English law when the enslaved African he had purchased from an English sailor refused "utterly" to "tarry and serve him"—might paradoxically attest as much to the *presence* of slavery in early modern England as to its illegality.[21] But despite the limited critical enquiry into the conditions and contingencies that attended the possibility of slavery, there has been renewed scholarly attention to the poetics and rhetorical politics of different forms of bondage (economic, erotic, affective), while there continues to grow a large field of work on servants and the performance of service in early modern texts, including discussions of the coarticulation of service and love; the interplay of agency and dependency; the emancipatory potential of service; and the (paradoxical) celebration of "bad" service.[22] In the pages that follow, however, I seek to excavate the place of slavery in early modern England's service society and literary discourse; by interrogating the intellectual, philological, and discursive prehistory of the British transatlantic trade in slaves, I argue that we recover early modern literary and cultural texts as a crucial vector by which the fictions and frameworks of slavery are conceived, articulated, authorized, and disseminated. Thus, *Fictions of Consent* revises and relocates the literary and cultural sites where we search for the genealogies of English and American discourses of slavery. In so doing, this book seeks to illuminate the origins of Atlantic slavery in English fictions of consent to servitude.

I therefore contend that in early modern England, freedom and servitude, far from being opposites, are mutually enabling concepts. Further, although service and slavery are located not on a spectrum of labor but rather as mutually distinct categories, they are also repeatedly coarticulated. This twinned appearance of service and slavery compels us to revise, definitively, not only where we look for the archives of histories of slavery but also how we understand the insistent conjunction of service and slavery, in sites ranging from the grammar school to the family, from the masterless man to the "spirited" or kidnapped one. These alternate genealogies, particularly as they pertain to the grammar schoolchild, generate another critical entry point to my study of early modern servitude: the changing understanding of the family in the sixteenth and seventeenth centuries. This book argues that the meaning of the family begins to undergo a crucial shift in this period, from denoting the members of a household to registering kin networks connected by blood. Thus, I explore the intimate spaces of the home and the family as loci for the negotiation of both race and servitude. The earliest meaning of the English "family" is "servants of a household," an etymology that knits together family and servitude in crucial ways, but the word also derives from *famulus*, a Roman household slave who lies etymologically and ideologically at the heart of the home. The reception of classical slaves in early modern England was therefore also inflected by the changing familial nexus of service and blood, particularly as it encountered emergent discourses of racialized slavery. Thus, drawing on recent work on race and blood, alienness and intimacy, this book also seeks to intervene in the genealogies of race-making in four central ways: first, by tracing the languages of racialized slavery through Roman comedies and their translations to the discourses around early modern "strangers" and slaves who must not only serve, but serve willingly; second, by considering the ways in which the nexus of service and blood in shifting understandings of the family also reconfigures both servitude and succession, intertwining natal genealogies with the futures of slavery; third, by positing that the condition of slavery and servitude recalls the problem of racial markers in the fundamental ineradicability of either in the early modern imagination; and fourth, by demonstrating how the English enactment of slavery both preserved its fictions of freedom, paradoxically, and underwrote more permanent forms of racialized slavery.[23] Thus, the Roman freedman's "stain of slavery" was conscripted in early modern England, I suggest, to secure slavery to somatic difference, and to presage its hereditability.

As the classical training early modern grammar schoolboys received provided the rhetorical and conceptual frameworks for slavery, it authorized the fictions of consent and the myths of benevolence that made slavery both possible and palatable. Thus, this book also articulates a prehistory to later narratives of "cheerful slavery," principally in North America. And if the futures of "cheerful slavery" are secured by the scaffolding of blood-based hereditability, not only does early modern natality begin to be yoked to the prospect of bondage; the figure of the child—so central in the schoolroom, in service, and in bloodlines of descent—also emerges as both a linchpin and a limit case for the practices of consent to servitude.[24]

Fictions of Consent employs two interwoven organizational logics. In the first instance, this book moves from a consideration of the meanings and early modern reception of the *servus* (slave) to an exploration of iterations of the *famulus* (household slave) in early modern England, turning in the final chapter to the problem of the *libertus* (freedman) in the early modern transatlantic world. These three sections thus together trace the inheritances of the most familiar forms of classical slaves, across the space of the stage, the schoolroom, the household, and the family, traversing the terrain from domestic intimacy to imagined freedom. In order to do so, and in the second instance, the first three chapters of the book establish the scope of practices and sites available for the fictions of consent across a range of texts, focusing in turn on liveried service, pedagogy, and the family. The latter chapters, meanwhile, attend to the tensions of contract, servitude, and manumission by placing single literary texts in conversation with the specific historical practices—of indenture, slavery, and emancipation—that they invoked, and in which they intervened.

Thus, the first chapter, "Marking Service: Livery, Liberty, and Legal Fictions in Early Modern England," explores the English languages of service to suggest that the tension between liberty and constraint resonant in the language and material forms of livery is an exemplum of and metonym for the larger paradox of "free service," of the commonplace of consensual servitude, in early modern England. A fraught term, "livery" both denoted the clothing that identified one as a servant attached to a particular household or patron (sometimes even operating as an unacceptable badge of servitude) and yet also conceptually suggested the "freedom" from which the word derived. Through readings of John Cooke's *Greene's Tu Quoque*, Thomas Dekker's *The Shoemakers' Holiday*, and William Shakespeare's *The Merchant of Venice* alongside contemporary popular and polemical literature, this chapter reveals the paradoxes of freedom and constraint apparent in both the linguistic histories and the material markers of livery. Even as it animates and sustains legal fictions of political and social liberty—the fiction, for instance, that players are liveried household servants, evoking the nostalgic world of feudal retainers—livery activates specific economic and material freedoms. Yet, as the prosthesis of clothing registers as a marker of complexion in the visual lexicon of the theater, livery also comes to anticipate the intersection of visible bondage and legible race.

Chapter 2, "'Leaue to Liue More at Libertie': Race, Slavery, and Pedagogy in the Early Modern Schoolroom," moves from the English languages of service to the Latin discourses of slavery that shape them. Reading Renaissance editions of Terence together with early modern English accounts of slavery and captivity as well as university plays such as Thomas Ingelend's *The Disobedient Child* and William Cartwright's *The Royall Slave*, this chapter examines the reception of classical bondage to argue for the schoolroom as a crucial site for the reception and reenactment of servitude. The early modern study of classical comedy's *servi*—and Renaissance (mis)translations of key Latin terms for slaves in early modern editions—not only navigate the schoolboy's vexed role as the dependent of his *magister* (master or teacher) while also a future master himself; they also ensure that slavery begins in the schoolroom. But the early modern English schoolroom also functioned as a crucial space for the pedagogy and performance of early modern race. In their reception of the Latin languages and literatures of blackness and bondage, I argue that early modern schoolboys mediated and molded contemporary conceptions of race, slavery, and family.

If Chapter 2 examines the pedagogical contexts that illuminate the cruxes surrounding servitude, slavery, and race, the next chapter, "'Am I Not Consanguineous?': The Foreign *Famulus* and the Early Modern Household," explores how they resonate in the intimate space of the family home, in readings of Ben Jonson's *Volpone*, Shakespeare's *Twelfth Night*, Thomas Middleton and William Rowley's *The Changeling*, and William Heminge's *The Fatal Contract*, alongside pamphlets, manuscript letters, and the 1593 Return of Strangers. The expansion of the understanding of the family in Renaissance England—from a community based on service to one also predicated on consanguinity—allows early modern writers to reimagine the Roman *famulus*, or household slave, in the figure of the "strange" servant, who was simultaneously foreign and familiar. Reading such "foreign familiars," this chapter argues that if English subjects overseas complicated contemporary understandings of slavery, racialized strangers serving in English households challenged the very nature of what it meant to be "English" and to be "barbarous," to be bound and to be "at libertie." But as we attend to the disjunctions and interstices between the meanings of *famulus* as both "slave" and "family," even English household servants appear as at once stewards and strangers, intimates and potential threats to the affective and discursive fictions of the household. The slave, it emerges, lies at the heart of the home.

The fourth chapter, "Faithful Covenant Servants and Inbred Enemies: Indenture and Natality in *Paradise Lost*," turns to the technologies of bondage which articulate and authorize the fictions of consent surrounding early modern service and, increasingly, servitude. Exploring early modern apprenticeship agreements alongside seventeenth-century Atlantic indenture contracts, I suggest that the architecture of contractual service retains the potential for the strategic manipulation of apparent operations of consent.

Chapter 4 reads Milton's *Paradise Lost* to argue that Adam's, Eve's, and Satan's languages of debt, gratitude, and dominion articulate an understanding of servitude that paradoxically lays claim to liberty, and of indenture that engenders indebtedness, to reinforce the political and affective fictions surrounding indentured servitude in early modern England and America. The chapter ends by reframing pre- and postlapsarian labor and servitude in *Paradise Lost* in terms not only of volition and indenture but also of blood and generation, arguing that by refusing insistently natalist readings of the text, we can illuminate the intercalibration of servitude and succession, natality and slavery, family and bondage.

My final chapter, "'Of a Bondslaue I Made Thee My Free Man': Servitude, Manumission, and the *Macula Servitutis* in *The Tempest* and Its Early American Afterlife," takes as its point of departure the paradox of "serving freely" (*servire liberaliter*) in Terence's *Andria* and its adaptation in Shakespeare's *The Tempest*, turning to the freed slave, or *libertus*, to argue that this classical figure provides a conceptual model for early modern—and, later, early American—notions of "happy slavery." Even as the *libertus* articulates free service as alternately nostalgic and fictional, consensual and coerced, a form of servitude and a paradoxical means to emancipation, he also reframes liberty as provisional, revocable, and contingent. Arguing against the teleology of liberty on which trajectories of manumission appear to turn, this chapter suggests that if Ariel is compelled by mutuality, Caliban is bound by *mancipatio*, a Roman enslavement ceremony. It thereby revisits a central crux in early modern studies—how do we read Caliban as a "thing of darkness"?—to demonstrate the imbrication of classical slavery and early modern discourses of race-making. The nexus of slavery, servitude, and race becomes particularly urgent in the late seventeenth-century case of Adam Saffin of Massachusetts, whose vexed status as simultaneously indentured servant and slave, consenting and coerced, cheerful and bound, demonstrates the ambiguity and urgency of the imperative to "consensual servitude" in early American negotiations of race and bondage.

Fictions of Consent ends with a brief epilogue locating the legacy of this discourse of "happy servitude" in the juvenile literature of the Atlantic in the eighteenth and nineteenth centuries about the willing American slave. If the Renaissance schoolroom introduces classical models of "willing servitude," later transatlantic discourses about slaves' cheer and gratitude reinforce the pedagogical and political links between slavery, liberty, and fictions of consent. Beginning with the early modern reception of "benign" Roman slavery in the comedies of Terence and ending with the afterlives of the authorizing discourses they introduce, this book argues that as we excavate early modern England's genealogies of servitude, we must also unearth its bound futures. As we recover the English Renaissance as part of the genealogy of English and American discourses of slavery and a key constituent of the imaginative frameworks of blackness and bondage, we discover in early modern literary and cultural texts a critical crucible for the conceptual architecture which generates early modern England's futures of racialized slavery.

CHAPTER 1

Marking Service

Livery, Liberty, and Legal Fictions in Early Modern England

In a letter from John Williams, later the bishop of Chichester, to the antiquary John Aubrey in 1694, Williams recounts a story of dubious credit from one Mr. Williamson. In the (unlikely) anecdote, Mr. Williamson's father meets a mysterious stranger who, claiming to be in "conversation with spirits," conjures up a liveried servant bearing gold: "And then taking a whistle out of his pocket, he set it to his mouth, & then came quickly in a Foot-boy with a Livery, & delivered him a purse, which was full of gold. Mr W. thought it had been a Foot-boy, his attendant, & which the stranger only called in to divert him. But he ^soon^ found there was no such servant belonging to him."[1]

That this almost preternaturally obedient and lavish servant turns out to be too good to be true, merely a phantasm, is unsurprising. But it is nonetheless revealing that the stranger's performance of authority includes the figure and fantasy of a liveried servant who *is* precisely phantasmatic. The "Foot-boy" manifests a fantasy of allegiance and of opulence: the sumptuary detail of the livery as well as the servant's purse of gold together mark his (apparent) master's wealth. Appearing on cue, the liveried servant engages an attractive fiction: the fiction of a "Foot-boy" who is as compliant as he is a credit to his master's reputation and renown. But perhaps most striking here is the fact that the *spectacle* of the sumptuous footboy comprises the *substance* of this fantasy. The spectacularly lavish nature of this seeming servant is significant; speaking in relation to the concept of "style," Amanda Bailey notes that "'publishing' one's ensemble involved constituting and reconstituting an ongoing sartorial conversation that included specific venues of display, collective standards of judgment, and a receptive audience."[2] The relation of the implausible if compelling tale of the footboy with the golden purse, "published" once purportedly in its oral narration and next in its written form, underscores both the legibility of this fantasy as well as its value as a form of nostalgic reminiscence. Framing his story as a memory—and not even his own memory at that, but rather that of his dead father—Williamson delivers the fantasy of the liveried footboy to a moment that precedes living memory, rendering him an altogether unrecoverable spectral figure: "[Mr. W] soon found there was no such servant belonging to him." By 1694, that is to say—at least according to this account—the fantasy of the sumptuously liveried attendant was tantalizingly out of reach. It was, quite literally, too good to be true.

But this anecdote, curiously, also relies on obscuring the question of the footboy's volition. According to this (tall) tale, the footboy appears "quickly" on command, answering with alacrity the whistle of this mysterious stranger. The phantasmatic, fantastic footboy appears to operate outside the framework of consent, in a realm where to summon service is automatically to receive it. Yet the whistle is impersonal, even somewhat dehumanizing. It mediates the relationship between master and manservant, refracting and reducing this dynamic to one which is performative, mechanical, economically driven (as the purse of gold would suggest), and, crucially, fictional.

The vexed interplay between memory and narration, consent and commerce, fantasy and fiction in this implausible anecdote undergirds, I argue, much of the earlier seventeenth-century cultural discourse and valences of the use and abuse of livery, as I will demonstrate in this chapter. In Williams's letter, the footboy's livery works both to affirm and to alienate his relationship with the stranger, marking him as ostentatious but not necessarily tied in any meaningful way either to his master or to his household. His livery is both central and essentially irrelevant to the tale related here, a detail both fundamental and superfluous, overwritten and under-signified. As I shall discuss in the pages that follow, this nexus of contradictions characterizes the very nature of livery as it was both enacted on the early modern stage and embodied in early modern culture.

As this book argues, early modern England was keenly concerned with the politics and poetics of servitude: what it meant, how to navigate both the necessity of service and the horror of bondage, and how to animate and articulate liberty instead. The central questions of this study, indeed, address the place of servitude in what was imagined as a pre-slavery economy—the early modern iterations, in other words, of slavery "without" slaves. In this service society, when was one actually in servitude? How could one discern servitude visually? And what marked one's bondage? For many in early modern England, the answer consisted in livery. Livery functioned as a social and familial referent: one announced, by one's livery, a network of allegiance and one's place in it. But for several writers, livery was a marker not merely of affiliation but also of servitude, a visual reminder that one was bound, that one wore the fabric of merely *fictive* consent to one's servile condition. In an early seventeenth-century English edition of Mateo Alemán's picaresque novel *The Rogue: or The Life of Guzman de Alfarache* (1622), for instance, the "rise from a *Picaro*, to be a Page" is described thus:

> I rest vpon my Lords loue and fauour, I referre my selfe to his discretion and goodnes. I eate of his meat, and drinke of his drinke; in Winter feeding on that which is cold; in Summer, that which is hot. And what I haue in that kinde, is but a poore pittance, and that little none of the best, and commonly some-what of the latest, that a man were as good goe without it. I weare what cloathes he giues me, such as you see; as a *Liuery rather of my seruitude* [emphasis added], then of deuotion to cloath mee; not giuen me to keepe me warme, but to doe my Lord honour: And those too must be made to their minde, and our cost. So that our money payes for it, and they choose the colours.[3]

In this passage, Alemán explicitly reads livery as a marker of servitude, but also distinguishes it from its function as clothing. Livery is not only or even primarily material "to keepe me warme," but rather "to doe my Lord honour"; thus, the body of the wearer is co-opted into his master's structures of status as well as his networks of allegiance. This is perhaps most apparent, according to Alemán, in the fact the servant bears the cost of the clothing that he must wear but to which he can never fully consent: "our money payes for it, and they choose the colours." Livery, as this chapter will discuss, did indeed comprise part of the servant's salary, and although it was sometimes coveted by servants, depending on the kind of livery in question, it was rarely expressly chosen. Even at its most sumptuous, livery "must be made to [the master's] minde," emphasizing its wearer's lack of volition.

But livery, as I will discuss, could also, paradoxically, signify not servitude but instead liberty, agency, volition, and possibility. In the parliamentary records of 1601, for instance, Edward Coke, "her Majesties Atturney," recounts an egregious *abuse* of livery:

[Edward Coke] sheweth that the Queene calleth her Parliament, & that her selfe is the cheife Doer thereof, & it was called for divers Waighty causes & matters, & further therein shewed that the Towne of Leycester in the County of Leicester is an Ancient Borough Towne, & that the said Towne send Burgesses to the Parliament house. And whereas the Parliament began *the* 27th of October, & they chose George Belgraue of Belgraue in the County of Leicester Esq*uire* to be Burgesse for the said Towne supposing the said George Belgraue to come with the good liking & free consent of the Earle of Huntington, (without whose advise the said Towne neither hath nor will chuse any Burgesse) where indeed he is a noted Enemy to *the* said E: of Huntington, & finding & fearing they would not chuse him because of the same, he the said Belgraue ag*ainst the* said Elleccion prepared to putt on his back a blew Coate with a Recognizaunce being a Bulls head sett upon the sleeue of *the* same, and thereby imagining him to be the said Earles man, chose him as aforesaid, & the rather to make him selfe sure of *the* said elleccion, hee offereth to affirme upon his Corporall Oath that he was servant, & in good fauour with the said Earle being much greived & offended the same being greatly to his prejudice....⁴

George Belgrave's illicit use of the Earl of Huntingdon's "blew Coate with a Recognizance" underscores the possibilities as well as the problems of livery. Although livery could operate as a stigma, a legible and tangible signifier of the servile state of its wearer, as Alemán's novel suggests, livery in the case of George Belgrave is a marker less of servitude than of affiliation, with real political benefits. Although Belgrave affirms that he is the Earl's "servant," the rhetoric of service here is strategic, designed to signify the Earl's "good fauour" rather than any "real" household allegiance or affiliation. And this "good fauour" is central to the town's choice of its "Burgesse."

This anecdote exemplifies early modern readings of livery—as a clear indicator of the wearer's social affiliation and authorization—while troubling precisely the legibility of livery. Far from being straightforwardly constitutive of service, a "blew Coate with a Recognizaunce"—the blue coat with a badge that functions on the stage as a metonym for liveried service—here emerges as a fraught symbol of the contradictions between liberty and servitude, consent and constraint. Although livery sometimes registers as a humiliating badge of service, as I have noted, in this case it is voluntarily assumed without the volition or even the knowledge of its owner. And it precisely *fails* to act as an accurate signifier: although everyone "imagin[es] [Belgrave] to be the said Earles man," Belgrave is actually his "noted Enemy." Rather than denoting dependency or social subjection, the blue coat and livery badge are intended here both to enhance Belgrave's social prestige and to gain political authority as "Burgesse" of the town. Coke's account of the case, finally, emphasizes the issue of consent: George Belgrave is assumed to "come with the good liking & *free consent* of the Earle of Huntington" (emphasis mine); yet the use of his livery is precisely *non*consensual. Far from being free, it is manipulated.

This account compels us to question how the use, or abuse, of livery can shape forms of freedom or volition in service. I therefore begin my study of "free service" in this book by examining the contingencies of livery in order to introduce the paradox of willing servitude and fictional consent as well as the problem of reading service—or bondage—on the body, and to demonstrate how these tensions obtained in one of the most quotidian and ostensibly unremarkable aspects of early modern service. Livery operates simultaneously as a litmus test of servitude and as the subversion of such a legible (and tangible) gauge. As I will discuss, discourses around livery centered on not only the extent to which it marked one's bondage, but whether it registered a capacity for consent at all. In its linguistic and social history as well as its literary and cultural representations, I suggest, the languages of livery engaged, resisted, and problematized fictions and depictions of free service and consensual labor. In so doing, livery capitalized not only on its social and aesthetic currency, but, more importantly, on the legal fictions it persistently created and ensured.

As this chapter will make clear, in speaking of livery's legal fictions, I refer less to the juridical practice of accepting false statements as putatively true than to a legal apparatus that cloaks or colludes in the operations of livery as enabling or binding.[5] But what in fact are the different functions of livery in early modern England, and where and why is it important? In order to address these questions, I begin by examining different concepts and practices of livery in this period, and the ways in which they negotiate their (etymological and material) associations with service, attachment, constraint, protection, and freedom. Within and across these different understandings of livery we see negotiated the persistent synchronic tensions between the overlapping economic and social systems—which I hesitatingly and reluctantly term "feudal" and "nascent capitalist" even as I remain aware of the anachronistic limitations of these terms—which livery mediates and materializes. At the same time, I want to pressure the categories of livery and to argue for the disjunctions and interstices between these disparate meanings and functions of livery in early modern England and the ways in which they navigate different understandings of servitude: from feudal fealty to affective obligation, from servility to servitude. The problem of livery, as I shall discuss, rests both in its legibility, or lack thereof, and in its tenacity: does it mark servitude, or merely secure reciprocal obligation? Does it register a marginalizing stigma, or rather a sign of civic inclusion within England's "service society"? Does it mark the body indelibly, or is it simply an accessory to indicate a temporary, strategic alliance? Is it given, or is it assumed? And what are the complications of consenting to livery? Livery, I suggest, constitutes a limit case for the slippages between consenting service on the one hand and bondage on the other; between the capacity and the compulsion to serve. It addresses both the contingencies and the possibilities of marked servitude, even as it presents the dangers of failing to mark one's servant.

The (il)legibility of livery, indeed, speaks to one of the principal concerns of this study: the persistence of markers of servitude, and the ways in which they might obtain on the body. To what extent are such markers transitory or indelible, and how might these markers of servitude (written either on or adjacent to the body) mirror the representation of epidermal race and anticipate racialized designations of slavery? Speaking of the "textile body," Ian Smith has vitally noted in his analysis of racial performance that "black cloth functioned as an epidermal prosthesis in the theater of racial cross-dressing," with textile prosthetics fabricating the representation of epidermal race.[6] Thus, livery might also work suggestively to materialize the body itself, also looking ahead—or across—to the ways in which complexion comes to suggest, and sometimes in specific contexts to signify, servitude. Although I do not address this nexus of somatic signifiers and marked bondage as such in this chapter, I want to draw attention to the ramifications of the use and abuse of livery for a larger understanding of the ways in which servitude might be signaled amidst service, and how bondage is marked through the very enactment of fealty. The idea of announcing one's allegiances through visible signifiers, as I will discuss, is not a new one; rather, it hearkens back to quasi-feudal modes of rendering service. But if we understand livery as both a proxy for the body and a prosthetic, I suggest that we might also read livery as a central mechanism for negotiating and anticipating the inscription of service on the body. Such textile inscriptions on the body were not unusual, as Steve Hindle's discussion of the badges distributed to vagrants and beggars as "technologies of identification" makes clear.[7] But such sartorial signifiers were already implicated in a sinister material practice of marking racial difference. Geraldine Heng reminds us that "In 1218, Jews in England were forced by law to wear badges on their chests, to set them apart from the rest of the English population"; this practice continued for the remainder of the thirteenth century, amid more extensive rulings pertaining to the badge's "size, its color, and how it was to be displayed on the chest in an adequately prominent fashion," until the expulsion of Jewish people in 1290.[8] Livery materializes the tensions of consent and servitude, but it always does so, I argue, in relation to both the genealogies as well as the afterlives of these "technologies of identification."

The etymology and history of "livery" reveal the complexities and contradictions that are embedded in the concept. "Livery" itself can refer both to marked and to unmarked clothing, and the use of the word or concept frequently evokes a kind of semantic and cultural nostalgia. "Liverie," according to John Cowell in his *The Interpreter: or Booke Containing the Signification of Words* (1607) is the term "vsed for a suite of cloth or other stuffe, that a gentleman giueth in coates, cloakes, hats or gownes, with cognisaunce or without, to his seruants or followers"; the *Oxford English Dictionary* notes that livery is "a suit of clothes, formerly sometimes a badge or cognizance (e.g. a collar or hood), bestowed by a person upon his retainers or servants and serving as a token *by which they may be recognized*" (emphasis mine).[9] With cognizances, usually in the form of a badge, collar, or hood, a servant or retainer in early modern England was visibly marked as belonging to a specific household. Sir Thomas Overbury could consequently claim that a servant "tells without asking, who ownes him, by the superscription of his liuery."[10] Conversely, livery could denote not only unmarked forms of clothing but also more generally the food or provision which a master gave to his followers.[11] In this latter sense, livery was defined as a form of protection whose genealogy could be traced back to God's protection of Adam and Eve: "Vnto Adam also and to his wife did the Lord God make coates of skinnes, and clothed them." Lancelot Andrewes writes, "This verse is, as it were, the opening of Gods warehouse, and giving thence his liverie and aparrell, wherein is mercy and favor even in judgement, for after the Sentence God promiseth life, and here giveth aparrell . . . They came hereby into Gods favour, by wearing his liverie they became his servants, and so of his houshold: They are of the Princes house, to whom he giveth bread and cloathing."[12] If livery is described as a form of protection, it also denotes servitude. But "livery" is derived from the Latin "liberare," so that this apparent signifier of servitude could paradoxically suggest "liberty." Indeed, one definition of "livere" in the *Middle English Dictionary* is "the delivery of a person, setting free," while "liveresoun" denotes "deliverance, freedom, redemption." In early modern London, "livery" in this latter sense was used to refer to the setting free of a journeyman when he was made a full member of one of the city livery companies.[13]

To unpack the complexities of livery both as a concept and as a range of material practices, I want to distinguish five kinds of livery. Since actors, in particular, stand at the crossroads of their liberty as professional players and the legal fiction and livery they inhabit as household servants (as in, for instance, the case of the Lord Chamberlain's Men, Shakespeare's company), this chapter explores how these different forms of livery intersected in contradictory ways both in the performances that actors staged and in the professional lives of those actors. The first kind of livery was the most feudal form, wherein servants and retainers wore clothing in the heraldic colors of the aristocratic households which they served. The second form articulated the relation of a servant to a particular master or household through badges, usually sewn onto clothing. But with a decline in household servants as well as in liveried retainers, contemporary disapproval of livery as an unacceptable sign of servitude and, finally, Elizabeth's and James's efforts to clamp down on these "badges of factious dependence"—including restricting the number of noble retainers at court—this kind of "marked" livery was on the decline in the sixteenth century.[14] Yet, if in London marked livery was less significant and visible, away from London such feudal markers acquired greater resonance. As the "household Servants" (at least nominally) of their patrons, actors on tour were protected by the license and livery of their patron from being arrested as vagabonds.

Livery also denoted the clothing given to the members of livery companies (actors and playwrights among them) when they became freemen, but in these instances marked livery connoted not attachment to a household but rather elite, often wealthy, and independent membership in a company. As opposed to the livery of a household, this third form of livery was an explicit *release* from service, the last step through which an apprentice who had become a journeyman could finally become a master. And while the marked livery of a nobleman comprised a threat to the centralized power of the Crown, the livery of the companies did not, so that liverymen of a company participated in processions through the city, for instance when European ambassadors visited London.[15] Such processions allowed for a sort of feudal spectacle of London's histories that posed little threat to the power of the Crown. At the same time, the structures and rhetoric of these London companies revealed their origins in the medieval guilds. While the liverymen were free, the companies themselves remained rigidly hierarchical.[16] Moreover, despite the commercial nature of these companies, they were frequently framed in terms of brotherhoods.[17] The liveries of the London companies, then, mediated between their own independence and their affiliation with the strictly hierarchical successors to medieval guilds, between the commercial nature of the companies and their fraternal rhetoric.

While suits of colored, marked livery were on the decline, blue coats with badges came to denote more widely and generically both the occupation of their wearer—a "bluecoat" was a term for a servingman—as well as the household to which he belonged, by virtue of the badge. Like suits of colored livery, blue coats with badges had difficulty circulating as clothing due to the inscription of the badge. But this badge could be removed to create a fourth category of livery that could circulate quite easily: the blue coat itself. A blue coat without a badge marked the wearer generically as a servingman, but it did not specify the household to which he belonged. It was only with a badge or "cullison" that it identified a particular patron. Blue coats could be lent and borrowed, bought and sold; they participated fully in the economy of circulation. Later in this chapter I will argue that blue coats come to act as a metonym for livery in general, while also comprising a point of tension between marked and unmarked livery. In this early modern context, when there is so much anxiety regarding the identifiability of clothing and livery, depictions of marked versus unmarked blue coats, and of blue coats as at once conventional and not generic enough, come to register contemporary concerns about the growing inability of clothing to act as an accurate indicator of station and patronage. At the same time, I suggest that blue coats and the badges they sometimes bear materialize the persistent tension we see at this time between different understandings of labor and livery, in part by metonymically depicting the circulation of unmarked livery while evincing a form of nostalgia for the idea of marked livery.

The fifth and final category of livery bore no visual marker of servitude. "Cast" clothing was often given by masters to servants as payment or gift, and seriously challenged the identifiability of livery since it effectively erased the sumptuary and sartorial difference between master and servant if the servant actually wore, rather than sold off, the clothing. Yet while cast clothing provided no outward sign of affiliation, it functioned as "a form of bodily mnemonic, marking the wearer's indebtedness to [his or her] master or mistress."[18]

Without the visual markers of affiliation, cast clothing also circulated easily, and could be converted into money, disassembled, and reassembled.

"Guarded" Liveries and Legal Fictions

Actors were, of course, themselves servants—the Queen's Men, for instance, were known as the Queen's Servants—and as such were given livery. But scholars are divided over the extent to which actors' use of livery and their designation as servants was merely nominal. Leeds Barroll, for instance, contends that this dual status of actors as professional players and as household servants was simply a useful legal fiction. Their designation as servants did not, in his view, "enhance or even create social prestige." Barroll argues that they did not receive "bed, board, pay," and that even the red cloth that the King's Servants received on James I's coronation was "the lowest grade of such cloth awarded to crown servants," although the poor quality of the cloth might not distance actors from their function as servants so much as mark them as especially lowly members of the royal household.[19] Scott McMillin and Sally-Beth MacLean acknowledge that to call actors "servants" is partially fictional, but contend that actors were sometimes used by their patrons as messengers. Moreover, McMillin and MacLean also make the stronger claim that the actors made particular use of their liveries when they traveled:

> a travelling company of Queen's Men would not only carry the name and influence of the monarch through the country but would also give the impression of a watchful monarch, one whose 'men' ranged over the land. They would perform useful fictions before crowds throughout the country, but they would also be something of a fiction themselves, coming into town dressed in their vivid livery coats, drums and trumpets heralding them: . . . the impression given by the Queen's Men on tour was that of a central government whose influence was active and penetrating.[20]

The "fiction" of the Queen's Men thus served both an authorizing function—it literally allowed the travel and mobility of the players—and a disciplinary one: it suggested the "influence" of a central government. In order to unravel the complex meanings and uses of actors' marked livery, it is worth examining the functions of this "fiction" within and outside of London. The designation of actors as servants and the receipt of their patrons' livery may have been primarily nominal in London, but if it was something of a fiction in London, it served both legal and financial functions outside of it. The 1572 "Acte for the Punishemente of Vacabondes" required that all players on tour have a noble or royal patron.[21] The designation of actors as household servants was thus crucial to their geographical mobility, protecting them from the vagrancy laws. Moreover, being liveried servants brought specific economic rewards: the touring companies were paid by the towns they traveled to on account of their aristocratic patrons, and in the records of early English drama the rewards paid out to traveling players are in fact annotated by the name of the patron.[22] Thus, the Chamberlain's Accounts for 1560-61 for Sussex note twenty shillings "paid the same daye to the quenes plaiers And Sir Robert Doodleys plaiers," while in 1563–64 somewhat less—six shillings, eight pence—is "p*aid the xxvijth Daie to my Lord Robertes* plaiers in reward," and, in 1569-70, ten shillings were "paid to the Erele of Laysters pleyers when they were here."[23] Peter Greenfield emphasizes that while in London theater companies and even particular actors could draw audiences, on tour it was the troupe's *patron* who was significant, with the welcome given to their servants often dependent on the national status or the local influence of the noble patron in question: "civic authorities thought of the players primarily as representatives of their patrons.... If the patron's reputation helped to guarantee traveling players a welcome and a large reward, at the same time the players' travels helped to spread and reaffirm their patron's reputation ... patronage was an effective means of preserving and enlarging their influence."[24]

This emphasis upon the players' patronage also recalls feudal politics in the desire of certain lords to reassert their regional and national influence and of the towns receiving their retainers to placate powerful figures.[25] At the same time, it underscores how actors undertook something of a step back in time when they toured outside of London. Moreover, the Records of Early English Drama (REED) volumes repeatedly demonstrate that towns not only viewed the actors as the servants of specific patrons—as I have noted above—but also paid them according to the relative status of those patrons. Thus, larger rewards were given to the servants of more locally or nationally influential patrons, or those of higher rank. In 1582-1583, for instance, Gloucester disbursed the sum of thirty shillings to the Queen's players but gave only sixteen shillings and eight pence to the Earl of Oxford's players. Meanwhile, since Lord Chandos "lived at nearby Sudeley Castle and had represented the county in Parliament," his players received twenty shillings that year, as opposed to Lord Stafford's players, who received the lesser sum of ten shillings.[26]

Significantly, there were also payments given out for *non*performance; in Cambridge, for instance, where "all assemblies in open places" were "expresslye forbidden in this vniuersitie and towne or wi*th*in fyue myles compasse," the town paid players to go away without performing. The Vice-Chancellor of Cambridge wrote to Lord Burghley: "of late wee denyed ye lyke [right to perform] to ye right Honorable ye Lord of Leiceter his servantes. . . . [But] being willing to impart somthinge from the liberalitie of ye vniuersitie to them I could not obtayne sufficient assent therto, and therfore I delivered them but xx s towardes their charges."[27] The payment of nonperforming players reflects the dual desire of the town to uphold its own statutes while behaving respectfully toward the servants of powerful patrons.[28] At the same time, it reveals the very different functions of marked livery within and outside of London. If the Queen's Servants and other "Servants" were commercial actors in London, accepting payment for performance, the fact that they could be paid for not performing outside London underscores the way in which they were *not* simply commercial players when they toured, and the extent to which their designation as liveried household servants was more than nominal.

Indeed, the actors' feudal livery would have been the more marked because it was on the decline in the sixteenth century, beginning with Henry VII's attempt in 1504 to "put teeth into Edward IV's statute of 1468, restricting the use of livery to household servants."[29] Subsequently, both Elizabeth and James restricted the number of liveried retainers that lords could bring to court so as to avoid the impression and the reality of decentralized power. Writing early in the seventeenth century, Fynes Moryson noted that the "great trains and large howse keepinges of lords and gentlemen" were things of the past.[30] It is thus the more striking that actors repeatedly emphasized their status as liveried servants. Writing to their patron in 1572, the Earl of Leicester's Men asked him to grant them a license "to certifye that we are your *houshold Servaunts* when we shall have occasion to travayle amongst our frendes as we do usuallye once a yere" (emphasis mine).[31] To circumvent the injunction that "no persone . . . geve or take eny clothynge or lyuereys, for mayntenaunces or otherwise, but only accordynge to the Statutes," players needed to reassert their feudal bonds.[32]

"Rare New Liveries": In Pursuit of Service

If the theater companies themselves made use of marked livery, they also staged the significance of such livery in their plays. The promise of a master who gives "rare new liveries," as well as livery in the broadest sense of provisions, is central to Lancelet Gobbo's desire to change masters in *The Merchant of Venice*: "My master's a very Jew ... I am famished in his service. You may tell every finger I have with my ribs. Father, I am glad you are come. Give me your present to one Master Bassanio, who, indeed, gives rare new liveries. If I serve not him, I will run as far as God has any ground. Oh, rare fortune! Here comes the man: to him, father, for I am a Jew if I serve the Jew any longer."[33] Bassanio's reputation is founded on his ability to dispense "rare new liveries" (there is cachet, as well, in the liveries being "new" rather than old or "cast"). Considering that Lancelet has just proclaimed that "my master's a very Jew ... I am famished in his service," the word "liveries" also takes on its larger sense of "provision," the expectation that with "rare new liveries" Lancelet will no longer be "famished." Moreover, the sense of "delivery" that John Cowell argues is present in "livery" is evident here;[34] the phrase "new liveries" gestures toward freedom or delivery from the service of Shylock but also carries connotations of delivery or deliverance in a religious sense from a Jewish master and household to a Christian one: "to him, father, for I am a Jew if I serve the Jew any longer."

In proffering his service in return for "new liveries," Lancelet is displaying an understanding of livery as a form of currency that can buy his labor. At the same time, however, Bassanio must still "give" his livery, a word that underscores the notion of livery as the master's conferral or even gift rather than as payment. A gift, we note, particularly a material one, creates obligation; a payment for goods or services does not.[35] Moreover, while a gift from master to servant denotes top-down largesse, payment or salary for services suggests mutually fulfilled exchange. Yet, while James Shapiro points out how common the construction "I am a Jew ... else" was in the early modern period as a form of negative emphasis, Lancelet's use of the phrase here also contains a play on a more constrictive concern about livery marking and molding its wearer.[36] Lancelet's "livery" marks him as a member of a Jewish household and—as Chapter 3's discussion of the meaning of the family will make clear—a Jewish *family*; the "[de]livery" he seeks is, as Ian Smith notes, racial and religious as well as economic.[37] That is, Lancelet's anxiety about "becoming a Jew" through his livery suggests a complicated understanding of livery not just as currency but also as material that can inscribe and reshape the identity of its wearer, including in terms of race and religion.

One strand of critical thought has usefully read this moment in *Merchant* as Lancelet resisting rational economic choice by choosing the service of "so poor a gentleman," as Bassanio calls himself, over that of the "rich Jew."[38] But Bassanio is not truly poor at this moment, having borrowed "three thousand ducats'" with which to win the heart, and further wealth, of Portia.[39] The point, though, is that whether or not Bassanio is less wealthy than Shylock, he is represented as a more generous master—his generosity framed as a racial and religious virtue—who is ready to give Lancelet "a livery / More guarded than his fellows'" (2.2.139–40). "Guarded" is a particularly telling word in terms of livery, suggesting elaborate ornamentation. Lancelet will be visually marked by his "more guarded" livery, but at the same time such ornamentation displays Bassanio's largesse. In pre-banking, cash-short early modern societies, conspicuous consumption rather than hoarded wealth could create social credit.[40] In order to woo Portia, and to enter into the feudal world of Belmont, Bassanio must create the impression of feudal prosperity. Thus, even before he meets Lancelet, Bassanio instructs a servant to "See these letters delivered, *put the liveries to making*, and desire Graziano to come anon" (2.2.103–5, emphasis mine). In having new liveries made, Bassanio is creating an impression of both his power and his wealth. And while Bassanio enters in 2.2 "with [Leonardo and] a follower or two," in Belmont he appears with Portia "and all their trains" (3.2). "Trains," meanwhile, is a term that nostalgically evokes the world of feudal retainers: it is Lear's "train" that is "cut off,"[41] while by 1620 the "great trains and large howse keepinges of lords and gentlemen" were being talked about as things of the past.[42] Moving from the mercantile world of the city, which informs Lancelet's understanding of his labor, to the feudal domain of Belmont, Bassanio must "enguard" himself appropriately with liveries and "trains."

Yet these marked liveries also acquire complex meanings in the context of mercantile city life. In selling his services for "rare new liveries," Lancelet is also effectively entering into an "economy of obligation," in Craig Muldrew's terminology.[43] Bassanio, at the beginning of the play, has "great debts / Wherein my time, something too prodigal, / Hath left me gaged" (1.1.128–30). Living beyond his means, he reveals, is to blame: "I have disabled mine estate / By something showing a more swelling port / Than my faint means would grant continuance" (1.1.123–25). The largesse that distinguishes Bassanio in racial and religious terms from Shylock—that underwrites his "prodigal" Christianity, in other words—has also "disabled" his "estate." Rather than practicing thrift, Bassanio borrows money from Antonio to clear his debts and court Portia. As it turns out, his risky venture pays off, and he is instated by Portia as lord of her feudal estate: "But now, I was the lord / Of this fair mansion, master of my servants, / Queen o'er myself; and even now, but now, / This house, these servants, and this same myself / Are yours, my lord's" (3.2.167–71). Yet, even as Bassanio—and, tacitly, Lancelet—is inscribed within this domain, the fact that Lancelet is attaching himself to a master who has difficulty repaying his debts, who is essentially "uncreditworthy," is significant. In this nascent capitalist economy, when, as Muldrew notes, so much commercial exchange was conducted on credit, one's reputation and trustworthiness were key: "To be a creditor in an economic sense still had a strong social and ethical meaning."[44] And since "in early modern England, as in classical times, the household with all its members, and not the individual or firm, was considered to be the basic unit of economic consumption and production," the reputation of the members affected that of the household, and the reputation of the household attached to each of its members—including its servants wearing the household livery.[45] Bassanio's lack of credit is underscored at the end of the play, when Portia responds to his broken oath never to part with the ring with an ironic challenge to "Swear by your double self, / And there's an oath of credit!" (5.1.245–46), emphasizing the way in which "credit" attaches to personal credibility while starting to assume greater economic resonance in this nascent capitalist economy. Once again, Antonio must act as Bassanio's "surety" (5.1.254), this time for his marriage. "Rare new liveries," then, and Lancelet's desire for them, participate in complicated ways within a larger framework of credit and nascent capitalism while negotiating their feudal resonances.

And even this apparent ability to change households by donning "new liveries" is not available to all. It is perhaps telling that in seeking to flee from a Jewish household and family to a Christian husband, Jessica herself assumes not just the habit of a boy, but specifically a "page's suit" (2.4.31), adopting the livery of a page in order to effect and sanction her move. Yet although Jessica partakes in what seems a form of Christian profligacy, "gild[ing]" herself with "ducats" (2.6.50–51) and squandering her father's "turquoise" ring (3.1.101), her failure—as Janet Adelman argues—to relinquish her Jewish identity or truly be accepted in Belmont underscores the inability of livery, as I will argue later in this chapter, to overwrite what are increasingly read as more immutable racial markers.[46]

"A blew coat without a Cullizan will be like Habberdine without mustard": The Circulation of Blue Coats

In *The Merchant of Venice*, livery seems clearly marked. To change masters is to change livery. But in early modern England, the more common form of livery for a servant was a blue coat. And while a blue coat marked the generic status of a servant, it was only the addition of a badge or cognizance that signified that a servant belonged to a specific household.[47] A blue coat could be bought and sold at pawnbrokers' shops and could circulate on the market, from servant to servant, without regard to any specific master. But when blue coats circulate on the stage, it is often to comment in conservative ways on livery as a visual marker of servitude and the transformative potential of clothing, and to uphold social and sartorial hierarchies imagined as intrinsic.[48] In John Cooke's *Greene's Tu Quoque* (1611), the transfer of a blue coat frames the whole play.[49] At the beginning of *Tu Quoque*, the gentleman Staines, who is heavily in debt to a usurer, becomes the servingman of his former servant, Bubble. Bubble, meanwhile, is elevated by an inheritance upon the death of this same usurer, his uncle, to the position of a gentleman himself. Bubble's upward mobility is confirmed by his acquisition of sumptuous clothing: he instructs Staines to "buy me seuen ells of horse flesh colour'd taffata, nine yards of yellow sattin, and eight yards of orenge tawney veluet."[50] Bubble's seemingly instantaneous ascension to the position of a gentleman, exemplified by the change in his wardrobe, seems tacitly to underscore concerns about the way in which clothing can construct a false identity all too easily, and can often obscure one's "true" standing in society. But the whole play works against any notion that clothes can truly transform servant into master and master into servant. Bubble consistently fails to act like a gentleman despite dressing like one and constantly needs to be helped out of his social awkwardness by the "true" gentleman Staines. In a classic conservative move, Staines argues that "a seruing-man liues a better life then his Master, . . . weares broad-cloth, and yet dares walke Watling-streete, without any feare of his Draper: and for his colours, they are according to the season, in the Summer hee is apparelled (for the most part) like the heauens, in blew" (sig. D2r–D2v).

The plot is designed to affirm Staines's assertion of the contented life of a servant. Staines himself assumes various disguises to goad Bubble into terrible debts, and then "rescues" him from the Counter at the end of the play by taking him back into his service and, significantly, returning his own blue coat to him, in an ending that seems to comprise a nostalgic fantasy about the protections of servitude as well as a reaffirmation of conservative social and sumptuary hierarchies.[51] Bubble's attempt to properly inhabit the life of a gentleman ends in debt and potential humiliation, and he is all too happy to regain his livery and profess himself once again "a man in a blew coate" (sig. M1v) at the end of the play.

The conservative comedy of *Greene's Tu Quoque* depends upon the privileged knowledge of the audience, who can always distinguish the gentleman from the servant, regardless of what clothes they wear. The audience's reactionary laughter is directed at the folly of those who cannot make such a distinction. Joyce, who is wooed by Bubble, "wrongly" believes that Staines is "really" a servant. So when she sees Staines wearing gentlemen's garments, she scorns him as an upstart servant who is dressing above himself:

Ioy: What are you? why doe you stay? who sent for you?
You were in Garments yesterday, befitting
A fellow of your fashion; has a Crowne
Purchast that shyning Sattin of the Brokers?
Or ist a cast Suite of your goodly Maisters.
Staines: A Cast suite, Lady?
Ioy: You thinke it does become you: fayth it does not,
A Blew Coat with a Badge, does better with you. (sig. H3v)

Joyce's anxiety in this speech concerns the identifiability of clothing. "A Blew Coat with a Badge" is readily identifiable, emphasizing the subservient position of the wearer, but also, by virtue of the badge, the specific household to which he belongs; without such "Garments ... befitting / A fellow of your fashion" onlookers are compelled to ask, as Joyce must, "What are you?"

"Cast suites," as I shall discuss in the following section, can obscure true origins. But Joyce also suggests that pawnbrokers are responsible for the spread of inappropriate clothing. The problem is that at a pawnbroker's shop one can buy clothes belonging to a different class, that one can effectively purchase a new station. When she asks, "has a Crowne / Purchast that shyning Sattin of the Brokers?" Joyce depicts money, in this instance a "Crowne," as the agent rather than the medium of such an exchange. Joyce thus underscores the extent to which the circulation of clothing—and the attendant extent to which it can obscure a servingman's true status—is driven by money.

Joyce's objection to Staines's new clothing is visual as much as it is driven by concerns about class signification. "You thinke it does become you: fayth it does not": in arguing that his new clothing does not "become" him, Joyce attempts to measure aesthetic infelicity as class dissonance. That is, Joyce asserts a lack of "becoming" in order to read disorienting and potentially misleading sumptuary signs as accurate class indicators once more. But the irony here is that when she argues that "A Blew Coat with a Badge, does better with you," she is in fact misreading: Staines does regain the status of a gentleman, and so, in a system wherein clothing operates as social signs, Staines's clothes *do* suit him. Although for Joyce the livery of a "Blew Coat" would simply confirm what is already clear to her—that the servile Staines can never transform himself by purchasing clothes above his station or by appropriating his master's "cast Suite"—the play as a whole, as we have seen, seeks to assuage the anxiety that pawnbrokers and aspiring servants can subvert social hierarchy. Whatever clothes the servant wears, the audience is reassured by the action of the play that he will always remain a servant, just as Staines, even in a blue coat, is still a "natural" master. To laugh at Joyce's error is to be complacently reassured that shifts of clothing can never undermine the realities of a deeply inscribed social hierarchy. The apparently "fitting" garment, in her view—a "Blew Coat with a Badge"—is precisely a *mis*fitting.

Thomas Dekker's *The Second Part Of The Honest Whore* (or *The Honest Whore, Part II*, ca. 1605, printed 1630) is another play in which a gentleman appears as a servant, but here it is as a deliberate strategy. In order to masquerade as a servingman, Orlando procures the necessary blue coat from one of his own servants:

> Orl. How now knaues, whither wander you?
> 1. To seeke your Worship.
> Orl. Stay, which of you has my purse, what money haue you about you?
> 2. Some fifteene or sixteene pounds, sir.
> Orl. Giue it me, I thinke I haue some gold about me; yes, it's well; leaue my Lodging at Court, and get you home. Come sir, tho I neuer turned any man out of doores, yet Ile be so bold as to pull your Coate ouer your eares.
> 1. What doe you meane to doe sir?
> Orl. Hold thy tongue knaue, take thou my Cloake, I hope I play not the paltry Merchant in this bartring; bid the Steward of my house, sleepe with open eyes in my absence, and to looke to all things, whatsoeuer I command by Letters to be done by you, see it done. So, does it sit well?
> 2. As if it were made for your Worship.
> Orl. You proud Varlets, you need not bee ashamed to weare blue, when your Master is one of your fellowes; away, doe not see me.
> Both. This is excellent.[52]

This exchange, I would argue, reveals the tension we see in the early modern period between livery's participation in a mercantile economy and the nostalgia it evokes for its feudal resonances. The scene begins with a depiction of economic trust and monetary circulation—Orlando's servants hold his purse and disburse his funds—yet quickly shifts to a reassertion of feudal dynamics. In divesting his servant of his blue coat, Orlando is temporarily dismissing him; it is the blue coat that binds the servant to his status as a servingman, and even, it seems, to Orlando's specific household. Moreover, the manner in which Orlando obtains the blue coat is startling in its physicality: he "pull[s] [his] Coate ouer [his] eares," in a move that asserts the master's power to treat his servant as he likes.

In fact, to pull a servant's coat over his ears is a conventional formula for dismissal. In Ben Jonson's *The Case Is Altered* (1609), the Count dismisses Onion with the words "away with him, pull his cloth ouer his eares," establishing the material cloth as what binds the servant to a particular master, even if the garment itself is conventional, as in the case of the blue coat.[53] But despite the comic fiction of a master and servant exchanging clothing in *The Honest Whore, Part II*, the blue coat seems at once generic and not generic enough—enough of a convention that the blue coat will identify Orlando, to other characters within the play as well as to the audience, as a servingman, yet specific enough that the servant who temporarily loses his coat must return home until he can get his coat back.[54] The feudal resonances of Orlando's reclamation of the servant's blue coat in exchange for his "Cloake" are articulated in explicit opposition to monetary exchange. Orlando's desire not to play the "paltry Merchant" constructs the master-servant relation as one of both gift-giving and violence even as he simultaneously recalls and refuses the resonance of proto-capitalist economic exchange.

In early modern plays, I have suggested, we discern an understanding of livery not just as goods that can buy service or labor but also as actively participating in a nascent capitalist economy. Within this framework, blue coats metonymically materialize many of the tensions between these different (feudal and capitalist or mercantile) understandings of livery. A blue coat is, of course, the visual signifier, on the stage and within the plays, of the male domestic servingman, and itself carries a kind of authorizing provenance. In his satiric attack on Gabriel Harvey in *Haue with you to Saffron-walden*, Thomas Nashe claims that Harvey is both lowborn and penurious. To pay back his debts to his printer and publisher, John Wolfe, Harvey returns home to Saffron Walden to collect money. But if actors needed livery to travel, gentlemen needed liveried servants to accompany them on their journeys so as to manifest their status, and so "[Harvey] concluded it better policie ... whereas he was to make a iourney to *London* within a weeke or such a matter, to haue his blue coate (being destitute of euer another trencher-carrier) credit him vp, though it were thrid bare."[55]

Although the "blue coate" may be "thrid bare," it is enough to imbue the wearer with a certain "credit" in public. Livery in general, of course, carries an authorizing provenance and the implicit suggestion of a master's protection and the "credit" that he himself bears.[56] The point about blue coats in this passage by Nashe is that it is not the state but the simple fact of the blue coat that allows it to imbue its wearer with "credit," unlike in the case of sumptuous clothing where it is the quality and condition of the clothing that reflects on the wearer and the wearer's master.

In the above passage by Thomas Nashe, we also note that the "thrid bare" blue coat has already been used and discarded: it is "destitute of euer another trencher-carrier."[57] Earlier in *Haue with you to Saffron-walden*, Nashe reveals the place of a used blue coat in Harvey's relationship with his servingman: "that poore *Iohn a Droynes* his man, whom he had hyred for that iourney, a great big-boand thresher, put in a blue coate too short wasted for him, & a sute made of the inner linings of a sute turnd outward, being white canuas pinkt vpon cotton" (sig. P1v). This is of course an instance of a literal, material misfitting; the blue coat is "too short wasted" for John a Droynes. But we note here that the individual wearing the blue coat is not himself a servingman; he is a "thresher" who has been "hyred for the iourney," with the blue coat acting as a quick and easy signifier of his new, temporary position as a servant—although the wearer himself is an inappropriate servingman.[58] Moreover, in the suit that he wears we see materialized the process of clothing circulating and being disassembled and reassembled; his suit is "a sute made of the inner linings of a sute turnd outward."

This is not the only instance in Nashe's text of a blue coat translating its wearer into a servingman. But if blue coats circulate fairly easily in the passages above, the problem of circulating a blue coat *with* a badge is central to another instance when the penniless Harvey depends upon Wolfe to outfit him for his trip: "*Wolfe* procur'd him horses and money for his expences, lent him one of his Prentises (for a seruing creature) to grace him, clapping an olde blue coate on his backe, which was one of my *Lord of Harfords* liueries, (he pulling the badge off) & so away they went" (sig. P2r). This is a striking moment. Harvey is unable to afford a servant "to grace him," so Wolfe lends him one of his apprentices. But to transform the apprentice into a liveried servant, it is first necessary to reclothe him by "clapping an olde blue coate on [the apprentice's] backe." However, the only blue coat that Wolfe has to hand is "one of my *Lord of Harfords* liueries," which is marked as such by the Earl of Hertford's badge. Only after "pulling the badge off" does the blue coat become sufficiently generic to use as a marker of Harvey's servant.

It is thus the livery badge that allows or prevents a blue coat's economic and material circulation. Marked with a badge, the servant declares the master to whom he belongs. In Q1 *Hamlet*, two of the "ieasts" that Hamlet forbids the clown to speak specifically relate to service: "you owe me / A quarters wages: and, my coate wants a cullison."[59] If "wages" provide economic surety, a "cullison" or cognizance offers a measure of protection, both indicating that the master or patron "recognizes" the wearer as his servant and providing a legible marker to the world by which to "recognize" the wearer and, by extension, his master. A "coate" without a "cullison" is inscribed within a larger network of social and economic instability, and suggests here the uncertainty of a servant's future, a future in which the servant will need to subordinate the idealized gift-economy of benevolent masters and grateful servants to the naked economics of "you owe me / A quarters wages."

But if fully liveried servants were being phased out in early modern England, even cullisons were sometimes treated as an antiquated obsession. In Jonson's *The Case Is Altered* the servingmen Juniper and Onion come across the former servant Jacques's stolen, hidden gold:

> *Iunip.* S'bloud what shall we do with all this? we shall nere bring it to a consumption.
> *Oni.* Consumption? why weele bee most sumptuously attir'd, man.
> *Iunip.* By this gold, I will haue three or foure most stigmaticall suites presently.
> *Oni.* Ile go in my foot-cloth, Ile turne Gentleman:
> *Iunip.* So will I.
> *Oni.* But what badge shall we giue, what cullison?
> *Iunip.* As for that lets vse the infidelity and commiseration of some harrot of armes, he shall giue vs a gudgeon.
> *Oni.* A gudgeon? a scutheon thou wouldst say, man.
> *Iunip.* A scutcheon or a gudgeon, all is one.[60]

Juniper and Onion's immediate desire is for finer clothing—"weele bee most sumptuously attir'd"—seeming to confirm contemporary anxieties about servants buying clothing that masks their true origin and station, and about the monetary economy within which the circulation of clothing participates. But the second wish, that now that they are rich they should, as gentlemen, "giue" a "badge" or "cullison" to their own newly acquired retainers, denotes a nostalgic desire to revert to feudal markers, even as it is mocked as a mystified obsession, a comic confusion between "gudgeon[s]," "scutheon[s]," and "scutcheon[s]."[61]

But the persistence of feudal modes of servitude in an economy of circulation is also curiously captured by Nashe in his account of "my Lord of Harfords liuer[y]" after the badge has been removed. Harvey, Nashe writes, "ran in debt with *Wolfe* the Printer 36. pound & a blue coate which he borrowed for his man, and yet *Wolfe* did not so much as brush it when hee lent it him, or presse out the print where the badge had been . . ." (sig. L3v). While Wolfe materially removes the livery badge from the blue coat, the imprint of the badge persists—along with the accumulated dirt of the unbrushed coat—so that the memory of the coat's previous ownership remains materially embedded in the fabric. The word "presse" is a curious one: it usually means to *im*press, to press an image or object *into* a material. In its use here to describe pressing *out* a print, it seems that an equal effort is required to *remove* the imprint of a badge. In this instance, while the blue coat functions as the conventional garb of a servingman—generic enough to be used by one servant and adopted by another, and also to "re-create" its wearer as a servingman quickly—the traces of (and perhaps nostalgia for?) its previous owners and allegiances, and of an older system altogether, remain inscribed on and in the fabric. The blue coat is here a palimpsest, its history legible to those, such as Nashe, who wish to read it. Yet the blue coat also reveals the intractability of the traces of servitude, of the vestiges which persist into the afterlives of service.[62]

At the same time, it is precisely the removal of the livery badge that enables the blue coat to circulate and to participate in a monetary economy, to be bought and sold at pawnbrokers' shops, and to be lent and borrowed for cash—in *Haue with you to Saffron-walden*, the blue coat is calibrated in a system of loans, debts, and expenditures, although only *after* the badge has been removed. Yet, in its material retention of the print of prior alliances, the blue coat can complicate its own circulation as a commodity; even as it circulates from servant to servant, it can retain its specifically feudal inscriptions. If the absence of the livery badge is what removes the specific identifying markers of the blue coat and allows it to circulate, the visual and tactile reminders of that absence recall the role of the badge both in the history of the coat and in its current circulation.

If contemporary plays engage a kind of nostalgia for the livery badge, they also manifest a nostalgic desire for the protections and comforts of "blue coats": *Greene's Tu Quoque*, *The Merchant of Venice*, and *The Honest Whore, Part II* all evince a fantasy about the pleasures of service. Orlando declares that "My blue coate sits on my old shoulders well" (although the word "my" also puns on the idea that the blue coat is his to give as well as to wear), while Staines argues that "a seruing-man liues a better life then his Master," and Bubble is happy to regain his own livery at the end of *Greene's Tu Quoque*.⁶³ But these are in part fantasies about not being one's own man, and, in the case of Staines, Bubble, and Lancelet Gobbo, negotiate a problematic participation in a nascent capitalist and credit-based society—which for all its seeming opportunities appears in these plays to disallow real economic or social mobility and to complicate the vending of labor—with nostalgia for the idea of livery as provision and protection. This nostalgia, as I have suggested, seems in part to be centered around the idea of the livery badge as identifying marker as well as intractable feudal inscription.

Moreover, an equally powerful rhetoric sees blue coats as the sign of a new order that subverts "old English ways." This latter rhetoric repeatedly sets the plowman in opposition to the servingman. The fantasy about becoming a "blue coat," after all, is often problematically realized in the early modern period with plowmen becoming servingmen and thereby giving up their life of sturdy independence for a life of dependency and diminished responsibility. In contemporary writings, the russet coats of yeoman farmers are associated with firm ties to the land and with military service to one's country.⁶⁴ In the debates between and about "russetcoats" and "Blewcoates," the rewards of the servingman include "pleasures," "dainty fare," and, tellingly, good clothes—in one ballad, Richard Crimsal's *A pleasant new Dialogue* (1640), the servingman boasts that "Our parell many times is silke, / our shirts as white as any milke"—while those of the plowman are those of "labour toyle and care."⁶⁵ And although the russetcoat wins the debate with the servingman about whose occupation is more desirable in *A pleasant new Dialogue*, with the latter eventually conceding, "I would I were a Plough man now," there is still considerable anxiety in the early modern period about plowmen turning in their russet coats for the blue coats of domestic servingmen, and concern that they will trade their "labour toyle and care"—along with their independence—for the sumptuous pleasures of "silke" apparel and nice clothes, that in effect they will market their labor to buyers offering clothing in return. Markham complains that "First for the Yeoman, or Husbandmans sonne, aspyring from the Plough to the Parlor, I holde these the contempt of his vocation, Feare, to hazard his life in his Princes Marciall affayres, and, the ambitious desire of dignitie, to be the especiall occasions that hath mooued him to change his habite and cullour, from Ierkin to Coate, and from Russet to Blew" (sig. E3r–E3v).

Blue coats, according to Markham, are associated with the dainty domestication of the "Parlor," and they are derided both for their failure to engage in "Marciall affayres" and for their ambition. Markham goes on to note that although plowmen may be attracted by "this easie and pleasaunt lyfe of Seruingmen," yet their youthful desire to be comfortably provided for with "foure Markes and a Lyuerie" (a phrase that also explicitly calibrates livery with the cash currency of a wage) may backfire in later life, when, "ruinated, and almost cleane withered," these plowmen-turned-servingmen no longer have their independent living to sustain them (sig. E3v).[66] Blue coats, as opposed to russet coats, in Markham's view embody the false aspirations of a monetary economy: "The seconde occasion that made Blew so deare [is] . . . now falling out so that an Armie must be leauied, to be imployed at home or abrode, for the defence of the Countrey, or offence to the enemie, Robin Russetcoate must of necessitie be one of the number, as good reason that all sortes shoulde be assistant to such seruice. Now his Father, loth to part from his beloued Sonne, will giue Markes and Poundes to redeeme him, and keepe him at home from doing his Prince and Countrey seruice" (sig. E3v–E4r). Not only do blue coats fail to work the land for the common good, they can also literally buy their way out of "seruice" to their country with "Markes and Poundes," the "Markes" explicitly echoing the language of wages ("foure Markes and a Lyuerie"). As blue coats are incorporated into the terms of a wage economy, in Markham's view, their wearers refuse public "seruice" and forsake the national interest, and in the process become themselves vendible, able to be bought.

In *Love's Labor's Lost*, Biron "forswears" "Taffeta phrases, silken terms precise" (5.2.407) in favor of "russet 'yeas' and honest kersey 'noes'" (5.2.414).[67] "Russet," in this articulation, is associated with integrity and honesty. "Bluecoats" may enjoy the material comforts of their position, but they do so at the expense of their independence. In Boccaccio and Petrarch and in *The Pleasant Comodie of Patient Grissill* (1600) by Chettle, Dekker, and Haughton, Griselda's servitude to her husband is marked by her sumptuous clothes while her freedom is paradoxically asserted by her simple russet coat.[68] In an increasingly mercantile society, servants could more easily buy goods and material comforts, and "disguise" their station with sumptuous clothing. Yet their livery recalled and negotiated its feudal histories and, often, its feudal inscriptions. I have argued that the absence of the livery badge allowed the blue coat to circulate even as its invisible histories or material imprint remained embedded in the garment; the presence of a badge, however, signified servitude but also a measure of protection, geographical freedom, and access to the material goods and pleasures of the master's household. Such tensions between freedom and constraint materialized in the blue coat, with and without its livery badge, reflected the tensions between freedom and constraint in livery itself, as well as in the very histories and etymologies of the word "livery."

"Cast" Clothes

At the furthest remove from the "russet 'yeas' and honest kersey 'noes'" of the plowman are the representations of servants who, not content with blue coats, acquire the cast-off clothing of their masters. "Cast" clothing is both something of a critical problem for the study of clothing in this period and a contemporary conundrum. While "cast" clothing fell into the category of livery in its most general sense, it failed to mark its wearer as in any way a servant. "Cast" clothing, then, fundamentally problematized the function of livery as a legible marker of service. As a result, while masters and patrons often gave gifts and payments in clothing which were circulated quite widely, "cast suites" were notoriously problematic in early modern England, as indeed was any kind of old or used clothing. The word "botcher," for instance, used as an insult for a person of low birth and little skill, is understood in Richard Huloet's *Abcedarium Anglico Latinum* (1552) to mean "a mender, or patcher of olde garmentes."[69] "Cast suits" themselves are often placed in derogatory contexts in the plays of the period,[70] while the phrase itself carries negative connotations, with the word "cast" implying dismissal, as in "cast off" or "cast away."

Yet servants are repeatedly depicted as hungry for the economic value and social prestige of cast clothing. In Thomas Dekker's *The Shoemakers' Holiday*, Sybil promises to deploy her considerably greater geographical mobility in order to engage in an erotically charged fact-finding mission on behalf of her mistress, Rose, in return for receiving several items of Rose's own clothing. If clothing is "a form of bodily mnemonic," Sybil's new clothing serves as a mnemonic of obligation, gratitude, and indeed of her information-gathering mission itself.[71] But stitched within the clothing is also the privileged knowledge of her mistress's clandestine love affair. In the following passage, all the clothing which Rose offers Sybil (with the exception of the stomacher, a perhaps less intimate article of clothing than the others) is "my" clothing, and Sybil takes semantic and literal possession of the gift by repeating each item of clothing.

> *Rose*: Get thee to London, and learn perfectly
> Whether my Lacy go to France or no.
> Do this, and I will give thee for thy pains
> My cambric apron, and my Romish gloves,
> My purple stockings, and a stomacher.
> Say, wilt thou do this, Sybil, for my sake?
> *Sybil*: Will I, quoth 'a! At whose suit? By my troth, yes, I'll go. A
> cambric apron, gloves, a pair of purple stockings, and a
> stomacher! I'll sweat in purple, mistress, for you; I'll take
> anything that comes a' God's name. Oh, rich, a cambric apron!
> Faith, then, have at uptails all, I'll go jiggy-joggy to London
> and be here in a trice, young mistress.[72]

The valency of the clothing changes from conferred livery to economic compensation in the course of the transference. As the items of clothing semantically and materially switch ownership, the shift from Rose's possessive ("my" clothing) to Sybil's use of the indefinite article undermines the memory of the origin of the clothing. The clothes are no longer "*My* cambric apron, and *my* Romish gloves, / *My* purple stockings" but rather "*A* cambric apron, gloves, *a* pair of purple stockings." Semantically, at least, Sybil's language is already erasing the clothes' previous owner, and hence undermining the potency of the clothing as a mnemonic of obligation. Sybil does exclaim that she will "sweat in purple, mistress, for you," thus tying the color of sumptuous clothing—purple—to her efforts on behalf of her mistress. But the word "sweat" is an interesting choice, explicitly suggesting as it does physical toil and labor. The dynamic of exchange, then, may be read here as labor in return for clothing as much as clothing as reward. If clothing can be reward, bonus, or gift—the model that Rose espouses when she proffers her clothing as a thank-you gift "for thy pains"—it can also be payment, currency, or wage. It is this latter model that Sybil emphasizes through her hesitation in accepting Rose's offer, while she works out whether the clothes are an adequate compensation for her "sweat," or labor: "Will I . . . At whose suit? . . . By my troth, yes, I'll go." Sybil accepts her task not *at* her mistress's suit but because she *gets* her mistress's suit. In this exchange, service shifts into an economy wherein clothing or livery is a form of payment, currency, or wage—a rather different economy from one wherein clothing is reward, or the tactile reminder of mutual obligation and gratitude.[73]

Kate Mertes has argued that masters often dressed their servants in sumptuous clothing as a way of showcasing their own wealth and prestige, and Amanda Bailey builds on this idea to suggest that this convention often created the "conditions for young men to use the sartorial expectations of their position to outshine their masters and to potentially disobey them in other matters."[74] And contemporary writers such as Gervase Markham repeatedly lamented the problem of telling servants apart from their masters: "yf a Nobleman or Gentleman now adayes, could no otherwyse be knowne but by his Liberalitie, I feare mee, yf I should tread the Strand, I should often (for want of knowledge) vnduetifully iustle some of them, and scarse lende my Cappe, to whom a low legge should belong. For trust mee, I met (not long since) a Gentleman in Fleetestreete, whose lyuing is better woorth then .2000. Markes yeerely, attended with onely one Man, whose apparell was much better then his Maisters, though he was a Iustice of Peace i[n] his Countrey" (sig. D3r). This sumptuary confusion carried serious implications for modes of address and social legibility, since one might unwittingly slight one's superiors or be inappropriately obsequious to one's social inferiors.[75] And if strangers could mistake servants for their masters, certain plays express concern that wearing a master's "cast sutes" will render a servant forgetful of his proper place. In George Chapman's *Bussy D'Ambois* (1607), for instance, Barrisor claims, "I haue heard of a fellow . . . had a visible paire of hornes grew out of his forehead: and I beleeue this Gallant ouerioied with the conceit of Monsieurs cast suit, imagines himselfe to be the Monsieur."[76] And in semantically forgetting whence her cast clothing derives, Sybil's behavior in *The Shoemakers' Holiday* realizes contemporary anxieties that wearing one's master's "cast sutes" can lead a servant to forget her proper station.

As the story of Griselda demonstrates, fine clothing can denote servitude in a way that poor clothing does not.[77] Yet when servants dress too sumptuously, or, even more directly, receive their masters' clothing, servants can begin to turn into their masters. The attendant, unspoken concern in *The Shoemakers' Holiday* is that receiving her mistress's clothing literally turns Sybil into her mistress in a certain way; far from being marked as a servant in Rose's "cast" clothes, in her mistress's clothing Sybil will be visually indistinguishable from her mistress. If the decline in marked livery renders it problematic for strangers to read sumptuary signs accurately, there is the greater potential for servants not only to forget their own positions, but also to misread the way in which even unmarked livery is intended to bind them to their masters materially and emotionally.

This material and textile resistance to legibility as well as to affective bondage troubles the "economy of obligation" that underwrites the paradox of free service in order to compel forms of servitude, as I will discuss in the chapters that follow. I have suggested in this chapter that the fictions of consent which actors engage and perform in their status as simultaneously liveried servants and livery guild members, bound to aristocratic households and (sometimes) "free" within the compass of the London companies, provide not only the lived context for but indeed the very legal fiction that allows their dramatic stagings of livery. It is tempting, of course, to speculate too far about the capacity of plays to reflect their authors' own material contingencies and constraints. Nonetheless, plays such as *The Merchant of Venice*, *Greene's Tu Quoque*, and *The Shoemakers' Holiday* reveal—in very different ways—the limitations of livery in a mercantile economy of credit, and the social necessity as well as the danger of reading livery as an accurate indicator of its wearer's status, fealty, affiliations, and even (as I shall discuss in subsequent chapters) family. These works perform the pleasures of livery, its playful imprecision and its sartorial semantics; reveal the limits of livery's hermeneutic register as only provisionally legible; and expose its unsettling effects on credit, identity, and household. As playwrights contend with the contingencies of livery in their own theatrical pursuits—as costume and constitutive; enabling and binding; substitutable and singular—they also register the constraints that livery authorizes and anticipates.

For while both plays and rogue literature are full of the disruptive powers of servants who dress as their masters, it is surely the structural dissonances between conflicting livery systems that opened up the most radical possibilities for social transformation. Perhaps nowhere were those dissonances more immediate in early modern England than among professional actors. As I have already argued, actors, who were marked with the liveries of specific households, were both distanced from and dependent upon their designation as household servants and their marked household livery. Yet the richer actors were often members of the livery guilds, and hence freemen of the city. Even if many never attained the livery of their company, actors nonetheless mediated between the nominal and visual servitude of their "household livery" and the freedom of their livery guilds. If household livery afforded actors protection and freedom while on tour, their membership in the livery companies gave them both "privilege and protection" within the city of London.[78] Anthony Munday, for instance, was a member of both the Drapers' company and the Earl of Oxford's theatrical troupe. And while William Shakespeare wore the "bastard scarlet" of the King's Men on state occasions, Ben Jonson participated in the Merchant Taylors' pageant as a freeman of the city. It was actors who thus brought together most markedly and contradictorily the material forms of bastard feudalism (in their roles as liveried servants) and the new forms of nascent capitalism (in their establishment of stock companies that staged performances for profit). Indeed, in their role as shareholders of their own theatrical troupes, the leading actors, far from being nostalgic relics of feudal households, already performed functions that challenged their own "servile" status as well as the constraints of the London companies. For the theater companies were not, of course, livery companies, so not companies at all in the sense that had been legally defined within the city of London. If the actors' commercial practices belied their status as liveried servants, they nonetheless could use that status to establish a proto-capitalist industry that simultaneously depended upon aristocratic patrons and the London livery companies and threatened to use each against the other in the pursuit of profit.

But if actors' use of their material fictions of service insisted on marking livery as performative, malleable, unstable, and contingent, the uses and abuses of livery, as I have argued in this chapter, served both to reveal and to reimagine the materialized signifiers of consent and affinity in England. As it authorized forms of movement and mobility, operating as a legible register of personhood but also literally conferring the freedom to roam, marked livery functioned as a "passport" of sorts, ensuring that the distinctions between servant and vagrant, citizen and foreigner remained intact.[79] But this authorizing function also registered the ways in which such material markers anticipated the intersection of visible bondage and legible race by in part *resisting* the economy of circulation. Not only did the 1547 Vagrancy Act authorize the permanent and highly visible branding of bodies (a "V" on the breast for vagrants who refused service, an "S" on the forehead or cheeks for slaves who ran away), thereby transferring the lexicon of livery to the immutable, corporeal body, the prosthesis of livery also worked to demarcate the limits of malleable markers and circulatable clothing.

The concerns around volition and servitude which the everyday use of livery raised also had far-reaching consequences for contemporary understandings of the nexus of race and bondage and of the early modern theater's incorporation in a larger system of commerce, corporeality, and commodification. The practices of livery, I have suggested, encoded forms of civic inclusion and purported to register reliable methods of reading the liveried wearer yet were continually revealed as contingent, mobile, unstable—not least as they materialized on the stage itself. As the practices of livery attempted a lexicon and taxonomy of the material markers of servitude on the body yet placed pressure on the legibility of that body itself, as livery functioned as both a corporeal prosthetic and a proxy, it grappled with the fundamental question of how to mark service, bondage, family, or freedom on the body—and how to read for those markers accurately. In its association with servitude, livery, one might suggest, trains its beholder to read for bondage, and it purports to teach them how to do so.

At the same time, the incorporation of the practices of livery within systems of capitalism and commodification in the space of theater and its textile inscriptions on the body intersected both with the long-standing use of sartorial signifiers to mark race and with the contemporary practice of materializing epidermal race on the early modern stage.[80] It is perhaps no accident that the Prince of Morocco, the only staged black character in *The Merchant of Venice*, urges Portia to "Mislike me not for my complexion, / The shadowed livery of the burnished sun" (2.1.1–2; the other black character in the play, the unseen Moorish woman whom Lancelet has impregnated and who may herself be part of Portia's retinue, is never staged).[81] For Morocco, his "livery" signifies an authorizing provenance—the sun itself, to which he is "a neighbor and near bred" (2.1.3)—as well as his nobility, and he tries to teach Portia how to gloss his "livery" properly. Yet Portia refuses, repeatedly alluding to his (immutable) "complexion." The strategic transportability or circulation of "livery" that is often available to its wearer, as I have discussed in this chapter, is denied to Morocco, whose argument that his "blood is reddest"—that he is not essentially defined by his "livery"—has no purchase: as Ian Smith argues in his vital reading of this moment, "Morocco's liveried black skin announces his indelible incorporation in the social institution that is race."[82] The palimpsestic nature of livery's associations, and the liberty it often allows, become reinscribed here as the immutability of complexion, and presage the corporeal legibility of bondage. Even if the staging of Morocco's "complexion" operates through a textile prosthetic (black fabric), this theatrical fiction not only registers the visual exercise of reading the body—for legibility, for affiliation, for race, for signs of servitude—but also reminds us that even such fictions have deeply felt effects and are bolstered in and by the social institutions that enforce them. The black body as materialized in black fabric operates to commodify the black body—and also portends the racialization of bondage. For as the "prosthetic" of black fabric signals "racial embodiment construed as textile, livery, and uniform," Smith observes that "the black body as commodified thing does not only emerge in the colonial aftermath of a slave and plantation economy; it has a fully articulated discursive life in the early modern English theatre."[83] Not only must early modern English audiences and readers confront—and gloss—the ways in which strangers and foreigners assume the authorizing fictions that livery allows, as I discuss in the following chapter; livery's visual lexicon of bondage is mediated by the pedagogical and political economies of slavery which frame it. The slippages between the legibility of livery as a sign of both bondage and freedom, and its growing mediation by the lexical registers of complexion, commodification, and servitude that are at once more contingent and more constant, portend the problems of reading race and signifying servitude in early modern England.

CHAPTER 2

"Leaue to Liue More at Libertie"

Race, Slavery, and Pedagogy in the Early Modern Schoolroom

In the previous chapter, I explored the ways in which the fictions of liberty and volition attendant on the use of livery underpinned a number of early modern debates around service and bondage. These debates, I have argued, centered around the possibility of serving with consent and traced the strategic slippages between ideologies of obligation and economic recompense. They iterated and inscribed the material markers and the sartorial and somatic lexicon of servitude, and they established the frameworks for bondage and the strategies of racialization which, I suggest, were seeded in the everyday contexts of livery. A commonplace material practice in service, livery—and its discontents—thus mapped the contested terrain of servitude and bondage. I now turn to another quotidian yet crucial early modern site, one that I argue inscribed the English ideologies of slavery: the grammar school classroom. Although English encounters with captivity in the Mediterranean world established a vital cultural context for the reception of slavery, equally significant, I argue, were the representations of slavery in the Roman comic plays that English authors read and reimagined for the stage, and in the languages of epidermal race and slavery learned in the grammar schoolroom. Slavery not only informed schoolboys' everyday education; it underwrote it. Thus the schoolroom, I argue, emerged as a formative site for the conceptual strategies of racialized bondage and of the place of children and hereditability in the genealogies of slavery.

In this chapter, I thread together an examination of archival material pertaining to the captivity and redemption of English men in the context of the global Mediterranean world with an inquiry into the pedagogy of slavery in the early modern schoolroom imparted through Terence's comedies and early modern translations, lexicons, and cribs (the latter of which offered readers phrase-by-phrase English translations of the original Latin text). I therefore seek to demonstrate the ways in which slavery was brought home to England, and suggest that it was in the formative spaces of the schoolroom that the conceptual genealogies of slavery were seeded and authorized. As the grammar school pupil was conscripted into the conceptual and discursive frameworks for slavery, he also underscored the ways in which pedagogy was explicitly being used and exploited as the basis for bondage, as children more generally were increasingly implicated in their own fictions of consent (as in the case of apprenticeships and poor indentures, for instance). At the same time, I suggest, it was the very enactment of enslavement in the classroom, and the insistence on the fundamental nature of English freedom outside it, that underwrote and authorized the arguments for more fixed and even heritable forms of racialized bondage.

This chapter, which unfolds over four parts, thus begins by illuminating the place of slavery in the early modern classroom, as schoolboys both enacted and were interpellated—linguistically, dramatically, and pedagogically—by the rhetoric of servitude and the specter of slavery, and establishes how slavery was not a faraway phenomenon but woven into the quotidian fabric of the schoolroom, its languages and logics learned in childhood. The first section of this chapter explores the affinities between the schoolboy and the slave through early modern lexicons and cribs and examines two university plays which invoke the schoolroom's association with both discipline and bondage and reflect on the contingencies of servitude and the fictions of consent established in the grammar schoolroom. If the grammar schoolboy learns the scripts of mastery and bondage alike, the situation of children in relation to servitude more broadly is a vexed concern. This is the subject of the second part of the chapter, which moves to a discussion of the status of early modern children both in relation to the place of servants and in terms of their capacity for liberty. The question of the status of children becomes particularly pressing in the contexts of apprenticeship and indenture, which nominally served a pedagogical function—like the grammar school—yet frequently breached the border between service and servitude; the problem of indenture is one to which I return at greater length in Chapter 4. The susceptibility of English people to bondage, and the extent to which their liberty was essential, was a concern being addressed simultaneously in the schoolroom and in the contexts of global trade and traffic, with English captivity narratives and tales of kidnap and redemption circulating widely in early modern England; the third section of this chapter explores these larger contexts of captivity and slavery that both permeated the plays students performed and intersected with the classical slaves that schoolboys encountered and engaged in the grammar school curriculum. These larger contexts of captivity and bondage for the reception of classical slavery, I suggest, also work to authorize racialized slavery; if the schoolroom enactment of slavery operates to render bondage thinkable and even palatable, the English ability to both participate in and be redeemed from slavery paradoxically functions to justify the enslavement of *other* peoples. The question then becomes: what marks certain people as fit for bondage? The fourth and final section of this chapter addresses that question by returning to the Latin lexicons and Terentian comedies with which the chapter begins, demonstrating the pedagogical strategies and discursive ideologies that both normalize slavery and suture it to somatic difference, within the schoolroom as well as outside of it. Chapter 2 concludes by arguing that the early modern reception and translation of the classical languages of slavery and blackness in the schoolroom inflected and precipitated the frameworks for racialized bondage and proposed a more permanent marker or "stain" of slavery. Moving, in its organization, between contemporary discussions of captivity and the context of the English grammar school, this chapter reveals the interplay and aggregation of cultural contexts that catalyzed the forces of chattel slavery and secured the frameworks of racialized slavery.

Despite its fictions of freedom, it is important to remember, early modern England was no stranger to the spectacle of slavery. This was evident in the lavish procession which welcomed the Moroccan ambassador to London in 1637.[1] "[A]ttended by Thousands, and ten Thousands of Spectators" and "conveyed with his Maiesties Coach . . . and the chiefest of the Cittizens," the ambassador, or Alkaid, received the pomp and circumstance of an official progress.[2] His own rich retinue included the "choisest" horses "in all *Barbary*" and "foure *Black-Moores* in Red Liveries" as well as, perhaps, a less comfortable spectacle of global exchange and affluence—a group of former English slaves—"Eighthly, there passed the Redeemed Captives, cloathed all new by the *Alkaid*, who were in number 18. on foot, who were part of the 33. men which Master *Robert Blake* gat to bee redeem'd by his Intercession to the *Emperor* of *Morocco*; for they were the *Emperors* Slaves or Captives, of whom more shall bee said hereafter."[3] The blackamoors' "Red Liveries" may signify a legible marker of patronage even as they register their wearers' servitude, as the previous chapter has argued, but any straightforward association between complexion, clothing, and bondage is immediately complicated by the English captives who follow this portion of the procession.[4] Distinct from the "Black-Moores" in their red livery yet visually articulated in proximate relation to them, the "Redeemed Captives" engage, even as they trouble, both the nexus of complexion and captivity and the legibility of spectacular servitude. These "Redeemed Captives" represent the success of Blake's "Intercession" to the emperor of Morocco, the happy outcome sought by the many redemption petitions which circulated in early modern England to recover captives in Barbary or Algiers, among other far-flung sites of imprisonment. But although the rescued captives in the procession are no longer enslaved, they nonetheless continue to comprise part of the emperor's retinue. Described precisely in terms of their former bondage—"they were the *Emperors* Slaves or Captives"—these freed slaves are "cloathed all new" by their former master's emissary, framed within a visual, material, and discursive lexicon of bondage even as they performatively announce their liberation.[5] The contingencies of bondage are embodied not only by these returned slaves, but also by the former master whose munificence they seemingly celebrate: the term "*Alkaid*" "[means] Lord in the language of the *Morocco*," yet the ambassador is himself a eunuch and a former slave who "*was taken Captive in his Child-hood at the age of almost eight yeares*" and "*bought and sold*," before being elevated to his current position by the "*favour*" of the emperor of Morocco.[6] In its staging of race and redemption, of liveried "Black-Moores" and rescued English slaves, the Alkaid's procession provides a powerful visual metaphor for the adjacency of slavery and visible markers of servitude, of bondage and blackness, even as it complicates their conflation. It underscores the proximity of bondage and freedom, and the contingencies, slippages, and continuities between these states. But the procession also, quite literally, brings slavery home to England.

That is what this chapter—and indeed this book—also seeks to do. If the spectacle of the repatriated slave both assures and challenges the fiction that "England is too pure an Air for Slaves to breath in," the city procession was not the only crucially English institution to affirm even as it disrupted the nation's central claim to liberty. The progress in the Alkaid's honor may have celebrated the global commerce that also resulted in the kidnap of English captives by featuring "*Barbary-Merchants* bravely mounted on Horsebacke, all richly apparrelled," but as this chapter will argue by looking at a very different corpus of texts alongside redemption petitions and captivity narratives, slavery was not only a foreign phenomenon, located on strange shores and the high seas, a spectacular and exotic experience.[7] Rather, I suggest that we must disorient and disrupt the spaces and places where we search for the archives and the genealogies of slavery. The political and economic forces that catalyzed the capture of English captives and the development of chattel slavery were authorized, I argue, by conceptual groundwork laid much closer to home.

Thus, this chapter seeks to recover the foundational place of slavery in that most quotidian and English of arenas: the grammar schoolroom. The Roman slave plays which constitute the cornerstone of the grammar school curriculum work to socialize their early modern pupils into civic discipline and ludic resistance. But as they articulate the nexus of enslavement and manumission, servitude and redemption as a crucial but persistently uncertain conundrum, they also remind us that, put plainly, slavery is central to the humanist education.

The fiction that there was officially no slavery in early modern England's service society or on English soil was a robust one. Yet the specter of slavery was ubiquitous, and nowhere more urgent or immediate than in the early modern schoolroom. Written by a Roman manumitted slave from North Africa, the slave comedies of Terence, in particular, represented a model of clear, elegant Latin and thus comprised a crucial vector for Latin learning and speech in the early grammar school curriculum.[8] But schoolboys, as we know, not only read Latin; they also performed, ventriloquized, and vivified authors, plays, and stock characters—including slaves. Thus, this humanist curriculum did not constitute merely a voyage to a classical past and precedent, nor simply an attempt to gain credit through antiquity. Rather, I argue that part of the schoolboy's Latin training, often through the enactment of Terence, included the pedagogy and performance of slavery and strangeness. And the translations of Terence that these schoolboys read themselves mediated contemporary contexts of race and slavery, so that the (often elite) grammar school pupil is at once schoolboy and slave, English and strange. Terence's slaves, the "strangeness" of Latin, and the negotiation of contemporary English slavery thus found a particularly generative site in the textual spaces and the schoolhouse theaters of the *puer*, or schoolboy, and the pupil. The schoolboy, I suggest, is always already strange, even as he is learning how to become English; bound, even as he enacts the fictions of consent that underwrite slavery.

The spectacular proximity of redeemed English captives and liveried "Black-Moores" in the Moroccan ambassador's procession, of course, visually registers how the early modern English were both captives and enslavers in the late sixteenth and seventeenth centuries. But as I will suggest in this chapter by looking at the reception of Terentian slavery, Latin learning, and the enactment of servitude in the schoolroom, the condition and staging of English bondage and the specter of citizens being taken into captivity paradoxically yet strategically authorized the practices of racial enslavement. The rhetoric of redemption from captivity so spectacularly celebrated in the procession was a well-worn trope in early modern England, often adopted and adapted from the Roman slave comedies which frequently staged the fantasy of revealing and reuniting captured citizens with the families from whom they had been separated many years earlier by the vagaries of fate. *The Taming of the Shrew*, for instance, a work which playfully stages the performance of pedagogy and learning, explicitly invokes one of these Roman slave plays, underscoring the ways in which the pedagogy—and the problem—of classical servitude and redemption from bondage reverberates in popular early modern discourse. In the first scene of *Shrew*, Tranio advises his lovesick master Lucentio: "*Redime te captum quam queas minimo*" ("Ransom yourself from captivity at the lowest possible price").[9] His advice is derived from Lily's *Grammar*, that staple of the grammar school curriculum—but both Shakespeare's *Shrew* and Lily's *Grammar* slightly misquote their source, Terence's *Eunuchus*. In *Eunuchus*, a play I discuss at greater length later in this chapter, the slave Parmeno also dispenses counsel to his lovelorn young master, Phaedria, but he does so in the form of a rhetorical question, not a command. Confronted with his master's dilemma—that Phaedria's beloved, the courtesan Thais, has given him the cold shoulder—Parmeno muses, "What should you do? but redeeme your selfe being taken captiue, at the least [rate] you can: if you cannot for a little, yet for as little as you can."[10] Whereas Lucentio is reassured by Tranio's advice—"Go forward, this contents" (1.1.159)—Phaedria seems much less sure of his slave's counsel: "Dost thou persuade me so?"[11]

For Tranio, Lucentio's captivity is a condition which he enters and departs at will. Parmeno's advice, however, comprises not the instruction it will become in Lily and Shakespeare but rather a suggestion marked by uncertainty, revealing the way in which the slaves of Roman comedy are acutely aware of the contingency of redeeming themselves from bondage. *Eunuchus*, for instance, hinges on the redemption and return of Thais's sister, a kidnapped citizen who has been mistaken for a slave, in the context of a larger global economy of slavery which includes "Ethiopian" slave girls and eunuchs, who are exchanged as "fashionable" courtship gifts. The possibilities and problems of redemption from bondage explored in this classical play are encoded in the very language of Roman slavery, so that even the common term for a slave, *servus*, registered enslavement as a form of enfranchisement or deliverance: it denoted someone who had been preserved from death in battle and instead taken into slavery.[12] The philology of slavery, therefore, incorporates—indeed, it hinges upon—the sense of redemption, even freedom. Conversely, Roman freedmen, or manumitted slaves, performed their supposedly consensual service to their patrons under threat of being returned to slavery.[13] Even as they encountered and recalled the classical contingencies of redemption and manumission from bondage, *Shrew*'s audiences and *Eunuchus*'s schoolboy actors might well be familiar, additionally, with the contemporary petitions that circulated to ransom Englishmen captured and bound as galley slaves, and the popular captivity narratives that in turn told these slaves' tales of daring adventure and redemption from bondage, documents I will explore at greater length later in this chapter.

Schoolroom Slavery: The Pedagogy of Bondage

The humanist curriculum of the grammar school encouraged the pedagogy and performance of slavery through the reading of classical slave comedy. However, the schoolboy did more than simply encounter or enact slavery. Even as the schoolboy learned of the nexus of consent and servitude in classical drama, as he studied and spoke the words of Roman slaves and freedmen, he found himself already bound, for the affinities between the schoolboy and the slave are also registered lexically. John Véron's 1575 *A Dictionary in Latine and English*, for instance, "corrected and enlarged" by Ralph Waddington, specifically seeks an audience in grammar schoolboys, proclaiming on its title page its intention to work for "the vtilitie and profite of all young students in the Latine tongue."[14] Waddington's address "To the Reader" begins by extolling "*How profitable the skill of any forreine tongue is in these daies to such as seeke knowledge and desire conference with strange nations,*" adding:

> whilst the enioyers thereof haue so double adua[n]tage ouer the base and skillesse sort, as among them they are both worthily praised, and of the higher and skilfull daily aduanced and preferred: But aboue all how necessary the knowledge of the Latine tongue is to any of vs, that either desire to be entred into other bordering tongues, or to serch the depth of

any Science, or the assurance of our salutation through the true vnderstanding of holy Scripture, is so co[m]monly knowne, and so generally agreed on, that happie seemes he that may attaine thereto, or procure and leaue it to his child as a sufficient heritage.[15]

The preface takes it for granted that the "profit" of a "forreine tongue" lies in its ability to facilitate "conference with strange nations," an outcome so desirable that it "needs no enforcing." Latin is, however, most necessary of all to allow "entry" to "bordering tongues," an odd phrase that articulates English as proximate (linguistically? nationally?) to "tongues" that are oriented spatially on its borders. But there is no literal "bordering tongue"; thus, *any* nation that lies beyond the English Channel is a "strange nation" which nonetheless uses a "bordering tongue" and with which it is important to hold "conference." For the young readers of this dictionary, therefore, Latin facilitates access to "strange nations" and "forreine" tongues. It at once recovers the past and forges new national affiliations. At the same time as Latin distinguishes the elite schoolboy from the "base and skillesse sort" and lends him "true vnderstanding" of both "any Science" and "holy Scripture," it also articulates him as, potentially, "strange."

The schoolboy becomes even "stranger" when we look at the following dictionary definition of the *puer*: "*Puer, pueri*, mascu. generis, *a childe, a seruant.*"[16] The grammar schoolboy or *puer* who sought himself in this early modern lexicon would therefore have encountered himself not only as a "childe" but also, crucially, as a "seruant." At the same time, "seruant" is also the proffered definition of "*servus*," the common Roman slave (according to Véron, a *servus* is a "seruant of seruile condicion" or "a bondman").[17] In other words, the schoolboy is linked to slavery through the Latin *puer*, a connection that not only suggests the infantilization of the slave (we might think, for instance, of the degrading use of "boy" in later American contexts of slavery and segregation) but also constitutes a mutually identificatory mechanism for the boy and the slave.

The nexus of servitude, pedagogy, and kinship is invoked at the opening of another Terentian play, *Andria*, a staple of the grammar school curriculum. In one of the first English translations of this play, Joseph Webbe's 1629 edition, we encounter a relationship that is pedagogically, affectively, and structurally vexed. Speaking of his dissolute son to his freedman Sosia, the old man, or *senex*, Simo, deliberately plays on the languages of liberty and mastery in terms that I argue relate as much to the students enacting these plays as to his hapless son:

> For, when hee grew to be mannish, Sosia,
> He had leaue to liue more at libertie.
> For, before that time,
> How could you know or vnderstand his nature,
> whilest his yong age, feare, [and] [his] Master kept him vnder?
> *Nam, is postquam excessit ex ephebis*, Sosia,
> *Libertus vivendi fuit potestas.*
> *Nam, antea,*
> *Qui scire posses, aut ingenium noscere,*
> *Dum aetas, metus, Magister prohibebant?*[18]

The affinities between errant Roman sons and early modern schoolboys are clear, but the pun here—in both the Latin and the English—is on *magister*. *Magister* means "master," but the word also referred to the teacher who instilled "feare," by virtue of his beatings, into the "yong" boys in the classroom. For schoolchildren and Terentian sons alike, adulthood was a period of more "libertie."[19] But the "master" here is also the father. *Magister*, then, resonates as father, teacher, and master. And each keeps the son, the pupil, and the servant, respectively, "vnder." When grammar schoolboys encountered the world of their Latin texts, then, they did so from a position of familiarity. If the *puer* is both schoolboy and *servus*, to be a *puer* is always already to embody the valences of servitude; to be a schoolboy is to enact and vivify those contradictions.

The social and affective ramifications of the schoolboy's identification with the trickster *servi* and disobedient sons of Roman comedy have been persuasively discussed in recent scholarship, which has gestured toward the grammar schoolboy's potentially subversive performance of rebellious sons and wily slaves who will not be properly governed by their *magistri*. In his discussion of Tudor *vulgaria* in the schoolroom, for instance, Paul Sullivan has argued that because memorization and recitation were strongly emphasized in early modern pedagogy, the schoolboys' repeated enactment of slaves and freemen alike playfully disrupted the social hierarchy, instilling in them both empathy and ambition.[20] While they would eventually leave the schoolroom and become masters and fathers themselves, with "leaue to liue more at libertie," their education, oddly, centered on their ventriloquizing of and identifying with disenfranchised subordinates. Yet, I contend that the instabilities of hierarchy and the contingencies of bondage are not only enacted but are embedded in the very language of the Roman comedies, and that these contingencies and instabilities resonated most strongly in the terms for slaves.

The most popular word for a slave in Terence and Plautus is *servus*; much less often, *mancipium* is used. Less commonly used still are *famulus*—a word denoting a Roman household slave, to which I shall return later in this chapter—as well as other terms for slaves working in specific occupations. *Mancipium* denotes a slave who has been taken ownership of during the formal ritual of *mancipatio*, who is, in effect, property. *Mancipatio* was the legal process of transferring ownership of something in the category of *res mancipi*, which encompassed land, property, agricultural animals—and slaves, who were its only human component.[21] In its etymology and history, the word *mancipium* is thus imbricated in systems of financial exchange, physical ownership, and the commodification of human life. Meanwhile, as I have noted, *servus*, too, registers a slave, but its etymology denotes quite the opposite, implying liberation through its sense of having been saved or redeemed in war. Thus the history and etymology of *servus* emphasize not being taken *into* captivity, but rather being preserved *from* death. And indeed, although the term *servus* registered slavery, early modern translations almost never render *servus* as "slave": *servus* is translated not just as "servant" but also in the specific, and deliberately *anachronistic*, terms of early modern service. Thus, *servus* is frequently rendered not only as "servant," "man," or "boy," but even as "page," while *ancilla*, a female slave, is rendered as "wench," "maid," "waiting-maid" and even "waiting-wench." Even in translations of *servus* in a contemporary work of fiction, the word "slave" is rarely used; Ralph Robinson's translations of Thomas More's *Utopia*, for instance, elect to use the term "bondman," not "slave."[22] The strikingly anachronistic translations of Terence persist into the latter half of the seventeenth century; in a 1694 version of Terence's *Andria*, for instance, titled "The Fair Andrian," Sosia (Simo's freedman, given as "Socia" here) is described as "Simo's *Steward*" and Dromo (his slave) as his "*Footman*" in the list of characters.[23]

Yet the language of slavery, as we know, was well established by the sixteenth and seventeenth centuries. The word "slave" first appears in English usage around 1290, to mean "one who is the property of, and entirely subject to, another person, whether by capture, purchase, or birth; a servant completely divested of freedom and personal rights."[24] "Servant," meanwhile, appears to originate from a slightly earlier period (ca. 1225) to mean "A person who is engaged to attend or wait upon, or to obey the directions and meet the needs of, a particular person, or to perform specified tasks or functions in a particular household or establishment . . . a person who is in the service of another ... or of a household."²⁵ If "servant" and "slave," then, occupy such distinct semantic spaces by the sixteenth century, why do these early translations take slaves for servants?²⁶ And what does the use of these deliberately anachronistic terms achieve, apart from inserting notes of either temporal disjuncture or, conversely, transhistorical immediacy?

In addition to "contemporizing" these Roman plays, I suggest that these translations also vivify them in specific ways for the early modern schoolboys who were their actors as well as their students. In Webbe's translation of *Andria*, for instance, *servolus* is rendered as "page." Webbe's choice of "page" conveys the slave's youth—a *servolus* was a young slave—but "page," a word which first appears in 1300, is particular to early modern usage. And while a "page" may signify simply "a seruaunt alway ready at his maisters commaundement" or "a waiting, or seruing boy," the word also carries specific class connotations as not only "a boy or youth employed as the personal attendant and messenger of a person of high rank," but also an elite one: "many pages were youths *of high rank* who were placed as attendants as part of their education" (emphasis mine).²⁷ Randle Cotgrave, indeed, somewhat haughtily observes that "in France, where he hath often good breeding, he ought to be a Gentleman borne."²⁸ This usage of "page" thus precisely obscures the status of classical *servi*, who were not only of low rank but who, as foreigners and noncitizens, failed even to register in the Roman polity in crucial ways.²⁹ What the use of the word "page" *does* achieve, however, is to render these *servoli* legible to early modern schoolboys, who, embedded within early modern structures of service, might themselves go on to become the "personal attendant or messenger of a person of high rank." The pages' youth is a point of commonality, while by tacitly evoking the pedagogical function of early modern pages' service (they were often placed as attendants as part of their education) the translation ensures that they resonate with their schoolboy readers as fellow *students*. Yet, early uses of "page" also simply registered "a boy, a youth. *Obs*."³⁰ Gesturing, like the word *puer*, to both service and childhood, the term "page" resists the *servolus*'s suggestion of slavery even as it reaffirms the imbrication of childhood, pedagogy, and servitude.

As we have seen, the early modern grammar school curriculum thus prompted the pedagogy of "social scripts" that used the enactment of mastery and slavery alike to inculcate in schoolboys the habits of mind that would accumulate in social and cultural capital.³¹ Yet early modern texts also provide clear counternarratives when they explicitly tie the situation of schoolchildren to discipline, violence, and even bondage. The early modern grammar schoolroom was a site of both intellectual and corporeal correction and punishment, visiting on the body of the schoolboy the beating he sometimes encountered in Roman slave comedies. Roger Ascham argues fervently against beating in his humanist treatise *The Schoolmaster*, suggesting that "loue is fitter then feare, ientlenes better than beating, to bring vp a childe rightlie in learninge," pointing out "what iniurie is offered to all learninge ... chieflie by the lewd scholemaster in beating and driuing away the best natures from learning."[32] Nonetheless, the threat of the rod in the schoolroom was pervasive and keenly felt, and discipline was commonplace. When, in Thomas Ingelend's contemporary university play *The Disobedient Child*, the "Peroratour" advises the audience to "Spare not the Rodde, but folowe wisdom," he echoes a widespread belief.[33] The play, indeed, stages the consequences of abandoning the rigors of grammar school study. At the beginning of the play, the "Sonne" explicitly analogizes the situation of the schoolboy to bondage when he argues, "Euen as to a great man, wealthy and ryche / Seruice and bondage is a harde thynge / So to a Boye both dayntie and nyce / Learnynge and studye is greatly displeasynge" (sig. A3v). But after he leaves the schoolroom for the anticipated pleasures of marriage, he realizes that he has simply entered a more onerous form of servitude, as his wife acts as his "mayster" (sig. F1v), compels him to "Laye these faggottes man vpon thy shoulder / And carye thys wood from streete to strete" (sig. E4v)—an instruction that might remind us of the "wooden slavery" of both Ferdinand and Caliban in *The Tempest*—and places him in the position of "Slaues that he hyred" (sig. E4v). As a didactic interlude, *The Disobedient Child* urges its audience to stay in school, acknowledging while complicating the association of the grammar schoolroom with excessive violence or servitude, and juxtaposing the "legitimate" discipline exercised by the schoolmaster over his charges with the "illegitimate" and—in gendered terms—"disordered" beating inflicted by the wife on her foolish husband.[34] Yet the schoolroom violence the "Sonne" recounts is nonetheless extreme, as he remembers "An honest mannes sonne hereby buryed / Which throughe many strypes was dead and colde" (sig. A4v).

Another university play, however, William Cartwright's *The Royall Slave* (1636), casts schoolboys within the terms not only of slavery, but of the global contexts of captivity and bondage, the subject of the third section of this chapter.[35] *The Royall Slave*, which was "Presented to the King and Queene by the Students of Christ-Church in Oxford," is set in (what is probably Achaemenid) Persia.[36] In the play, after the conquest of his country by Persia, the Ephesian captive Cratander is selected by the Persian monarch, Arsamnes, to be king for three days, after which he will be killed, following Persian custom. In the very first scene, however, the Persian jailer, Molops, threatens his Ephesian prisoners with death, "shew[ing] [th]em a halter" (sig. B1v), according to the stage direction, which he callously compares to "your Thread of Life." Molops thereby situates himself as "Destiny" and underscores the extent to which his captives' lives are, quite literally, in his hands, as he simultaneously analogizes his instrument of death to an instrument of pedagogy: "Come forth; and if you can endure to read, her's a Persian line in my hand will instruct you" (sig. B1v). The joke here plays on the extent to which pain is always a pedagogical device; Molops thus appears as both a captor and a pedagogue, whose "instruction," like that of schoolmasters, is as much corporeal as it is conceptual.[37]

Although it is a university drama, *The Royall Slave* frequently plays on the relationship between the pupil and the *magister*. The play is concerned most centrally with the demands on and of kingship and with the extent to which slavery might be considered a natural or innate state; when we first meet Cratander, for instance, the eponymous "royal slave," he is deeply immersed in "a discourse o' th' Nature of the Soule; / That shewes the vitious Slaves, but the well inclin'd / Free, and their owne though conquer'd" (sig. B2v). But *The Royall Slave* is also a text that is keenly attuned to the often fractious dynamics of the schoolroom. Cratander is originally selected for the dubious honor of being appointed (temporary) king of Persia because he is "Arm'd with a serious and Majestique looke" (sig. B2v), and although Molops originally dismisses Cratander as "unfit for any honour" because "he's wondrous heavy and bookish" (sig. B2v), the true king, Arsamnes, can properly discern his merits: "thou hast prov'd that he is best bestow'd / That best deserveth to be spar'd" (sig. B3r). Quiet and learned, Cratander seems far better suited than his more riotous companions in prison to the demands of kingship. And yet, when the Persian queen, Atossa, asks her ladies how the new "Three-dayes King" is faring, Mandane replies, "As Schoole-boyes / In time of Misrule, looke big awhile, and then / Returne dejected to the Rod" (sig. B4v). We are repeatedly reminded that the so-called "king" is enacted by a student little older than a grammar schoolboy, one who might vividly recall both the pleasures of "Misrule" as well as the pain of the "Rod."

Although Cratander displays the "dejection" of the chastised schoolboy, his erstwhile fellow-captives grumble resentfully about his reign: "Must we still thus be check'd? we live not under / A King but a Pedagogue: hee's insufferable" (sig. E2r). To the Ephesian prisoners Philotas and Stratocles, Cratander resembles nothing so much as an overbearing teacher—or perhaps even worse, a swotty schoolboy: "we suffer all this meerely because he hath a little familiarity with the Devill in Philosophy, and can conjure with a few Notions out of *Socrates*" (sig. E2v). But *The Royall Slave* also grapples with the extent to which slavery can be justified. Although Cratander's first act as king is to release his fellow captives from imprisonment, he immediately demands their "service," so that his countrymen complain that "we have left off shackles, / To be worse fetterd" (sig. E3r) and have simply substituted one form of servitude for another. And when they then plot to assassinate Cratander, whom they view as a "tyrannical" ruler, they must be summarily returned to their captivity. This second imprisonment is both more fitting and more humiliating than their former captivity; while they were earlier taken in battle, a condition that often "justifies" slavery, they are now banished from society. What Cratander's countrymen therefore reaffirm is not only the idea of the natural slave, whose very nature fits him best for captivity—it is surely not an accident that Cratander is staged perusing "a discourse o' th' Nature of the Soule," perhaps a text that addresses the notion of natural slavery, such as Aristotle's *Politics*—but also the idea that slavery can constitute a safeguard and a mode of moral protection, even amidst the bondage: "The Chayne and Fetter were your Innocence" (sig. E2r), Cratander charges. Liberty here emerges as peculiarly corrupting, whereas slavery comprises the realm of "innocence," a moral bulwark against the temptations of freedom.

The Royall Slave, we remember, is situated at the temporal moment both of English captivity and bondage in the Mediterranean and of contemporary English slaving practices. Despite their putative and public commitment to the concept of liberty, the English had participated in the slave trade in one way or another for several decades, from the slaving voyages of John Hawkins in the sixteenth century to—as Noémie Ndiaye, Gustav Ungerer, and Emily Weissbourd argue—tacit involvement with the contemporary Spanish and Portuguese slave trade.[38] In addition to its pedagogical resonances, the play therefore also grapples with the problems of whether slavery is justified, whether the condition of captivity is due to providence or personal responsibility, and whether conquest can elicit consent. In staging Cratander as both a slave and "naturally" free, whereas his fellow Ephesians are undeserving of liberty, and in rendering captivity in the rhetoric of the classroom, *The Royall Slave*, I suggest, traverses a complex terrain in which English men are both enslavers and captives—a terrain, I am suggesting, that is also mapped in the schoolroom.

Cratander, after all, articulates a near-fantasy of loyalty achieved through conquest. He refuses to betray the Persians to his fellow Ephesians, and not only is he eventually saved from death by divine intervention, he is rewarded by the Persian king at the end of the play: he is made king of Greece. The best he can procure for his Ephesian compatriots, however, who have already shown themselves undeserving of liberty, is to "live protected as a weakned friend / Under the Persian shelter: still preserving / Your Lawes and Liberties inviolate" (sig. F3v–F4r). Part conciliatory pragmatism, part threat, this seems an implausibly optimistic iteration of Ephesus's future status as a vassal state. Cratander's countrymen must accept this compromised liberty, bound to the Persians for military protection and to avoid "The tempest that is falling on their head, / Unlesse the Persian shield them" (sig. F4r). Yet, by the play's end, this Ephesian subjection in perpetuity, which is initially framed as an alliance of convenience, is reimagined as a form of willing servitude, as Arsamnes's queen, Atossa, demands of her husband:

> . . . you shall grant that the Ephesians may
> Still freely use their antient Customes, changing
> Neither their Rites nor Lawes, yet still reserving
> This honest Pow'r unto your Royall selfe,
> To command only what the free are wont
> To undergoe with gladnesse. I presume
> You scorne to have them subject as your owne,
> And vile as strangers, Tyrants conquer thus. (sig. H1r)

Atossa's insistence that Arsamnes's "command" be limited to "only what the free are wont / To undergoe with gladnesse" not only is a paradoxical directive, belied precisely by his very "command," but also redraws the boundaries of that "command" according to the extent of the Ephesians' willingness to receive it. In other words, Arsamnes's "command" is, by definition, not only beneficial but desired, and his Ephesian subjects maintain a fiction of freedom under his aegis—a fiction necessitated by their compulsion to consent to his command. Yet, we soon discern the real reason for this elaborate narrative of "gladness" under "command": to shore up the legitimacy of Arsamnes's rule, and to distance his reign from that of "Tyrants." The last words in the play, indeed, belong to Arsamnes as he asserts, "Let others / When they make warre, have this ignoble end / To gaine 'em Slaves, *Arsamnes* gaines a Friend" (sig. H4v). Resolutely insisting on the mutual amity between the two nations and their rulers, Arsamnes reimagines Cratander as a "Friend" even as he reviles those "ignoble" conquerors who aim only "to gaine 'em Slaves."[39]

Cratander's true liberation, of course, can be realized only by the royal audience of this play; and so, in the play's epilogue, Cratander pleads for his "real" manumission:

> *The Slave though freed by th' King, and his Priest too,*
> *Thinkes not his Pardon good, till seal'd by you:*
> *And hopes, although his faults have many beene,*
> *To finde here too the favour of a Queene.* (sig. I1r)

Cratander here strategically reminds us that the dramatic play-monarch, and a Persian one at that, can never supplant the true (English) ruler of the land; his plea for "pardon" recalls the strategic relationship between acting company and patron discussed in the previous chapter, wherein the actor is both servant and supplicant. "Cratander" is, however, neither a servant nor an actor in the conventional sense, and the play's Epilogue to the University (sig. I1v) underscores the distinctions "'twixt a Colledge and a Court," emphasizing that "We are not trayn'd yet to the Trade, none's fit / To fine for Poet, or for Player yet." Indeed, at the conclusion of the epilogue, "Arsamnes" reassures the university audience that "Though rays'd from Slave to King, he vowes he will / Resume his former Bonds, and be yours still" (sig. I1v). Cratander's readmission into the pedagogical community appears as a form of "bondage," both affective and intellectual.

The Royall Slave's multiple epilogues thus underscore both the metaphoricity and the malleability of slavery, evoking the schoolboy and the player as imbricated and implicated in the literary navigation of servitude. But in a curious moment in the Epilogue to the University, "Arsamnes" expresses the players' hope that, although they are untrained, "you'le like it then, although rough fil'd; / As the Nurse loves the lisping of the child" (sig. I1v). The monarch and the master become the "Nurse" to the "lisping . . . child" that is both the play and its players. They therefore stand in for the schoolmasters who, though often depicted in paternal terms, "sometimes represent themselves as mothers or nurses." As Lynn Enterline points out, "In Lily's *A Short Introduction of Grammar*, the first lesson is how to decline the noun *magister*. The noun with which it is paired is *parens*."[40] The scripts of servitude the schoolboy speaks and learns, I have suggested, conscript him into the structures of bondage and compel him to confront the global contexts of captivity. In the next section of this chapter, I will turn to the way in which the nexus of pedagogy, servitude, and kinship in the grammar schoolroom underpinned a larger question in early modern England, around the status of children themselves and the ways in which they, too, might seek yet fail to attain the rights which obtained to the *civis*, or full citizen, and be subject not only to service, but possibly even servitude.

"Neither Free-men nor Servants": Children, *Servi*, and *Famuli*

Early modern commentators explicitly wondered how to situate not only schoolboys but children more generally in relation to servants. Writing in the seventeenth century, the theologian Dr. Thomas Jackson sought to clarify the affinities between childhood and servitude. Emphasizing that "*Servitude* is opposed to *Freedome*," Jackson asserts that "As for *Children* or such as are under Yeares, though borne to be Lords over others, yet whilest they are under yeares, they are properly *neither Free-men nor Servants*."[41] He then goes further, insisting "*that the Heire as long as he is a Child, differeth nothing from a Servant, though he be Lord of All, but is under Tutors and Governours, untill the time appointed of the Father*. For this Reason, one and the same word in the Original is promiscuously used for Children and for Servants, because Neither of them are at their own disposals, but at the disposals of their Guardians or masters."[42] Children, for Jackson, are both in a state of unfree limbo, neither "*Free-men nor Servants*," yet simultaneously in the same category as, and "*differ[ing] nothing from*," a servant. Echoing the potential slippage between the meanings of *magister* as father, teacher, and master, Jackson rehearses the child's subservience to his "*Tutors and Governours*," echoing Simo's metaphorical situation of his son kept "under" the control of the "Magister" who denies him his freedom.[43]

How, then, might we understand the status of children in relation to the *servus* or the *famulus*?[44] And if servants must fundamentally consent to be bound—even if, as I shall discuss, that consent is sometimes also fictional—how can it be that a child "*differeth nothing from a Servant*" without undertaking such contractual consent? The answer, for Jackson, seems to lie in the distinction he draws between partial and full abdication of consent:

Though our English [*Servant*] may be derived from the Latin *Servus*: yet servants in our English tongue we call many, which a good Latinist would rather call *Famuli* then *Servi*: being indeed *Servants*, that is, at other mens disposals, but in part only, not in whole; whom for Distinction sake we call *Apprentices* or *Hired Servants*: Over whose Actions or Imployments their Masters during the time of their hire or *Apprentiship*, have full right and Interest; and Authority likewise over their Bodies or Persons, to correct or punish them, if they take upon them to dispose of their Actions or Imployments otherwise then for their Masters Behoof, or as they shall appoint: But over their Persons, their Bodies, their Goods or Children, their Masters have no Right nor Interest. They may not take upon them by our Laws to dispose of These, as they do of their Day-Labours or bodily Imployments. Yet are these properly called *Servants*, as having made themselves such, or are so made by their Parents or Guardians, upon some Contract, or by some *Branch or Title of Commutative Justice*, in which there is always *Ratio dati & accepti*, somewhat given and taken, that binds both the Parties: As in this particular case, The *Master gives* and the *Servant receives* meat, drink, and wages; And in Lieu of these Benefits received, the *Servant* yields up, and the Master receives a Right or interest in his bodily and daily Labours, and a Power to dispose of these. Yet are they *Servants* (as we said) only *in part*, not *meer servants*.[45]

Jackson here acknowledges the provenance of "servant" as originating in *servus*, yet he is careful to distinguish between "*meer servants*" and servants "*in part*," the latter denoting both apprentices and servants engaged in *ratio dati & accepti*, the contract of mutuality that technically binds masters as well as servants. As "meat, drink, and wages," livery in its broadest sense is precisely what fixes a servant as a "hired" rather than a "meer" servant, affirming the *ratio dati & accepti* that characterizes the servant "in part."[46] But, Jackson insists, "the Bodies or persons of hired *Servants* are their own: Their mindes and Consciences are *Free*, even during the time of their *service*," even as he acknowledges that the masters of apprentices and "hired servants" have "Authority likewise over their Bodies or Persons, to correct or punish them, if they take upon them to dispose of their Actions or Imployments otherwise then for their Masters Behoof, or as they shall appoint."[47] Jackson thus distinguishes between "hired" and "meer" servants both along the lines of reciprocity, the *ratio dati & accepti*, and in terms of the difference between the master's claim to the "Actions and Imployments" of his servants and a more absolute power over their bodies and their children (raising the specter of hereditary servitude). Although Jackson notes that the "mindes and Consciences" of hired servants are "Free," they nonetheless remain subject to punishment. Children, moreover, can be "made" servants by "Parents or Guardians." More troublingly, child actors were sometimes kidnapped and impressed into acting.[48] But even under the conditions in which children could and would enter a state of "hired servant-hood" or apprenticeship, their capacity for free consent and their relationship to liberty, as I shall demonstrate, remained uncertain.

"Honestly, Orderly and Obediently": Apprenticing the Child

In 1577, John Fit John's conduct book *A Diamonde Most Precious* was published to "[Instruct] all Maysters and Seruauntes, how they ought to leade their lyues." Included within is a commentary on apprentices, structured as a dialogue between a *civis* (citizen) and a *puer* (boy). The significance of this discussion is signposted by an early modern reader's manuscript index on the title page of the Folger Library's copy of this text, which helpfully directs the reader's attention to the text's specific discussion of apprenticeship.[49] In response to the *puer*'s question about the process of apprenticeship, the *civis* replies:

> you shall goe with [your master] to the Hall [tha]t he is free of. . . . Also you must be bound by a payre of Indentures, for so many yeares as your Mayster and you can agree for, alwaies prouided whe[n] you come out of your yeres, before you haue the liberties of London, you must be of the age of foure and twenty yeres, & the same maister . . . must teach you or cause you to be taught your occupation, & he to find you meat, drink, linnen, wollen, hose, shoes and all other such necessaries. And if you haue serued your mayster truely, then he wil make you a freeman of London.[50]

The pedagogical function of apprenticeship is clearly delineated, in the explicit instruction that the master "must teach you or cause you to be taught your occupation." In addition, the apprentice's master must furnish him with livery in its broadest sense (food and general provision as well as clothing). In order to attain "the liberties of London," the apprentice must be "of the age of foure and twenty yeres" at manumission, a detail not unnoticed by the manuscript hand, who offers marginal glosses noting the discussion of "app*ren*tises" and assiduously records the age of emancipation: "Aged 24 y. free." But age alone is not the prerequisite for manumission: it is only "if you haue serued your mayster truely" that "he wil make you a freeman of London." The emphasis on the *manner* of service, particularly the contingencies of "pleasing" service, are even more explicitly underscored on the next page: "You must be . . . willing and dilligent to please your Mayster and Mistresse, in which doing, you shall fynde great commoditie and profyte" ("profit" being at least in part a euphemism, one imagines, for freedom itself).[51] How might this insistence on "willing" and "dilligent" service complicate the freedom over their minds and bodies that Jackson insists apprentices retain? Although apprentices might be understood in early modern England as *famuli*, household servants, and members of the family, *A Diamonde Most Precious* underscores the ways in which London apprentices pave the way for their contractual kin and ideological successors, the transatlantic indentured servants who so troublingly encroach upon the terrain of the *mancipium*, whose bodies can be transacted and vended along with their indentures.[52] Children and the apprenticeships they often assume thus deeply disrupt the boundaries between pedagogy and bondage, service and servitude.

Nowhere was this more apparent than in the use—and abuse—of poor indentures, which served to bind out poor children in order to relieve their parents (and by extension the parish) of the cost of their upkeep and to discipline them into work. In his discussion of pauper apprenticeships, Steve Hindle underscores the very real ways in which the notional parental consent which authorized these contracts was quite often coerced not merely financially or socially but even legally: "Although the poor laws had not *explicitly* obliged either masters to receive apprentices or parents to give up their children, rulings by the Jacobean and Caroline judiciary emphasized that the statutes *implied* compulsion."[53] And when we turn to Folger X.d.646 (1696), which binds out a "poor Child of the said Parish" of Clutton in Somerset as an apprentice until the age of twenty-four, we note that the terms of such poor indentures specifically work to mitigate financial risk for the parish and to minimize the potential for resistance or refusal (Figure 1). In this contract, Jeremie Feere is bound out to William Redman, a broadweaver, whom he is legally enjoined to serve "honestly, orderly and obediently," and whom Redman "in the Science Art or Trade of A Broadweaver in the best manner as he may or can he shall ^& will^ teach and informe or cause to be taught

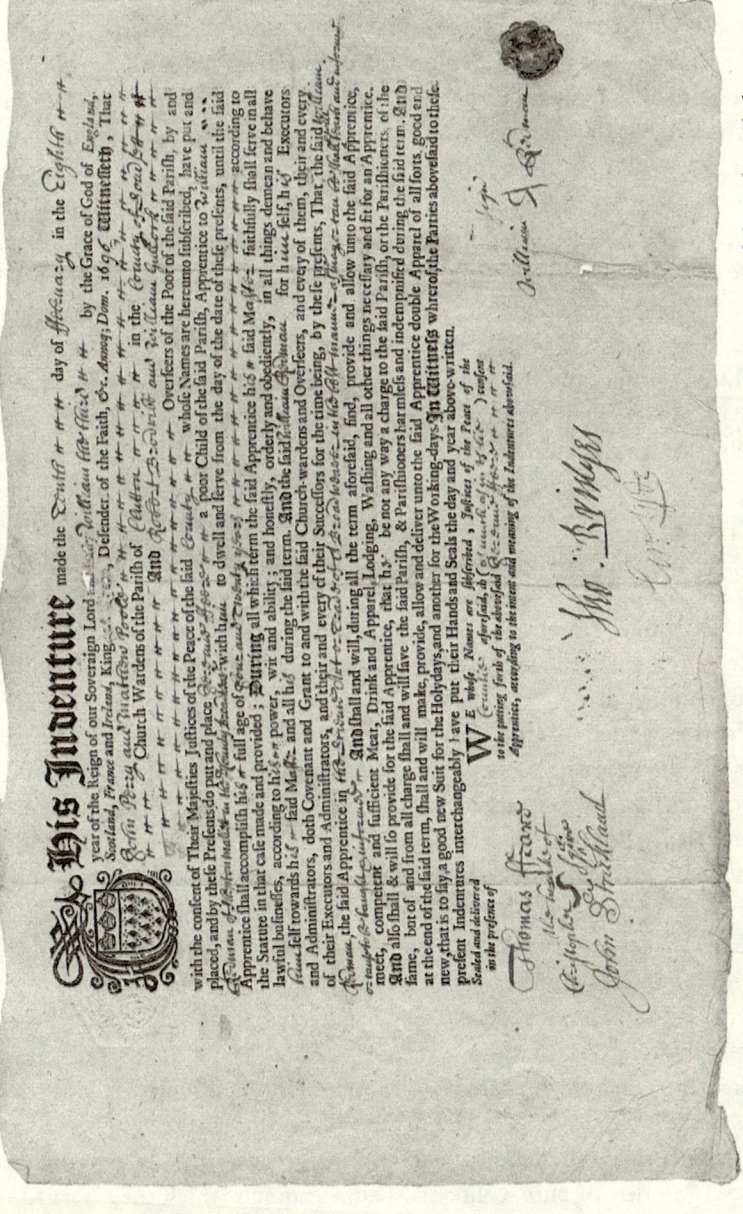

Figure 1. Apprenticeship indenture for Jeremie Feere (1696). X.d.646. Used by permission of the Folger Shakespeare Library under a Creative Commons Attribution-ShareAlike 4.0 International License.

and informed." Thus, although Feere "his said Master *faithfully* shall serve" (emphasis added), the indenture contract emphasizes the pedagogical payoff of his servitude—"servitude" being a provocative term I use deliberately here, for Feere does not, after all, sign this contract himself; rather it is (presumably) his father, Thomas Feere, who records his consent to the terms of the document.[54] But even the notion of consent is cast into disarray by the conventional yet obfuscatory language employed by the very legal apparatus that authorizes the contract. The contract is ratified by the Justices of the Peace, whose authority is textually inscribed in the document as follows (I have italicized manuscript annotations): "We whose Names are subscribed, Justices of the Peace of the *Countie* aforesaid, do (*as much as in us lie*) consent to the putting forth of the abovesaid *Jeremie ffeere* Apprentice, according to the intent and meaning of the Indentures abovesaid." The phrase "as much as in us lie[s]" is not uncommon during this period, but its use signals contingency, uncertainty—and in this instance, the clear suggestion of abdication of responsibility for the child who is only ostensibly willingly bound, so that he "be not any way a charge to the said Parish, or the Parishioners." The blank space that occupies the parentheses preceding the word "consent" invites a formulaic textual annotation ("as much as in us lie") even as it materially registers the affective and legal lacunae surrounding the operation of consent in pauper indentures.[55]

I have suggested that the binding of children to labor and the legal instruments for the apprenticeships so many assumed fundamentally destabilize the boundaries between service and servitude. And yet we remember that in Renaissance England, slavery was seen not as an extreme form of service, but rather as opposed to it. To be a slave was categorically *not* to be a servant; slavery was marginal and threatening. The 1547 Vagrancy Act's utter distinction between service and slavery—one can occur only in the absence of the other—underscores the ideological and social marginality of the slave to early modern England's service society, as well as his dangerous proximity. It is for this reason, I suggest, that the schoolboy translations of Terence discussed earlier in this chapter rendered *servus* for their young, often elite readers not as "slave" but rather as "page" or some other Renaissance designator of service. Grammar schoolboys read Terence because his elegant language provided "models of pure, colloquial Latin" through which they learned to speak.[56] For all the potentially transgressive ramifications of enacting (and maybe identifying with) disobedient sons and wily *servi*, for these schoolchildren, themselves sometimes future masters of servants, to ventriloquize rebelliousness was one thing; to embody the slave, that most marginal and disenfranchised of figures, quite another.[57]

But as we know, by this point slavery was a feature both of European and even English trade and of English captivity by Barbary pirates and Turks.[58] Othello claims that he was "taken by the insolent foe / And sold to slavery" (1.3.137–38), a fact that he not only acknowledges but capitalizes upon in his narrative seduction of Desdemona, suggesting the conflicting associations of slavery in the early modern period.[59] On the one hand Othello's use of his slave story as an instrument of seduction suggests the narrative and fetishistic power of this encounter; his "redemption" (1.3.138) from slavery is economic as well as religious, but it also signifies his passage from the margins of society (as a slave) to membership in its community (as a servant proffering his military services to Venice). Yet Othello is literally commodified by the sale of his body into slavery, and when Brabantio laments that "if such actions may have passage free, / Bondslaves and pagans shall our statesmen be" (1.2.98–99), he explicitly links slavery to irreligious otherness, both marking Othello as foreign and marginalizing him by echoing Othello's own account of enslavement. But with reports circulating in early modern England of European traders and seamen themselves being taken into captivity, slaves could no longer be so easily "othered."[60] Nor could the distinctions between master, servant, and slave be so easily sustained.[61] And while white English schoolboys and captives alike navigated their (sometimes flickering) experiences of bondage, slavery was at the same time already linked to racial and epidermal difference. Thus, the coat of arms granted to the English enslaver John Hawkins in 1565, for instance, prominently—and famously—featured an enslaved African whose arms were bound with rope, explicitly linking bondage with blackness. In Hawkins's crest, depicted on the cover of this book, the figure of the bound African is placed on top of, and juxtaposed with, the heraldic English lion. The grant of this coat of arms registered Hawkins's ennoblement: even as it commemorated Hawkins's indelible ties to bondage, this "badge of slavery," far from condemning these connections, instead secured Hawkins's entry to an upper echelon of English aristocratic status by celebrating them, once again signaling the foundations of racialized slavery to (at least some of) the English nobility, and situating slavery at the heart of "Englishness."[62] In recording the origins of Hawkins's aristocratic status in the traffic in enslaved persons, this crest attests, for the future, to the genealogies of "Englishness" which are so often hidden in plain sight, and illustrates the embeddedness of slavery in English life.

It is in part English captivity, I suggest, that paradoxically works to sanction this form of bondage. The next part of this chapter turns to an examination of early modern English captivity narratives and redemption petitions to explore how, in their accounts of bondage, English captives navigated the slippages between service, servitude, and slavery, and precipitated both the problems and the possibilities of "English" slavery. As these accounts detail the contingency of manumission, they also seem to place under scrutiny the idea of "innate" English freedom and resistance to "real" enslaveability. But in such accounts, I suggest, the strategic coarticulation of service and slavery also *ratifies* the ideologies of slavery in order to later secure them with racial difference. The trope of "redemption," so central to English captivity narratives, is also invoked by but is ultimately unavailable to Othello, who is redeemed from slavery only to be perpetually remembered as—in Brabantio's words—a "bondslave" and a "pagan." And the logics of (white, English) enslavement and redemption, I propose, paradoxically work to render palatable the structures of slavery; while Othello is "redeemed" from slavery, therefore, like so many others in early modern England taken captive by the "insolent foe," I suggest that his tragic end underscores how, in the logic of the play, unlike other captured and redeemed Europeans or Englishmen, he is indelibly marked, his blackness registering a more permanent debasement, a sort of stain of slavery.

"One of the Most Remarkable Occurrences Which Hath Happened in the Memory of Man": Slavery, Captivity, and Redemption

The problem of the *civis* or citizen being captured and taken into slavery had a dual resonance, and a dual provenance, in early modern England. The slave comedies of Terence and Plautus frequently derived dramatic tension from the prospect of citizens being captured, commercially transacted, and finally returned to their status as fully legible members of a civic community. But Tranio's advice to Lucentio to "*Redime te captum quam queas minimo*" ("Ransom yourself from captivity at the lowest possible price") in *The Taming of the Shrew*, discussed at the beginning of this chapter, not only registered its grammar school inheritance, via Lily; it also echoed the literal petitions for the redemption of kidnapped Englishmen which circulated widely in the seventeenth century. In 1680, a group of twenty signatories delivered a petition to Sir Thomas Carew and other "Justices of the peace for this County of

Devon" on behalf of one Hugh Mudge, who "beinge on boarde the Parragon of Dartmouth whereof William Sare was Master on the ffifth day of November 1679 was taken by an Algerine Man of Warr And Carried into Sally where hee is deteyned vnder most Cruell Slavery."[63] Since Mudge's mother was unable to pay the requested ransom, the signatories requested a contribution from the "County Stocke":

> hee cannot bee freed without the payment of Nynety pounds (as wee are Credibly informed) And wee knowinge the Inability of the said Mary Mudge shee not beinge able to pay soe greate a summe for the Redempcion of her son at her request doe hereby certifie the trueth of her deplorable Condicion & on her behalfe doe desire your Worshipps to take into your serious Consideracion the sad estate of the poore Captive. And to Contribute somethinge out of the County Stocke towards his Redempcion for which wee shall bee verry much obleiged to your Worshipps...[64]

The redemption petition drawn up and delivered at least rhetorically on behalf of an impecunious family member was a common trope; thus, the petition functions both as a request for funds and as a ratification of the "Cruell Slavery" being endured by the "poore Captive" in question.[65] In 1685, for instance, Elizabeth Terry wrote to William Sancroft, the Archbishop of Canterbury, requesting his assistance on behalf of her husband Abraham Terry, who

> being Master of a Vessell & bound for the West-Indyes in October 1684 was unfortunately taken by a pirate a Sally man of War who seazed upon the vessel & all the goods & Merchandice therin, & upon your petitioners said husband, & all the men that were in the said vessell, & carryed them all as Captiues into Sally & from thence to Mackanes in the Kingdome of Morocca wher your petitioners said husband remaines in great slavery & misery being allowed only bread & water & where he is likely to continue during all his life unlesse he be releiued by the Charity of well-disposed Christians.[66]

In the case of Terry's husband, "the King of that place" demanded the higher payment of three hundred pounds for his redemption and refused to "release him under [that sum] being Master of a Vessell." In both petitions, the excessive and onerous nature of the bondage is emphasized—"Cruell

Slavery," "great slavery & misery"—while the "bread & water" on which Terry is forced to subsist registers the depth of his wretchedness, a condition which may "continue during all his life" unless the petition is successful. Yet, although for both Mudge and Terry the state of captivity is not only a "sad estate" but also—barring redemption—perpetual, captivity narratives often depicted such slavery as fluid, revocable, and even potentially emancipatory. In so doing, they also disrupted the boundaries between service and slavery, emphasizing not only the slippages between but also the coarticulation of these supposedly very different states and estates.

Captivity narratives were a perennially popular genre in early modern England, containing stories of daring escape and redemption as well as more far-fetched accounts that traced scandal and intrigue across several seas. The year 1676 saw the publication of a tale that records, in the hyperbolic words of its title page, "One of the most Remarkable Occurrences which hath happened in the memory of Man" as it recounts the "True and Perfect" story of the "Examination, Confession, Tryal, Condemnation, and Execution of *Joan Perry*, and her two Sons, *John* & *Richard Perry*, For the Supposed Murder of William Harrison, Gent."[67] According to Sir Thomas Overbury's account, Harrison, a steward to Lady Campden, was out collecting "his Ladys Rents" when he disappeared; his manservant, John Perry, who had been sent to meet him, was accused of murder. Perry, in turn, charged his mother and brother with the crime, claiming that they had repeatedly asked him to "help them to money, telling him how poor they were, and that it was in his power to Relieve them, by giving them notice when [Harrison] went to receive his Ladys Rents, for they would then Way-lay and Rob him."[68] All three were executed for murder, and, for good measure, Joan Perry was accused of having bewitched her sons, "being Reputed a Witch."[69]

But Harrison resurfaced two years later, well after his supposed murderers had been executed, and, in an account that echoed other popular early modern captivity narratives, claimed to have been kidnapped, transported across the seas, and sold into slavery. He had, he said, been ambushed while collecting Lady Campden's rents, sold for "seaven pounds," and transported in a Turkish ship.[70] Upon landing,

> then came to us eight men to view us . . . and examined us of our Trades and Callings. . . . One said he was a Chyrurgion, another that he was a Broad-cloath-Weaver, and I . . . said I had some skill in Physick: We three were set by, and taken by three of those eight men that

came to view us: It was my chance to be chosen by a grave Physitian of Eighty-seaven years of Age, who lived near to *Smirna*, who had formerly been in *England*, and knew *Crowland* in *Lincoln-shire*, which he preferred before all other places in *England*: He employed me to keep his Still house, and gave me a Silver Bowl double gilt, to drink in; my business was most in that place; but once he set me to gather Cotton-Wool, which I not doing to his mind, he struck me down to the ground, and after drew his Steletto to Stab me; but I holding up my hands to him, he gave a stamp, and turned from me, for which I render thanks to my Lord and Saviour Jesus Christ, who staid his hand, and preserved me.[71]

Harrison's account is chilling for the way in which it depicts the possibility of being kidnapped and enslaved while performing everyday duties—collecting rents, undertaking one's duties as a steward, and so forth. England, in this telling, becomes not a protected terrain but a vulnerable one, subject to the kind of "ambush" and swift descent into slavery that redemption petitions often portray as taking place offshore and at sea. The slippage between freedom and bondage, England and Turkey, is exacerbated by Harrison's master's unusual familiarity with and affection for his home county of Lincolnshire, situating Harrison as both a stranger and at home in this distant land. In a departure from other, more violent accounts of capture in contemporary narratives, there is no possibility of "turning Turk" in this tale (on the contrary, Harrison is "preserved" by Christ, in his telling).[72] Rather, and strikingly, the narrative instead casts Harrison's master in an almost *emancipatory* register. Indeed, after his death, Harrison uses the silver bowl his master gave him to procure passage on a Portuguese ship to Lisbon, where he has the happy if somewhat implausible fortune to run into a gentleman who was born in Lincolnshire, and who "provided for me Lodging and Dyet, and by his Interest with a Master of a Ship, bound for *England*, procured my Passage."[73] Thus, it is the very man who buys and enslaves him who ironically enables Harrison's passage to freedom, by means of his gift of a "silver bowl" which Harrison exchanges for his journey home to liberty. This account underscores the affective networks in conditions of bondage, positing that modes of faithful service meriting extravagant gifts might also carry other, more far-reaching rewards. But it also suggests that the possibility of redemption from slavery lies *within* slavery. If fictions of consent frequently organized the depiction of bondage, this incident proffers the fantasy of freedom in servitude.

Overbury's *A True and Perfect Account* does acknowledge that "many question the truth of this Account Mr. Harrison gives of himself," but nonetheless argues for the veracity of his story. After all, it insists, "[Harrison] liv[ed] plentifully and happily in the Service of that Honourable Family, to which he had been then Related above fifty years, with the Reputation of a just and faithful Servant."[74] Indeed, the *Account* finally ends with the delicate suggestion that Harrison's *son* may have contrived his removal in an attempt to assume Lady Campden's stewardship for himself, as he in fact did. Overbury's *Account*, as we see, condenses into one intriguing pamphlet some arresting and salacious ingredients: crime, domestic disorder, betrayal, captivity and redemption, even witchcraft. But the narrative also capitalizes on the real and rhetorical economy of servitude, and the different kinds of potential affective and remunerative dynamics within these service relationships. Harrison's "happy service" to the family to whom he was "related" for more than fifty years is the principal piece of evidence to support his unlikely story of captivity; it is his loyalty as a "just and faithful Servant" that bolsters his literally outlandish claim that he was also a slave. But Harrison is also a master vulnerable to the scheming of his *own* manservant; his position as steward is both covetable and coveted—so much so, in fact, that his son may have masterminded his kidnapping. Both Perry's master and Camden's steward, servant and slave, Harrison simultaneously inhabits the roles of both citizen and stranger, *civis* and bondman.[75] Bought and enslaved, subject to beatings if he fails to undertake his task properly, Harrison is nonetheless redeemed, emancipated, and repatriated by his master's gift.

The idea that a man could be both master and servant at the same time was hardly polemical; this, after all, was the very premise of early modern England's service society, wherein everyone was articulated as a servant of some sort, where indeed service was a precondition of civic and political legibility and inclusion. Nor was the understanding of one's master as the locus of both obligation and freedom unfamiliar. Thomas Jackson, for instance, discussed earlier in this chapter, notes Christ's role in man's emancipation from "*Servitude* to Sin," emphasizing that "*whosoever committeth Sin is the servant of Sin*," a bondage from which only the "Son of God" can manumit us.[76] The imperative to serve freely, and to serve in order to attain freedom, was a well-worn trope, ratified by the *Book of Common Prayer*, which enjoined God's "humble servau[n]tes" to worship him "whose seruice is perfecte fredome."[77]

A problem arises, however, when such servants are rendered slaves, when "hired servants" turn into "meer servants," when *servi* assume the register of *mancipia*. If the genre of captivity narratives is structurally organized around the *telos* of manumission—the narrator must, by definition, have been freed in order to recount his story—Harrison's (rather embellished) account underscores the coarticulation of slavery and service, the ways in which one can be simultaneously not only a master and a servant (which is after all not only common but frequently necessary in early modern England's service society) but master, servant, *and slave*. And while the structure of captivity narratives might propound the notion that Englishmen are essentially free—that even in Turkey, one might say, one continues in Lincolnshire—contemporary letters suggested something rather different.[78]

In 1684, Henry Raines, "prisoner in Ludgate," wrote to William Sancroft, Archbishop of Canterbury, for help in securing his release from prison:

> your pet*itione*r is a very poore man aged 78 yeares and hath a wife and children residing in Huggin Lane in Theamestreete London and was soe unfortunate that hee was taken at sea by *the* moores and carryed into Barbery where hee remayned 7 yeares in Captivity and after his discharge & returned home hee was Arrested for a debt of 20 [pounds] And thereupon hath continued a close prisoner almost 2 yeares last past, And yo*u*r pet*itione*rs Creditor finding yo*u*r pet*itione*r is very poore & aged is now contented to take 5 [pounds] in full for his debt & charges & to release yo*u*r pet*itione*r out of prison hee being detayned for noe other cause, Wherefore yo*u*r pet*itione*r humbly prayes that yo*u*r Grace wilbee pleased . . . to bestow upon him yo*u*r Charity towards his discharge as yo*u*r Grace in pitty shall thinke fitting.[79]

As this letter attests, Raines's Barbary captivity ends in debt bondage, exchanging one form of enslavement for another. The structure of his letter highlights the irony of following the path of emancipation back to England only to find oneself once again imprisoned.[80] Raines's unfortunate account exposes the contingencies (and the fiction) of the *telos* of manumission, but, significantly, it also connects Barbary captivity to English debt capture, suggestively returning slavery to English soil.

But Raines's letter also emphasizes the way in which, even at this point, poverty underwrites seizures of the body.[81] As early as 1617, Ralph Winwood wrote to Sir Thomas Edmondes to try to persuade him to intercede on behalf of "one Mathew Burghe who hath bene these two yeares a gally slaue at Marseilles" to "the Generall of the Gallies there for his release."[82] Unlike others of his Company who had also been captured, Burghe could not afford to redeem himself, remaining in slavery simply because he could not buy himself out: "the said Burghe was but a servant to Captaine Bennington and so poore that he could not ransome himselfe as the rest of that Company did."

Burghe, like Raines, is a victim of desperately bad luck, but his status as "servant to Captain Bennington" underscores the extent to which his master's fate is also his own. Burghe's service is thus not only closely imbricated in his servitude, it also unwittingly binds him into bondage itself: his present enslavement is on his master's account, calling into question the limits of consent even within a service relationship in which one engages "freely." The operative fiction here seems to be that one can ransom oneself from a slavery into which one might be ignominiously and suddenly cast. Yet, this narrative disintegrates in Burghe's case. What his continued enslavement exposes, therefore, is the crucial fiction that underwrites slavery at this time: that it is, if not consensual, then revocable. His indigence reveals the ways in which slavery, at least in popular captivity narratives and at least for white Englishmen, *should* resemble debt bondage—in which the body can be redeemed for cash—but here it fails to do so. And it underscores the very real ramifications when the premise of revocability comes under pressure, when the wrong player unwittingly wanders into a rigged game.

Slavery, Pedagogy, and the Problem of *Eunuchus*

The premise of redemption in captivity narratives, petitions, and classical plays is that slavery is a fundamentally revocable condition, that the slave can be bought out of bondage and restored to his or her native liberty. At the same time, I have argued, this corpus of texts repeatedly and deliberately blurs the boundaries between very different forms of labor: slavery, servitude, debt bondage, and service. And it repeatedly returns the workings of slavery to England, defying the crucial distinction between liberty and bondage. As I shall argue in the remainder of this chapter, this move insistently resituates slavery as English, reveals the quotidian conditions and everyday environment of compromised consent, and, in coarticulating service and slavery, works to authorize the ideologies of slavery even as it affixes them to racial difference.

The slippage between bondage and freedom was perhaps most urgent and perplexing in the early modern schoolroom. The contingencies of captivity are particularly acute in Terence's *Eunuchus*, a text to which I now return in the fourth and final part of this chapter not only on account of its status as one of the staple texts of the humanist curriculum, but also, and more importantly, because it stages one of the only legibly "racialized" slaves in classical drama, an "Ethiopian" maid situated at the nexus between classical and contemporary racialized slavery, whom I shall discuss in this final section. *Eunuchus* also, unusually, presents four other kinds of slaves: a native (and generically conventional) *servus callidus* or "wily slave," a "fake" slave, a foreign slave, and a eunuch. In the play, Chaerea, the son of an Athenian gentleman, falls in love with the slave girl Pamphila, who never speaks during the play. Chaerea's older brother, Phaedria, has been courting the courtesan Thais, wooing her with extravagant gifts of exotic slaves: a eunuch named Dorus, and an Ethiopian maid. Meanwhile, Phaedria's rival, the boastful soldier Thraso, has himself bought Pamphila as a gift for Thais. In order to gain access to Pamphila in Thais's house, Chaerea disguises himself as a eunuch (upon the *servus callidus* Parmeno's suggestion) and takes Dorus's place. But Chaerea rapes Pamphila, and soon after it transpires that she is not a slave at all, but rather a free-born citizen who belongs to one of the noble families of Attica and who was wrongfully sold into slavery. Chaerea escapes the punishment of castration for his transgression (which, it is clear, is not the act of rape itself, but rather the rape of a *free citizen*) by marrying Pamphila.

In the figure of Pamphila, we encounter a citizen—indeed a gentlewoman—who has been stolen into captivity and who is in danger of being violated sexually. Pamphila has been "stoln ... out of Attica" (*ibi tum matri parvolam puellam dono quidam mercator dedit ex Attica hinc abreptam*) and given to Thais as a gift.[83] However, Pamphila's status remains slippery; she is, variously, a "Maide", (*virgo*, sig. I2v), a little serving-maid (*ancillula*, sig. E1v, translated as "little we[n]ch"), a "fellow seruant" (*conserua*, sig. Aa2r), and, finally, a "slaue" (*mancipium*, sig. H1v). Simultaneously gentlewoman and kidnapped slave, a virgin in danger of forced sexual access, Pamphila mutely embodies various contradictions. And *both* the Latin and the English find it difficult to render her status. At once *mancipium* and *ancilla*, *virgo* and the affectionately diminutive *ancillula*, the figure of Pamphila silently navigates the different resonances of slavery, service, and gentility. Although she is named, unlike the Ethiopian *ancilla*—"Pamphila" can mean both "loved by all" or "loving all"—she never speaks during the play, nor is her character included in any of these translators' lists of characters.[84]

In light of the contemporary contexts of English captivity, I suggest that the character of Pamphila would both have resonated with and troubled English readers. As a free-born citizen who is "stolne away by Pyrats," "sold . . . to a Mercant" and later violated by Chaerea, the story of her capture by pirates and her sale to a merchant might have been uncomfortably reminiscent of English captivity narratives, such as the one discussed earlier, which told of English merchants being captured by pirates and sold in foreign markets. Although at the end of the play Pamphila is discovered to be of free birth and thus a suitable wife for Chaerea, the terms consistently used to refer to her in Webbe's translation are "wench"—the word also used to describe the unnamed, racially "othered" Ethiopian slave-girl—"maid," and "virgin." But Pamphila is also spoken of as property: "*Whose* is the virgin?" Parmeno asks (sig. I3v, emphasis added); a little later, Chaerea instructs Parmeno to "procure [her] that I may enioy [her]" (sig. K3v). The transactional valences of "procure" situate Pamphila as property or chattel, and the manner in which Chaerea asks Parmeno to "procure" her reinforces her lack of volition and her status as property: "This [Maid] see thou deliuer vp to mee either by force, or secretly, or by entreatie, I am indifferent, [or, I care not which,] so I may enioy her" (sig. I3r). Pamphila's foreignness is, moreover, emphasized when Chaerea claims that "the Maide is not like our Maids" (sig. I2v), delineating a distinction between "*our* Maids" (emphasis mine) and those of Pamphila's native land. The difference demarcated is primarily a physiological one: "their mothers study [our Maids] to haue low sholdered, narrow brested, that they may become slender: If there be any a little more full bodied they say she is made to be a Wrastler, they withdraw [their] diet: albeit their constitution be good, they make them like rushes by their ouer much care, and they are beloued accordingly therefore" (sig. I2v–I3r). Part of Pamphila's appeal is that she is exotic and unspoiled, that the cultural conventions that alter a woman's natural physiognomy in Chaerea's society are absent in hers. In Roman society, slaves could look similar or dissimilar to free citizens; for an early modern society that would come to associate physiological difference with slavery, however, Pamphila's physical difference would have seemed on the one hand alluring and exotic and on the other hand problematically symptomatic of her foreignness as well as, given Chaerea's "indifference" to how she is "procured," of her status as property.[85]

Pamphila, the noble slave, has to my knowledge thus far been overlooked as a source for *Pericles*'s Marina. Marina, too, is sold as a slave for the purpose of sexual exploitation, but Marina is Pamphila redeemed, not the silent victim of rape but rather the tutor of virtue. Thaisa, Marina's mother, recalls Thais, Pamphila's adoptive sister. It is to her that Pamphila—who, like Marina, is sold by "Pirats"—is given by the merchant who purchases her, but Pamphila is sold again after her mother's death:

Her couetous brother, heire to her estate,
Nothing the wench was faire, and skilled well
In Musique; hop'd her at good rate to sell:
So forth he brought her, sold her to my friend.[86]

If Pamphila is "skilled well in Musique," Marina "sings like one immortal." transacting her talent for gold just as Pamphila does.[87] Marina may avoid the sexual violation of which Pamphila is a victim, but she nonetheless must vend her wares within the economy of slavery. If Marina recalls the beautiful slave Pamphila, so too does Paulina in Philip Massinger's *The Renegado*.[88] In the figure of Paulina—whose name itself recalls Pamphila's—we encounter another noblewoman who has been stolen into captivity and who is in danger of being violated sexually. But while Pamphila recalls the threat of enslaved Englishmen and women to Renaissance readers and audiences, *Eunuchus*'s other slaves also evoke the specter of *European* slave trading, of an incipient trade in racialized chattel slavery.

The Racialization of Bondage in the Early Modern Schoolroom

I have argued that the humanist curriculum that socialized elite schoolboys into civic obedience and authority also, paradoxically, interpellated them as slaves. At the same time, the enactment of bondage in the schoolroom ensured that the apparent paradox of English slavery was not after all an oxymoron but rather an antecedent, rendering the schoolroom the foundational terrain for English slavery. But grammar schoolboys' Latin learning not only served to navigate the vexed legibility of English slavery, it also came to mediate, and authorize, the languages and logics of racialized servitude. Schoolboys, as I have demonstrated, embodied the nexus of pedagogy and bondage as they interpellated early modern ideas of slavery. But the servitude these schoolboys mediated also authorized the racialization of bondage. The pedagogical instruments and aids—such as dictionaries and cribs—that imbricated schoolboys in the nexus of servitude and scholarship also generated discourses of race, color, and complexion, an intersection illuminated by the lexical capaciousness around the language of blackness in Véron's dictionary, which, according to Ralph Waddington, early modern schoolboys use and from which they "profit." An extensive lexicon outlines the meanings of "black," the contours of blackness, and the gradations of color. And lists such as the one below suggest that early modern schoolboys read, learned, and adopted the language of color differentiation, and that they encountered in particular the varieties of blackness (Figure 2):

> Niger, a, um. *blacke.*
> Nigella, ae, f.g. *an herb called gith, of sweet sauor, good against reumes.*
> Nigellus, a, um, dimin. *browne, a collour some what blacke.*
> Nigrior, & hoc nigrius, hui, oris, co[m]parat. *blacker, more blacke.*
> Nigerrimus, a, um, Superlat. *blackest.*
> Nigritia, ae, f.g. *blackenesse.*
> Nigrities, ei, Idem.
> Nigritudo, nigritudinis, foem. g. *blakenesse.*
> Nigredo, inis, f.g. Idem.
> Nigror, oris, m.g. Idem.
> Nigrans, huius, antis, adiect. *that which is blacke.*
> Nigrefacio, facis, factum, facere. *to make blacke.*
> Nigreo, es, ui. *to become blacke.*
> Nigresco, nigrescis, nigrui, nigrescere. *to waxe blacke, to become blacke as a coale.*
> Nigricans, nigricantis, Adiectiuum. *drawing to blacke collour, some what browne.*
> Nigro, as, are. *to make blacke.*
> Nigrico, as, are. *to be somewhat blacke.*[89]

Black, blacker, blackest; to wax black; to make black; to be somewhat black; drawing to black "collour": the list is extensive, and includes not only fine gradations of blackness, but also synonyms for these terms. Thus, *nigritudo*, *nigredo* and *nigror* all denote, in English, "blakeness," the term "idem" suggesting here a rhetorical richness for an incipient concept. But we remember that "idem" also lies at the etymological root of "identity." The descriptions of black people in early modern records not only as "blackamoors" but also as "negars" or "negres" meanwhile adopt the word for "black" that we see here, *niger*, to ascribe such identity.[90]

We find similar catalogues of blackness in other contemporary lexicons, including Thomas Cooper's *Thesaurus Linguae Romanae & Brittanicae* of 1565. But there seems to be somewhat less attention to varieties of whiteness. *Candidus* is explicated in Véron's dictionary, but the word can also mean "bright,"[91]

"Leaue to Liue More at Libertie"

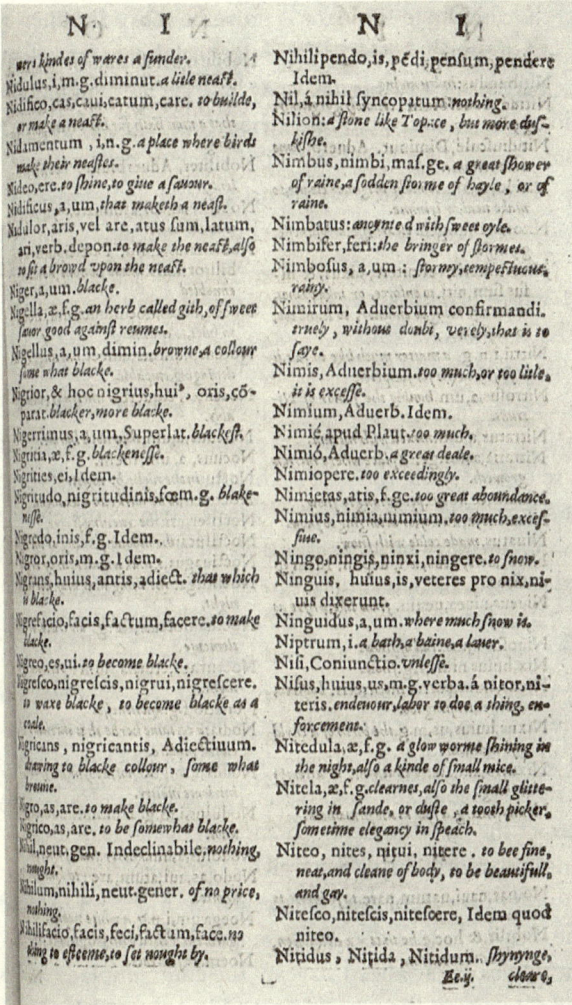

Figure 2. John Véron, *A Dictionary in Latine and English* (London, 1575), sig. 2E2r. RB 69723, The Huntington Library, San Marino, California.

and we find little under *albus* in Cooper's lexicon: *Albus, Adiectiuum,* is rendered as "white," followed by a list of Latin commonplaces featuring the word *albus*, sometimes in relation to whiteness.[92] Strikingly, "*Albus an ater sis, nescio.* Cic." is translated as, "I know not what thou art: I know not whether thou be white or blacke." But this is also how the Elizabethan schoolmaster John Conybeare renders this Ciceronian commonplace: "*Albus an ater sis nescio*: I knowe not whether thou be whyte or blacke; A proverbe spoken of them whose manners be to us unknowen."[93] Since, as the Folger catalogue for his miscellany notes suggests, papers such as this one "may have been exemplars he used in teaching," it is likely that many grammar schoolboys received this translation. What is notable here is that, again, an Elizabethan translation of a Ciceronian proverb about "manner" turns on the naturalized dichotomy of white and black. Although *albus* and *ater* can refer to invisible attributes rather than to skin color, the association between moral corruption and blackness also denotes the way in which blackness, by this point, had come to resonate as a legible register of the inscrutable. Indeed, Cooper's definition of *ater* reinforces this sense: "black, brown, dreadful, horrible, deadly, sorrowful, heavy."

But Conybeare's pedagogical exercises also index the ways in which classical blackness resonates within the terms of early modern race. In a fascinating moment, Conybeare conflates the classical Aethiopian with the early modern Moor in ways that suggest the confluence between the two in the early modern imaginary as well: "*Aethiopem lavas*: Thou washest a Mooren, or Moore. A proverbe applied to hem that prayseth a thinge that ys naught, or teacheth a foole wisedome."[94] The famous trope of "washing the Ethiop white" registers as a proverb about "labouring in vain," or, in Conybeare's words, "teach[ing] a foole wisedome" (Figure 3). In the ambiguity of both "Moor" and "Ethiop" as racialized descriptors, two apparently distinct geographical terrains become conflated in designating a marker of complexion. If the early modern stage, to quote Stephen Orgel's famous and foundational formulation, took "boys for women," the theater of the early modern schoolroom apparently took Moors for "Aethiops."[95] This is extraordinary, if not exactly surprising to us; we already know the capaciousness of apparent descriptors such as "Moor" or "Aethiop."

I want to argue, however, that this slippage also indexes a crucial intervention in the genealogies of racialized slavery. The commonplace of "washing the Ethiop white" turns on the sense that the blackness of the "Aethiop" is an exemplar of blackness; that is to say, that exemplary blackness becomes rewritten on the bodies of Moors to render them legible *both* in terms of classical precedent *and* in terms of the immutable black body. To wash the "Aethiop" white, then, is also to wash the *Moor* white, collapsing the historical and geographical distinction between Moor and "Aethiop" in the rewriting of this commonplace, and ensuring that the "Aethiop" is read *as* Moor, the Moor *as* "Aethiop."[96] In moments such as these, I argue, classical slaves were not relegated to antiquity by early modern schoolboys, but were rather urgent and exemplary, comprising not merely literary precedent but

Figure 3. Geffrey Whitney, *A Choice of Emblemes, and Other Devises* (Leiden, 1586), 57. RB 79714, The Huntington Library, San Marino, California.

intellectual and political analogues and kin. My use of the word "kin" here is deliberate, for ideas about kinship and "kind"-ness allow us to keep both familiarity and estrangement in view. Both kin and unkind, alike and dissimilar, (Roman) "Aethiops" and (early modern) Moors are simultaneously interchangeable even as the proximate translation (from "Aethiop" to Moor) comprises a temporal, spatial, and linguistic disruption.

These proximate translations from Aethiop to Moor become particularly urgent in editions of classical slave plays which were grammar school favorites—for instance, in *Eunuchus*, where we find a similar slippage. Phaedria's extravagant gifts of "exotic slaves"—the eunuch Dorus and the Ethiopian *ancilla*—are commodities in a classical slave trade, but they also invoke the language and logistics of the European commerce in chattel slavery. Thus, Thomas Newman's 1627 translation of *Eunuchus* literally transposes the language of slave trading to an early modern context; in the following passage, having obtained these expensive slaves for Thais, Phaedria admonishes her for requesting his absence:

> when late you said
> You had a great mind to an Aethiop maid;
> Did not I, laying all else care aside,
> Cast out for one? and *Eunuch* too beside
> Thou wishedst; cause great Ladies haue
> Such creatures; I found one; yesterday gaue
> Twentie pounds for 'hem.
> (*nonne ubi mi dixti cupere te ex Aethiopia*
> *ancillulam, relictis rebus omnibus*
> *quaesivi? Eunuchu[m] porro dixti velle te,*
> *quia solae utuntur his regina: repperi.*
> *Heri viginti minas pro ambobus dedi.*)[97]

An Ethiopian *ancillula* is a "maid" here, the "queens" who traditionally owned eunuchs in their courts are now called "great Ladies," and the anachronistic reference to "Twentie *pounds*" converts *minas* into contemporary currency, invoking the specter of the early modern slave trade by recalling the real economy founded on the sale of humans for pounds.[98] But I suggest that we must also attend to the language of the Ethiopian slave, who is never named. In Newman's translation she is described as a "wench," as she is in Webbe's edition, but in Newman's version she is specifically called a "*Blackemore* Wench":

Enter Blackemore Wench and Eunuch.
Parmeno: Come you here forward. This same wench was brought
   From Aethiopia.
Thraso: Some three halfe penie purchase.[99]

Newman's use of "*Blackemore* Wench" is significant, for "blackamore" is a word that has particular resonance in terms of early modern servants. At the turn of the seventeenth century, Elizabeth I's Privy Council drafted "open warrants" to remove English "blackamores" on the spurious grounds that black servants were depriving white English citizens of employment as servants, and that Elizabeth's white subjects were as a result "greatly distressed in these hard times of dearth."[100] In a vital essay on early modern polyglot dictionaries, meanwhile, Susan Phillips traces the term "knave" across its Italian, Dutch, Spanish, and Portuguese translations to argue its association not just with "menial labor" but with Africans, noting that it suggestively denotes both the possibility that "in the imagination of schoolmasters and by extension, their students, English knaves might at times be black servants or, indeed, slaves" and "the ways in which black laborers participated in the social and economic life of early modern England."[101] Elizabeth's "open warrants" may not have been "real" proclamations, but their rhetoric certainly played on the fear of black servants overrunning English households, crowding out white subjects.[102] Terence's Ethiopian slave girl, then, is portrayed as at once desired and commodified, an apt servant and a problematic one who, in an English context, supposedly disrupts the proper employment of England's servants.[103]

Yet *Eunuchus*'s Ethiopian slave is *not* always differentiated by color. In a woodcut of Act 3's characters in Johann Grüninger's 1496 printing of Terence's plays, she is clearly black (Figure 4),[104] but in the title woodcut, *ethiopissa* herself appears no different from her Athenian counterparts (Figure 5).[105] Yet her turban-like headdress is markedly different from that of the other women in

Figure 4. *Terenti[us] cu[m] directorio vocabuloru[m] sententiaru[m] artis comice glosa i[n]terlineali come[n]tarijs Donato Guidone Ascensio* (Strasbourg, 1496), fol. 39v. RB 31147, The Huntington Library, San Marino, California.

Figure 5. *Terenti[us] cu[m] directorio vocabuloru[m] sententiaru[m] artis comice glosa i[n]terlineali come[n]tarijs Donato Guidone Ascensio* (Strasbourg, 1496), fol. 28v. Folio Inc. 473, Newberry Library, Chicago.

the woodcut, similar only to that of the slave Pamphila, Thais's long-lost kidnapped sister, who is herself a foreigner and described in the play as desirable yet physiologically "different" from the local women. By the early seventeenth century, however, as we see in Thomas Newman's translation and John Conybeare's teachings, the Ethiopian slave comes to inhabit the signifier of physiological difference—"blackamore"—of both unwanted English subjects and early Renaissance enslaved people. And if we turn to the Huntington Library's copy of the Grüninger Terence, we discern a small but immensely significant addition to the Ethiopian slave.[106] A reader, clearly unhappy with *ethiopissa*'s white visage, has taken it upon himself to correct her complexion: he has inked in her face (Figure 6). In marking *ethiopissa* as a blackamoor, an exotic slave who is also a familiar face, our mystery doodler articulates race as both additive and inherent, intimate and alienated, a vestige of classical precedent and a symptom of contemporary mores and Moors, something that can be learned and something which must be repeatedly marked, remarked, and

Figure 6. *Terenti[us] cu[m] directorio vocabuloru[m] sententiaru[m] artis comice glosa i[n]terlineali come[n]tarijs Donato Guidone Ascensio* (Strasbourg, 1496), fol. 28v (detail). RB 31147, The Huntington Library, San Marino, California.

manufactured, as they literally ink the mark of slavery onto the face of *ethiopissa*. In so doing, of course, they simultaneously attempt to secure a place for *whiteness* as unmarked and unmarkable and assert—however tacitly—that white people, even in bondage, are safe from the stain of slavery, from a permanent and immutable signifier of unfreedom.[107]

I have argued, in this chapter, for the figure of the "blackamore wench" as a crucial early modern fulcrum for the association of slavery and blackness. Yet, if the blackamore of Elizabeth's so-called "expulsion edicts" is a strange interloper, depriving loyal, local subjects of their livelihoods, the "blackamore wench" of Terence's early modern readers is also a familiar figure in more ways than one, for, as I shall argue, the word "family" derives not only from the Latin for "household" (*familia*) but also from *famulus*, a Roman household slave. The spectacle of the "blackamore" may have invoked both the burgeoning slave trade and domestic labor problems, but she also crucially challenged conceptions of and distinctions between "foreignness" and "family," rethinking what it meant to be an *English* family, even as she was firmly ensconced within the English household. As I have suggested earlier, in Renaissance lexicons the term *mancipium* denotes "a mannes propre goodes or catell, sometyme a bondeman"[108] or "a prisoner taken in warre, a captiue, a bondman, a slaue, a drudge, anie thing taken with the hande,"[109] and a *servus* is a "seruant, a slaue, a drudge, a bondman" who is "in bondage or subiection: that oweth or is bound to certaine seruice."[110] I turn finally to the *famulus*, a slave with a greater degree of domestic access or intimacy: he is "a *housholde* seruant" (emphasis mine), a slave who specifically serves "in the hous."[111]

The *famulus* is thus central both to the history and to the different meanings of the family. But in early modern England, these understandings did not center on consanguinity; the word "family" itself, as I've noted, comes both from the Latin for "household" (*familia*) as well as, of course, from *famulus*. Indeed, the first meaning of "family" was "the servants of a particular household or establishment"; and although the modern understanding of "family" as "a group of people consisting of one set of parents and their children, whether living together or not ... any group of people connected by blood" was present as early as the fifteenth century, it did not become *prevalent* until much later, while service-based understandings of the family persisted into the eighteenth and even the nineteenth century.[112]

The etymological and historical resonances of *famulus*, then, emphasize the centrality of the *famulus* to the meaning and the makeup of the family. Who, then, comprised the family in early modern England? In the complaint of the

"Cittie of London" against "the Multitude of straungers that are setled amongst vs" of "three kindes ffirst Marchants 2. Retaylers 3. Artificers" who "Carrie all to the benifit of their owne Nations and render vs nothinge," servants are not named among those who disrupt English opportunities for labor.[113] But Emily Bartels notes that in her letters to the Lord Mayor of London regarding expelling "Negars and Blackamoors," Elizabeth I expresses concern that these racial groups are monopolizing opportunities for service in England: "manie [Englishmen] for *want of service* and meanes to sett them on worck fall to idlenesse and to great extremytie" (emphasis mine).[114] Through his comprehensive study of parish records, Imtiaz Habib confirms that "domestic service is what Africans brought into England initially or permanently often ended up in."[115] And the parish register entries of the London Metropolitan Archives and Habib's own *Chronological Index of Records of Black People, 1500–1677* document several early modern black servants: "Domingo, a black neigro servaunt unto Sir William Winter," "Suzanna Peavis a blackamore servant to John Deppinois," and "Cassango a blackmoore servaunt to Mr Thomas Barber a merchaunt," to name just a few.[116] Some strangers, Habib suggests, performed services of a different kind, looking particularly at "Barbary Moore," a presumably black woman coerced into an act of prostitution: "Barbary Moore's blackness is self-evident from both her names, each of which is identical to informal ethnic descriptors seen many times in this book, although unusually she has two of them, of which the first may be a deliberate punning conflation of the Christian English name of Barbara with the African coastal place name of Barbary."[117] Elsewhere, "Barbaree, servant to Mr. Smith," is glossed as a "likely black individual with an obviously given nickname resonant of West Africa."[118]

Habib's insights into the name "Barbary" as a moniker for black servants are particularly resonant for *Othello*. We remember that "[Desdemona's] mother had a maid called Barbary: / She was in love, and he she loved proved mad / And did forsake her" (4.3.25–27). Michael Neill notes the variance of "Barbara" that also evokes the "'Barbary Moors" of North Africa, and Iago's description of Othello as a "Barbary horse" and an "erring barbarian," but he also gestures toward a reading of Barbary as a black maid: "Interestingly enough this was the assumption made by Le Tourneur whose French translation (1776) adds the words '*C'étoit une Moresse, une pauvre Moresse*' ('She was a Moorish woman, a poor Moorish woman') to Desdemona's speech."[119] Barbary evokes not only the "wheeling stranger" at the heart of the play, but also the figure of the "blackamore wench" and those "strange" servants who were racially and legally distinct in English society yet quite literally members of "English" families.

Thus, when Roderigo urgently asks Brabantio, "Is all your family within?" we know the family is incomplete, not because Desdemona has fled, but because she is in a sense no longer a member of Brabantio's family at all. Yet her familial relationship with Barbary is both evoked and reaffirmed in her familial affinity with Othello, marking a point of contiguity between these two "foreign families." Forsaken, like Barbary, by "he she loved" and seeking solace in the Willow Song, Desdemona's identification with her childhood servant delineates the nexus of family, foreignness, and service in the play: Barbary the maid both anticipates the "Barbary Moor" whom Desdemona will marry and pre-scripts Desdemona's articulated anxiety about her crumbling family.[120] Desdemona's "familiar" affinity with a "foreign" member of first her service family and second her marital family is thus marked by the text.

But at the same time as the *famulus* is an intimate, he is of course still a slave. The *servi* that early modern schoolboys encountered in their Terence recalled to them not only the larger world of slave trading and English captivity, but also those *famuli* at home who were at once intimate and foreign, who would come to be associated with racialized slavery but who were also, quite literally, members of the family. These familial fictions and frameworks of service and slavery are the subject of my next chapter. The subjection of *pueri* to their *magister* both trained them to "liue more at libertie" and compelled them to confront the contingencies of liberty and subjection alike in a new global economy of servitude. Yet it also revealed the presence, and the promise, of English slavery. As grammar schoolboys encountered, mediated, and ventriloquized the slaves through whom they learned to speak, to act and to enact their place in society, to consent to their own subordination and practice their elevation, they also, paradoxically, further entrenched slavery within a kin network and nexus of family, lineage, and schooling. But they also ensured that English slavery—a legal fiction, both impossible and persistent—was not an oxymoron but an antecedent. And in originating slavery in the figures of children, in mediating bondage through the bodies of schoolboys, and in untangling racialized servitude in the pedagogical instruments of the grammar school, early modern texts not only located the schoolroom as an essential space for the pedagogy of bondage; they also ensured that the future would be rooted in slavery.

CHAPTER 3

"Am I Not Consanguineous?"

The Foreign *Famulus* and the Early Modern Household

On New Year's Day of 1511, Catherine of Aragon gave birth to a son and heir. To celebrate the birth of the new Prince Henry, a joust was held in February 1511, which was memorialized in an illuminated roll nearly sixty feet long. This Westminster Tournament Roll is notable in featuring "the only identifiable black person portrayed in sixteenth-century British art": John Blanke, a trumpeter in the courts of Henry VII and Henry VIII (Figure 7).[1] Records of monthly wage payments and gifts made to "John Blanke, the blacke Trumpet" and of his successful negotiation for higher wages, as well as the composition of this painting, suggest that he occupied a position of status and importance in the court. His depiction in the painting is striking: Blanke is differentiated from his fellow musicians not only by his dark complexion but also by his black horse. The only musician who is not bareheaded, Blanke wears a yellow and green cap.[2] Yet, structurally and compositionally, Blanke is indistinguishable from his companions: he and his horse occupy the same stance and space as his peers; he performs the same royal musical duty as his fellow trumpeters; he wears the same gray and yellow livery as the other musicians; and he bears the same royal quarterings.[3]

Nearly 170 years later, in 1680, the English émigré Richard Mulleneux wrote to the Oxford antiquarian Anthony Wood to boast of his life in Montserrat, which he was soon to leave behind.[4] "My parishoners which are all *the* protestant part of *the* Island are mighty kind & obliging," he writes as he contemplates his return to England, and "they are very unwilling to part with me." "I live here in some respects better *than* I shall in England," he muses as he describes the pleasures of Montserrat, including his lavish clothes: "I wear broad cloth, of which I have two suits, silk stockins, black spanish leather shoos, and shoos

Figure 7. College of Arms MS Westminster Tournament Roll, 1511. Reproduced by permission of the Kings, Heralds and Pursuivants of Arms.

covered with black cloth, Holland shirts, + an hat of 50s price. These are my garments, when I go abroad." But in addition to his sumptuous clothing, Mulleneux also records some more disturbing aspects of his position: he rides "as good an horse as *the* countrey affords . . . [and] I have a negro boy to look after him, which cost me 25 L [pounds]." This enslaved person "proves very well, looks after my horse carefully, speaks indifferent English, & curses & swears," in Mulleneux's sparse description of him. Just five lines after recording the "cost" of this enslaved boy, Mulleneux notes that he has "had my boy about five months, ~~bought out of,~~" before striking through this second allusion to the slaving economy that allows Mulleneux to "buy" this person.

Although Mulleneux gestures twice to his involvement in the traffic in chattel slavery, the status of this "negro boy" whom Mulleneux has purchased is now uncertain. "He runs with me according to *the* custom of *the* countrey in a livery," Mulleneux notes, suggesting that the simultaneously authorizing and binding possibilities of livery (discussed in Chapter 1) might extend to this person too, while the reference to "*the* custom of *the* countrey," as I will discuss in Chapter 4, is a common phrase in contracts for indentured servants. Mulleneux thus draws on the recognizable rhetorics of both early modern English service (in the granting of livery) and of indentured servitude (in his allusion to "*the* custom of *the* countrey"). Yet at the end of his discussion Mulleneux makes clear this "negro boy's" position: "I would bring him home with me," Mulleneux admits, "but am afraid of loosing him, because *the* laws of England admit of no slave there."

Mulleneux's admission is extraordinary for the way in which it explicitly articulates his "negro boy" as an enslaved person and thus disrupts the myth of English liberty. England may have "too pure an Air for Slaves to breath in," and although I have argued for the expedient fictionality of this claim, Mulleneux's letter makes clear the ways in which it carried legal if not ideological heft: Mulleneux clearly has no objection to purchasing and enslaving a person and, perhaps surprisingly, to naming him as a "slave," even as he is well versed in the laws and legal fictions of his "home" country. His hesitation, rather, is in regard to the potential of loss of property, framed also as the loss of one toward whom he appears to express some attachment. "I would bring him *home* with me," he states, suggesting that "home" is where this slave boy, in Mulleneux's eyes, belongs.

Mulleneux's letter places under pressure precisely the problem of what "home" is. The place of the enslaved person, particularly the racialized enslaved person, within early modern England's borders and English homes and families is one that remains heavily contested, although such contestation sometimes also performs the work of strategic elision.⁵ As I have argued, the family owes its etymology to the Roman *famulus* and thus to slavery, and indeed the earliest understanding of the family alludes to "the servants of a household." Yet if the servant and even the slave lie at the heart of the family, etymologically and philologically, early modern audiences must nonetheless contend with the place of strangers in early modern families. John Blanke and Mulleneux's unnamed "negro boy" represent two very different instances of black servants and family members (in the broadest sense of those terms) across the sweep of early modern English cultural history. How, then, do literary and cultural depictions of servitude, especially servitude imagined as foreign or racialized, account for this shift? This chapter argues that as early modern texts grapple with the philological possibilities and problems of the servant as both "family" and "slave," they also confront the place of the *English* servant as simultaneously foreign and familiar, who enacts the affective fictions that secure his position in the household but which challenge the structure of the family. Thus, the intimacy of the "secretary," affectively bound and privy to his master's secrets, paves the way for the exploitation of the networks of recompense, gratitude, and obligation which seemingly structure networks of household service. The *famulus* lies at the heart of the home; but the texts I examine in this chapter must also contend with understandings of the family oriented not only around service, but also, increasingly, around sanguinity. As they do so, I suggest that they crucially register and intervene not only in the representation of racialized bondage, but in reimaginings of the racialized subject.

Even the archive of John Blanke, one of the most notable and elevated black people in early modern England, turns out precisely to obscure even as it unearths his identity. For Blanke's name presents a puzzle. Critics have suggested that "blanke" may be a joke or nickname of sorts, a play on "blanco" or white. As Patricia Parker has argued, "English 'blank' was also part of the racialized lexicon of color, in which Spanish *blanco* or white (counterpart of Italian *bianco* or *bianca* and French *blanc*) figured the opposite of *negro* or black."⁶ Blankness may lexically denote whiteness, but we think of Othello's anger that "this fair paper" is "Made to write 'whore' upon" (4.2.70–71). Indeed, on the manuscript of the Westminster Tournament Roll, Blanke's right hand appears white, not black, suggesting a vestigial white prototype which has been overlaid with Blanke's distinctive, black representation. Whiteness or blankness, then, can be inscribed, overwritten, defaced, tainted, modified. And although it is likely that Blanke's right hand appears white because it is gloved, the visual dichotomy of white and black here registers not only the distinction as well as the proximity of whiteness and blackness, but also the way in which "blankness" tacitly anticipates the appearance of somatic—and epidermal—markers. In so doing, it denotes whiteness as a racialized positionality, and as I shall argue, also metonymically affirms that very whiteness as a quality that must be deliberately naturalized as central and essential.

Blackness, conversely, registers as immutable, such that the very famous *topos* of "washing the ethiop white" becomes a commonplace about laboring in vain (Figure 3).[7] We might think of Aaron's argument in *Titus Andronicus* that "Coal-black is better than another hue / In that it scorns to bear another hue" (4.2.98–99). But "blanke" is also tantalizingly proximate, aurally and typologically, to "black." As Parker notes, "early modern English 'black' and 'blank' were not only polarities—like 'white' and 'black'—but synonyms, capable of turning 'tropically' into one another."[8] In the figure of John Blanke, we have a black man with a white name; a white name that both disguises and denotes a black man; a man whose name renders his racial identity both hyper-legible and inscrutable; a blank laden with possibility.

In the case of John Blanke, then, the rhetoric of race obscures as much as it illuminates, underscoring the ongoing problem in early modern race studies of, as Kim F. Hall puts it, "reading what isn't there."[9] To return to a familiar question: in a pre-Atlantic moment, how then do we excavate and delimit the presence of black people in sixteenth- and seventeenth-century England?[10] How do we understand early modern blackness when the languages used to denote black people—including "negar," "moor," "blackamoor," "Barbary," and even "blank"—serve both to delineate identity and to demolish fixity, and comprise even different kinds of black people: Indians, Africans, Moors? As Imtiaz Habib has vitally argued with regard to "the un-seeability of early modern English black people," "Racial naming proceeds not from the fixity of essence but from its very ambiguity, which is to say that it fixes difference on that which resists difference, on that which is human/white but not quite."[11] In the previous chapter, I argued that rather than exploring the problem of slavery and racialized bondage solely in the terms of foreign encounter, we must excavate its roots in early modern England, in the early modern schoolroom which engaged and activated the crucial nexus between childhood and servitude. In this chapter, I suggest that we must also attend to the ways in which the intersection between servitude and kinship animates a reading of not just slavery but also somatic race, not as a "strange" phenomenon but rather as situated *within*. Bodies corporeal, political, and social claim to cohere family, kinship, and consanguinity even as they reveal—and indeed rely on—the alien at their core.

In the process, I suggest, early modern literary and cultural contexts conscript the logics of difference to construct, on the one hand, the white, English family and, on the other, the conceptual scaffolding for the underpinning of that very family by the structures of not just service, but slavery. This chapter therefore moves across a range of dramatic and popular texts as well as private correspondence to trace the convergence of tensions between service and sanguinity in the early modern family with the fictions of consent mobilized and manipulated by the "native," English servant to render palatable—and even inevitable—both the structures of slavery and an association between blackness and bondage. I begin by tracing tropes of "incorporated blackness" in two paired poems, moving to Jonson's *Volpone* to suggest that the dramatic blueprint for the "stranger within" is already generically available through the classical figure of the parasite, a dramatic convention pressed into the service of racialized difference in this play. I then turn to Middleton and Rowley's *The Changeling* to explore the ways in which the languages of debt and obligation, amity and reciprocity in service collide and collude with the discourses of "blood," dynamics which—as I shall discuss—underpin the cases of Mary Wylbram and John Daniell as well as *A Letter sent by the Maydens of London*. This latter text demonstrates how the corporeal logics of body and family are often already embedded within the languages of service. Turning next to *Twelfth Night* and then to Heminge's *The Fatal Contract*, and finally through brief readings of *The Comedy of Errors* and *A Midsummer Night's Dream*, I suggest that these texts also stage the collusion of kinship and service to limn the boundaries of the family along sanguinal and racialized lines. As early modern plays and popular discourse grapple with their registers of mutuality, amity, care, and reciprocity, they mobilize the fictions of consent to render palatable—and to presage—the operations of servitude, bondage, and slavery. The tension between service and blood in understandings of the family, I end by suggesting, simultaneously lays the groundwork for strategically imagining the enslaved person as a member of the "family" and for inscribing the very familial fictions which secure slavery.

"Portends More Terror Than Delight": Strange Servants in Early Modern England

In its depiction of John Blanke, the Westminster Tournament Roll registers not only an elevated blackamoor but also, possibly, a Spanish immigrant servant and "stranger" in the court of Henry VIII. Meanwhile, a late sixteenth-century census, the 1593 Return of Strangers, attests to the number of non-English "strangers" in London by the end of the sixteenth century. The Return of Strangers confirms the centrality of servants to the early modern meaning of the household, but also suggestively outlines what constitutes "strangeness," making clear the number of strangers or foreigners who comprise those London homes.[12] "Straungers borne out of the Lande" (which is to say, "Aliens, borne over sea") are distinguished in the Return from "straungers borne within the Realme" ("ther Children, borne since their Arivall heare"), and are further subdivided according to their household or family situation: "Houshoulders," "wives" who "keepe houses with ther husbandes," "Inmates," "The wives of the married men Inmatts," "Children," and, strikingly, "Seruantes," which include both "Men servaunts, Jornymen & Apprentices" as well as "mayden & women seruants."[13] "Strangers" in turn employed English subjects in their homes, further muddying the distinction between English and "foreign" households. In "Blackefriers and St: Martines le graunde," for instance, out of 5,545 strangers, "Seruantes" accounted for 574. But the number of "Englishmen & boys servaunts in theire houses [of strangers]," of "English women, maidens, & Girles," and of "Englishe" subjects "sett . . . on worke" added up to 1,345 (Figure 8). The 1593 Return of Strangers depicts a London whose households are becoming, to put it plainly, less and less English.

The Return does not specify here how many "straungers borne out of the Lande" are specifically black servants, as differentiated through nonwhite somatic markers, although Elizabeth I's edicts and contemporary parish records (addressed in Chapter 2) tether the presence of black denizens in early modern England to their role as servants and members—in the sense of both etymological provenance and lived experience—of early modern English families. But it is the nexus of race and servitude, in particular, that remains a vexed scholarly problem. To yoke them together—to read early modern blackness in the terms of slavery—may be anachronistic and essentializing; yet to overlook their confluence is naïve and possibly disingenuous, ignoring the ways in which English writers subscribed to their own legal fictions around slavery, and in so doing replicated them. As I attempt to show

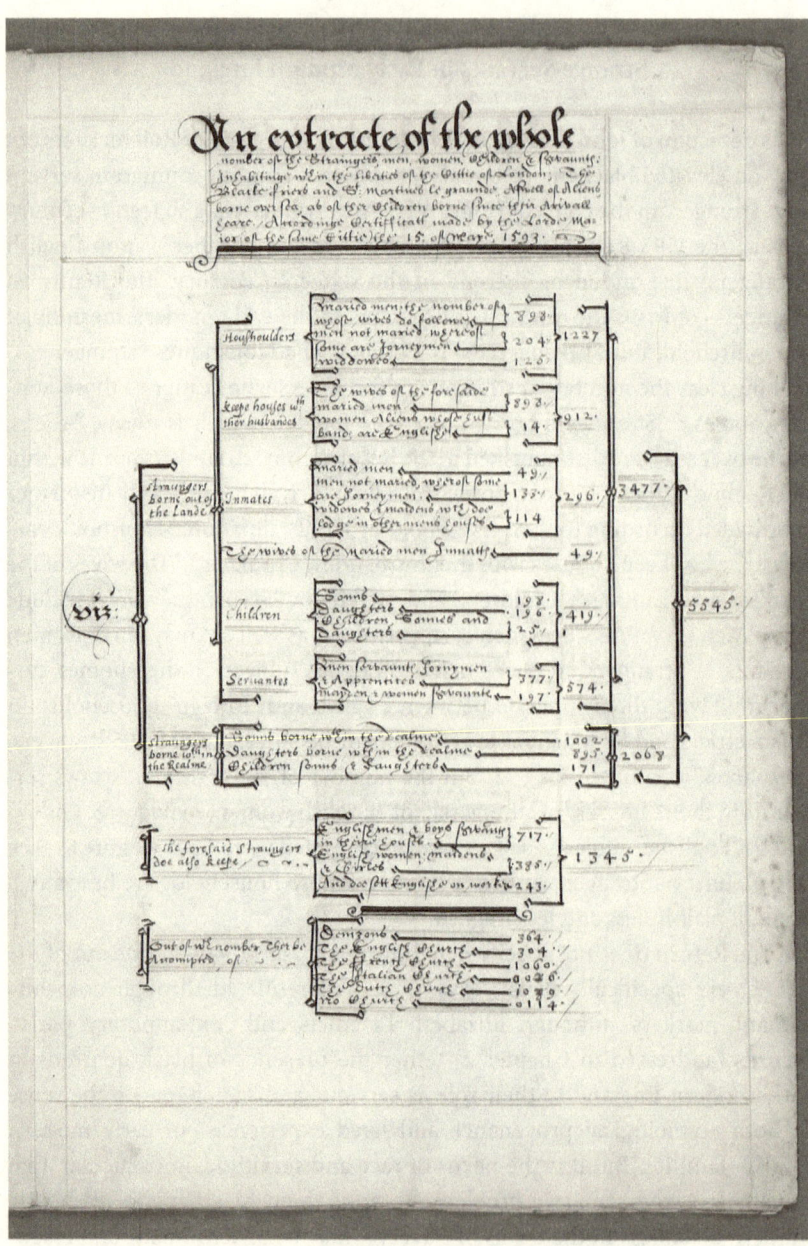

Figure 8. "Straingers 1593," Ellesmere MS 2514, The Huntington Library, San Marino, California.

both in this chapter and across the book as a whole, by mining the intersections of family, race, service, and slavery, we may excavate the strategies by which race was constellated in a complex nexus of power relations around "free service," bondage, and servitude in order to inscribe the "stain of slavery" only onto particular bodies and thereby to implicate them within the terms of hereditability. It is undeniably true, moreover, that some "blackamoors" in early modern England occupied the social and rhetorical place of enslaved people, even as slavery was, officially, a legally uninhabitable status. Thus, in 1662, a parish record in St. Benet Fink notes the burial of "Emanuell Feinande, Mr Adams' friend's slave, a blackmore," while in 1740, a parish entry in St. Katherine Coleman notes the burial of "Jacob, Mr Currie's negro boy," elsewhere recorded as "Jacob, Mr Currie's negro *slave*" (emphasis mine).[14] Both entries situate these black servants in a system of social and affective affiliations—"Mr Adams' *friend's* slave" (emphasis mine), "Currie's negro slave"—yet the possessive also marks them as property at the same time as it registers an authorizing social provenance.[15]

These entries demonstrate the slippages between the legal status of and the rhetorical tropes surrounding black servants in England, and the precisely unfixable ways in which black servants navigated the terrain between service and servitude. A now well-established scholarly tradition, however, reads early modern black denizens in terms *not* of axes of difference but rather of proximate relations.[16] Thus, the figures and fears of early modern racial representation are reimagined as not only Moorish marginalization or Dutch doubleness but as a crucial component of—to use a well-worn term—Renaissance self-fashioning, national formation, and imperial ambition.[17]

But I want to argue that an equally powerful rhetoric resisted the discourse of differentiation or the politics of mere proximity by situating the raced subject as the figure *within*, collapsing the binary framework of distinction and similitude as an interpretive and conceptual blueprint and instead, and increasingly, articulating the (white) English subject as both mediator and palimpsest of difference. Just as the conceptual origins of English slavery are located in the quotidian sites and spaces of early modern life, so that early modern English literary, cultural, and classical inheritances contain the ideological seeds of slavery, this book argues, the framing of racial difference as incorporation, I suggest, reflects and reveals a similar strategy. In the foundational work *Things of Darkness*, Kim F. Hall demonstrates how early modern "trope[s] of blackness" register not merely "aesthetic concerns" but rather a "semiotics of race" at a vital moment in England's colonial history.[18] I therefore propose that these rhetorical frameworks of incorporation—a word I use advisedly, as this chapter will explore how bodily metaphors take hold across and within the scope of service to manifest in the context of sanguinity and hereditability—hold England responsible for these racial discourses, rather than framing them in terms of encounter, and identify the pressure points that compelled these writers to demarcate—and distinguish—the racialization as well as the boundaries of whiteness. In Chapter 2, I suggested that the early modern schoolboy embodies and enacts both the languages of slavery and the affinities between classical and contemporary bondage; in this chapter, I demonstrate that early modern literary and cultural discourses also underscored how blackness is already inscribed within the white body. This, indeed, is the "blackamore wench's" contention in Henry Rainolds's "A Black-Moor Maid wooing a Fair Boy," transcribed as "The Blackamore wench to the boy" in Sloane MS 1792 at the British Library:

> Why louely boy why flyest thou mee
> Who languish in thes flames for thee
> I am blacke, tis tru; why soe is night
> And in darke shade^s^ ~~wes~~ is loues delight
> All *the* world; but close thyne eye
> Will appeare as blacke as I
> Or veiw they selfe how foule a shade
> Is by thyne owne faire body made
> Which followes thee where ere thou goe
> Oh Who allow'd would not doe soe
> Lett mee for euer dwell so nigh
> And thou shalt neede noe shade but I.[19]

The "blackamore wench" pines for her "faire" lover, acknowledging that while "tis tru" that she's "blacke," so is not only "night," but also the "louely boy" himself, under certain conditions: when he closes his eyes; when he casts a "foule" shade. The paradoxical marriage of "faire" and "foule" is hardly unusual, but we often see this dichotomy evoked in the tension between visage and virtue—for instance, in verse where the "fair" lady is "really" black, or foul. Here, however, the fair youth is himself generative of darkness, in the form of the shadow which he casts.[20] But the "foule . . . shade" made "by thyne owne faire body" also evokes the specter of the miscegenated child, the "foule" offspring sired by the "louely boy's" own body. Blackness, here, is distinguished by its very *proximity* to fairness; indeed, the "blackamore wench" ends her poem, and her argument, by suggesting that she might take the place of her lover's shade, that she can supplant the darkness of his own corporeal form, which, being a shadow, "followes thee where ere thou goe." Always already generated by fairness, blackness is always a *part* of the fair body: after all, even closing one's eyes elicits darkness.[21] The relationship between light and dark, then, is marked by not only proximity but also incorporation. In the most literal of ways, blackness is inscribed within the white body.[22]

In Henry King's "Reply," however, the "lovely boy" turns precisely the "blackamore wench's" claim to proximity on its head:

> Blacke made complayne not that I flye
> Since fate commands Antipathy
> Prodigious might that vnion proueth
> When night and day together moueth
> And the coniunction of our lipps
> Not Kisses makes but an Eclipse
> Where in *the* mixed blacke and white
> Portends more terror than delight
> Yet if my shadow thou wilt bee
> Enioy thy dearest wish, but see
> Thou take my shadowes property
> That hasts away when I come nigh
> Else stay till death hath darkned mee
> And Ile bequeath my selfe to thee.[23]

"Take my shadowes property," the boy commands, and "[hast] away when I come nigh." Refusing the "blacke made's" argument about an incorporate darkness, the boy instead reads his shadow not as essential, but rather as elusive, always fleeing. For this particular fair youth, the conjunction of black and white can only be theorized in terms of an eclipse: the white eclipsed by the black in a kiss, or in death. In the terror that accompanies the thought of their potentially "prodigious union," the lovely boy hints at the fear of a dark, miscegenated future.[24]

And yet ironically, the boy nonetheless imagines the "blacke made" as his successor. Darkened in death, he offers to "bequeath my selfe" to his "blackamore wench." At once a brutal rejection of his lover's advances—she can have him only when he is dead—and an odd reimagining of courtship as inheritance, the "lovely boy" also proffers himself not only when he is dead, but when, as a result, he is dark. "Bequeathing" in this context offers a new lineal framework, even as it remains a deeply ironic one: while it evokes generation, the dead body is, it goes without saying, fruitless. And if a bequeathal normally suggests the transfer of property, here the heir receives nothing except a body.[25]

As Kim F. Hall has noted, the imperative to "fair" reproduction (in Shakespeare's procreation sonnets, for example) also encodes the transfer of property, dynastic heritage, and other material constituents of inheritance systems which are reserved for and as white property and which secure the continuance of white supremacy.[26] The "louely boy's" bequeathal of his newly "darkened" "selfe" comprises a troubling move which gestures on the one hand to the chilling ways in which black bodies can indeed be transferred, bequeathed, inherited, possessed, and on the other to the precise fruitlessness of this particular "inheritance." It also imagines a lineal, even familial, relationship reliant on phenotypic parity. Otherwise, as the fair youth insists, we are left with only the possibility of eclipse.[27]

Although these paired poems do not explicitly allude to the structures of service—even as they do invert the gendered conventions of Petrarchan courtship-as-servitude—they redound in striking ways on the relationship between consanguineal familiarity and the bonds of service. If the incorporation of darkness within the white body insists on marking what appears to be familiar as always already strange, it also reflects the ways in which, as I have suggested, the English household finds the "alien" at its core. In the next section of this chapter, I turn to a common early modern inheritance from Roman comedy, the figure of the parasite, to demonstrate how even that most quotidian of dramatic tropes stages the threat of the stranger within, and of the foreign body at the heart of the family.

"The True Father of His Family": *Volpone's* Familia

In closing Chapter 2, I argued that the *famulus* embodies the slave at the heart of the home, as well as what I call the "foreign familiar," the stranger within who is both intimate and alien. This figure, I have suggested, becomes particularly urgent at the crossroads of subtle shifts in early modern understandings of the family as it moves from a service- to a blood-based register.[28] These slippages between the family of consanguinity and the family of service reverberate particularly strongly in Jonson's *Volpone*, in the parasite Mosca's gossiping conflation and subsequent disruption of the different understandings of "family." Early in the play, Mosca introduces Volpone's "dwarf," his "hermaphrodite," and his "eunuch" as members of Volpone's household, "trifle[s]" which give him "pleasure."²⁹ But when the inheritance-hunter Corvino asks Mosca whether Volpone has children, Mosca replies in the affirmative:

> Bastards,
> Some dozen or more, that he begot on beggars,
> Gipsies and Jews and black-moors, when he was drunk.
> Knew you not that, sir? 'Tis the common fable.
> The dwarf, the fool, the eunuch are all his;
> He's the *true father of his family*,
> In all save me—but he has given 'em nothing. (1.5.43–49,
>   emphasis added)

The family of service and the family of consanguinity map onto one another here in unusual and disastrous ways. In a pun on the meanings of "family," not only is Volpone the patriarchal father of his household, he is also the "true" blood father of its members "In all save [Mosca]." Mosca casts his master's paternity in terms of miscegenistic sex, emphasizing that Volpone has fathered monstrous servants, which, as a long tradition of monstrous birth pamphlets would attest, bear witness to the social and sexual transgressions that Volpone has enacted. In excluding himself from the blood lineage, Mosca subordinates the family of blood to the family of service (even as he paradoxically seeks to *remove* himself from service through his parasitical stratagems) and creates a space for himself to be the true inheritor and "heir" (5.3.22) precisely because he is *not* "proper issue" (1.4.103), which in this play signals both illegitimate and monstrous consanguinity. In excluding himself from the "true" family to argue for new lines of succession, Mosca also parodies both the fetishization of lineage and, I would suggest, the inclusiveness—which is perhaps also racial—of the early modern English "family."

But the form of Mosca's revelation about his master's monstrous children is also troubling. At first, Mosca displaces and deindividuates the rumor; it is simply the "common fable," he remarks airily. But in Mosca's formulation, the rumor has no source; moreover, the word "fable" both signals something factually unlikely and accords with the magical and monstrous nature of these supposed children, "The dwarf, the fool, the eunuch."³⁰ Yet then the fable, in

Mosca's telling of it, becomes consolidated into fact: "He's the *true* father of his family," he states, "In all save me." Not only does Mosca disseminate this rumor about his master, then, deliberately voicing the "fable" even as he attributes it to a larger and unidentified "common" mouthpiece, he also reconfigures it into a much more categorical, "true" statement in a matter of just a few lines. When he not-so-innocently asks, "Knew you not that, sir?" he works to cast the rumor as common knowledge, something he assumes his listener already knows, and simultaneously distances himself from its dissemination.

Mosca's indiscretions, then, undermine his master's authority and compromise the integrity of his household, at the same time as they construct an alternate lineage for his patron. In describing Volpone's monstrous servants as his "family," Mosca literalizes the metaphor of the household *as* a (blood) family. But in this play about disinheritance, "true fathers" disown true sons; Mosca convinces Corbaccio to disinherit his son Bonario in favor of Volpone "without . . . least regard, unto your proper issue" (1.4.102–3). Mosca's rhetoric thus destabilizes the lines of succession between true fathers and proper issue, utterly denying blood relatives (albeit illegitimate ones).[31] His engineering of Bonario's disinheritance foreshadows Mosca's own usurpation of Volpone's wealth. Master and servant do reverse roles, at least briefly, as critics have pointed out,[32] but I also want to suggest the larger repercussions of Mosca's disruptive discourse. As a member of Volpone's household gossiping about private affairs in a public capacity, Mosca underscores early modern anxieties about servants trafficking in privileged information. Even more troubling, however, is the speed with which his new, brief position of wealth is publicly recognized. Despite "Being a fellow of no birth or blood" (5.12.112), when he announces himself Volpone's heir he is immediately and opportunistically pronounced by the 4th Avvocato "A fit match for my daughter" (5.12.51), a claim that underscores the fictions of lineal and consanguineal integrity by authorizing a matrimonial match based not on familial "fitness" but on a recent usurpation that dismantles the very notion of what makes a family "fit." Mosca's economic mobility is accompanied by a dizzying, if momentary, social ascension that not only exposes and parodies the social and sexual fault lines in early modern England's service society, but also bears out Mosca's cynical pronouncement that "All the wise world is little else in nature / But parasites or sub-parasites" (3.1.12–13), just waiting to feed off someone else's good fortune.

Mosca's own depiction as a parasite is particularly significant. Although the biological sense of the parasite as a harmful "foreign body" did not become prevalent until the eighteenth century, early modern understandings of the parasite as "a base flatterer, or soothing companion," "a trencher friend," evoked its classical antecedents, the parasites of Terence and Plautus.[33] Parasites, as much as strangers, are foreign familiars, and in speaking of them as such I want to establish a discursive and dramatic framework for those "alien" bodies who paradoxically occupy positions of intimacy and service in early modern English households and on English stages. In their peculiar role as foreigners and family members, strangers serving in early modern English homes resist their legal and political distinction by reimagining the English family. But if the stranger is marginalized as a national interloper co-opting English labor and resources, the parasite—with his more trusted literary and cultural provenance in classical comedy—estranges systems of friendship and family in ways that reorient the "extravagant" foreignness— recalling Othello's description as "extravagant and wheeling"—of nationally or racially differentiated strangers.

But the early modern parasite's *subversion* of his literary predecessors in Jonson's *Volpone* also enacts a relationship of strange affinity or "foreign familiarity" with his classical provenance which disrupts the very networks of friendship and family on which he has formerly depended. The classical parasite transacts information for food—the word derives from the Greek *para* (beside) and *sitos* (grain, food)—and relies on the integrity of the household for his livelihood. The parasite Mosca, however, distorts this model, peddling slander to upend his patron Volpone's family and to become the master of the household he has served.[34] It is by disrupting the very parasitical tradition it explicitly borrows—by undermining the generic "family" to which the trope of the parasite belongs, as it were—that *Volpone* problematizes the structure and succession of the early modern household.

Perhaps the best-known classical parasite is the figure of Gnatho in Terence's *Eunuchus*, who had become by the early modern period synonymous with parasitism. For Thomas Thomas in 1587, a "Gnatho" was "A parasite, a smel-feast, a flatterer"—a definition that marries the parasite's appetite for food with his association with excessive flattery and sycophancy.[35] Thomas Newman's 1627 translation of *Eunuchus* includes this description of the parasite and his master: "*Thraso.* & *Gnato*. These I couple: for what good Musique makes a trumpet without its ecco. . . . The souldier a bragging sot, of necessitie therefore a Cowheard; the other a Clawbacke rubbing his proud itch. The Parasite thus farre wise, that he can make vse of his foolish Master: for he pickes matter of mirth and meanes out of him."[36] The master and his parasite are here figured as a couple, framed (sarcastically) in specifically aural and musical terms; the parasite is an echo of his patron. But at the same time the echo is itself a means of manipulation and sycophantic parasitism and parasitical sycophancy, allowing the parasite to "[pick] matter of mirth and meanes out of" his master.[37]

Jonson's Mosca, however, articulates an explicit turn away from this understanding of parasitism, denouncing those who "fawn and fleer, / Make their revenue out of legs and faces, / Echo my lord" (3.1.20–22). For Mosca, parasitism is innate rather than learned, talent rather than tradition, nature, not nurtured: one must have

> ... the art born with him;
> Toils not to learn it, but doth practise it
> Out of most excellent nature; and such sparks
> Are the true parasites, others but their zanies. (3.1.30–33)

This is an explicit departure from both Terence and Plautus, whose parasites have "trained" themselves to act as they do. Not only does Mosca present a naturalized and naturalizing rather than a professional view of parasitism, he also rejects the tradition of echo as a form of parasitical sycophancy. Rather than deploying the mimetic form of echo, Mosca claims another skill: to be an "observer" to Volpone (1.1.63). But "observe" is itself a fraught term, suggesting both to "treat with respect, worship, honour," "pay attention to, watch, or notice," "preserve, retain," "watch over," and "keep safe," but also to "watch attentively or carefully" and "make observations" upon others; it suggests a gaze that can be protective and respectful, or excessive and evaluative.[38] And indeed, as Volpone's "poor observer," Mosca both judges and protects, honors and appraises. Appearing to protect his "patron" from inheritance-hunters, Mosca in fact embodies a troubling understanding of "observing" as very vocally "remarking" or "making observations upon" him, and in so doing realizes two competing but simultaneous literal meanings of ob-serve: his doublespeak works *against* the imperative to service even as he appears to be laboring *toward* it.[39]

Performed nearly contemporaneously with *Volpone*, *Othello* offers a parasite who evokes Jonson's, and who, like Mosca, both recalls and subverts the classical parasitical tradition from which he derives. The classical roots of Iago's parasitical nature perhaps lie most directly in Terence's Gnatho, whom I have discussed above. At the conclusion of *Eunuchus*, Gnatho tricks his patron Thraso into a course of action which exploits his wealth for another master's end. Thraso has begged Gnatho to procure him access to the woman he loves, the courtesan Thais; in return, Gnatho extracts a promise that Thraso's "house may stand open to me in your presence, [and] [in your] absence, that there be a place for me alwayes vnbidden."⁴⁰ But Thais is beloved of the comic hero, Phaedria, whom she loves in return. By manipulating both men's feelings for Thais, Gnatho ensures that he will remain well provided for:

> *Gnatho*: I am of opinion that the souldier [your] riuall is to be receaued.
> *Phaedria*: Ha, to be receaued?
> *Gnatho*: Doe but thinke vpon it: you liue with her by *Hercules Phadria* & at great expence, for [indeed] you keepe a bountifull table. And [you haue] little to giue and it is of necessity that *Thais* receiue much, that shee may apply herselfe to your loue, without your cost. For all these things there is no man more fit, nor more for your turne. First of all he both hath to giue, and he giueth, no man more plentifully: He is a foole, a [fellow] without falt, a dull [coxcombe:] he snoreth both night and day. Nor need you feare him lest the woman fall in loue [with him] that you may easily driue him away when you will ... Moreouer, this likewise, which I esteeme to be the verie chiefest, he entertaineth a man no man better, doubtlesse, nor more abundantly ... this one thing likewise I intreat you, that you receiue me into your companie. I rowle this stone long enough now.⁴¹

Gnatho here persuades Phaedria to exploit Thraso's foolish generosity—and secures in the process a reliable source of food and "companie" for himself. Although he has thus effectively betrayed his patron Thraso to his rival, Gnatho convinces Thraso that he has in fact carried out his orders: "After that I had informed them of your fashions, and praised [you] according to your actions & vertues, I obtained [my request]."⁴²

If Thraso is "a foole," "a dull coxcombe" distracted by love, so too is *Othello*'s Roderigo. Indeed, Iago calls him "my sick fool Roderigo," whom, like Thraso, "love hath turned almost the wrong side out" (2.3.44–45), and boasts, "Thus do I ever make my fool my purse" (1.3.361).⁴³ And while at the beginning of the play Roderigo reminds Iago that he "hast had my purse / As if the strings were thine" (1.1.2–3), he later regrets the fact that "[his] money is almost spent . . . I shall have so much experience for my pains. And so, with no money at all and a little more wit, return again to Venice" (2.3.335–39); like Thraso, Roderigo has foolishly pursued a woman devoted to another man. But although Roderigo is his parasite's "fool," Iago also intends to "Make the Moor thank me, love me, and reward me / For making him egregiously an ass" (2.1.291–92), as he suggests in his declaration of false, and parasitical, intimacy with Othello:

> In following [Othello], I follow but myself.
> Heaven is my judge: not I for love and duty,
> But seeming so for my peculiar end.
> For when my outward action doth demonstrate
> The native act and figure of my heart
> In complement extern, 'tis not long after
> But I will wear my heart upon my sleeve
> For daws to peck at. I am not what I am. (1.1.56–63)

Iago's divided duty to Roderigo and Othello in order to follow "but [himself]" mirrors Gnatho's comic strategies, but it also exemplifies the parasitism vilified in a contemporary pamphlet, M.B.'s *The Triall of true Friendship; or perfit mirror, wherby to discerne a trustie friend from a flattering Parasite* (1596). In his discussion of "the double dealing of men, how they carried most commonly two faces like Ianus under one hood" (dissimulation strikingly evident in Iago's boast that "I am not what I am"), M.B. argues that "thou canst haue but one true friend":[44] "But how can a man that is said to haue many friends, execute this office of true friendship, when in the same instance one friend inuites him to a banket, and another sends for him being sicke: . . . he can do his dutie to no more but one . . . it appeareth, that true friendship can bee onely in the duall number, namely an unfained consent of two mens willes and affections, & a transportation of two hearts into one body: and therefore a frend is called *alter idem*, another moity, or another selfe."[45]

This strikingly intimate ideal of friendship, in which a "trustie friend"—as opposed to a "flattering parasite"—is "another selfe," is ironically subverted in Iago's pledge to "follow but myself" in his friendship with Othello.[46] Othello is "another selfe" not because he has "transport[ed]" "two hearts into one body," but because for Iago to follow Othello is simply to follow his *own* "selfe." Without the "love and duty" of the "*unfained* consent of two mens willes and affections" (emphasis mine), Iago distorts this model of friendship into a destructive parasitism that is reinforced both by his "Ianus"-like qualities and by his divided seeming-loyalties to both Othello and Roderigo.[47] Iago, like Mosca, disseminates slander; like Mosca, who disdains those who "with their court-dog-tricks, that can fawn and fleer, / Make their revenue out of legs and faces, / Echo my lord" (3.1.20–22), Iago has only contempt for "Many a duteous and knee-crooking knave / That, doting on his own obsequious bondage, / Wears out his time" (1.1.43–45). And while Gnatho's parasitic deceit effects familial reconciliation, Iago, like Mosca, destroys his master's "family," both that of blood and that of service, by disseminating rumor and in his violence toward another member of Othello's family, Desdemona's servant Emilia.[48]

For Iago to resist the bonds of service, as for Mosca, is to situate himself outside the nexus of family. And since the "strange" suggests both that which is "not of one's own kin or family," as well as something "Of or belonging to another country; foreign, alien," to be "unfamiliar" is to be "strange."[49] But when Iago refuses to "demonstrate / The native act and figure of my heart" (1.1.59–60), he unwittingly underscores the service he owes even as he denies it: the word "native" suggests not only something inherent as well as national or racial belonging (as opposed to Othello's dubious provenance in "here and everywhere" [1.1.133]), it also in the early modern moment carries, in specific instances, particular resonances in relation to servitude: "Of a servant, bondsman, etc.: having that status from birth; born in servitude," even as the word also registers an association with the proximity of birth, belonging, and family.[50] Yet it is precisely the "extravagant and wheeling stranger['s]" (1.1.132) tale of being "sold to slavery; of my redemption thence" (1.3.138) that enables Othello to become "familiar" with Desdemona in the first instance. The peculiar nexus of nativity and service, strangeness and familiarity, asks us not only to resituate servants—and servitude—at the heart of early modern debates about foreignness and familiarity but also to understand even the citizen of one's own nation and the native member of one's family as the "foreign familiar," the parasite, the stranger within. And as I will discuss in the next section of this chapter, early modern plays also staged the danger of the native servant and household intimate who could precisely exploit the fictions of consent and mutuality embedded in service to mount a threat to the discursive fictions of the service-based family by insisting on its potential for "blood."

"This Last Is Not Yet Paid For": Servitude and Recompense in *The Changeling*

Early modern texts, the previous section of this chapter suggests, posited the possibility that the "native" citizen or family member can be "bound," despite English fictions of freedom, and the parasite can be as alien as the stranger. Despite this—or, perhaps, because of this—some early modern discourses nonetheless insisted on asserting the precedence of "blood" over the affective ties of service. Middleton and Rowley's *The Changeling* stages one of the most dangerous iterations of this problem, wherein the servant refuses the economic and political terms that would mark his labor as service rather than a different kind of erotic and even familial relationship altogether: one based on blood. This blood-based relationship both looks to the desire for consanguinity and registers the blood*shed* which compels return and creates a perpetual indebtedness in its beneficiary. *The Changeling* not only indexes the social imperative to "free service"—as volitional, willing, affectively generous—while emphasizing that such service can never truly be *gratis*; it also underscores the horrific ends to which that fiction of consent can be placed by "native" servants who exploit the family's philological slippage between service and sanguinity.

When Beatrice-Joanna first decides to entrust the "horror ... blood and danger" of her "service"—the murder of her betrothed, Alonzo—to De Flores, she seduces him with affectionate language, abruptly relinquishing her former harshness toward him.[51] If De Flores was previously a "Slave" (2.1.68), now he is "*my* De Flores" (2.2.99). But although De Flores interprets her words as loving, even erotic—"She calls me hers already, *my* De Flores!" (2.2.99)—the possessive signals both affection and a master's control of her servant's will. De Flores is not, however, Beatrice's servant; he is her father's. "[A] gentleman / In good respect with [her] father," he "follows him" (1.1.138–39). Although he is a man of gentle birth "thrust ... out to servitude" by his "hard fate" (2.1.48), De Flores refuses to allow his service to be defined in fiscal terms, elevating him to the position of steward, as distinct from a waged hireling.

And so when Beatrice attempts to set the terms of her future recompense, De Flores prevents her from doing so. Beatrice promises him, "When the deed's done, / I'll furnish thee with all things for thy flight" (2.2.141–42), but De Flores refuses to enter into the contract she proposes, deliberately delaying any discussion of pesky compensatory details: "Aye, aye, we'll talk of that hereafter" (2.2.144). Rather, he repeatedly emphasizes that he serves

Beatrice-Joanna *freely*, assuring her, "How sweet it were to me to be employed / In any act of yours" (2.2.121–22), and affirming his willingness to undertake the murder in insisting, "It's a service that I kneel for to you" (2.2.117). In the fiction of consent De Flores iterates, he sidesteps the question of recompense altogether. But De Flores simultaneously exploits the semantic slippages of Beatrice-Joanna's language. When Beatrice reassures him that "[his] reward shall be precious" (2.2.130), using "precious" to mean "of great monetary value,"[52] De Flores reveals that he has "assured [him]self of that beforehand, / And know[s] it will be precious" (2.2.131–32), apparently echoing Beatrice's language but actually glossing "precious" as "beloved" or "held in high esteem."[53] And while Beatrice-Joanna deploys the language of dependence in addition to the language of love—"I throw all my fears upon thy service" (2.2.140)—she fails to understand how De Flores's volitional service can be intended to realize their *mutual* amity and dependence, how it can simultaneously comprise a labor of love and a form not of monetarily and volitionally free service but rather of recompensed—and billable—work. De Flores's service creates an outstanding obligation, and in denying Beatrice the opportunity to determine the repayment, he himself retains control of the return. It is only after having killed Alonzo that De Flores asserts the payment he desires—Beatrice herself—claiming that the murder is but a small price to pay for the munificence he is about to receive:

De F. [*Aside*] My thoughts are at a banquet for the deed;
I feel no weight in't, 'tis but light and cheap
For the sweet recompense that I set down for't. (3.4.18–20)

The word "recompense" carries a range of meanings, suggesting both compensation for an injury and repayment for a favor or gift, the making of amends as well as a reward for service.[54] "Recompense" thus comes to signal the conflicting registers of service: an outstanding obligation and a duty fulfilled, sexual possibility and monetary return. It is clear what this recompense is *not*: De Flores maintains a crucial distinction between his "recompense" and any form of economic return. When Beatrice offers a ring worth "near three hundred ducats" (3.4.43) from the dead Alonzo's dismembered finger (a remarkably phallic transfer in precisely the way De Flores might wish, since he hopes also to assume Beatrice's sexual "ring"), De Flores accepts it as his "fees" (3.4.46).[55] But when Beatrice clarifies that "'tis not given / In state of recompense" (3.4.49–50), De Flores seems angered at the very suggestion:

"No, I hope so, Lady, / You should soon witness my contempt to't then!" (3.4.50–51). The ring may be conceptualized in terms of its financial value of "three hundred ducats," but in reading the ring as payment, Beatrice reveals her understanding of it both as a marker of De Flores's servile status and as a means to discharge her debt to him for his service. Yet to De Flores, the ring taken from the hand of Beatrice's betrothed is a sign of affection. While a ring is frequently used in early modern plays as a signifier of courtship, this ring is also "the first token [Beatrice's] father made [her] send" (3.4.33) to Alonzo.[56] By bestowing upon De Flores her betrothed's ring, then, Beatrice seems to mark him not only as Alonzo's (and her) social equal but also as her sexual partner. Yet valuable personal objects—such as clothes and jewels—were of course also given by masters to their servants as livery, and such livery was (or was sometimes intended as) a "material mnemonic" of the servant's obligations to his master.[57] Alonzo's ring is thus freighted with the conflicting intentions and desires of both Beatrice-Joanna and De Flores: it is simultaneously a payment and livery, an attempt to discharge a debt and a reminder of the inadequacy of that repayment. It also signifies opposing obligations: while Beatrice means for it not only to repay De Flores but also to incite his gratitude—if it is not given as "recompense," it can be a gift or livery, which always creates a debt—for De Flores the ring confirms an affective relationship with Beatrice, and, precisely since it is not recompense, it signals Beatrice's outstanding obligation to him.

The ring thus becomes an ambiguous signifier of both amity and servitude, and De Flores's angry response to Beatrice's talk of "recompense" reveals his conviction that the ring is the former, a sign of love. Oblivious to his reaction, Beatrice explains that the ring does not comprise his recompense only because she is prepared to give him a greater financial reward:

> Bea. Look you sir, here's three thousand golden florins.
> I have not meanly thought upon thy merit.
> De F. What, salary? Now you move me.
> Bea.   How, De Flores?
> De F. Do you place me in the rank of verminous fellows,
> To destroy things for wages? Offer gold?
> The life blood of man! Is anything
> Valued too precious for my recompense?
> Bea. I understand thee not.

> *De F.*   I could ha' hired
> A journeyman in murder at this rate,
> And mine own conscience might [have slept at ease],
> And have had the work brought home.
> *Bea.* [*Aside*]   I'm in a labyrinth;
> What will content him? I would fain be rid of him.
> [*To De F.*] I'll double the sum, sir.
> *De F.* You take a course to double my vexation, that's the good you
>   do. (3.4.61–74)

Beatrice believes that the amount of her reward will convey her high estimation for De Flores: since her payment is not "mean" in the sense of "modest," or "thriftie,"[58] it will suggest that her opinion of her servant is neither "low" nor "poor," that she does not "meanly" judge his "merit." But the money here would be a *false* signifier, for far from esteeming him, Beatrice in fact "would fain be rid of him." And De Flores, who disdains "salary" and "wages," is insulted rather than gratified by Beatrice's offer of money. Although "wages" and "salary" later come to denote quite different forms of payment, at this point the terms are interchangeable, with contemporary lexicons defining "salary" as "hire" or "a servant's stipend or wages" and "wages" as "salary."[59] Yet there is clearly a distinction between the "recompense" given to an esteemed servant and the "fees" paid to a mere "hireling." We remember that De Flores has lost a formerly elevated station; he might well bristle at the lucre that marks him as a "fee'd post."

De Flores thus seeks to distinguish himself from a mere "journeyman" in his determination—and his ability—to dictate the form of his own recompense. Yet the terms in which he does this are themselves slippery. He insinuates that he is due extraordinary recompense on account of "the life blood of man" that has been sacrificed. In so doing, De Flores argues that his reward should be measured by his own actions as well as against the value of another man's life. Despite the clear obligation to "recompense" De Flores, therefore, Beatrice's compensation reflects on and repays two parties (even if one of them is dead), subverting what seems to be a straightforward relationship between the act and the recompense, the debtor and the debtee. Moreover, De Flores makes clear that he and Beatrice are joined by blood; even if "the life blood of man" that binds them has been shed through an act of murder, it nonetheless represents the relational space that De Flores now seeks to fill—that of her sexual and marital partner—and simultaneously underscores the means by which he stakes his claim to a new mode of familial membership: blood.[60] The "life blood of man" that has been spilled also suggests, ironically, a generative, life-*giving* blood that can engender new affective alliances and affiliative spaces.

For De Flores to reject Beatrice's coin, then—and to do so despite the fact that he "want[s]" it "piteously" (3.4.112)—is to reframe the dynamic of their relationship altogether. As I have suggested, De Flores's fiction of free service creates an outstanding obligation for Beatrice. And if this obligation cannot be discharged with money, it remains an outstanding debt, which can be dispensed with only as De Flores's "pleasure"—and not simply some form of "wealth"—dictates:

> *De F.* Soft, lady soft;
> The last is not yet paid for! Oh, this act
> Has put me into spirit; I was as greedy on't
> As the parched earth of moisture, when the clouds weep.
> Did you not mark, I wrought myself into't,
> Nay, sued and kneeled for't. Why was all that pains took?
> You see I have thrown contempt upon your gold,
> Not that I want it not, for I do piteously:
> In order I will come unto't, and make use on't,
> But 'twas not held so precious to begin with;
> For I place wealth after the heels of pleasure,
> And were I not resolved in my belief
> That thy virginity were perfect in thee,
> I should but take my recompense with grudging,
> As if I had but half my hopes I agreed for. (3.4.105–19)

A Maussian reading of the gift offers a useful model here for theorizing De Flores's recompense and understanding the logic by which he seeks to reframe his place in the family.[61] By rejecting (for now) the money that he needs "piteously," De Flores is demonstrating his "power,"[62] while in emphasizing the value of his initial gift—"the life blood of man!"—he reminds Beatrice-Joanna that her recompense must, according to the rules of gift exchange, match or exceed the value of his initial gift.[63] But because De Flores's "opening gift" is so "precious," money can never comprise an adequate "reciprocating gift."[64] If Beatrice earlier used the language of dependence to persuade

De Flores to her service, now she is literally subject to his will and to his determination of an appropriate repayment. Should she fail to return a "sufficient" present—her virginity—his "insult" to her (in Maussian terms) will be to "confess all" (3.4.149). The repeated evocation of the specter of blood—from the "life blood of man" (3.4.66) to the proposed "payment" in virginal blood—underscores, again and again, the genealogical and familial violation De Flores portends. And due to the inestimable value of a man's "life blood," there is always the danger that Beatrice's debt can never be properly repaid, that her virginity will be not a true reciprocating gift but merely an "advance present" that affirms the outstanding debt even as it attempts to recompense it. Since Beatrice is now the "deed's *creature*" (3.4.137, emphasis mine)—re-"created" by her part in the murder to a person of little value, a "thinge made of nothynge"[65] who has "lost [her] first condition" (3.4.138) and must now "settle . . . In what the act has made [her]" (3.4.134–35)—in this postlapsarian world her virginity, while more valuable than money, may well be less "precious" than the prize De Flores once deemed it to be. Both recompensed work and loving service, De Flores's actions are also a gift than can perhaps never be repaid.

In refusing to accept the economic terms of his labor, De Flores presses a fiction of consent into the service of reimagining his place in his master's family as no longer a steward but rather a son-in-law, at least structurally. As we have seen in the multivalences of Beatrice's ring, the refusal of payment or even of livery immediately ruptures not only the financial but also the (fantasy of the) affective bond between master and servant, supplanting it with something much more amorphous and dangerous. And as I shall discuss in the next section of this chapter, the invocation of an outstanding debt and of the politics of obligation proves a surprisingly effective strategy for servants who wish to exploit the slippages between families conjoined by blood and families bound by service.

"We Are to You Very Eyes, Hands, Feete & Altogether": The Body of the Family

In 1567, a pamphlet was published that articulated a striking affirmation of servants' rights. *A Letter sent by the Maydens of London, to the vertuous Matrones & Mistresses of the same,* signed by "Your handmaydens and seruants Rose, Iane, Rachell, Sara, Philumias & Dorothy" but written by anonymous writer(s) who were most likely not themselves servants, responded to a published pamphlet (since lost) entitled *The Mery Meeting of Maydens in London*.⁶⁶ *The Mery Meeting* had accused maidservants of abusing their excessive leisure time by frequenting the theaters and engaging in other activities resulting in laziness, moral laxity, and the dereliction of domestic labor, concluding that servants should no longer be allowed this time away from their work. In their *Letter*, however, the "maidservants" write back against these accusations, emphasizing how indispensable they are to the citizenry of London. The "handmaydens" paint an ominous picture of what will happen if they are denied their "lawful libertie," their temporary reprieves from their labor: "in a verie shorte time and space, ye shoulde haue gotten very fewe or no seruants at al, when such as are born in the countrey shoulde choose rather to tarie at home, and remaine there.... Then, the less inured and accustomed that euery matron and mistresse were to toyle and drudge ... the lesse paines that the mistresse were able to take, the more neede should she haue of hir handmaid or seruant."⁶⁷

Once the maidservants leave, their mistresses, unaccustomed to such arduous labor, will learn the "paynes" of "toyle":

> But ye (good Matrones and Mystresses) withoute your maides what coulde ye doe when now ye are paste paines taking youre selues, some by reson of age waren vnweldie, some by the grossenesse of your bodies, some by lack of bringing vp in paines taking, and som for sundry and diuers other reasonable respects and causes, we are to you very eyes, ha[n]ds, feete & altogether. If ye byd vs go, we run, & are as loth in any thing to offe[n]d you, as ye are to be grieued.... The more & the greater that your businesse are (right worthie Matrones) and the lesse able that ye your selues are to accomplishe them, the more merite those your poore maidens, that take that toyle for you.⁶⁸

The *Letter* acknowledges the important "businesse" of these "right worthie Matrones," underscoring the maidservants' "merite"—indeed, their indispensability—in working to "accomplishe" it. But the *Letter* also emphasizes the mistresses' vulnerable dependency, ascribing this not only to their lack of habituation to labor but also to their physical incapacity; they are "waren vnweldie" by age and by "the grossenesse of [their] bodies." As a result, their servants must take "paines" on their behalf; but they also redeem their mistresses' physical deficiencies, becoming literally indispensable to their employers by supplying the "very eyes, hands, feete & altogether" of their masters and mistresses. This is a strikingly intimate portrait of the master and the servant as a *single*, corporeally conjoined entity, of servants supplying the most essential faculties of their weakened and dependent employers. Ironically, however, the *Letter* moves from emphasizing the mistresses' dependency to invoking their care, arguing for affective as well as corporeal closeness by articulating the relationship between mistress and maidservant as mutual and indivisible: "For as ye [masters and mistresses] are they that care & prouide for our meat, drinke and wages, so we are they that labor and take paines for you: so that your care for vs, and our labor for you is so requisite, that they can not be separated: so needeful that they may not be seuered."[69]

This somewhat idealized portrait strategically underscores the mistresses' mutual dependency on and mutual benefit from their maidservants. The exchange of "labor" for "meat, drinke and wages" is clear, but this transaction is framed not as remuneration but as "care" and provision, recalling the larger rhetoric around livery. Indeed, the language of the *Letter* here emphasizes the supposed affective underpinnings of service relationships, so that the maidservants "labor and take paines *for you*" while their masters and mistresses "*care* & prouide for" them (emphasis added). "Labor," in other words, derives less from duty than from devotion, and is here calibrated in terms of "care," "paines" in terms of "provision"; indeed, the incorporated bodies of mistress and maid are now reimagined as the indivisible union of "care" on the one hand and "labor" on the other, "so needeful that they may not be seuered."[70] By describing themselves as corporeally conjoined, the maidservants invoke the metaphor of both the true friend as "another moity, or another selfe" as well as the stranger within the incorporated self.[71] Yet, even as the *Letter* emphasizes mutuality and intimacy in one passage, it threatens to abandon the mistresses to an unaccustomed and arduous "toyle."

A Letter sent by the Maydens of London may only ventriloquize servant perspectives, but if the affective bonds described in the *Letter* are a rhetorical strategy manipulated by an impostor narrator, however, it is a strategy employed in the letters of servant supplicants more generally.[72] In 1626, Mary Wylbram, the former "gouernes" of the Earl of Bridgewater, wrote to him to ask that he remain neutral in a case concerning her father's will, a case with significant financial ramifications.[73] In her letter, Wylbram evokes not only her past intimacy with the Earl of Bridgewater but also the specific form of her past relationship to and even authority over him in an attempt to remind him of his obligation to her, using both affective and mnemonic rhetorical strategies to influence the economic outcome.

Wylbram had reason to be concerned: it was the Earl's "kinesman," Sir Richard Egerton, who was threatening to "heape charges and trobles" on the Wylbram family. In effect, Wylbram asks the Earl to take the part of his family of service, not of his "kinesman . . . off [his] name," his consanguineal family. She nonetheless writes to ask for the Earl's help, opening her letter by recalling her past service: "my humble dutye remembered may ytt please your honor to geue mee Leaue to open my my [sic] trobles vnto you as on whous noble fauor I make most account off." She also urges the Earl, in turn, to remember her own blood kinsmen's service to him: "and in rememberence off my latte husband and hes cheldren who are no strangers to your lo*rdship* w*i*th my selfe wonst your gouernes, thus nothing doutting of your L*o*rd*ship*s faver. . . . W*i*th my vmble seruece remembered to your selfe and my Ladey." Wylbram here recalls not only her own "humble dutye" but also draws on a larger network of familiarity and service by evoking her "latte husband and hes cheldren." In urging the Earl's "rememberence" of her family's service, Wylbram effectively compels his obligation to help by invoking his gratitude. "Thus," once he remembers, there can be "nothing doutting of" his "faver" toward his "poor frende and olde gouernes," she asserts, her use of the word "thus" underscoring the fact that "rememberence" *must* lead to "faver."[74]

Wylbram's evocation of her prior role as "gouernes" is mirrored in the Earl's reply, which is addressed to "My Good Gouernesse" and which attests both to the intimacy of his association with his "olde gouernes," in Wylbram's words, and to her former position of authority: "I thinke fitt a little to quarrell my Gouernesse, who coulde be so suspicious or Jealous of her Charge, as to thinke it requisite to haue desired him to stand indifferent betweene party & party, (especially so louing and kinde frendes,) in suites w*hi*ch concerne particuler Interests."[75] The Earl protests against Wylbram's skepticism that he might not be a "louing and kinde frende" and promises not to take his cousin's side against her family's interests. Just as Mary Wylbram ends her letter by invoking her former role in their relationship, so too does the Earl, who signs his epistle, "*y*o*ur* very affectionate frend & respectfull charge."

The language of this epistolary exchange might ventriloquize the relationship of "charge" and "governess" very effectively, but it does not obscure either the fact that Mary Wylbram is now the supplicant nor the material considerations that underlie Wylbram's request, despite the rhetorically affectionate language. After all, the Earl's position is precisely what allows him to "thinke fitt a little to quarrel" with Wylbram. Yet by insisting on the recollection of her former authority and of their intimacy—a recollection effectively realized and tacitly acknowledged in the Earl's epistolary language in turn—Mary Wylbram successfully reminds the Earl of his obligation to her, compelling his help. The economies of memory, of obligation, and of intimacy thus animate networks of financial transaction through the persuasive vector of an epistolary mnemonic. If Wylbram's "vmble seruece" is a gift which obligates the Earl's "stand[ing] indifferent"—a slight misnomer, since he denies his own kinsman his support and hence his "indifference" comprises a considerable recompense for Wylbram's family—it is a gift that both compels return and in Derridean terms simultaneously denies its own capacity as gift by insisting on "rememberence."[76] The Earl's generosity and *caritas*—his "faver" and charity—in turn reinforce his relationship with Wylbram as *carus*, both affectively and economically dear, while revealing that very affective economy as strategic, if not altogether fictional.

This tension between monetary and affective economies is readily apparent in the 1599 forgery case of John Daniell of Daresbury, a "servaunte" to the Earl of Essex who stole some letters belonging to the Earl's wife.[77] Daniell took these stolen letters

> to one Mr Peter Bales a scrvyenor for to make coppies of the same le*tt*res and procured the said Bales to write expresse and counterfaite the same le*tt*res as neere and like as he possible could to the said Earle of Essex proper hand writing and to observe the same length and distaunce of the lynes the scantling of the margent and the proporc*i*on of the paper wherw*i*th the said Daniell had fitted him very conveniently; So that thoriginall and the coppies mighte not be different or discerned one from another; and the rather to provoke the said Bales thervnto the said Daniell moste falsely abused the name of the said Countesse and told the said Bales a counterfaite and vntrue messuage pretending that the said Countesse had sent him to the said Bales purposely to gett him the said Bales to coppy the same le*tt*res for her self in such manner as they mighte resemble one another in all likelyhood (verbatim) and w*i*thout any alterac*i*on.

Although the letters were "only le*tt*res of affecc*i*on" to the Countess from her husband, when she discovered that they were missing she was very anxious to retrieve them, for "when her Lorde should knowe that his le*tt*res should be exposed to the view of the world only by her Credulity and want of Care, it mighte for ought she knewe hazarde his vnkindenes towardes her wh*i*ch if she could she would prevent with all she were worth." Daniell, however, refused to return the letters, instead demanding three thousand pounds for their safe return, claiming that "he was become very much ympouerished of late and decayed in his estate above three thousand pounds during his service with the said Earle, the said Earle having had small respecte of him."

Daniell's unauthorized copying and forgery of the Countess's letters (through the proxy of Peter Bales) evokes and parodies the role of the secretary with its attendant claims to both authority and intimacy in the early modern period: "The Secretorie, as hee is a keeper and conseruer of secrets, so is hee by his Lorde or Maister, and by none other to bee directed. To a Closet, there belongeth properlie, a doore, a locke, and a key: to a Secretorie, there appertaineth incidentlie, Honestie, Care, and Fidelitie."[78] Daniell not only usurps and violates the function of the secretary—his "counterfaite and untrue messuage" to the "scryvenor" mirrors his "counterfaite" authority—he also dismantles the fiction of labor for "care" (in the sense of provision and intimacy as well as solicitude) and of the relationship between supplicant and patron. Far from providing for his servant, Daniell argues, the Earl "ympouerished" him, costing "his estate above three thousand pounds." The "gift" of his free service and his subsequent impoverishment, in other words, is met with ingratitude and "small respecte"; without the receipt of either "care" or *caritas*, and in the absence of the relationship of supplicant and patron with its concomitant exchange of labor and provision, Daniell must exploit the Countess's "want of care" to demand not remembrance, but recompense.[79] Daniell's case thus reveals even as it dismantles the fictional exchange of "willing" service in return for paternalistic provision.

As we see, Mary Wylbram's letter places pressure on the distinction between intimacy and economy, recompense and care by compelling the "rememberence" of her closeness with the Earl of Bridgewater.[80] But although Wylbram invokes the fiction of supplication by underscoring its reliance on Maussian "gift" exchanges, the case of John Daniell exposes those very fictions of supplication and generosity, of labor in return for *caritas*. If Wylbram compels the Earl to remember the family of service—not merely of consanguinity—in which he is imbricated, and the authors of *A Letter sent by the Maydens of London* insist on the rhetorical incorporation of the corpus of servants into the bodies of their mistresses, Daniell, like De Flores, not only reveals the difficulty of receiving proper recompense in the absence of remembrance, but also exposes precisely the dangers of servile intimacy and familiarity. As the next section of this chapter demonstrates, however, strategies of willing service can be conscripted by the structures of kinship when they serve the ends of consanguinity.

"Am I Not Consanguineous?": The Recompense of Blood in *Twelfth Night*

I now turn to the ways in which some early modern discourses themselves insisted on reimagining the servant as the kinsman. For Malvolio, the steward in *Twelfth Night* who must maintain order and prevent unnecessary household expenditure, who has the "power . . . to direct and order the gouernement of [the] houshould," Sir Toby's profligacy and riotous behavior violate the claims of hospitality.[81] Although Malvolio is Olivia's steward, while Toby is her kinsman, Malvolio nonetheless possesses the authority to "turn [him] out of doors" on his mistress's orders.[82] When Malvolio chastises him, however, Toby is furious, asserting his blood relationship with Olivia to justify his behavior and his high status: "Am I not consanguineous? Am I not of her blood?" (2.3.72).

Toby's bluster, though, exposes his anxiety that although he is Olivia's kinsman, he has no more and perhaps rather less authority than her steward. In emphasizing his claim to Olivia's hospitality and his superiority over Malvolio by speaking of "consanguinity" and reminding him that he is "of [Olivia's] blood," Sir Toby reveals his concern that his place in the household is insufficiently recognized, suggesting that it is deeply uncertain, that he could, in fact, be "turn[ed] . . . out of doors." Malvolio is not the only member of Olivia's household who objects to Toby's excesses. Olivia's gentlewoman, Maria, also attempts to persuade him that he "*must* come in earlier a-nights. Your cousin, my lady, takes great exceptions to your ill hours" (1.3.3–5, emphasis mine) and again that he "*must* confine [himself] within the modest limits of order" (1.3.7–8), although admittedly not with very much success.

Nonetheless, Malvolio must be punished for his officiousness toward Sir Toby. The epistolary forgery that both shames and humiliates him is plausible in part because it so readily rests on the affective and economic bond between mistress and steward. Its opening line—"I may command where I adore" (2.5.104)—evokes precisely the dynamic of intimacy and authority we see navigated by Wylbram and the *Letter sent by the Maydens of London*. Malvolio accurately glosses the letter's use of "commands"—"Why, she may command me. I serve her, she is my lady" (2.5.104–5)—but, like De Flores, he reimagines "my lady" in the terms of courtship, not service, misreading the interplay of "command" and "adore" as *particular* rather than as inherent in the rhetorical tension between duty and devotion central to the discourses of service.[83] The letter's promise mimics this; when it assures Malvolio that "thou art made if thou desir'st to be so" (2.5.135–36), it suggests both erotic and economic remuneration. Malvolio's extravagant daydreams of the "daybed where I have left Olivia sleeping" (2.5.43–44) on the one hand and "play[ing] with my—some rich jewel" (2.5.54) on the other indulge precisely these fantasies.

The irony, of course, is that once Olivia learns of Malvolio's troubles, she articulates again the language of intimacy in emphasizing that Malvolio is *carus*, "dear" in both affective and material terms: "Let some of my people have a special *care* of him. I would not have him miscarry for the *half of my dowry*" (3.4.58–59, emphasis added). It is Olivia herself who calibrates affective "care" in economic terms, who recognizes Malvolio's worth to her home and her estate as "half of my dowry." But of course it also tethers Malvolio's value to her marital worth, slipping uneasily between his place in her household and his ramifications for her kin networks, ironically bolstering Malvolio's claim to be marriage material—if not quite in the way he had intended.

Yet Malvolio's final letter, wherein he "leave[s] [his] duty a little unthought of, and speak[s] out of [his] injury" (5.1.296–97), troubles the exchange of duty and devotion, insisting on remembrance even as he denies it, but he dismantles this dynamic entirely when his supplication is unmet. "I'll be revenged on the whole pack of you" (5.1.364), he claims, collapsing "my lady" into a "pack," but not before accusing Olivia of doing "notorious wrong" (5.1.316) to him. Like Daniell, Malvolio abandons the fiction of supplication; yet Olivia's last words suggest sympathy, even *caritas*, for the maligned servant who is the focus of her final words in the play. "He hath been most notoriously abused" (5.1.365), she asserts, echoing his language of "notorious" wrongdoing and thereby incorporating him linguistically, dramatically, and affectively into the body of her final utterance, evoking the corporeal conjoining of mistress and maid in *A Letter sent by the Maydens of London* and leaving us with a striking reminder of the problematic slippages between duty and dependency, insubordination and inseparability in early modern service.

For Olivia's reckoning of Malvolio's worth—"half of my dowry"—also, of course, underscores his indispensability to her household. Malvolio may be a Puritan and a prig, but even Sir Toby realizes that he may have gone too far in his taunting of his adversary: "I would we were well rid of this knavery. If he may be conveniently delivered, I would he were, for I am now so far in offense with my niece that I cannot pursue with any safety this sport to the upshot" (4.2.63–66). To redeem himself, he marries Maria. This is Fabian's brief history of the events preceding this marriage:

> Most freely I confess myself and Toby
> Set this device against Malvolio here,
> Upon some stubborn and uncourteous parts
> We had conceived against him. Maria writ
> The letter at Sir Toby's great importance,
> In recompence whereof he hath married her. (5.1.347–52)

But as the audience knows, this narrative simply isn't true. If we return to Act 2, we remember that it is *Maria* who conceives of and executes the epistolary forgery: when Sir Toby asks, "What wilt thou do?" (2.3.142), Maria immediately outlines a fully developed scheme: "I will drop in his way some obscure epistles of love, wherein by the color of his beard, the shape of his leg, the manner of his gait, the expressure of his eye, forehead, and complexion he shall find himself most feelingly personated. I can write very like my lady, your niece. On a forgotten matter we can hardly make distinction of our hands" (2.3.143–48).

Maria's boast to Sir Toby that "On a forgotten matter we can hardly make distinction of our hands" suggests that there have been many occasions on which Maria has written for Olivia, has (legitimately) assumed her identity, perhaps even as an amanuensis or a secretary in a more official capacity.[84] The proximity of their scribal and lexical discourse is certainly clear: Maria claims that her hand is "very like" Olivia's, and Olivia herself concurs that it is "much like the character" (5.1.334). Malvolio, who, as Olivia's steward, would know her hand intimately, is also fooled by the forgery: "It is in contempt of question [Olivia's] hand" (2.5.79–80).[85] But if Fabian's account is accurate, then it is by acting at Sir Toby's "commandement" that Maria particularly compromises her singular allegiance and therefore her secretarial duty and her "Honestie, Care, and Fidelitie" to Olivia.[86] Except, as we know, Maria doesn't act at Sir Toby's behest. So why do we have these conflicting accounts of the forged epistle, and why is Maria's part in the letter trick so thoroughly effaced?

Reading either a queer or a homosocial alliance between Maria and Olivia, several critics have pointed out that not only does Toby's so-called recompense of marriage protect Maria from punishment at the hands of Olivia and Malvolio, it also spares *Olivia* from punishing Maria—a punishment that would rupture the "homosocial alliance" between them—by incorporating Maria into Olivia's kin network.[87] Certainly the marriage resolves Maria's abuse of her secretarial intimacy, very deliberately resituating her within a consanguineal family rather than one bound by service. But Maria's part in the letter trick also suggests that, since she did not undertake her role "at Sir Toby's great importance," there is no call for the "recompense" of marriage. Maria's forgery, indeed, operates as a perfect Derridean gift, to be neither repaid nor remembered; her assertion that "On a forgotten matter we can hardly make distinction of our hands" (2.3.147–48) confirms this, framing her letters not as mnemonic calls for recompense but as the opposite, as "forgotten matters." Yet, I argue, Maria's gift of the forged letter, which begins as perfectly Derridean, absent even its own memory, is rendered, through Toby's insistent "recompense" of marriage, something closer to a Maussian dynamic, with its attendant structure of exchange. Transliterated into a patriarchal ("rudimentary" or crypto-capitalist) gift exchange of letter for bridegroom, Maria's Derridean gift-*as*-gift is forgotten, Maria herself absented, and her former familial relationship with Olivia supplanted.

Maria's forgery emerges as a gift that is especially unsettling outside a clear affective framework. If both De Flores and Mary Wylbram wield the memory of past fealty to secure future recompense, Maria's refusal to participate within that economy ensures that reinscribing her as kin emerges as the only means of resolving her unauthorized use of familial intimacy in her role as a servant. The long critical tradition of unquestioningly accepting Fabian's account situates readers and audiences of this play as similarly complicit in the text's depiction of marriage and of new kin networks bound by blood rather than service. This play and its readers mobilize the fictions of consent in service to map the boundaries of the family along the lines of consanguinity, and at the same time they anticipate "familial" depictions of servitude which import and rely on such fictions of consent. In so doing, they establish the framework for the way in which, as I will discuss in the next chapter, the nexus of blood, service, and natality lays the groundwork for Atlantic servitude. And as we shall see with regard to Milton's *Paradise Lost*, the politics of obligation and Man's "debt immense" paradoxically demand the performance of fictions of consent even as they secure the move to servitude, bondage, and even slavery.

Yet, the framing of Maria's marriage as recompense works to reveal and ratify her move from servant to secretary to "consanguineous" family member even as it distinguishes and secures these different understandings of the "family." For as I shall discuss in the next section of this chapter, if the "native" servant emerges as both foreign and familiar, the sanguinal family member is also revealed as unknowable, their affiliations of blood both ratifying and threatening to familial futurity and the legibility of lineage. In William Heminge's *The Fatal Contract*, I shall argue, the specter of the racialized servant who is also a slave underscores the slippages, tensions, and assonances between slavery and somatic difference even as it discloses the threat, and the promise, of servitude as and at the heart of the home. In staging a white woman, played by a boy actor, in the guise of a blackamoor eunuch—a masquerade that is narratively disclosed to the audience at the end of the play but never visually revealed—*The Fatal Contract* invokes a number of tropes this book has mentioned: the parasite, the classical slave eunuch, the privileged Ottoman slave eunuch, the blackamoor servant or slave, and the classical slave who is "really" a long-lost member of the family. As it combines these tropes in a single figure, *The Fatal Contract* stages a "sootie" blackamoor servant and slave who is altogether *too* familiar to play on the titillating yet ultimately foreclosed prospect of miscegenation and to suggest that slavery is seeded in the native and natal home.

"Mingl[ing] with These Sootie Limbs": Slavery, Sanguinity, and Miscegenated Bodies in *The Fatal Contract*

William Heminge's *The Fatal Contract* (1638–39) features a blackamoor servant who is a eunuch, a plotter and a schemer who drives much of the action of the play. Although named Castrato, *The Fatal Contract*'s eunuch is most frequently referred to simply as "Eunuch," repeatedly recalling the generic dramatic trope of the eunuch and the plays that feature them; the Queen's eunuch servant evokes the representation of Turks and of Ottoman households in early modern plays, in which eunuchs are simultaneously sexualized and literally desexed, depicted as lascivious by virtue of proximity to women who are normally secluded from public view.[88] Thus, implicit in the relationship between mistress and eunuch in *The Fatal Contract* is the possibility of sexual access. The Queen promises to "unclaspe my soul to thee, / I've alwaies found thee trusty, and I love thee," but the physical intimacy she attempts to generate falls flat:

> Now by this light I'm taken strangely with thee,
> Come kiss me, kiss me sirra, tremble not.
> Fie, what a January lip thou hast,
> A paire of Iscicles, sure thou hast bought
> A paire of cast lips of the chast *Diana's*
> Thy blood's meere snow-broth, kiss me again.[89]

This is an unnerving spectacle of apparent interracial intimacy between a blackamoor eunuch and his white mistress, the kind that—to an audience familiar with similar scenes in *Titus Andronicus* and *Othello*—might well foreshadow a tragedy. Such a spectacle must engender both fascination and fear in its audience, not to mention the titillation of witnessing such intimate contact with a eunuch, a figure both alien and sexually inaccessible.

It is not until the end of the play that we learn that the eunuch is in fact Chrotilda (the daughter of Brissac, "an old Peer of *France*"), who has been raped by Clotair, King Childerick's son, before the action of the play begins. Described in the list of characters as "*Crotilda*, by the name of *Castrato*, as an *Eunuch*," Chrotilda appears "as herself" only in the very last scene of the play, and "her" part is noted as "eunuch" in the 1653 playtext even after "her" true identity is revealed. Thus, when the Queen appears to seek sexual gratification from her servant, without success, the joke is that the blackamoor eunuch is "actually" a white woman, and her "blood" may indeed resemble "meere snow-broth." This is a joke that perhaps the audience could be party to: a few lines earlier in the scene, the eunuch declares,

> Were but *Chrotilda* here, and these two youngsters,
> It were a pastime for the Gods to gaze on.
> Oh were I but a man as others are,
> As kind and open-handed nature made me,
> With Organs apt and fit for womans service. (sig. B4r)

We imagine, perhaps, a moment of stage business in the first line, where the eunuch, Castrato, makes it quite clear that Chrotilda *is*, in fact, "here" on stage—but maybe not, for nothing else in the play's dialogue alerts us to this disguise plot. When the eunuch expresses "his" regret that he is not "a man as others are," the audience assumes that this is a reference to his lack of male organs. The eunuch's last remark, that "he" wishes that he could be "fit for womans service," seems in a similar register to comprise a lewd comment about his supposed inability to "serve" women sexually. And yet, the joke rebounds on the audience; "womans service," it transpires, simply alludes to the offices that women perform. The audience is caught wrong-footed in its desire for titillation, revealed to be poor readers of the body of the blackamoor eunuch, and, by extension, of his language as well.

But as the eunuch also notes, if "he" were truly a man,

> I'd search the Deserts, Mountaines, Vallies, Plaines,
> Till I had met *Chrotilda*, whom by force
> I'd make to mingle with these sootie limbs,
> Till I had got on her one like to me,
> Whom I would nourish for the *Dumaine* line;
> That time to come might story to the world,
> They had the Devil to their Grand-father. (sig. B4r)

This explicit and alarming threat of rape—Castrato plans to "get" on Chrotilda, "by force," "one like to me"—is considerably altered by our (eventual) awareness that this threat is hollow, that he is himself Chrotilda, and that rather than "*making* [her] to mingle with these sootie limbs," Chrotilda is already intermingled with "his" body: it is one and the same. This conflation of both whiteness and blackness may recall the poems discussed at the beginning of the chapter, which traced the inscription and incorporation of blackness within white bodies. But *The Fatal Contract*'s eunuch "constantly *performs* his blackness," a performance that is permitted by his "real" whiteness and "real" femininity and one which also rests on the racist trope of sexual rapaciousness.[90] It is thus all the more troubling that Chrotilda, speaking as Castrato, imagines the future of the Dumaine line—her line—as testifying to a "devilish" ancestry originating in the blackamoor eunuch "getting" on her "one like to me." Chrotilda readily reproduces the logic first of racial pollution and second of the conflation of blackness with sin. But she also anticipates the narrative force of this move, so that the mark of blackness persists two generations later to "story to the world" the true provenance of these descendants' "Grand-father."[91] Indeed, the imagined baby will be "nourished" not for its own sake but rather for the "Dumaine line," nurtured in order to reveal lineal corruption rather than to secure familial futurity.

This prospect of unacceptable mixture does not only evoke racial miscegenation; rather, it also raises the prospect of class-based lineal degeneration. *The Fatal Contract* is, indeed, one of the few plays of the period where the use of the word "slave" is applied to an apparently somatically marked and differentiated figure, when the "banished Lord" Lamot enquires of the whispering Castrato, "What sayes the slave?" (sig. C2v). Although "slave," as we know, would more often signify a pejorative insult than denote a "literal" slave in this period, the use of the word here registers "a term of contempt" even as it articulates the body of the blackamoor servant in the very terms of *racialized* slavery.[92] Thus, when in Act 3 Clotair wonders about the veracity of the eunuch's prediction regarding the Queen's and her favorite Landry's desire for Aphelia's—Old Brissac's daughter's—death,[93] he wonders whether "This carries shew of truth, or is't a lie / Well shadowed by the slave? I cannot tell" (sig. E2r–E2v). The "slave" is imagined as casting a significant "shadow" over the truth, once again invoking the language of darkness and obliquely reinforcing the sense of the slave as a vector of "shadowed" blackness, a figure who embodies and imbues a dark and "shadowed" aspect.[94]

For all this, the "slave" eunuch is nonetheless offered the quintessential early modern compliment granted to a domestic servant: "Thou art a faithful servant," Clovis remarks (sig. H2r). The irony, of course, is that he is entirely wrong: Castrato is neither a servant nor is "he" faithful. And indeed, the Queen herself comes to understand this soon enough; having learned that Castrato has administered poison both to her and to her lover, Landry, she berates him as an "Inhumane slave, treacherous Rascal" (sig. H4v). It is, therefore, no surprise that in fact "no *Eunuch* she; / No sun-burnt vagabond of Aethiope" (sig. K1v).[95] The Queen's outburst curiously conflates the eunuch and the blackamoor; but what is more striking here is the recovery of a raped, white woman, the "lost" daughter of a prominent family, as the blackamoor servant. If, as I have suggested, the English household inevitably finds the alien at its core, Chrotilda demonstrates the ways in which the family of blood and the family of service are collapsed and confused. The labile and fluid identity of the violated daughter, which arises precisely as she removes herself from a traditional economy of marriageable women, allows Chrotilda to move laterally into a different familial role: that of the *famulus*. It is, perhaps, no accident that the "eunuch" of *The Fatal Contract* recalls the "false" eunuch—Chaerea—of Terence's *Eunuchus*.[96] The representation of the eunuch, as I have noted, raises the specter of a cross-gender emotional and sexual relationship, but without any danger of lineal contamination: the eunuch cannot engender offspring. The spectacular representation of a blackamoor eunuch, that is, raises the prospect of miscegenation, a titillating possibility, only to foreclose that potential threat.

But in staging the racialized servant who is also a eunuch and then revealed to be the violated, unmarriageable daughter of a nobleman, *The Fatal Contract* not only plays on the sense of the slave at the heart of the home; it also literalizes the bodily metaphor of the servant-master and familial corpus, portending a miscegenated mingling which mirrors the violation the raped and discarded Chrotilda has suffered. As it collapses the figure of the black servant and slave into that of the white daughter and threatens a rape which would establish an enslaved ancestry for a nobleman's line, *The Fatal Contract* traffics in the fear of lineal degeneration, uncertain bloodlines, and a racialized future—not least by situating a white woman as simultaneously the agent of this racial disguise and the mouthpiece of a rapacious black servant and slave *and* as his potential victim. Even as this prospect of miscegenation is preemptively denied—both because of Castrato's status as a eunuch and because he is "really" a white woman—the play attempts to secure the attachment of slavery to somatic difference and to situate it at the very heart of the family, making clear the white, "native" agents of that process (a white woman, embodied by a white boy) and the indeterminate future it presages. The play's racial masquerade ultimately remains unresolved; it is debunked at the end of the play, yet never visually clarified for the audience by returning Chrotilda to her "real" form. But even as *The Fatal Contract* thus places pressure on ideas of racial "legibility," it locates both blackness and slavery at the heart of the home in order, I suggest, to anticipate the generation of hereditable slavery, the production of marked bodies, and a stain of slavery which, I shall argue, is as frequently invisible as it is perpetually ineradicable.

"Mark[s] Prodigious" and the Futures of Slavery

Early modern race and slavery, I have been suggesting, are intertwined with that most intimate, quotidian, and seemingly English concern: family, bloodlines, and the imperative to natal generation. In Chapter 2, I argued that the figure of the schoolboy is interpellated by, and authorizes, the frameworks of racialized bondage. The "blackamore wench," meanwhile, mediates the imbrication of blackness and the social body, even as the gendered term "wench" signals contemporary contexts of service and anticipates the racialized connotations of the "wench" in the contexts of American slavery. And *The Fatal Contract* stages the fear of a miscegenated, enslaved future through the body of the "strange" servant. As the early modern family increasingly encompasses its modern sense of sanguinity, the specter of sanguinal heredity and of the child itself serves to secure the futures of slavery, as I will examine in brief readings of two Shakespeare plays.

At the end of *A Midsummer Night's Dream*, Oberon proposes to proceed "to the best bride-bed" for a final benediction. This "bride-bed," he says,

> ... by us shall blessèd be;
> And the issue there create
> Ever shall be fortunate.[97]

Oberon here explicitly links the creation of "fortunate" issue to the location of the "blessèd bride-bed," underscoring the inevitable teleology from matrimony—the happy generic resolution of comedy—to maternity. "So shall all the couples three," he assures us, "Ever true in loving be," and

> ... the blots of nature's hand
> Shall not in their issue stand;
> Never mole, harelip, nor scar,
> Nor mark prodigious, such as are
> Despisèd in nativity,
> Shall upon their children be. (5.1.393–400)

Yet, in this fantasy of futurity, the fortunate issue that Oberon promises are simultaneously framed in terms of the numerous misfortunes that may befall them.[98] Each successive assurance that the children will not be "blotted" generates more anxiety that they *might* be. Generation emerges as both inevitable and unknowable; couched within the promise of spotless children lies the uncontrollable prospect that one's offspring might instead be marked, scarred, and despised. "Moles" and "harelips" may be legible and ineradicable "blots," but the "marks prodigious" that render children "Despisèd in nativity" are more sinister. The word "prodigious" signals not just something unnatural, abnormal, and strange, but also something "monstrous,"[99] something that "giu[es] an ill signe."[100] Both capacious and inexact, the word "prodigious" activates a range of imaginative associations, authorized by the language of "blotting" (as in "the blots of nature's hand") that recalls the spectacle of staining, of black ink on white paper, of Terence's *ethiopissa* turned "blackamore" in Chapter 2, and—according to early modern lexicons—of defacing as well as erasing and e-*race*-ing. As the blotted copy that defaces and dismantles its own progenitors—one reason, perhaps, that such a child might be "Despisèd in nativity"—the specter of the prodigiously marked child portends a future that does not look like our present. We remember here Henry King's "lovely boy's" warning, at the beginning of this chapter, that "Prodigious might that vnion proueth / When night and day together moueth."

In examining the meaning of *Midsummer*'s "prodigious mark," I follow both Miles Grier's illuminating work on "inkface" as a racial strategy inscribed in and by the histories of print and textual materiality and Patricia Akhimie's invaluable reading of the bruise in *The Comedy of Errors* as a "stigmatized somatic marker" which is unnatural yet seemingly carried from birth and (mis)read as morally legible.[101] The Dromios' slavery, Akhimie notes, is articulated from birth and "in nativity," persuasively revealing "the intersection between hereditary servitude—a class system—and somatic signs—a racialized system of identification."[102] But the Dromios' slavery is also the metronome of their masters' lives. Dromio of Ephesus's early joke that "My mistress made it one upon my cheek," marking time with a mark, paves the way for his poignant revelation in Act 4 that he has served his master "from the hour of my nativity to this instant."[103] This is not, of course, literally possible—Dromio could hardly have "served" as a baby—but the obfuscatory language of service not only rehearses the logic of hereditary slavery, it also locates the anchor of Dromio's slavery in his very birth and links slavery with natality: to be born of slave blood is to be bound. But if *The Comedy of Errors* demonstrates how the bondage of blood ensures an enslaved future, it also provides an equally disturbing revelation: that the slave also *underwrites* the work of civic and familial generation. He is an essential, shadowy record of his obverse, the fully included and legible civic member. Emilia celebrates her reconciliation with her family—"After so long grief such nativity!" (5.1.408), she says—by framing it as another parturition: "Thirty-three years have I but gone in travail / Of you, my sons, and till this present hour / My heavy burden ne'er deliverèd" (5.1.402–4). But this deliverance is also, crucially, a re-enslavement for the Dromios. Here, the play's departures from its principal source, Plautus's *Menaechmi*, become particularly poignant; for Shakespeare's adaptation doubles not only the masters, as in *Menaechmi*, but also the slaves—a literal multiplication and regeneration of slavery. But perhaps more significantly, *Menaechmi*'s slave, Messenio, is manumitted at the conclusion of that play.[104] *Menaechmi* ends in emancipation, but its "offspring" *The Comedy of Errors* ensures that "nativity" and the continuation of familial and consanguineal networks are contingent, and indeed conditional, on the perpetuation of bondage.

As the language of natality authorizes the biopolitics of bondage in this play, it underscores how slavery is always philologically and intellectually central to how we must understand generation and nativity, kinship and bloodlines. If the family comes to register the sense of kindred and consanguinity, and even of a "race," the slave, as I have argued, nonetheless lies at the heart of the family, indeed is foundational to the family; etymologically, and as *The Comedy of Errors* reveals, one quite literally cannot have the family without slavery.[105] In these brief readings, I have suggested that *A Midsummer Night's Dream*'s and *The Comedy of Errors*'s seeming imperative to marriage and natality portends the "prodigious" specter of racialized futures. As the biopolitics of blood insist on yoking generation itself to bondage, this association crucially animates the nexus of generation, slavery, and race in the early modern Atlantic world. Thus, for instance, as Joyce MacDonald reminds us, in seventeenth-century Virginia, a free Englishwoman who gave birth out of wedlock to a child who had been fathered by a black man would be fined, and could be indentured for five years; her child, however, "would be indentured until the age of thirty."[106] The stain of slavery works its way into bloodlines of descent, registering the heritable markers of bondage in blood at precisely the moment both when the family increasingly organizes itself along the vector of sanguinity and when the somatic logics of slavery are founded on an unsustainable premise of legibility.

It is this fantasy of legibility that Heminge's *The Fatal Contract* interrogates. Yet Chrotilda's Castrato ultimately emerges as a fiction. Like Richard Mulleneux's Montserratian "negro boy," by the mid-seventeenth century, the blackamoor "servant" cannot be at home in the English family, a family simultaneously underwritten by bondage and a fantasy of racial bloodlines. Meanwhile the English servant, as I shall discuss in the next chapter, must contract himself into a global network and negotiation of servitude, sanguinity, and somatic difference to secure the fictions of consent that both catalyze and protect him from the development of racialized chattel slavery.

CHAPTER 4

Faithful Covenant Servants and Inbred Enemies

Indenture and Natality in *Paradise Lost*

In a pamphlet published in 1641, English "Gentlemen" as well as "Labourers" were offered a brave new world. *A Direction for Adventurers* promises an opportunity for "Gentlemen, and all Servants, Labourers, and Artificers to live plentifully" in North Virginia, even to get "good land freely."[1] Bountiful, free land should be enticement enough, but the pamphlet lists other advantages to a transatlantic transfer: "Here a ship may go; and returne in four moneths laded and comfortably see their freinds; making three voyages a yeer, in a healthy ayre freed from enemies, and Turks, and get two for on each voyage."[2] The rewards proffered to the brave adventurers who cross the Atlantic are material—the laden ships—but also political: the ships allow their passengers to be "freed" from "Turks." Playing on fears of Barbary piracy and captivity, accounts of which circulated widely, as I have discussed in Chapter 2, the pamphlet situates the English planter in America as the alternative to the English slave in the Ottoman Empire, locating Virginian labor and husbandry as the welcome respite from (the constant threat of) Turkish slavery.

Nonetheless, the arrivals to America are accounted for and (e)valuated in fiscal and economic terms, as *A Direction* notes: "All Adventurers of 500 l. to bring 50 men, shall have 5000 Acres and a Manor with Royalties at 5. s. Rent, and whosoever is willing so to transport himselfe or servant at 10. l. a man, shall for each man have 100 Acres freely granted for ever."[3] For ten pounds a head—or per transported man—this pamphlet promises an "adventurer" a hundred acres granted in perpetuity, with more to come. As the title notes, each "adventurer" will also receive a considerable return on his initial human investment; the pamphlet includes "*a briefe of the charge of victuall, and necessaries, to transport* and buy stocke for each Planter, or Labourer, there to get his Master 50 l. *per Annum*, or more in twelve trades, and *at 10 l. charges onely a man*."[4] Moments like these might suggestively anticipate the economic discourses of chattel slavery in its unabashed economic valuations of potential "labourers." Yet the financial assessment for potential "adventurers" of planters and laborers does not anticipate slavery's reification of labor so much as it works to distinguish Atlantic bounty from Mediterranean bondage. Virginian servants and laborers may enable that bounty, but they can also hold it: "All which after 5 yeeres service, are to have 31, Acres of free land and some stocke and bee freeholders."[5] "Freeholding" and the promise of economic and political freedoms are articulated at the teleological end of indentured service, but a form of freedom must also precede such service: the presumed freedom to attach oneself to an "adventurer" and transport oneself across the ocean, for instance. Less than thirty years later, the Company of Royal Adventurers of England Trading Into Africa would issue an unsettling invitation to "all His Majesties Native Subjects" to "become Sharers in their Joynt-stock" in order "to furnish His Majesties *American* Plantations with *Negroes* at certain and moderate Rates," enjoining English people to exercise their economic liberty not by investing in the labor of their fellow countrymen, but by supporting a joint-stock corporation that would traffic in the bodies of enslaved peoples.[6]

In the attempt to persuade planters to settle America, we have seen, pamphleteers not only articulated the land as a "new Albion"; they also played on fears of the East, on the captivity that might befall the Mediterranean adventurer. At the same time, North Virginia not only offers shelter from potential Turkish captors; it also allows liberty from an *English* form of unfreedom, debt bondage: "Here the kind Gentleman that in *England* doth not live without debts, mortgages, suretiship, Lawsuits, & troubles, may here settle."[7] Thus, planting in America does not just achieve economic and material liberties; it is itself a deliverance from various forms of bondage.[8]

This chapter argues that the early modern and early American indentured servant, who binds himself into bondage and whose liberty underwrites his servitude, anticipates the "stain of slavery" alongside the imperative to consent, even at the very moment of his redemption. If service and slavery are legally and civically exclusive categories, despite their peculiar and repeated coarticulation, the indentured servant marks the terrain where each category must, for the first time, *explicitly* impinge on the other, and not only in instances of "spiriting," the illicit practice of coercing servants to bind themselves into servitude across the sea or kidnapping workers altogether.[9] The indentured servant has, after all, been sold, however provisionally, sometimes even from master to master, and the moment of the vending of the body is the moment of absolute corporeal ownership. To transact something—even an indentured servant—one must have claim to it.

But the corporeal claim which underwrites the practice of indenture also recalls the logic of *res mancipi*, a Roman category of transferable property. As Amanda Bailey has vitally argued, the provenance of the indenture contract is the debt bond (in indentured servitude, one binds oneself, and the labor of one's body, as surety for the incurred debt), and Bailey notes that "The very language of the [debt] bond [in "*teneri et firmiter obligari*"] invoked the physical act of bondage. *Teneri*, the passive infinitive of *teneo*, meant to hold onto or to grasp something in one's hand."[10] This sense of "taking in hand," however, is not only located in the language of debt and indenture via *teneri*; as it relates to the word *manus*, or hand, it also comprises the provenance of *mancipium*, the Roman slave who formed part of the category of *res mancipi* and whose transfer took place during the ceremony of *mancipatio*. *Res mancipi* were, by definition, items to which the vendor had incontrovertible title; a *mancipium* (slave) was therefore held with absolute ownership.[11] It is the vendibility of the *mancipium*, in other words, that seems to authorize the transaction of labor articulated by the indenture contract, and which therefore organizes the very logic of indentured servitude.

At the same time, to situate the indentured servant along the spectrum of slavery (to argue, in other words, that indentured servitude sets the precedent for slavery) is to ignore the discourses around indenture which explicitly articulated it as an *alternative* to slavery, and as a function of consent.[12] This chapter therefore examines English apprenticeship indentures to reveal the fictions of consent that undergirded the legal and conceptual antecedents of the Atlantic indenture contract. By mining the genealogy of Atlantic indentured servitude rather than looking to fix it on a spectrum of servitude, I seek to excavate the apparently unthinkable ideologies of early modern English slavery, to trouble the teleologies of liberty, and to unearth the fictions of consent which sustained both. The technologies of bondage that enabled emergent forms of Atlantic servitude, I argue, were inscribed in the fictions of service which organized early modern labor. And these fictions were reaffirmed and negotiated in the literary texts I discuss. In the second half of this chapter, I turn to Milton's *Paradise Lost*, a text deeply concerned with the contingencies of consent and the capacity for freedom and bondage alike, in order to read the "voluntary service" which God requires in light of indentured labor on the one hand, and of the futures of Atlantic slavery on the other. As these futures relied on genealogical succession, this chapter closes by exploring how children, and the reproductive imperative that generated them, both secured the fictions of voluntary servitude and ensured the futures of bondage.

Ties That Bind: Contracting Early Modern English Apprentices

The English apprenticeship contract was a formal document, its terms and tenor bound by legal and social precedent. Thus, the 1607 edition of *A Booke of Presidents* offers a template for an apprenticeship indenture, in both Latin and English, nestled between "An Indenture made betweene partners" and "An Indenture of marriage." By the terms of "An Indenture for a Prentice," the apprentice is instructed to "serue" his master "well and faithfully," and

> his secrets shall keepe, his commaundements lawfull and honest euery where shall do, no fornication in the house of his said master, nor without hee shall commit, hurt vnto his said Master he shal not do, or consent to be done . . . Tauerns of custome he shall not haunt, but if it bee about his maisters busines there to be done: At the dice, cards, or any other vnlawfull games he shall not play: The goods of his said master inordinatly hee shall not wast . . . Matrimony with any woman within the sayd terme hee shal not contract nor espouse: Nor from his seruice neither by day nor by night shal absent or prolong himselfe, but as a true and faithfull seruant ought to behaue himselfe, aswel in words, as in deeds.[13]

The apprentice's master, in turn, must not only "teach & informe, or cause to be taught and informed" the "craft" to which he belongs; he must also provide livery in its broadest sense, "finding vnto his said seruant meat, drinke, linnen, woollen, hose, shooes, and al other things to him necessary or belonging to an apprentice of such craft, to be found after the maner and custome of the city of London."[14]

The conventional terms of the indenture contract persist across shifts in the material forms of these legal instruments. Thus, while Figure 9 depicts

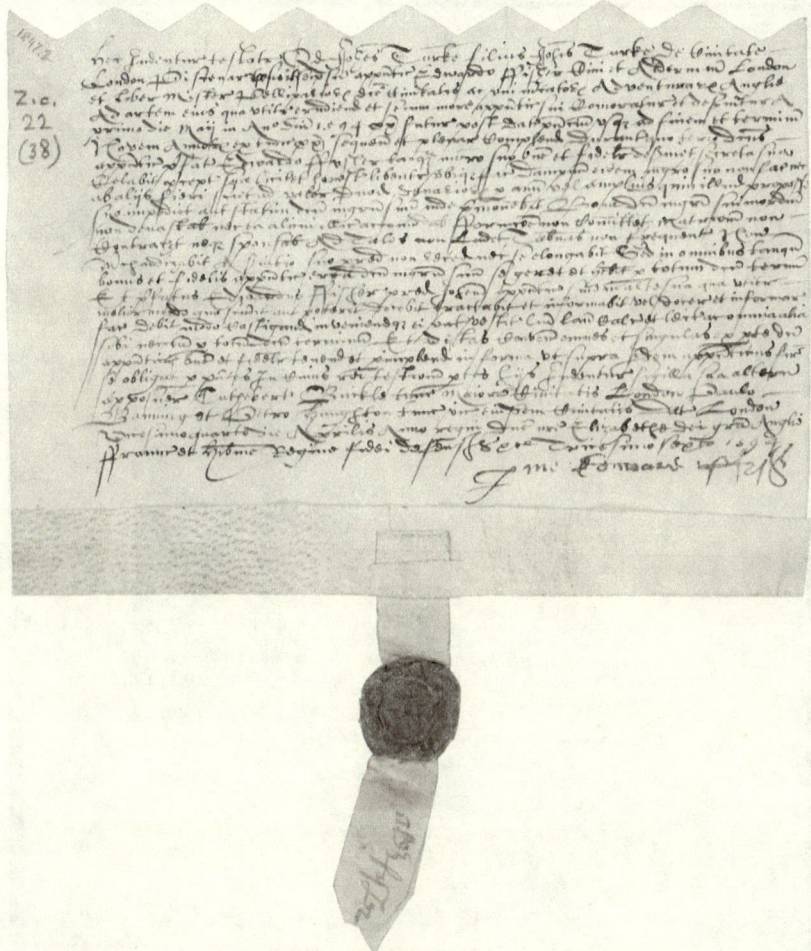

Figure 9. Apprenticeship indenture between John Turke and Edward Fisher (1594). Z.c.22 (38). Used by permission of the Folger Shakespeare Library under a Creative Commons Attribution-ShareAlike 4.0 International License.

a manuscript indenture on vellum binding John Turke to Edward Fisher, a master skinner and merchant adventurer of England, for a period of nine years in 1594, by the middle of the seventeenth century the apprenticeship contract had assumed a familiar form: a printed document with blank spaces for manuscript annotations (see, for instance, a printed and "blank" apprenticeship form for the University of Oxford in Figure 10).[15] Yet, as I shall

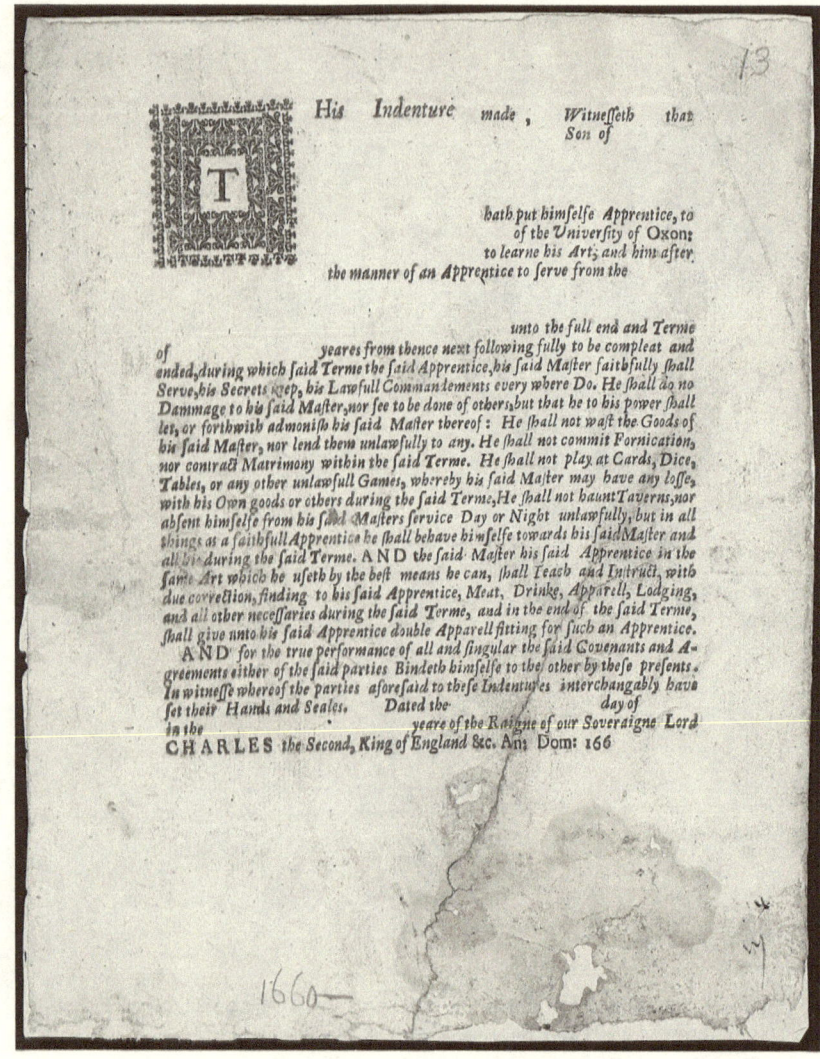

Figure 10. Apprenticeship form, University of Oxford (1660). G. A. Oxon. b. 111, fol. 13r, Bodleian Libraries, University of Oxford.

suggest, despite the conventions that dictated the form of the indenture contract, the deliberate lacunae in the printed instrument ensured its strategic manipulability.

In 1683, an apprentice named James Holden, son of Humphrey Holden, was bound to the cutler Thomas Spencer for a period of seven years

(Figure 11). A few years later, in 1688, James Holden's brother John Holden was bound to the salter John Purdue, also for a period of seven years (Figure 12).[16] As younger sons, excluded from their family succession, these brothers needed to secure apprenticeships to wend their way in the world, to procure the freedom of the city, and eventually to ply their trade.[17] The contracts that legislated their labor were relatively standard, with blank spaces in which to note, by hand, names, dates, and the number of years of service to be performed; these documents sought to regularize both the terms and the tenor of service. Thus, the apprentice may not enter into marriage or "commit Fornication," "haunt Taverns or Play-houses," or "absent himself from his said Masters service day nor night unlawfully."[18] In return, the apprentice receives "meat, drink, apparel, lodging, and all other necessaries." So far, so typical.

But rehearsing the tenets of apprenticeship published in *A Booke of Presidents*, the terms of these indentures also compel the apprentice to serve his master "faithfully," "his Secrets keep, his lawful Commandments every where gladly do." The "secrets" that the apprentice must keep may refer to the mysteries of their master's trade, but they also gesture to the apprentice's role as an intimate, a member of the family—discussed in the previous chapter—whose "secrets" he is privy to and must protect. The indenture is more explicit about the manner in which the apprentice must perform his work—"faithfully," "gladly"—but how *can* a contract compel "glad" servitude, or ensure the enactment of "faithful" service?

In attempting to enjoin or enforce an affective tie, the contract of apprenticeship not only mandates the performance of regulated forms of labor; it also enforces the enactment of mutuality. A servant or apprentice must not only undertake work, in other words; that labor must be willing, "glad," and "faithful." What these legal instruments attempt to require is the fulfillment of work that is paradoxically free. And yet, as I have argued, that is not a paradox at all in early modern England; rather, service is understood as fundamentally willing, cheerful, free, while to be free is, by definition, to be a servant.

But although "service is perfect freedom," the documents that contract labor, including apprenticeship contracts, insist on the persistent articulation of fictions of consent, which reimagine even as they deliberately obfuscate the terms and tensions of servitude.[19] Thus, while in Folger X.d.734, the fiction of consent obtains in the insistence on serving "faithfully" and "gladly," on the performance of contracted work according to an affective framework,

Figure 11. Apprenticeship indenture between James Holden and Thomas Spencer (1683). X.d.734. Photograph by Urvashi Chakravarty, from the collection of the Folger Shakespeare Library.

Folger X.d.735 makes clear how such a fiction also operated in less mutual circumstances. In this indenture, the usual transaction of service for housing and provision is troubled by a change to the standard terms of this engraved form: in the list of provisions to be supplied by "the said Master" to "the said Apprentice," the word "apparel" has been quite deliberately and noticeably effaced. Since apparel would almost certainly have been the most expensive and valuable component of the apprentice's payment, this erasure significantly alters the terms and value of what is a supposedly conventional exchange, and violates the "Custom" of the city. For a period of "seaven" years, John Holden must serve without that most quintessential (as Chapter 1 demonstrates) of livery's provisions: apparel.[20]

The case of John Holden suggests that, even at their most generic, the legal instruments that frame and authorize the performance of service and articulate the fiction of mutual legal protection reveal strategic lacunae which raise the unsettling possibility that the servant may inadvertently bind himself not only into an inequitable contract, but even, possibly, into servitude.[21]

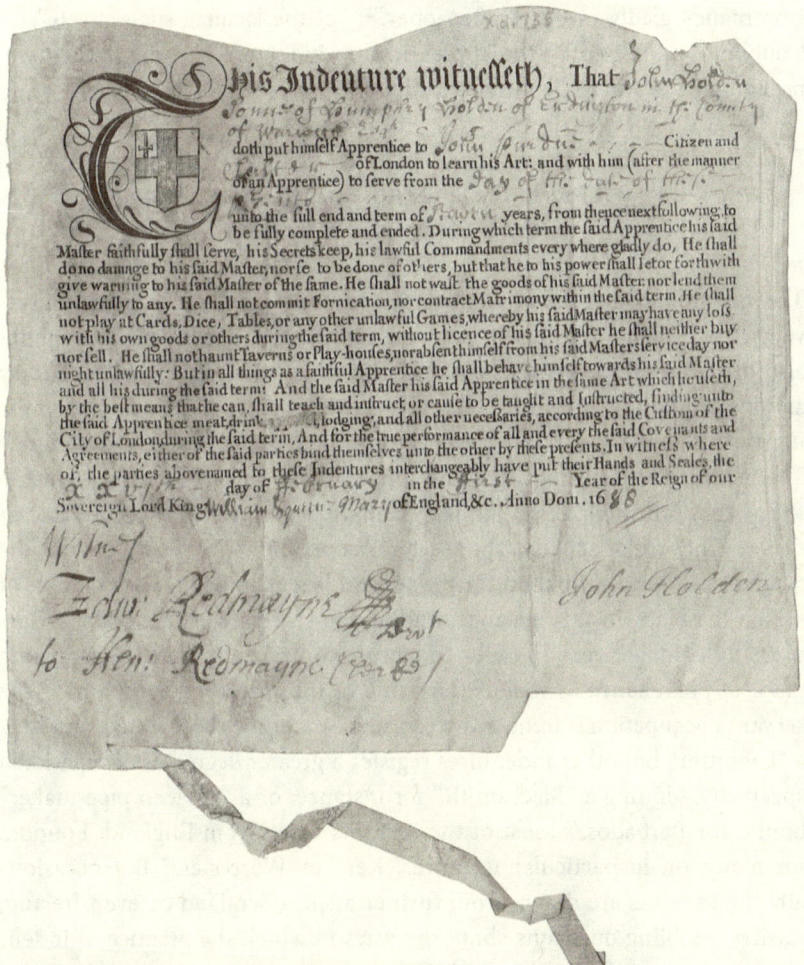

Figure 12. Apprenticeship contract between John Holden and John Purdue (1688). X.d.735. Used by permission of the Folger Shakespeare Library under a Creative Commons Attribution-ShareAlike 4.0 International License.

This is the unsettling prospect we increasingly confront when we cross the Atlantic. The frameworks and fiction that organize the architecture of early modern English apprenticeship certainly persist in their Atlantic afterlives; thus, in 1765, the apprentice Joel Norton was bound out to Ebenezer Talman in New Haven, on terms almost identical to those of the Holden brothers: Norton must "faithfully serve [his master] his Secrets keep his lawfull

Commands gladly every^where^ obey."²² Yet the lacunae suggestively and troublingly indicated by the apprenticeship indenture become particularly pronounced in Atlantic contracts for indentured servitude.

X Marks the Spot: Absenting Consent in the Transatlantic Indenture

The indenture contract that set the terms for the transatlantic transfer of servants, I shall suggest, precisely troubled not only the capacity for consent but also the material forms of its own enactment.²³ A late seventeenth-century archive of Atlantic indentures tellingly illustrates these pressure points, raising critical questions about the meanings and limits of these contracts.²⁴ The indentures, like their legal and material antecedents in apprenticeship forms, follow printed templates, with blank spaces in which to record at least the servant's name and age, the master's name, the term of service, and the gender-appropriate pronoun for the servant (see Figure 13 for an example of such a template, in this instance binding the servant for four years in Barbados).²⁵ A longer version of the indenture contract also notes the servant's place of provenance as well as the name of the ship conveying him.²⁶ The servant's occupation is frequently recorded; sometimes he is noted simply as a "Labourer," but other indentures register a greater degree of occupational specificity, binding a "Blacksmith," for instance, or a "tobacco pipe maker" bound for Barbados.²⁷ Most of the servants come from England: London, for many, or, in particular instances, Kent or Worcester.²⁸ But occasionally the servants are drawn from further afield—Scotland or even Ireland, raising troubling questions about the ways in which the practice of indenture was being inflected by particular national, ethnic, or non-phenotypic racialized formations.²⁹ Although most of the to-be-indentured servants are men, there are some women, and most are in their twenties, although occasionally there are older servants; one indenture, for instance, binds a "bricklayer" who is the unusually advanced age of thirty-eight years old.³⁰ Troublingly, there are also some younger subjects binding themselves: one servant is identified as sixteen years old; meanwhile, another bound servant aged eighteen must swear that both parents are dead before being allowed to contract himself (Figure 14).³¹ Although servants are usually bound for four years, there are occasionally longer terms of indenture in this collection: five years, seven years, or even, in one extraordinary instance, nine years; this,

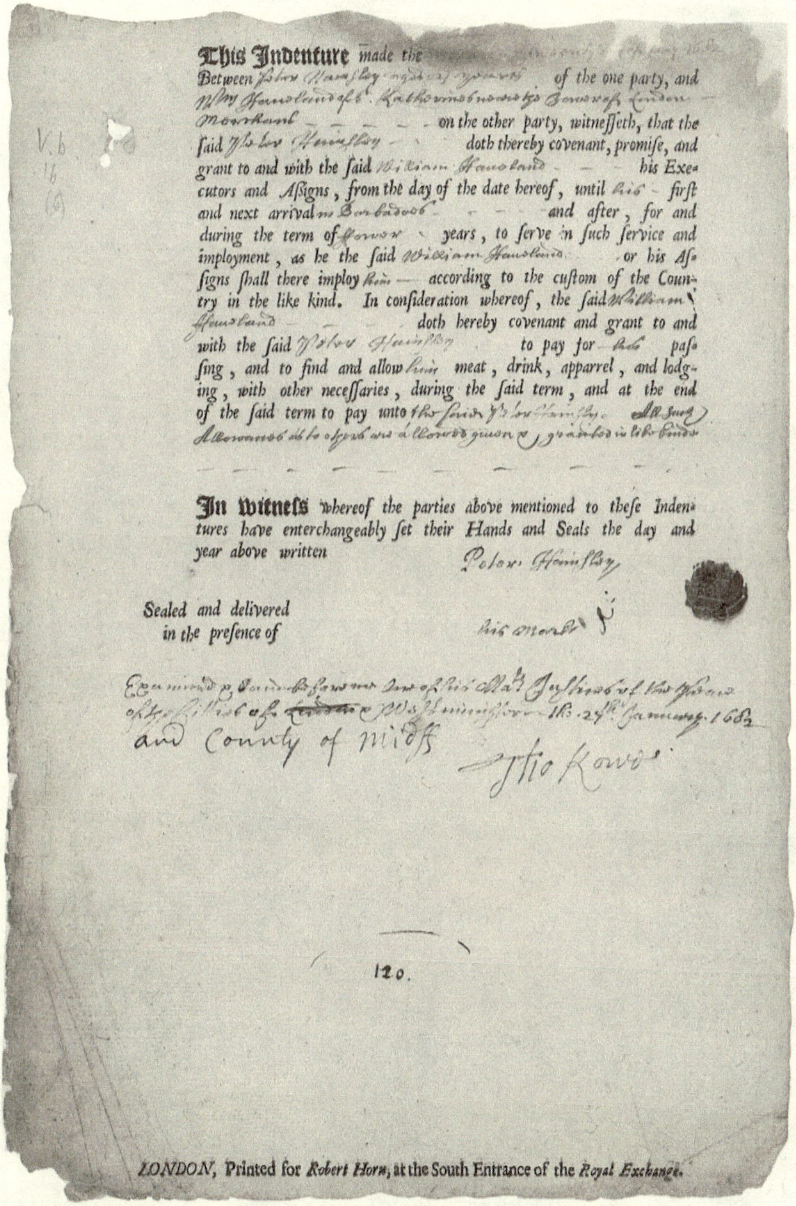

This Indenture made the ⟨_____⟩ ⟨_____⟩ 1682
Between *Peter Hainsley* ⟨aged __ years⟩ of the one party, and
Wm Hausland of St Katherines neere the Tower of London
Merchant _____ on the other party, witnesseth, that the
said *Peter Hainsley* doth thereby covenant, promise, and
grant to and with the said *William Hausland* _____ his Executors and Assigns, from the day of the date hereof, until *his* first
and next arrival *in Barbados* _____ and after, for and
during the term of *four* years, to serve in such service and
imployment, as he the said *William Hausland* or his Assigns shall there imploy *him* _____ according to the custom of the Country in the like kind. In consideration whereof, the said *William*
Hausland _____ doth hereby covenant and grant to and
with the said *Peter Hainsley* to pay for *his* passing, and to find and allow *him* meat, drink, apparel, and lodging, with other necessaries, during the said term, and at the end
of the said term to pay unto *the said Peter Hainsley such*
Allowances as is to other are allowed given or granted in like kinds

In Witness whereof the parties above mentioned to these Indentures have enterchangeably set their Hands and Seals the day and
year above written
                                        Peter Hainsley

Sealed and delivered
in the presence of   *his mark*

Examined ⟨___⟩ Before me one of his Maj Justices of the Peace
of the Citty of ⟨___⟩ Westminster the 24th January 1682
and County of Midd
                                        Jno Rowe

120.

LONDON, Printed for *Robert Horn*, at the South Entrance of the *Royal Exchange*.

Figure 13. Contract for indentured service in Barbados for Peter Hainsley (1682/3). V.b.16 (6). Used by permission of the Folger Shakespeare Library under a Creative Commons Attribution-ShareAlike 4.0 International License.

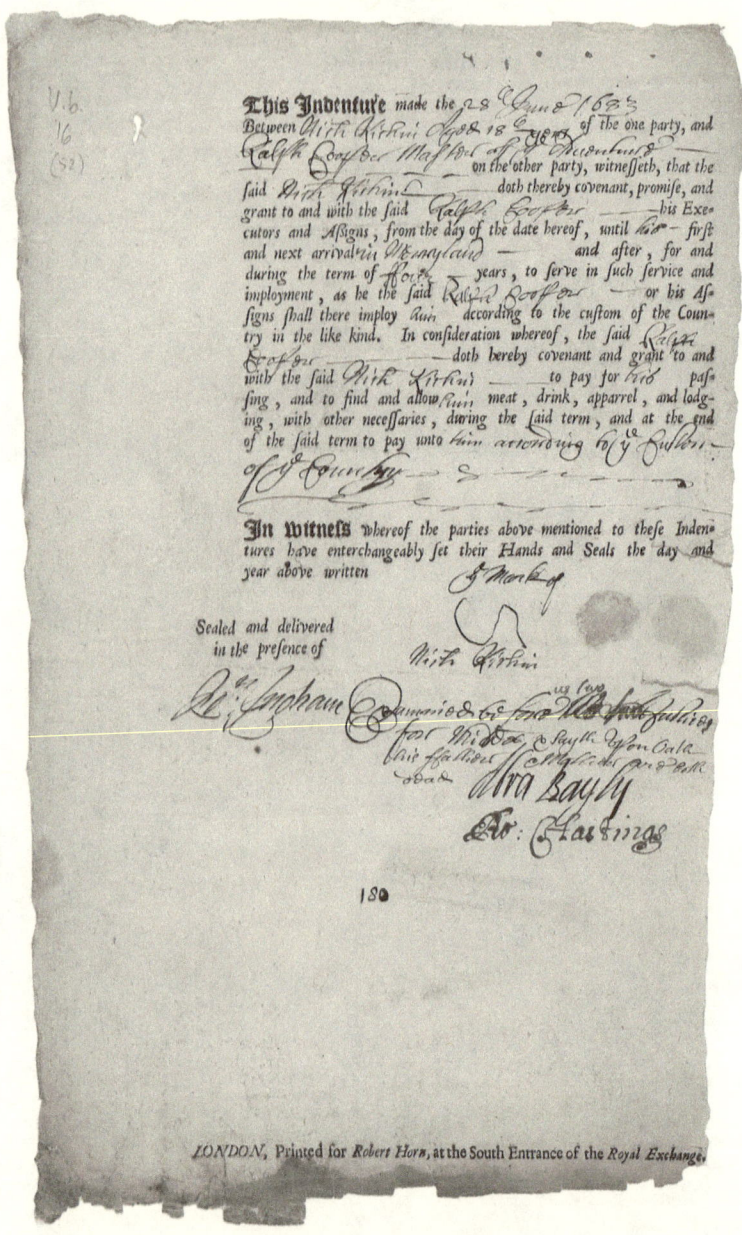

Figure 14. Contract for indentured service in Maryland for Nich[olas] Kichin (1683). V.b.16 (52). Used by permission of the Folger Shakespeare Library under a Creative Commons Attribution-ShareAlike 4.0 International License.

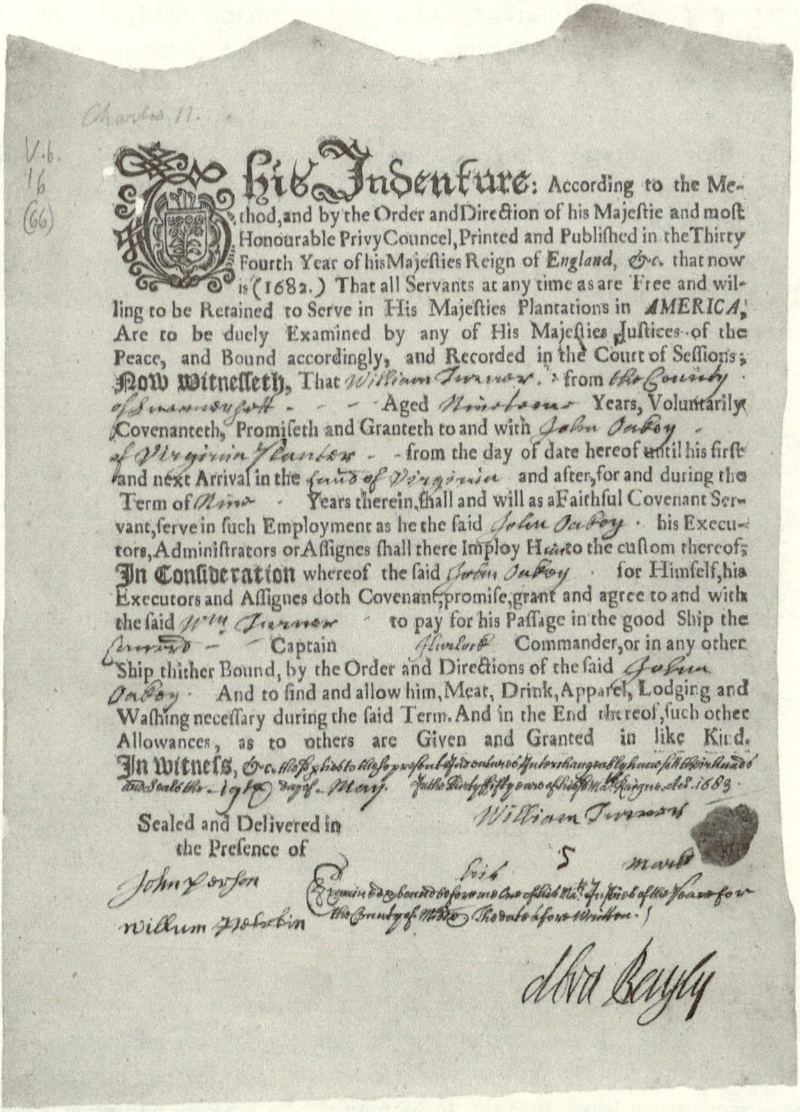

This Indenture: According to the Method, and by the Order and Direction of his Majestie and most Honourable Privy Councel, Printed and Published in the Thirty Fourth Year of his Majesties Reign of *England*, &c. that now is (1682.) That all Servants at any time as are Free and willing to be Retained to Serve in His Majesties Plantations in *AMERICA*, Are to be duely Examined by any of His Majesties Justices of the Peace, and Bound accordingly, and Recorded in the Court of Sessions; **Now Witnesseth,** That *William Turner* from the County of *Summersett* Aged *Nineteene* Years, Voluntarily Covenanteth, Promiseth and Granteth to and with *John Oakey* of *Virginia Planter* from the day of date hereof until his first and next Arrival in the *Land of Virginia* and after, for and during the Term of *Nine* Years therein, shall and will as a Faithful Covenant Servant, serve in such Employment as he the said *John Oakey* his Executors, Administrators or Assignes shall there Imploy Him to the custom thereof; **In Consideration** whereof the said *John Oakey* for Himself, his Executors and Assignes doth Covenant, promise, grant and agree to and with the said *W:m Turner* to pay for his Passage in the good Ship the _____ Captain _____ Commander, or in any other Ship thither Bound, by the Order and Directions of the said *John Oakey*. And to find and allow him, Meat, Drink, Apparel, Lodging and Washing necessary during the said Term. And in the End thereof, such other Allowances, as to others are Given and Granted in like Kind. **In Witness,** &c. _____ 1683.

William Turner

Sealed and Delivered in
the Presence of

John _____
William _____

Figure 15. Contract for indentured service in Virginia for William Turner (1683). V.b.16 (66). Used by permission of the Folger Shakespeare Library under a Creative Commons Attribution-ShareAlike 4.0 International License.

the longest of the indentures, is also the only one to specifically contract the servant to a "planter" in Virginia, but it is also for one of the youngest servants bound in this collection, one William Turner, aged just nineteen years (Figure 15).[32] Only one contract promises specific remuneration at the end of the term of service.[33] Otherwise, there is sometimes (but not always) only mention of the "custom of the country" which will determine the servant's "freedom dues."

What this fascinating archive compellingly elucidates is the way in which the indenture form is both intended to assert—and yet repeatedly destabilizes—the very contract to which the hired servant consents. These indentures, after all, are founded upon the premise of mutuality. Thus, in one indenture, the servant, Thomas Norton,

> Voluntarily Covenanteth, Promiseth and Granteth to and with *Joseph Ball of Rodorith In the County of Surrey Marriner* from the day of date hereof until his first and next Arrival in the *Island of Barbadoes* and after, for and during the Term of *ffower* Years therein, shall and will as a Faithful Covenant Servant, serve in such Employment as he the said *Joseph Ball* his Executors, Administrators or Assignes shall there Imploy H*im* to the custom thereof. In Consideration whereof the said *Joseph Ball* for Himself, his Executors and Assignes doth Covenant, promise, grant and agree to and with the said *Thomas Norton* to pay for his Passage in the good Ship the *Hopewell* Captain *Joseph Ball aforesaid* Commander, or in any other Ship thither Bound, by the Order and Directions of the said *Joseph Ball* And to find and allow him Meat, Drink, Apparel, Lodging and Washing necessary during the said Term.[34]

As we see, the indenture rests, primarily and crucially, upon volition; the laborer "Voluntarily Covenanteth," in the language of covenant that signals not just an agreement but also God's "covenant" and the redemptive "better covenant" of Jesus. In order to be bound, one must be willing, but one must also be free. But the promise to be a "faithful covenant servant" articulates this service in not only a legal but also a religious register of contract and consent, raising the question of whether a *lack* of "faithful" service (or lack of service that is *perceived* to be "faithful") would actually invalidate the contract. As I shall discuss in the next chapter, the answer, in at least some instances, is, chillingly, "yes."[35] Yet the covenant is technically enjoined upon both parties; the master must also "covenant" with his servant to fulfill the terms of a mutual bond, providing "Meat, Drink, Apparel, Lodging" in ways that nostalgically evoke the benevolent patriarchalism of master-servant relationships as well as, specifically, the terms of the apprenticeship agreement. Both forms of contract explicitly insist on the performance of "faithful" service in return for the provision of "livery" in its most capacious sense: food, drink, clothing, houseroom. Yet there are two crucial differences. The first, of course, is that while the apprenticeship agreement contains at its core the stipulation that the master must "teach & informe" his servant—indeed, this provision precisely legitimates the lack of payment—the indenture contract requires no such pedagogical benefit. The second is the conspicuous inclusion of the term "voluntarily" in at least one printed indenture form (the servant "Voluntarily Covenanteth, Promiseth and Granteth to and with [his master]"), a word which does not appear in the apprenticeship contract. "Voluntarily" does not need to appear in the apprenticeship contract, but the indenture contract must include it because, as I shall demonstrate, the agreement to and sealing of the instrument does not ensure the operation of volition. The servant's confirmation that he covenants "voluntarily" paradoxically underscores the potential for the *lack* of volition.

For as we see again and again, the indentured servant cannot fully consent to or often even understand the terms of the contract. Indeed, many servants merely make a mark, usually in the form of an "X," rather than signing the contract with their name (Figure 16).[36] The "X," in this instance, becomes both a signifier of acquiescence or even nominal consent and simultaneously a lacuna, an *absence* of specific assent. In replacing a signature, it apparently offers the mark of an individual, but it does *not* individuate the supposedly consenting party to the contract. The "X" is, at its core, a fiction of consent that marks a contractual bond even as it undermines its own authorizing capacity. But the "X" also signals the larger problem of literacy; since the servant frequently cannot *read* the contract, it constitutes a signifier of the *ruse* of the mutual contract, which is predicated on reciprocal volition but repeatedly reveals its own structural instabilities and lacunae.[37]

If the "X" of the indentured servant comprises a fiction, the final master who must actually provide his servant with "Meat, Drink, Apparel, Lodging and Washing" in the colony does not, of course, himself sign or ratify the agreement; the servant is instead frequently bound to a ship's captain, "merchant," or agent who will sell the contract on to another master.[38] And unlike apprentices (for the most part), indentured servants could have their

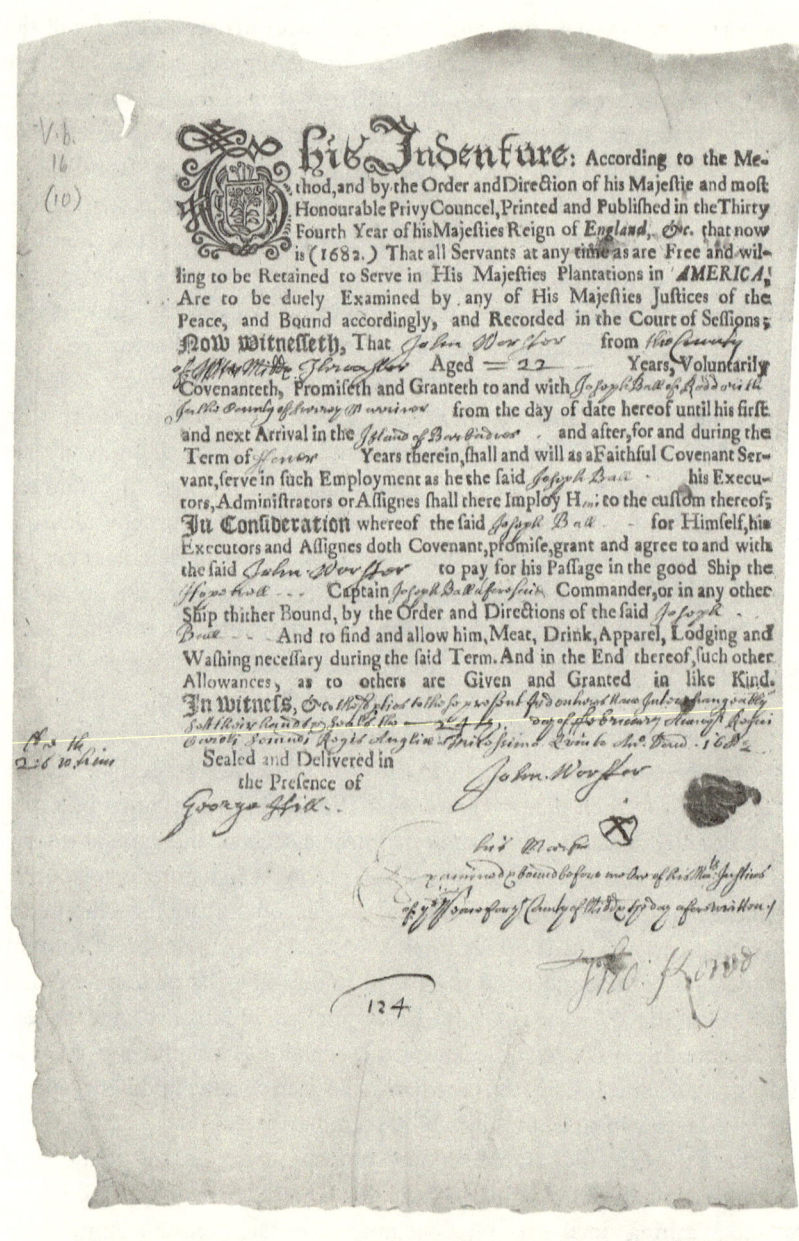

Figure 16. Contract for indentured service in Barbados for John Worster (1682/3). V.b.16 (10). Used by permission of the Folger Shakespeare Library under a Creative Commons Attribution-ShareAlike 4.0 International License.

contracts bought and sold without their consent, with little say over or even knowledge of the person(s) they might eventually serve. This uncertainty, tellingly, does not affect the efficacy of the contract, but it might suggestively compromise the mutuality which technically undergirds it, while contracts nevertheless repeatedly insist on servants' "willingness" to embark on them. When in 1682/3 John March contracted to serve William Emberly for four years, for instance, the indenture contract contained an additional and somewhat unusual manuscript statement from a witness that March "acknowledged him selfe being free and att his owne Disposall willing & Contented to goe into Berbadoes to serve the within named William Emberly his Master for the terme of years."[39] Even more troubling are the oversights and "mistakes" in even this limited collection of indentures, which underscore the myriad opportunities for abuse. In one indenture, for instance, the servant, Richard Cheffhere, apparently contracts with himself when he "doth thereby covenant, promise, and grant to and with the said *Richard Cheffhere*...."[40] More amusingly—and, perhaps, presciently, given his eventual imprisonment for spiriting—in another indenture, William Haveland "doth Covenant, promise, grant and agree to and with the said *Wm Haueland* to pay for his Passage ... by the Order and Directions of the said *William Haueland*," thereby effectively binding *himself*.[41] But perhaps most troubling of all is a contract binding John Ellis, "Aged *Twenty One* years," to a merchant and to service in Barbados, where the term of servitude has been accidentally omitted (Figure 17).[42] Legally bound for a potentially indefinite term of servitude, John Ellis can once again sign only with a mark, a stark reminder of the fictions of consent that underwrite these contracts, and of the finer and finer distinctions between *famulus*, *servus*, and *mancipium*, between servant and slave.[43]

If indentures disrupted in practice the boundaries between service and bondage, the provisions for binding children in particular as indentured servants exposed some of early modern England's larger fictions around slavery. Some indentures, we have seen, bound quite young servants, who must in turn attest that their parents are deceased; but if children embody the slippage between youth and servitude, as I argued in Chapter 2, they also comprise the limit case for the exercise of indenture as bondage, which dispensed with the organizing and authorizing logic of apprenticeship: that masters were also teachers, and children were pupils. The problem of how to regulate children in servitude is therefore addressed in a Privy Council order about spiriting issued in 1682 and renewed in 1686:[44]

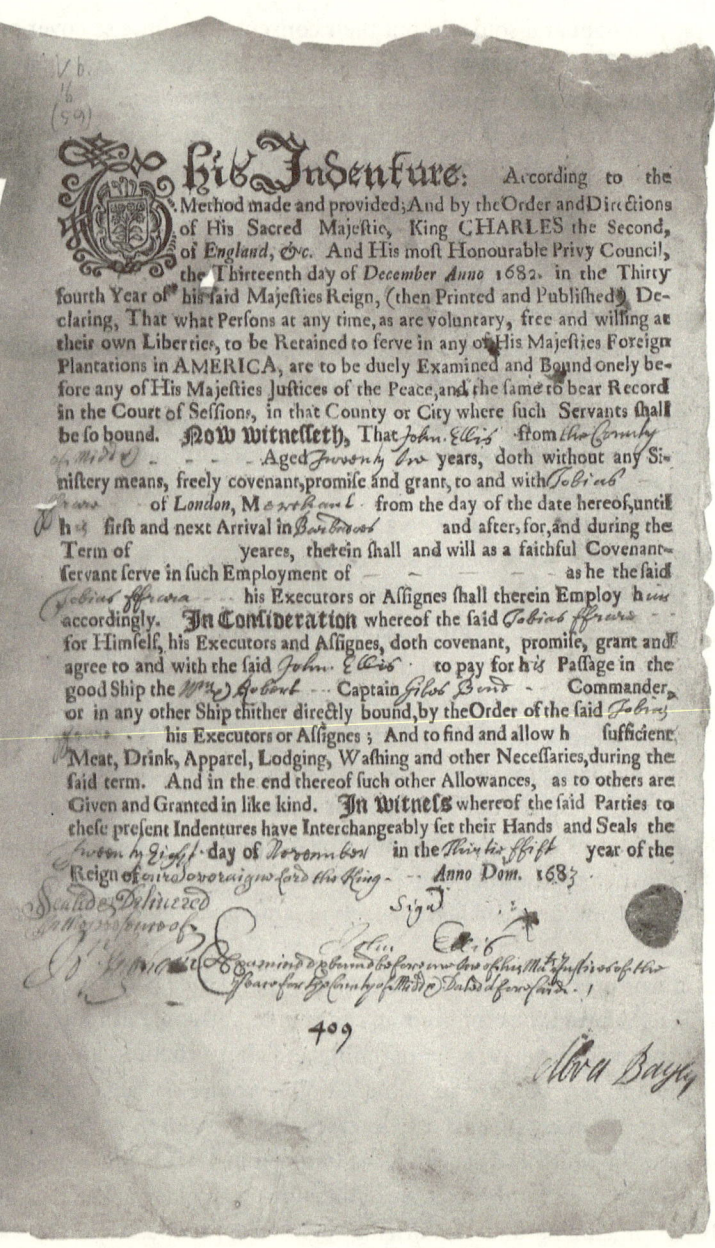

Figure 17. Contract for indentured service in Barbados for John Ellis (1683). V.b.16 (59). Used by permission of the Folger Shakespeare Library under a Creative Commons Attribution-ShareAlike 4.0 International License.

IV. If any person be under the Age of One and twenty years, or shall appear so to be, he shall be Bound in the presence of the Lord Mayor of *London*, or one of the Judges, or an Alderman of *London* being a Justice of Peace, or the Recorder, or Two Justices of the Peace of any other County or Place, who shall carefully Examin whether the Person so to be Bound, have any Parents or Masters; And if he be not Free, they are not to take such Indenture, unless the Parents or Masters give their Consents, and some Person that knows the said Servant to be of the Name and Addition mentioned in the Indenture, is to Attest his said knowledge upon the said Indenture.[45]

In this 1682 order, masters and parents are effectively interchangeable; either can give their consent to the child being bound into indentured servitude, reminding us of the pun on *magister*—as parent, master, and teacher—that Terence's *Andria* illuminates.[46] Under the age of fourteen, however, parents become more central to the legal framework of indenture: "V. If the Person be under the Age of Fourteen years, unless his Parents shall be present, and consent, he is not to be carried on Shipboard till a Fortnight at least, after he becomes Bound, to the intent, that if there be any Abuse, it may be discovered before he be Transported."[47]

Although lack of parental consent supposedly prevents the transportation of children under fourteen, these protections remain rather half-hearted. While children *not* released by their parents must wait a fortnight after being indentured and before being transported, they are, nonetheless, bound, and bound effectively without consent (the fact that parents must authorize the bond suggests that the child under fourteen does not have sufficient capacity for consent; the lack of parental consent gestures to its legal absence altogether). Moreover, the temporal delay of two weeks hardly seems sufficient provision against the possibility of "Abuse." Rather, it delays the discovery of "Abuse" to the moment of transportation or even later, when any child in servitude has left England's shores, when the ship bearing them has, quite literally, sailed. The 1682 order simply displaces the possibility of slavery to a different geographical terrain, securing England's claim to freedom within its borders and ensuring that the legal claim that "England was too pure an Air for Slaves to breath in" might technically be upheld.

The affinities between childhood and servitude, and the mediation of servitude by the figure of the child, are only strengthened when we realize that our modern word "kids" is closely tied to indentured servitude. Turning to Hugh Jones's *The Present State of Virginia* (1724), we find the following passage: "The Ships that transport these Things often call at *Ireland* to victual, and bring over frequently white Servants, which are of three Kinds. I. Such as come upon certain Wages by Agreement for a certain Time. 2. Such as come bound by Indenture, commonly call'd *Kids*, who are usually to serve four or five Years; and 3. those Convicts or Felons that are transported, whose Room they had much rather have than their Company."[48] "Kid" was already in limited seventeenth-century use to refer to children; the *Oxford English Dictionary* notes its use in the "American Colonies" and suggests that its meaning as "a child, esp. a young child" comprised "low slang."[49] By 1699, "kid" was glossed in B.E.'s *A New Dictionary of the Terms Ancient and Modern of the Canting Crew* as "a Child; also the first Year of a Roe, and a young Goat."[50] The association between childhood and "kids," and the context of indenture in which "kids" are so clearly imbricated, situates the specter of children at the heart of discourses of servitude.

If those subject to indenture become, by the early eighteenth century, collapsed with the rhetoric around childhood, the material form of the indenture would come to anticipate, chillingly, the more explicit traffic in children. The legal instrument of the indenture had, of course, been used for centuries to transact and transfer property. It would continue to be used for this purpose within a new global economy of slavery. Thus, in 1709 in Pennsylvania, in an "indented schedule" attached to an indenture for the receipt of goods, "One Negro Boy named Yarmouth" was listed as an "Item" and transacted along with not only six other "Negro" men and women—a "man named ffrank," a "woman named Nanny," a "man named Blackboy"— but also "Three old Iron Saws," "Six Steel Bitts," "One Grindstone," "A parcel of working tools." In the process, he and the other enslaved people with whom he was catalogued and conveyed were legally and visually rendered a piece of property, mere *mancipia*, in a devastating instance of the chillingly quotidian economic and legal business of racialized chattel slavery (Figure 18).[51]

Only thirty years later, in a bill of sale which in its use of both print and manuscript mirrored the mixed media of the Atlantic indenture contract, John Burr of Fairfield, Connecticut, "For the Consideration of *one hundred pounds*," sold to one Thaddeus Gregory "*one Negro boy named Robin about ten year old*" (Figure 19).[52] In this explicit sale of a child, we see the inevitable

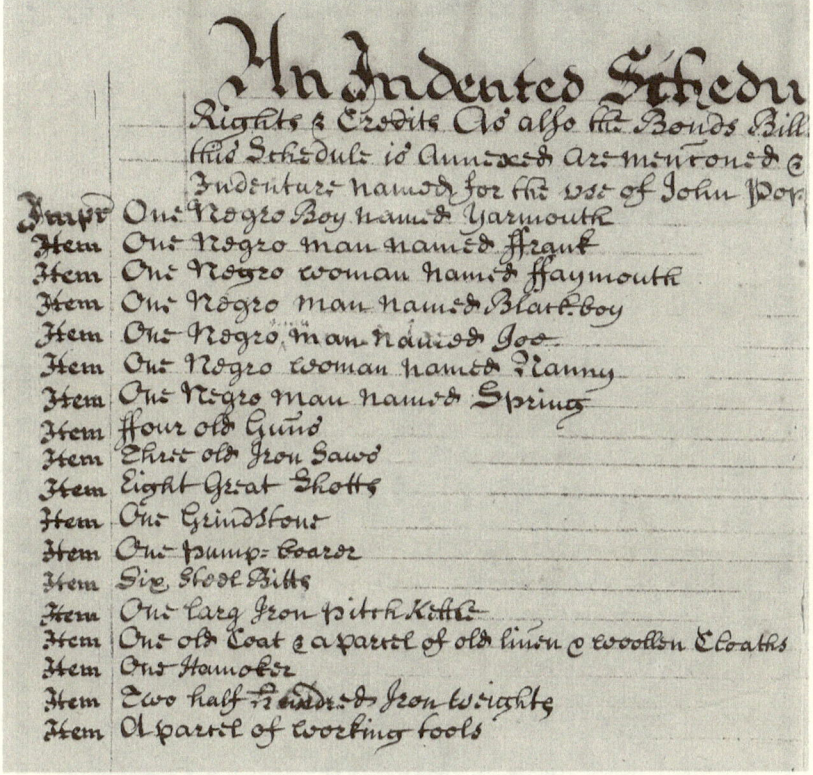

Figure 18. Indenture between Pentecost Teague, John Popel, and Robert Quary (Philadelphia, 1709), leaf 2 recto (detail). Y.d.554. Used by permission of the Folger Shakespeare Library under a Creative Commons Attribution-ShareAlike 4.0 International License.

result of the semantic and conceptual slippage between childhood and servitude, and of the authorizing fictions of the indenture contract. These legal fictions came under particular pressure in cases of children trafficked and transported across the ocean. If indentures contractually bound their nominally willing participants, sometimes they lacked even the fiction of consent, laying bare their workings as instruments of bondage. And the legal status of children, both vexed and vulnerable, illuminates the crucial role of generation in securing the future of servitude. As I shall argue, children do not only expose the fictions of early modern voluntary servitude; they also emerge at the heart of the logics of slavery.

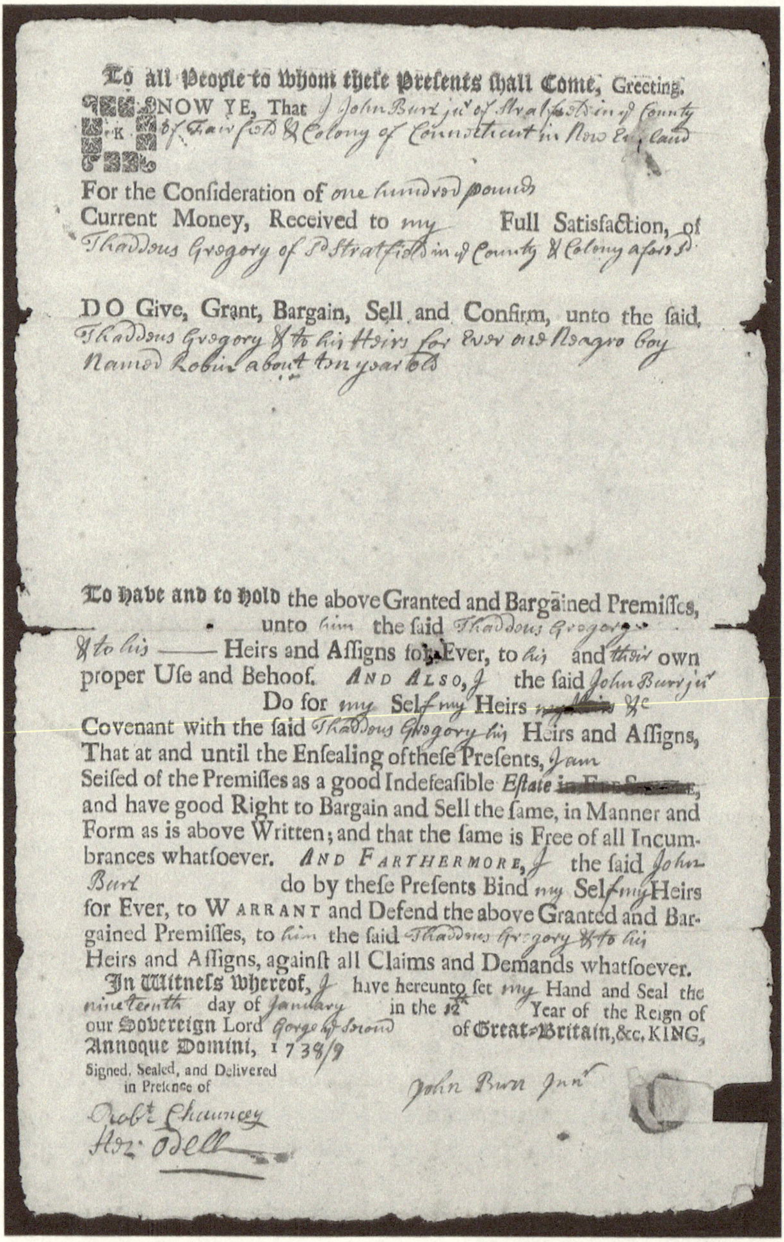

To all People to whom these Presents shall Come, Greeting.

KNOW YE, That *I John Burr jr of Stratfield in sd County of Fairfield & Colony of Connecticut in New England*

For the Consideration of *one hundred pounds* Current Money, Received to *my* Full Satisfaction, of *Thaddeus Gregory of sd Stratfield in sd County & Colony aforesd*

DO Give, Grant, Bargain, Sell and Confirm, unto the said *Thaddeus Gregory & to his Heirs for Ever one Negro boy Named Robin about ten years old*

To Have and to Hold the above Granted and Bargained Premisses, unto *him* the said *Thaddeus Gregory & to his* Heirs and Assigns for Ever, to *his* and *their* own proper Use and Behoof. AND ALSO, *I* the said *John Burr jr* Do for *my* Self *my* Heirs *&c* Covenant with the said *Thaddeus Gregory his* Heirs and Assigns, That at and until the Ensealing of these Presents, *I am* Seised of the Premisses as a good Indefeasible Estate ~~in Fee Simple~~, and have good Right to Bargain and Sell the same, in Manner and Form as is above Written; and that the same is Free of all Incumbrances whatsoever. AND FARTHERMORE, *I* the said *John Burr* do by these Presents Bind *my* Self *my* Heirs for Ever, to WARRANT and Defend the above Granted and Bargained Premisses, to *him* the said *Thaddeus Gregory & to his* Heirs and Assigns, against all Claims and Demands whatsoever.

In Witness whereof, *I* have hereunto set *my* Hand and Seal the *nineteenth* day of *January* in the *12th* Year of the Reign of our Sovereign Lord *George ye Second* of Great-Britain, &c. KING, Annoque Domini, 1738/9

Signed, Sealed, and Delivered
in Presence of

Robt Chauncey
Jos. Odell

John Burr Junr

Figure 19. Deed of sale for an enslaved child named Robin (Connecticut, 1738/9). Gen. MSS Misc., Grp 1223, Item F-1, Beinecke Rare Book and Manuscript Library, Yale University.

"Our Voluntary Service He Requires": Indenture in the Garden of Eden

The centrality of children and natality to servitude itself is anticipated by the politics and poetics of *Paradise Lost*, an epic that addresses the problem of the theological imperative to serve freely at precisely the moment at which it encounters the necessity of indenture to the aims of economic and imperial expansion. Adam and Eve have been suggested as planters by some previous critics, and I want to situate them clearly in the terms of indentured servitude.[53] But the question that animates my study of *Paradise Lost* is: where do we locate the place of slavery? The problem of a "voluntary service" that God "requires" is expressed as a theological one, which deploys the discourse of willing servitude but only tacitly evokes the specter of slavery. In the remainder of this chapter, I shall argue that not only does the prelapsarian language around labor problematize the volitional nature of work, it also reimagines the place of consent to generation, dynasty, and family, reframing the semantic discussion around the family of service and the family of blood. As *Paradise Lost* exposes the fictions of consent that undergird the imperative to faithful service, it also reveals the ways in which the future of humanity is contingent on a generativity that will underwrite structures of slavery. For reproduction not only guarantees the future of humanity; it also secures the future of slavery.[54]

The rhetoric of indebtedness and gratitude in *Paradise Lost* underscores how the Miltonic "debt immense" (4.52) participates within larger discursive and affective fictions surrounding servitude and obligation in early modern England and America.[55] As we have seen, contracts of indenture in the seventeenth century frequently emphasize mutual obligation between master and servant. Concomitantly, the practice of servitude often insists on the performance of "free," willing, and "faithful" service together, paradoxically, with iterations of gratitude and indebtedness to the master by the servant. Adam and Eve's languages of debt, gratitude, and dominion articulate an understanding of servitude that paradoxically lays claim to liberty, and of indenture that engenders indebtedness, in rhetoric resonant of the political and affective fictions surrounding indentured service in the early modern transatlantic world.

Milton's Sonnet 19 and its peculiar negotiations of labor and service prepare us for the paradoxes of *Paradise Lost*. "When I consider how my light is spent" is perhaps best known for its concluding lines, its principal lesson that

"They also serve who only stand and wait."[56] As Milton would have it—or so we understand—faithful "waiting" and readiness to "serve" is not a form of impotence or mere inaction, but rather a legitimate form of obeisance. Whether it subscribes to a pedagogy of patience or reflects a turn away from passivity, the final line certainly underscores that "They *also* serve who *only* stand and wait," that "serving" can consist of something other than, and more than, "standing and waiting." We need only look earlier in the sonnet to discover what that other mode of service resembles. The blind Milton's "light is spent," he claims, "Ere half my days," leaving

> that one talent which is death to hide,
> Lodged with me useless, though my soul more bent
> To serve therewith my Maker, and present
> My true account, lest he returning chide. (lines 2–6)

The "talent" to which Milton alludes refers, of course, to Matthew 25 and to the parable of the talents, wherein the slothful servant, who neglects to put his talents to profit, is punished when he gives his "account" to his master. But the parable of the talents, in Sonnet 19, is then rendered as not an account of investment or profit, but rather a commentary on a different kind of work. "'Doth God exact day labor, light denied?'" Milton "fondly ask[s],"

> ... but patience to prevent
> That murmur soon replies, "God doth not need
> Either man's work or his own gifts; who best
> Bear his mild yoke, they serve him best; his state
> Is kingly." (lines 7–12)

The investment of the talents, then, comes to resemble a kind of "day labor"; and yet, patience replies that "'God doth not need / ... man's work.'"

Sonnet 19 sits uneasily with Adam's own description, in Book 4, of his task in Eden. Adam observes that he and Eve

> ... at [God's] hand
> Have nothing merited, nor can performe
> Aught whereof hee hath need, hee who requires
> From us no other service then to keep

> This one, this easie charge, of all the Trees
> In Paradise that bear delicious fruit
> So various, not to taste that onely Tree
> Of knowledge (4.417–24)

Adam repeats the rhetoric of *need*: they cannot perform "Aught whereof [God] hath need," echoing Sonnet 19's assertion that "God doth not need / ... man's work." Their only prohibition, Adam goes on to reiterate, is that "God hath pronounc't it death to taste that Tree, / The only sign of our obedience left" (4.427–28). Death, we note, attaches itself to the tasting of the tree as to the hiding of the talent in Sonnet 19.

Yet, while Adam claims that the injunction is their "One easie prohibition" (4.433), "The only sign of our obedience left / Among so many signes of power and rule / Conferrd upon us" (4.428–30), an injunction that they must therefore not "think hard" (4.432), it becomes clear that they do not, in fact "enjoy / Free leave so large to all things else" (4.433–34), as he claims. Rather, they must "ever praise [God], and extoll / His bountie" (4.436–37); in addition, they must undertake their "delightful task / To prune these growing Plants, and tend these Flours, / Which were it toilsom, yet with thee were sweet" (4.437–39). The description of Adam and Eve's labor is conflicted. Adam describes it as a "delightful task," yet he himself notes that the only thing that prevents it being "toilsom" is Eve's company. It is Eve, not the nature of the work nor the "work-master," who makes the day labor "sweet."

More tellingly, the register of Adam's speech shifts as he describes their "easie prohibition." The subject of his discourse, at the beginning, is the nature of their service. God "requires" from them, he says, no other service than "this easie charge ... not to taste that onely Tree / Of knowledge" (4.419–24). The proscription, then, is itself a form of service. But then it alters slightly:

> God hath pronounc't it death to taste that Tree,
> The only sign of our *obedience* left
> Among so many signes of power and rule
> Conferrd upon us. (4.427–30, emphasis added)

In addition to comprising their sole service to a master, then, the injunction also becomes their sole obedience, the only exception to their dominion. By the end of his speech, however, in 4.433, the proscription is no longer "one ... easie charge," as in 4.421, but rather "One easie prohibition." It is, moreover, the crucial exception to their liberty, they "who enjoy / Free leave so large to all things *else*" (4.433–34, emphasis added). Given how commonly early modern service is paradoxically articulated as a form of freedom, that the exception to their freedoms is synonymous with Adam and Eve's only service seems particularly odd. "But let us ever praise him," Adam concludes in 4.436, completing the "then ... but" construction begun in 4.432, but also inserting a grace note of reluctance into the word "but," a note amplified in the suggestion that, but for Eve, the task "were ... toilsom."

It is Eve who accommodates and attempts to reconcile Adam's conflicted discourses of toil and liberty. "[W]hat thou hast said is just and right," she allows, but adds, "For wee to him indeed all praises owe, / And daily thanks" (4.443–45). Eve, therefore, invokes the rhetoric both of perpetual indebtedness and of gratitude. In so doing, she echoes Satan's own comment, earlier in Book 4, about the "debt immense of endless gratitude, / So burthensome, still paying, still to ow" (4.52–53). But Satan misunderstands that "a grateful mind / By owing owes not, but still pays, at once / Indebted and dischargd; what burden then?" (4.55–57). The "debt immense" of "endless gratitude" can never be paid off in the conventional sense, but it can be discharged by the "grateful mind."[57] As David Hawkes notes, "Satan had conceived of his debt to God in the same terms as the opponents of usury described moneylending ... [but] it is not a temporal debt that God has unfairly extended in duration to the point that it can never be paid. The debt can never be paid because it is Satan's essential quality.... In fact the debt is forgiven as soon as its nature is acknowledged."[58] For God, the failure of man is a failure of *gratitude*. Man will heed Satan's "glozing lyes," he proclaims, "And easily transgress the sole Command, / Sole pledge of his obedience" (3.93–95). This renders Man not only a disobedient subject but also, crucially, an "ingrate" who "had of mee / All he could have" (3.97–98) and failed anyway. But God upholds the crucial conflation of service and freedom, insisting that "I formd them free, and free they must remain, / Till they enthrall themselves" (3.124–25). After all, "Not free, what proof could they have givn sincere / Of true allegiance" (3.103–4)?

The paradoxical yoking together of freedom, obedience, and allegiance in this way echoes the *Book of Common Prayer*'s edict that God's "seruice is perfecte fredome."[59] "[D]efend vs thy humble seruau[n]tes," the prayer continues, "in all assaultes of our enemies; that we surely trustyng in thy defence, may not feare the power of any aduersaries."[60] "Free service," therefore, will protect man from his adversary—or, in Hebrew, Satan. But Adam, as I have suggested, tacitly contests this paradoxical paradigm of free service. And however exceptional the nature of the "debt immense" of gratitude owed to God, its affinities with quantifiable debts become particularly pronounced when we also take into account the slippages in Adam's speech between task and toil, service and subjugation. Eve's account of the "thanks" they owe reconciles these tensions to some extent, but also underscores, I suggest, the peculiar conflicts between servitude and consent, indenture and indebtedness, that we see in seventeenth-century contracts of indenture. As J. Martin Evans has noted, "Adam's situation in *Paradise Lost* resembles nothing so much as an idealized form of indentured servitude. Placed in an earthly Paradise by the 'sovran Planter' (4.691), he is destined to serve out a fixed term of 'pleasant labour' (4.625), at the end of which, by 'long obedience tri'd' (7.159), he may be given the status of an angel and allowed to dwell permanently in the terrestrial or the celestial paradise" (5.500).[61] If God is the "sovran Planter" (the word "planter" recalling the colonial settlers who were planted in, and planted, the land), the indentured laborers who actually tilled the soil were, as I have noted, themselves frequently persuaded onto the ships to the New World by "spirits," a word which also evokes the many different kinds of "spirits" who inhabit the cosmos of *Paradise Lost*.

Unlike the toil of indentured servants, however, Adam and Eve's labor is, as Evans has noted, idealized: they can rest from their work "after no more toil / Of thir sweet Gardning labour than suffic'd / To recommend coole Zephyr" (4.327–29), while Adam argues that

> . . . not so strictly hath our Lord impos'd
> Labour, as to debarr us when we need
> Refreshment, whether food, or talk between,
> Food of the mind, or this sweet intercourse
> Of looks and smiles. (9.235–39)

After all, Adam claims, "not to irksom toile, but to delight / He made us" (9. 242–43). Yet we note again the contingencies of Adam's description: "our Lord" has still "*imposed*" Adam and Eve's labor upon them. Allowing them the refreshment they "need" hardly seems a significant concession under the circumstances. Moreover, the work they undertake is both essential and overwhelming. As Eve points out, they may

> . . . labour still to dress
> This Garden, still to tend Plant, Herb and Flour,
> Our pleasant task enjoyn'd, but till more hands
> Aid us, the work under our labour grows,
> Luxurious by restraint. (9.205–9)

God may not "need" "man's work," according to Sonnet 19, but the Garden certainly demands it. The Sisyphean image of their "labour" generating more and more "work" fails utterly to delimit the nature of their service. Adam and Eve are both willing to undertake and "enjoyn'd" to a task at once pleasant and ever-increasing, which may never be discharged. Labor is, it seems, a trap that leads not to the resolution but to the multiplication of toil, intended not for the end of work but for the progress of service and even servitude—in effect, a form of bondage. Performing obedience in their own dominion, Adam and Eve are both indebted and redeemed, both indentured and free.

These tensions characterize the legal, political, and economic situation of seventeenth-century indentured servants, who volitionally contracted themselves into servitude, who were both in debt and indentured, and who labored so that they might eventually earn dominion over some part of the land they worked (not to mention over their own bodies).[62] Adam and Eve evoke the tensions in the institution of indentured servitude between consent and contract, liberty and obligation, not only in the nature of their work, but also in their political and affective rhetorics of gratitude and gift. What animates this performance of willing service and grateful bondage is the construction of the service-based family that knits together God the "sovran Planter" and his toiling laborers as forcefully as the rhetorics of familial organization: God the Father and his fallible human children, whose filial duty also consists in their "voluntary service." But if Adam and Eve are figured as God's children, *Paradise Lost* also contains a curiously insistent and perverse anti-natalist strain that both sutures the family to work and yokes natality to the prospect of slavery.

"He My Inbred Enemy": Anti-Natalism in *Paradise Lost*

In an essay on *Macbeth* and early modern futurity, Luke Wilson begins with a provocative pronouncement: "An heir is a peculiar sort of person," he asserts, because "an heir comes into existence only when the person whose heir he or she is is dead. . . . As the common law maxim runs, *nemo est heres viventis*: no one is heir to a living person."[63] An heir, therefore, is pure potential, radical futurity: because one can never coexist with one's heir, an heir is always presumptive or, in Wilson's words, "contingent." To take this argument further, an heir is a conceptual impossibility. But to read early modern literature is often to take for granted the teleology of reproductive futurity. If the project of early modern reproduction is determined by the need for heirs, as it is so often understood, then it is a project that is at the very least founded on a semantic as well as a legal fiction. In the remainder of this chapter, I build on my earlier discussion in Chapters 2 and 3 of the fallacies of blood lineage and the changing definitions of the family in order to argue that the legal fiction of the heir and the concomitant potentialities of anti-natalism—a term I understand to register the refusal of the reproductive imperative—inform and transform the representation of bodies in servitude in *Paradise Lost* and in the early modern transatlantic world. If, as I have argued, the figure of the child is philologically imbricated within the rhetorical frameworks of service, it also secures the futures of slavery.

Although later American blood policies, including the infamous "one-drop rule," as well as affective discourses binding slaves and the families they served, would adumbrate and regulate the workings of servitude according to the legal and rhetorical frameworks of family, the connection in this earlier period between lineage and labor is harder to discern. I have already suggested that early modern definitions of the family did not center on consanguinity, even as, of course, lineage remained organized by dynastic succession in early modern England. But an attentiveness to the role of service in meanings of the family also reconfigures readings of reproductive futurism. Depictions of anti-natalism, I suggest, are particularly urgent for standing at the crossroads of the different definitions of what constitutes family, blood, or service. Returning to *Macbeth*, Luke Wilson argues that the play paradoxically locates Macbeth's journey toward kingship *in opposition to* the project of begetting heirs and ensuring one's own lineage.[64] This seems extraordinary; if there is one question on which succession crises are founded, it is this: what is the point of being a king if one doesn't have an heir? An attentiveness to anti-natalism marks a radical reimagining of the dynastic and familial imperative, queering teleological modes of kinship. In larger terms, it also compels us to ask: what happens to the blood-based family when it is resituated within an anti-natalist framework? As I shall demonstrate by addressing the poem's anti-natalism in light of the different resonances around the meanings of family, *Paradise Lost* precipitates the coarticulation of servitude and sanguinity by suggesting that (reproductive) futurity portends merely bondage.

Although there has been little critical discussion of *Paradise Lost*'s antinatalism, this scholarly lacuna is unsurprising. After all, how can this retelling of Genesis, a narrative which purports to give us a provenance which is both providential and fundamentally corporeal, which explains our lineal and familial origins, be in any way anti-natalist, when its very title announces its natalist imperative? Isn't genesis the *sine qua non* of, well, Genesis?

Not exactly. Even the first allusion to lineage—the poem's first mention of "parents"—is deeply vexed:

> Say first, for Heav'n hides nothing from thy view
> Nor the deep Tract of Hell, say first what cause
> Mov'd our Grand Parents in that happy State,
> Favour'd of Heav'n so highly, to fall off
> From thir Creator . . . (1.27–31)

While the "Grand Parents" are at first associated with a "happy State," swift mention is made of their "fall[ing] off," the enjambed line again "falling" into a rhetorical void before we learn what they have fallen off *from*: "thir Creator." Not *our* Creator, we note, but *theirs*, drawing an association, deliberately, between their natality and the natality of their (human, embodied) descendants. The descent of the "Grand Parents" from their "happy State" evokes familial, lineal descent; even the visual inscription and organizational logic of a family tree necessarily occasions a "fall" in the direction of the eye as we read it, a fall that increases with the length of the family, with an increase of the natality of the reproductive project. The greater the natality, the longer its history, and the longer the fall.

But while the *Oxford English Dictionary* affirms the meaning of "grand parent" as "A parent of one's father or mother," the word carries other valences, too.[65] If we turn to Timothie Bright's *Characterie An Art of Short, Swift, and Secret Writing by Character* (1588), we see the word "Parent" described thus: "Aunt Brother Cosen Father Grandfather Grandmother Kinseman Mother Nephewe Sister Vnkle."[66] A parent, then, can be a range of different kin relationships. In other words, "Grand Parents" here contains a play on words; Adam and Eve are not only "grand" parents, but also grandparents, one kin relationship removed from "us," the readers of the poem. This articulation traces parentage not to Adam and Eve directly, but rather as mediated via Christ. While in this section of the poem the reader is still learning about the "falling off" of these "Grand Parents," they nonetheless already know of his redemption by "one greater Man" (1.4), through whom they can trace an alternate ancestry.

Book 1's description of the fallen angels coming to attention also rehearses extensive analogies to unfilial sons and unhappy parents: the "barbarous Sons" (1.353) of the "populous North" (1.351); the "parents tears" (1.393) of those sacrificed by Moloch, "Thir childrens cries unheard" (1.395), a particularly gruesome image; and of course the "Sons of *Eve*" (1.364), an allusion both to mankind and to the "Sons of God" who "cohabited with the 'Daughters of Men' and begot a race of demonic giants. Christian commentators associated these 'Sons of God' with the fallen angels."[67] The language, in other words, has changed from the "Sons of God" to the "Sons of *Eve*," explicitly couching this lineage in the terms of human generation, while also underscoring the inevitable corruption of this line. Meanwhile, the allusion to

Th' *Ionian* Gods, of *Javans* Issue held
Gods, yet confest later then Heav'n and Earth
Thir boasted Parents; *Titan* Heav'ns first born
With his enormous brood (1.508–11)

evokes the violence, incest, and brutality of the Greek gods, couching this description again in the language of natality, but also mocking the imperative to succession in that very same language. The "first born," who usually assures and secures dynastic succession, is here Titan with his own "enormous brood," a grotesque rather than laudable image.

It is in Book 2, however, that we get one of the most horrific images of generation, in Satan's (re)encounter with Sin, when we first learn of the brutal birth of Death, an act of natality that literally deforms the bearer. As Sin relates the tale, "this odious offspring" (2.781), Death, Satan's

. . . own begotten, breaking violent way
Tore through my entrails, that with fear and pain
Distorted, all my nether shape thus grew
Transform'd: but he my inbred enemie
Forth issu'd, brandishing his fatal Dart . . . (2.782–86)

This is hardly an advertisement for childbirth, although it does prefigure a (thankfully, horrifically exaggerated) version of the travail that human labor will necessitate. Our introduction to natality in the poem is therefore grim, to say the least. Then, however, there is another violent act of conception and natality: the rape of Sin by Death, which, as several critics have pointed out, parodies the virgin birth of Christ, but also simultaneously evokes, disrupts, and corrupts the Holy Trinity of the Father, the Son, and the Holy Spirit:

> Mee overtook his mother all dismaid,
> And in embraces forcible and foule
> Ingendring with me, of that rape begot
> These yelling Monsters that with ceasless cry
> Surround me, as thou sawst, hourly conceiv'd
> And hourly born, with sorrow infinite
> To me, for when they list into the womb
> That bred them they return, and howle and gnaw
> My Bowels, thir repast; then bursting forth
> Afresh with conscious terrours vex me round,
> That rest or intermission none I find. (2.792–802)

The opening phrase, "Mee overtook his mother," describes Death's terrible action, but also signals his lineal disruption, marking him as the overreaching offspring. This passage, indeed, gestures toward forms of corruption throughout; the "Ingendring" leads to "rape," and what is "begot" is not a legitimate heir but rather "Monsters." The natal process is itself deformed, with the "Monsters" "hourly conceiv'd / And hourly born," a grotesquely accelerated natal cycle. But perhaps the most horrifying image in this whole passage is that of the hounds returning to Sin's "womb / That bred them," "gnaw[ing]" her "Bowels," an image which is both incestuous and even cannibalistic, a gross distortion of the teleology of childbirth and of the narrative of natalist nurture. If the virgin birth occludes the messiness of parturition, this description of the incestuous Trinity is disturbing in its evocations of the horrors of childbirth.

And yet, this passage also foreshadows the effects of the fall: the site of postlapsarian suffering is, precisely, natalism and childbirth. The pain of parturition will therefore echo if not exactly repeat Sin's gruesome travails.[68] Eve's children will also be an "inbred enemie" of sorts, marking by their very birth the continued site and evidence of man's fall. The "inbred enemie" will cause their mothers pain, but will also, writ large, continually necessitate and jeopardize mankind's salvation. The worst enemy is the enemy within.

And yet, the corporeal family constituted by God, Adam, and Eve is explicitly intended for expansion. And expand it does: Eve is "our general Mother" (4.492). But her children are located in the future, as Adam and Eve remind God when they pray "unanimous" to him (4.736): "thou hast promis'd from us two a Race / To fill the Earth" (4.732–33). Ten lines later, the text infamously describes a scene of conjugal union, which it vigorously defends:

> Our Maker bids increase, who bids abstain
> But our destroyer, foe to God and Man?
> Haile wedded Love, mysterious Law, true source
> Of human ofspring. (4.748–51)

In other words, "wedded Love" is desirable because it leads directly to "increase" and "ofspring," dovetailing nicely with God's "promise" to engender a "Race." Adam and Eve certainly seem to be doing what they can to bring this "Race" about. But the word "promise" situates "ofspring" in the terrain of the future, endlessly deferring this promised reproductive moment. What is God waiting for?

We will of course see the children of Adam and Eve later, although the vision of what happens to mankind is certainly grim. But as we know, part of the punishment of Eden is the very difficulty around children. It is childbearing and reproduction, in other words, that is the site of the Fall, something God explicitly emphasizes in the pronouncement of his punishment: "Thy sorrow I will greatly multiplie / By thy Conception; Children thou shalt bring / In sorrow forth" (10.193–95). But why is Eve's penalty so closely centered around childbearing, specifically? Even Adam, on discovering the repercussions of his transgression, laments:

> O why did God ... not fill the World at once
> With Men as Angels without Feminine,
> Or find some other way to generate
> Mankind? (10.888, 892–895)

Woman is the problem here again, but more specifically it is reproductive generation that is to blame. Tellingly, the angels Adam wishes populated the world do have sex, but it is nongenerative, nonreproductive, non-natalist sex.

Eve for her part also responds to the prospect of a "cursed Race" by raising the specter of a nonreproductive futurity:

> If care of our descent perplex us most,
> Which must be born to certain woe, devourd
> By Death at last, and miserable it is
> To be to others cause of misery,
> Our own begotten, and of our Loines to bring
> Into this cursed World a woful Race,
> That after wretched Life must be at last
> Food for so foule a Monster, in thy power
> It lies, yet ere Conception to prevent
> The Race unblest, to being yet unbegot.
> Childless thou art, Childless remaine. (10.979–89)

We note the framing of negative potentialities (unblest, unbegot) here, and the sense of near-inevitability conjoined with a near miss. The injunction that "Childless thou art, Childless remaine" is particularly striking for the way in which it takes a current state of childlessness—the case, we know, only because God's natal promise has been relegated to the future—and argues that it should continue, that the temporality of reproductive futurity which had been both promised and assumed should now be revised and regauged, precisely because children have not *yet* happened in the past and present. The utopia of children has been replaced by another, queerer utopia: that of childlessness.

But what is striking here is that Eve locates in "descent" only the prospect of misery, situating in the "Loines" of natal potentiality only "certain woe." Animating Eve's fear of children is not just the ethics of preventing pain, but also the horror of creating it. Adam denounces such "wilful barrenness" (10.1042), but what ultimately prevents this ungenerative future is the attendant injunction against intercourse: "But if thou judge it hard and difficult [Eve says], / Conversing, looking, loving, to abstain / From Loves due Rites, Nuptial imbraces sweet" (10.992–94), then "Let us seek Death, or he not found, supply / With our own hands his Office on our selves" (10.1001–2). If they cannot engage in "Nuptial imbraces," that is to say, then they may as well commit suicide. Adam hastens to clarify that this is not a viable option, so they must accept the natal consequences of "Loves due Rites," without which life is not worth living. What assures Adam and Eve's reproductive futurity, then, is not the figure of the Child or the prospect of children *qua* children, but rather the horrors of abstinence.[69] In other words, Eve subordinates their deferred, reproductive future to their immediate, present desire: "Before the present object languishing / With like desire" (10.996–97) would, she says, be "miserie" (10.997).

Despite Adam's admonition against "wilful barrenness," he soon repeats this turn away from generation, from the teleology of the heir, from consanguineal linearity. When Adam realizes what Death means, as he witnesses in Book 11 the scores of painful and violent forms it can take, he immediately adopts an anti-natalist rhetoric: "O miserable Mankind, to what fall / Degraded, to what wretched state reserv'd! / Better end heer unborn" (11.500–502). This response has been read by some critics as advocating, as Eve had, for suicide; but I understand the words "Better end heer unborn" to register somewhat differently, not as negating present life but rather as acknowledging and simultaneously foreclosing on future lives, as articulating a radical argument for human extinction. Adam, like Eve, advocates for anti-natalism on ethical grounds, that it is better to spare "miserable Mankind" their inevitably "wretched state." If, as David Benatar argues, we have an obligation to spare future generations pain, Adam and Eve's anti-natalism signals not despair but rather a radical ethics of compassion.[70]

Even after Adam learns that the Flood, for all its destruction, will still spare "one Man found so perfet and so just" (11.876), Noah, his response is to express relief at the continuation of animal, not human, generation: "I revive / At this last sight, assur'd that Man shall live / With all the Creatures, and *thir seed preserve*" (11.871–73, emphasis mine). In other words, Adam assigns reproductive potentiality to the animals but not to himself, subordinating the preservation of human generative possibilities to nonhuman futures.[71]

But even in Book 10, as Adam desperately seeks the silver lining in his grim postlapsarian future, the best he can come up with is the prospect of . . . work. Trying to make the best of the punishment he must endure, Adam insists:

> . . . On mee the Curse aslope
> Glanc'd on the ground, with labour I must earne
> My bread; what harm? Idleness had bin worse;
> My labour will sustain me. (10.1053–56)

Work is not so bad, Adam ventures to suggest, even as the language he uses around labor betrays just how onerous it can and might be:

> No more be mention'd then of violence
> Against our selves, and wilful barrenness,
> That cuts us off from hope, and savours onely
> Rancor and pride, impatience and despite,
> Reluctance against God and his just yoke
> Laid on our Necks. (10.1041–46)

"Yoke" reflects a seventeenth-century metaphor for marriage, but the word had already come to register not only subjection or oppression but also servitude and even slavery, an association that would be cemented by 1721 in Nathan Bailey's *An Universal Etymological English Dictionary*, which notes that the term "yoke" "is figuratively taken for Subjection, Bondage or Slavery."[72] Given Adam's punishment, which is labor, and his own attempts to reconcile himself to the "work" which lies in store for him, it is difficult not to read the "yoke" that God "lays on their necks" as resonant not just of the yoke the master lays on his animals, but also of tyranny and indeed of slavery. If part of the punishment of the Fall is generation, despite all Adam and Eve's anti-natalist arguments, along with that natality comes the yoke of bondage. God's prelapsarian promise may be "a Race / To fill the Earth," but race is in this period vitally informed by conceptions both of genealogy and lineage as well as of blood.[73] Adam and Eve's anti-natalist rhetoric, and their assumption of God's "yoke," problematize changing meanings of the family from service to consanguinity, but they simultaneously precipitate the nexus of race, slavery, and kinship.

The reading of race in relation to blood has been persuasively advanced by Jean Feerick, who suggests that in addition to phenotypical understandings of race, early modern writers situated blood as a critical component of frameworks of race-making. In her provocative reimagining of early modern racial formations, Feerick argues that "Race was . . . a way of 'speaking the body' quite distinct from modern paradigms first and foremost because it defined the body primarily through the qualities of its *blood*. That is, it propounded distinctions of rank above all else. . . . To be 'of a race' was also to be 'of the blood.'"[74] Glossing the "widespread notion of degeneration that rose to prominence in the late sixteenth and early seventeenth centuries" as "conveying the fraying of the period's dominant system of racial identity,"[75] Feerick also reads the implications of dislocation, displacement, and migration on bloodlines in ways that are particularly resonant in the early Atlantic world in the context of English planters:

In revealing that the "fixed" lines of race that were a central feature of that social body were fallible, subject to dispersal under the pressure of migration, colonization had the effect of destabilizing the English social body.... what the newly planting English feared, obsessed over, and, in some cases, embraced in using this language were not merely cultural alterations but racial alterations—that is, alterations that had an impact on a system of race-as-blood. Through this language, they worked through the implications of inhabiting another soil, sorting through how their acts of "planting"—a term that they preferred to colonizing—would affect not only themselves but their descendants.[76]

The newly "planted" colonies, then, become the site of novel iterations of society, identity, and race, the places not only of imperial expansion but also of the performance of racial reformations.[77]

But as I have tried to argue in this chapter, the centrality of blood may in fact be working quite differently in texts like *Paradise Lost*, which crucially intercedes in arguments about what the family means in this period, pitting the familial fictions of the "sovran Planter" and his children and servants against consanguineal structures, thus complicating the family's semantic dependency on service (remembering again that the family's earliest and primary meaning is "servants of a household"). Coarticulating both planting and indentured servitude with bondage, Adam and Eve's fictions of volition and rhetorics of compulsion enable us to reimagine the nexus of the indentured servant and the family, and in so doing open up spaces for the futures of slavery. If the provenance of the family—in *famulus*, the Roman household slave—knits together family and slavery in crucial ways, so too does the insistence on natality and its less salubrious effects in *Paradise Lost*. The poem's counterintuitive depictions of anti-natalism expose the construction of natalist imperatives that accompany and even authorize postlapsarian bondage, yoking natality to slavery.

A consideration of race and blood also pushes us to interrogate the effect of natality on early modern racial formations. What happens when we reexamine and interrogate not just the meanings and valences of lineage, but the very lineal imperative, the natalist project itself? When we trace blood back to its origins, to birth not just as rank and race but also as imperative, to the "blood" of continued consanguinity as well as of class, we observe the ways in which the racialization of slavery is inscribed in the call to generation, and the tensions of the family between servitude and consanguinity enable the fictions of consent embodied by the framework of indentured labor. For "race" of course, a word which conspicuously appears twice in five lines in 10.984–88, is implicated in not only sanguinal but also somatically visible, epidermal, and religious formations. The "woful Race" (10.984) and "Race unblest" (10.988) which Eve fears to generate deliberately invokes a lineage and bloodline not only morally but, suggestively, somatically darkened by sin.[78] This "race unblest" in turn emerges as a *bound* race implicated, I propose, in anticipating the imperial projects of racial capitalism.[79] It is significant, perhaps, that in weighing the Son's request for Man's redemption in Book 11, the Father dismisses the possibility that Man might "longer in that Paradise ... dwell" (11.48), since although "I at first with two *fair* gifts / Created him endowd" (11.57–58, emphasis added), Man now bears a kind of stain which renders him unfit for Paradise: "Those pure immortal Elements that know / No gross, no unharmoneous mixture foule, / Eject him *tainted* now" (11.50–52, emphasis mine). The language of being "tainted" carries the suggestion of impurity as well a kind of darkening, a fall from the "fair" gifts of Man's origin to the "tainted" nature of his postlapsarian state. But this "tainted" nature, tied as closely as it is to natality and generation as the site of the fall, may also presage a "blot," "taint," or "stain" of slavery that can be inherited.

In Book 1 of *Paradise Lost*, Satan himself links generation to the colonial project:

> Space may produce new Worlds; whereof so rife
> There went a fame in Heav'n that he ere long
> Intended to create, and therein plant
> A generation, whom his choice regard
> Should favour equal to the Sons of Heaven. (1.650–54)

The language of generation here is attached to the land, so that one must plant a generation, the process of natality tied intrinsically to the rhetoric of "planting" the soil, thereby generating "new Worlds" or *the* New World. Although this is a Satanic association, it also anticipates postlapsarian iterations of an ungenerative earth. With the expulsion from the Garden will come toil and tilling; the gentle planting of the earth will be replaced by hard labor:

> Curs'd is the ground for thy sake, thou in sorrow
> Shalt eate thereof all the days of thy Life;

> Thorns also and Thistles it shall bring thee forth
> Unbid, and thou shalt eate th' Herb of th' Field,
> In the sweat of thy Face shalt thou eat Bread,
> Till thou return unto the ground, for thou
> Out of the ground wast taken, *know thy Birth*,
> For dust thou art, and shalt to dust returne. (10.201–8, emphasis added)

God here not only condemns Adam to an unfruitful earth, he also reminds him of his natal origins: the ground. Marking the site of his birth as the very place of his punishment, God himself renders barren Man's natal origins, the land itself, tying it to bondage instead.

At the same time as children are central to servitude and the family evokes the shifts that precipitate slavery, then, *Paradise Lost* offers a vision of a service-based family, not a natalist one. Natality, indeed, is death. If the place of gratitude in structures of indenture exposes the crevices in iterations of consent, it also underscores the fictions of family that anticipate the affective and structural logics of slavery. *Paradise Lost* is both a forecast and a warning, a reminder that bondage and natality are closely imbricated, that the work on which Adam relies can itself become merely an authorizing fiction of agency, and that the bondage that is intertwined with reproductive futurity implicates a "tainted" nature. In reproducing itself, Man's "race unblest" inevitably generates a heritable—and sometimes somatic—mark of slavery.

And yet, our last view of Adam and Eve offers the prospect of redemption:

> Som natural tears they drop'd, but wip'd them soon;
> The World was all before them, where to choose
> Thir place of rest, and Providence thir guide:
> They hand in hand with wandring steps and slow,
> Through *Eden* took thir solitarie way. (12.645–49)

The weeping and wandering Adam and Eve, who have squandered their talents rather than investing them in ecological and spiritual growth, might remind us of the exiled unprofitable servant of Matthew 25, to whom Sonnet 19 refers. This slothful servant is exiled utterly: "And cast ye the unprofitable servant into outer darkness: there shall be weeping and gnashing of teeth." But unlike him, Adam and Eve are redeemed by the "better covenant" and its "works of faith," a covenant whose benevolent fictions of filial duty, faithful service, and free servitude persist into the contractual rhetoric of the seventeenth-century transatlantic indenture.

The "better covenant" of Christ, of course, reminds us that while he is the Son of Man, he is also the son of God. In a closed consanguineal loop that folds back on itself, Adam and Eve are both heirs and progenitors, reluctant reproducers whose most famous progeny is not their own. These heirs, this family, is also a family of indentured servants, whose navigations and negotiations of servitude and succession manifest the nexus of service and blood, of the unfilial and the unlineal, in early modern understandings of kinship and family. God might helpfully secure his covenant in woman's seed (11.116), but that covenant promises not only salvation but servitude, a reproductive futurity mortgaged on the backs of fictions as well as fealty. If the "better covenant" entails a transition "from servil fear / To filial" (12.305–6), that better covenant also exposes the "servil fear" and the fear of servitude that grounds the edifice of the filial family, and of blood as well as bondage. If the figure of the child emerges as and at the limit case of willing servitude, he also serves to secure the futures of slavery.

CHAPTER 5
―――――

"Of a Bondslaue I Made Thee My Free Man"

Servitude, Manumission, and the *Macula Servitutis* in *The Tempest* and Its Early American Afterlife

Early in the Terentian slave comedy *Andria*, which was widely studied in the early modern schoolroom, the old man and master (*senex/magister*) Simo reminds his freedman (*libertus*) Sosia of his previous servitude: "of a Bondslaue," he declares, "I made thee my free man."[1] Simo's strategic reminder affirms Sosia's current, apparently free state even as it simultaneously recalls his earlier bondage. But in reminding Sosia of his reward of manumission, it also both enacts and ensures a dynamic of continued servitude. Sosia may no longer be a "Bondslaue," but he remains "*my* free man"; although apparently no longer subject to complete mastery, Sosia remains bound by (at least discourses of) mutuality. The condition of the freedman, as I shall discuss in this chapter, is thus one of both consent and contingency, problematizing the teleologies of liberty on which trajectories of manumission appear to turn. To be freed is not, it seems, truly to be *free*. *Fictions of Consent* has thus far explored the nexus of service and servitude in early modern England and its anticipatory fictions for the frameworks of slavery and for a more permanent "stain of slavery"; this final chapter turns to servitude *after* manumission, revealing the rhetorical and conceptual antecedents for the discourses of "happy slavery" and, more insidiously, for the logics of racialized slavery's somatic markers.

Sosia's servile dilemma in *Andria* is not unique; indeed, the freedman or *libertus* is himself something of a paradox. According to Thomas Elyot's 1538 *Dictionary*, the *libertus* is "he that of a bondeman is manumised or infranchised"; for Thomas Thomas in 1587, a *libertus* or *liberta* is "He or she that of bond is made free: a late seruant or bondman."[2] The *libertus*, then, is seemingly free, his journey from bondage to liberty apparently complete. And yet, the *libertus* bears the trace, constantly, of his former bondage. He is not a free man; he is, crucially, a *freed* man.[3] The *libertus* gestures, constantly and contemporaneously, to his current liberty and his past slavery. This vestige, this remnant, is not only a semantic one. In his study of the *libertus*, redressing the scholarly lacuna around the Roman freedman, Henrik Mouritsen underscores the *macula servitutis* or "stain of slavery" that attends the *libertus*, constantly undercutting and compromising his hard-won freedom. This *macula* gestures to the way in which slavery is less a temporally bound state than a perpetual, ineradicable, essential *stain*.[4] A naturalized trait rhetorically framed as a legible, bodily marker, the *macula servitutis*, I argue, comprises an antecedent and an analogue for early modern understandings of the incipient racial formations around slavery, and of the vestiges of a servitude that often proves to be ineradicable. In this way, I suggest, we might come to understand the *macula servitutis* as presaging the conceptual tenacity of early modern racial markers, even in the absence of their somatic or material counterparts. And as I will suggest later in this chapter, this "stain of slavery" also exposes and reflexively gives way to the ceremonial (re)enactment of one of the most unambiguous forms of Roman servitude, underscoring the slippage between a servile "blemish" and bondage, between manumission and enslavement. Even in its contemporary context, the *macula servitutis* gives the lie to the fiction of manumission that attends the *libertus*.

But if even a freed man is always attended by the "stain" of servitude, how can a servant become truly free? For early modern readers, this is something of an irrelevant question: to be a servant is *already* to be free. It is the condition of masterlessness, in contrast, that both renders one marginal and authorizes one's servitude.[5] Yet the question of how to serve freely remains an early modern discursive preoccupation, dramatically and rhetorically subtended by the classical slave comedies that comprise their political and pedagogical precedents. By exploring this early modern legacy of the classical paradox of "free service" in *The Tempest*, this chapter contends that the play reimagines the Roman *libertus* and the Roman *mancipium* (slave) in the figures of one of Shakespeare's most trusted servants, Ariel, as well as one of the most reviled, Caliban. In so doing, I argue that this play first articulates the performance of volition, gratitude, and liberty as the properties of "good service," demonstrating freedom's compulsion to bondage, and the fictions of consent inherent in the enactment of faithful service. Second, it reveals the revocability of manumission, and therefore the tenuousness of both the state of and the imperative to emancipation. And finally, it anticipates the racialized register of the stain of slavery that attaches to the supposedly manumitted servant. Thus, I end this chapter by reading the case of Adam Saffin, a "negro man" in seventeenth-century Massachusetts whose contracted date of manumission was subject to deferral, his master alleged, because Saffin had failed to act "as an Honest true and faithfull Servant ought to doe."[6] Even as it ascribes specific epidermal signifiers to servitude and slavery, the "stain of slavery" presages the perpetual indebtedness that undergirds structures of Atlantic slavery.

* * *

Before beginning my discussion of *The Tempest*, I want to turn to one of the most famous, and famously loyal, servants in the Shakespearean canon: *King Lear*'s Kent, whose first words in the play register Lear as not only a king but also a master, a father, and a patron:

Royal Lear,
Whom I have ever honored as my king,
Loved as my father, as my master followed,
As my great patron thought on in my prayers—[7]

Kent articulates Lear as a Roman *magister*: a father, a teacher, and a master.[8] This conflation is not unusual; but what is curious is what happens after the death of the *magister*. Just as Kent's first words declare his allegiance to his master, his last words in the play only affirm his loyalty to the dead Lear: "My master calls me. I must not say no" (5.3.298). This moment has been interpreted as an exemplum of the servant's loyalty, representing the play's nostalgic depiction of faithful, willing service. The question Kent's last utterance presents, however, is no more nor less than this: what does it mean to say no? For critics such as Richard Strier, Kent's refusal to obey Lear—a resistance recalled by his final "no"—is itself a form of faithful service.[9] Here, however, Kent denies the "no"; "I *must not* say no." In other words, he resists the kind of (disobedient) fidelity for which Strier argues, in effect rescripting the service he has demonstrated throughout the play, which has appeared as the paradoxically resistant fealty of the true servant.[10]

But what does one, or can one, say no *to*? Kent acknowledges and then forecloses the possibility of saying no to the "call" of his master, a call which can itself take many forms: to action; to renewed service; to the inaction of death. The "call" can also be to a particular narrative of service, to *recall*; to a history or memory of the particular service relationship. It is, in effect, a call waiting for a response, a response itself strategically scripted for specific ends. This "call," therefore, also represents a rhetorical charge, crucially raising the question of consent: how does consent impact the form of "no"—and when can a servant *really* say "no"? As I will suggest in my reading of *The Tempest*, service necessitates scripted speech. But in this instance, Kent's response occurs after his master has died, when, in effect, he is no longer a servant at all. And yet he still calls Lear his master, still follows his call. Kent demonstrates his greatest self-abnegation as a servant, his most essential servitude, when he is, technically, free. I move from the word *service* to *servitude* deliberately; it is in his freedom that Kent's dependence on his master—his servility, even—is at once most conventional and most shocking. It is both an act of the purest self-abnegation—an understanding of himself as socially, personally, and bodily incorporated in his master, so that the erasure of Lear must mean the disappearance of Kent—and a rich, perplexing negotiation of his own consent. He suggests that he has none—"I must not say no"—and yet, as I have suggested, his understanding of what he "must" do (that is, follow his master to his death) comprises a deliberate and decisive action. It is clearly a fiction that "My master calls me; I must not say no," but it is a fiction that Kent deliberately articulates and sustains. In other words, he demonstrates a consent he refuses to acknowledge, a liberty perversely exercised in self-abnegation.[11]

The journey on which Kent is called by his master, is, of course, also a spiritual one. Although the mercurial gods of *King Lear* have proved themselves "fickle," the play's end promises—or at least proposes—Christian redemption. The conflation of the spiritual and the secular in the word "master" was not novel for early modern readers, for whom the service relationships that authorized and identified them on earth also reflected and reified their allegiance to their Christian master in heaven. For Thomas Jackson, for instance, as earlier chapters have discussed, true freedom consisted in service to God, while no servitude was more absolute than servitude to sin: "So saith S. *Paul.* to the Romans, Cap. 6. 16. *Know ye not* (as if it were matter of gross ignorance or imputation, not to know) *that to whom Ye yield your selves servants to obey, his Servants ye are to whom ye obey: Whether it be of sin unto death, or of obedience unto righteousnesse.* So that there is a proper *Servitude* in yielding unto Sin: And whosoever yields his consent or obedience unto Sin, doth thereby make himself the true and proper *Servant* of Sin. . . . As absolute *Happiness*;

So absolute *Freedom* is only in God."[12] Notably, in Jackson's treatise, consent seems to be articulated as a synonym for obedience. To obey, in other words, is already to have consented; there seems little room for the practice of obedience *without* consent. To enact obedient service, that is, implies the (pre) operation of consent—in this case, consent to servitude to sin.

If Jackson is careful to distinguish between servitude (to sin) and service (to God), he also reminds his reader that it is in this service to God, as Thomas Cranmer famously asserts in the 1549 *Book of Common Prayer*, that freedom lies: "O God, which art author of peace, & louer of concorde, in knowledge of whom standeth our eternall lyfe, whose seruice is perfecte fredome: defende vs thy humble seruau[n]tes, in all assaultes of our enemies, that we surely trustyng in thy defence, may not feare the power of any aduersaries."[13] Cranmer's articulation that "seruice is perfecte fredome" posits a paradoxical provenance of freedom in service. But as we have seen, this paradox quickly gained widespread resonance, so that in the seventeenth century, Jackson could argue, "*Freedom consists in the service of God*":[14] "This Conclusion is as necessarie and true in the Argument whereof we treat: *He only is a true and perfect Free-man, which hath a power or Freedom to desire nothing but what he ought, and a power or Freedom to dispose of himself, and of his endeavours, for attaining or compassing what he thus desires.* So that *this Freedom consists in the service of God:* And that consists in a submission to his Will, and in reliance upon his most absolute Power to accomplish whatsoever he will, or whatsoever He shall think fitting for us to will or desire at his hands."[15] The utter self-abnegation for which Jackson argues reminds us of Kent, whose "submission to [Lear's] Will" is complete. But as I have suggested, Lear's death actually leaves Kent masterless. In other words, if indeed it is in service that perfect freedom lies, Kent suggests that the inverse may also be true: that in freedom lies perfect service.

This chapter explores the provenance of this idea not simply in the context of the *Book of Common Prayer*, but in what I suggest was the equally ideologically powerful figure of the *libertus*, or Roman freedman.[16] As I have noted, the *libertus* was a richly complex figure even by virtue of his name, which indicated a slave who had been freed even as it suggestively recalled the condition of bondage the slave in question had previously occupied. The *libertus* may have been manumitted, but it is in his freedom that he finds himself most bound to his master. But why? What is it about the condition of liberty that impels service even as it cannot compel subjection? To address this perplexing question, I argue that we must return to Terence's *Andria*, a play which was not only widely studied in early modern grammar schools in the Latin original but also translated into English for a wider audience in the late sixteenth century. The articulation of servitude in Terence, therefore, comprises not just a literary antecedent for service in early modern England, but also, I want to suggest, the intellectual and philosophical foundation for the problem of willing servitude with which early modern writers, readers, and audiences alike must reckon.

Andria opens with the central question of the contingency of liberty, with the *senex* Simo's suggestion that his *libertus* Sosia may have forgotten what he owes his former master:

> *Simo*: After I had bought thee, being then a little one, thou alwaies
>   knowest how iust [and] with me how gentle thy bondage was.
>   I caused that of a bondman, thou mightest be a freed-man
>   to me; because that, thou didst serue after the manner of a
>   freeman. I payed [thee] the highest price that I had.
> *Sosia*: I have it in memory.
> *Simo*: I repent me not of the deed.
> *Sosia*: I am glad, If I haue done any thing for you, or doe that may
>   please you, Simo; and, that it was gratefull to you, I hold it for
>   a fauour. But, this is troublesome to me. For, this putting in
>   mind is as it were an vpbraiding [of a man, as] vnmindfull of a
>   benefit.[17]

Simo recalls that Sosia, at the time of being bought, was then "a little one," his consent compromised not just by his vendibility but also by his youth. But it is this very youth that Simo emphasizes in narrating a long history of association. Sosia's "gentle" bondage, he reminisces, began in childhood, situating Simo not only as a benevolent master but, quite clearly, as a surrogate father; it is his conduct as well as his structural role that is paternal(istic). When Simo insists that Sosia "knowest" his treatment to be "iust" and "gentle," he imposes an epistemological certainty on Sosia which the latter has never expressed; when Simo claims that thou "*alwaies* knowest" (emphasis added), he forecloses the possibility of historical distinction, collapsing the child and the man in the certain knowledge of his own bondage as always already "gentle" and "iust." Simo "caused" Sosia's progression from "bondman" to "freed-man," he declares, locating the deliberate causality of this move in his own will to action, thereby simultaneously denaturalizing the journey from slavery to manumission. "I payed [thee]," he continues, inevitably recalling the fact that he also "payed *for* [thee]." At the same time as Simo affirms the narrative of the transformation, he also reveals the structural contingencies of the path to emancipation, disrupting the teleology of liberty.[18]

Sosia, in turn, can do no more than warily reply, "I have it in memory." For him, Simo's narration comprises a not-so-tacit rebuke; his "putting [Sosia] in mind" of his benevolence suggests that, contrary to the servant's assertions, Sosia does not "have it in memory." To be reminded, as Sosia points out, is to be accused of ingratitude, for it is when one is "vnmindfull of a benefit" that one must be literally re-minded. But Simo's rebuke is also a veiled threat. "I repent me not of the deed [of manumission]," he claims; and yet his very utterance suggests that he might. Startlingly, and ominously, Simo implies that Sosia's manumission is ultimately retractable. Far from denoting a departure from bondage, Sosia's "freed" state hinges on being "mindfull of a benefit," on the repeated assertions of his own *macula servitutis*, or stain of slavery. Is manumission, then, fundamentally yet paradoxically inseparable from this *macula*? How may we understand a liberty which can, apparently, be "repented" for and revoked? And what—as I will discuss next—is the role of both memory and gratitude in ensuring the continuity of the condition of freedom?

In his commentary on *Andria*, the humanist scholar Adrianus Barlandus explicitly glosses Sosia's claim *in memoria habeo* ("I have it in memory") as *ingratus non sum* ("I am not ungrateful").[19] Barlandus goes on to emphasize the dangerous consequences of a freedman's ingratitude, arguing that manumission could be revoked and the freedman (re)turned once more into a slave: *Libertus ingratus olim in seruitutem reuocabatur* ("At that time an ungrateful freedman was recalled into slavery").[20] When Sosia insists that he both bears Simo's kindnesses "in memory" and is "gratefull" to him, then, he is not simply mounting a defense of his own rhetoric or of his empathy. Rather, under threat of re-enslavement, of a master "repenting" of his former kindness, the freedman must repeatedly rehearse his remembrance of his master's benevolence, thereby enacting an affective dependency in order to repeatedly reauthorize his condition of liberty. This performance of gratitude is at once strategic and obligatory; it must be carefully staged yet, by necessity, convincing enough to ensure the continuity of a tenuous condition of freedom. Not only does the imperative to remember revivify the servitude from which the freedman has been released, it also creates another and perpetual obligation to one's master, constructing a new form of bondage for the freed slave.[21] And the specter of bondage is that much more urgent, the *macula servitutis* significantly more pronounced, for the ungrateful or the forgetful freedman. Should memory fail, that is, the *macula servitutis* must always supply its place.

Thus, in *The Tempest*, it is specifically in response to Ariel's so-called forgetfulness that Prospero threatens re-enslavement. In an exchange which echoes that between Simo and Sosia, Prospero manipulates the discourse of memory to forfeit his own promise of manumission even as he threatens Ariel with renewed bondage:[22]

> *Ariel*: Is there more toil? Since thou dost give me pains,
> Let me remember thee what thou hast promised,
> Which is not yet performed me.
> *Prospero*:   How now? Moody?
> What is't thou canst demand?
> *Ariel*:   My liberty.
> *Prospero*: Before the time be out? No more.
> *Ariel*:   I prithee,
> Remember I have done thee worthy service,
> Told thee no lies, made no mistakings, served
> Without or grudge or grumblings. Thou did promise
> To bate me a full year.[23]

Ariel adopts the language of memory to seek redress: "Let me remember thee." The construction is revealing, dwelling less on the sense of a contract violated than on a shared memory; when Ariel begins, "Let me remember," he evokes his own reminiscence, ostensibly framing the final "thee" simply as an invitation for Prospero to join his recollection.[24] The temporal markers here as well as the "since ... then" construction are striking; Prospero "dost give" pains, so Ariel employs the present perfect "hast promised" to enjoin him to share in a collective memory of the pledge "yet" to be performed. But Prospero, in turn, interprets Ariel's words as a "demand." By the end of this exchange, however, Ariel has adopted much more markedly the language of the supplicant: "I prithee," he pleads as he urges Prospero to "remember" his "worthy service." While he now employs the present perfect tense to remind Prospero that "I *have done* thee worthy service," Prospero's promised recompense rhetorically recedes into the perfect past: "Thou *did* promise to bate me a full year."

Further, Prospero declines to engage with either his former promise or Ariel's assessment of his service. Rather, he uses Ariel's requests for him to "remember" to recall instead the injunction against *forgetting* for a servant, and to levy an accusation of ingratitude against Ariel. And this charge, as I have suggested, encodes—in this case, quite explicitly—the threat of bondage:

Prospero: Dost thou forget
From what a torment I did free thee? . . .
Ariel   . . . I do not, sir.
Prospero: Thou liest, malignant thing! Hast thou forgot
The foul witch Sycorax, who with age and envy
Was grown into a hoop? Hast thou forgot her?
Ariel: No, sir.
Prospero: Thou hast. Where was she born? Speak. Tell me.
Ariel: Sir, in Algiers.
Prospero: O, was she so? I must
Once in a month recount what thou hast been,
Which thou forgett'st . . .
        . . . Thou best know'st
What torment I did find thee in . . . It was mine art,
When I arrived and heard thee, that made gape
The pine and let thee out.
Ariel: I thank thee, master.
Prospero: If thou more murmur'st, I will rend an oak
And peg thee in his knotty entrails till
Thou hast howled away twelve winters. (1.2.250–96)

Whereas Ariel claims that Prospero "dost give [him] pains," Prospero alleges that Ariel "Dost . . . forget," his use of the present tense suggesting that the process of forgetting is both ongoing and self-regenerating. In other words, Prospero must "Once in a month recount what thou has been" because Ariel (continually, it is suggested) "dost forget." Ariel's denial of this charge ("I do not, sir") only leads to its repetition. Indeed, ignoring completely Ariel's defense, Prospero uses this supposed failure of memory as a reason to "recount" again the tale of Ariel's rescue from Sycorax's captivity, at the end of which Ariel must, however laconically, "thank thee, master." As with Sosia, the accusation of forgetfulness both registers as the charge of ingratitude and authorizes the possibility of re-enslavement, so that Prospero can threaten to "rend an oak" and "peg [Ariel] in his knotty entrails." Not only would this bondage repeat the slavery from which Ariel was liberated, but Ariel will be returned to the same form of captivity as before; the "rend[ing]" of the oak recalls and reverses the way Prospero previously "made gape the pine." If Prospero "arrived and heard" Ariel's pleas on a previous occasion and released him from his bondage, he now refuses to hear Ariel's defense, portending an imprisonment that will make the former captive "howl away" twelve years. Indeed, the threatened re-enslavement will repeat exactly the same length of captivity as Ariel's former sentence: twelve years. Spatially as well as temporally, then, Prospero will repeat Ariel's bondage; if Ariel fails to remember the past as he should, Prospero will turn back the clock on manumission.

But in recreating the specific details of Ariel's first imprisonment, Prospero not only situates himself as a master who controls both servitude and liberation; he also threatens to recast Ariel into the state of *servitus* whose *macula* he, like Sosia, appears to bear indefinitely. Manumission, in other words, does not signal a departure from the master; rather, it, too, occurs at the master's pleasure, as part of an ongoing affective, affiliative, and performative relationship between *magister* and *servus/libertus*. Moreover, for Ariel as for the Roman freedman, freedom is not a teleological conclusion but rather deeply contingent and fundamentally provisional. At the same time, both Simo and Prospero valorize willing service, defining good service by its *volition*. Simo, for his part, paradoxically claims that it was because Sosia "didst serue after the manner of a freeman" (*seruiebas liberaliter*) that he was emancipated. In order to be free, then, one must first serve freely. But once the slave becomes free, he must continue to serve. Indeed, the Roman commentator Aelius Donatus's gloss on this line calls attention to the imperfect rather than the perfect tense of *seruiebas*, which raises the possibility of serving *still*.[25] The freedman's frequent articulations of gratitude not only constitute a form of discursive supplication and subservience or even servitude, they also constantly recall his former condition of bondage. In effect, there is no *discursive* manumission.[26]

But as we see in both these texts, service does not end with manumission either. Indeed, the Roman freedman frequently seems to articulate a sense of greater loyalty and obligation to his master than the slaves still in bondage. Ariel may "murmur" here, but his service is more effective and apparently more willingly rendered than that of Caliban. If it is true that in service lies perfect freedom, then it is also the case, as I have argued, that it is only in freedom (however tenuous) that we find "perfect" service.[27] Yet Ariel's status underscores the ways in which the *macula servitutis* persists into the supposed condition of liberty, working to inflect the rhetoric and discourse of both master and servant, and functioning not only as a stain but a specter that can be recalled to life at any moment.

If Simo recalls that Sosia served *liberaliter*, or "in a manner befitting a free man or someone of gentle birth," the word *liberaliter* also signifies other qualities which are attendant on "freedom": courteousness and kindness, as well as generosity and honesty. Just before this moment in *Andria*, Simo praises Sosia's trust and good faith (*fides*); in a copy of the 1493 Lyon edition of Terence's *Works*, this discussion of *fides* is highlighted by two different readers in their marginalia, suggesting its connection with serving *liberaliter*.[28] In 1565, meanwhile, Thomas Cooper translates *Propterea quod seruiebas liberaliter* in his lexicon as "Because thou diddest thy seruice like an honest man."[29] Thus, Sosia is freed because he "naturally" embodies the traits of a free man, but also, paradoxically, because these "free" qualities reinforce rather than compromise his service to his master, underscoring the ways in which "natural" freedom—in addition to the *performance* of freedom—enables legibly "good" service. When Prospero then threatens to re-imprison Ariel if he "more murmur'st" (1.2.294) even though Ariel claims that he has "served / Without or grudge or grumblings" (1.2.248–49) and has therefore served *liberaliter*—honestly, affably, without complaint—Prospero argues that his "murmur[ing]" has compromised his performance of "free" service, and that he should therefore be returned to a state of slavery. The oddity of service performed *liberaliter* but unable to avail itself of the liberty to speak freely is highlighted by the conceptual proximity of the *libertus* with *libertas*, a kinship signaled by the spatial proximity of these terms, only one entry apart, in Véron's *A Dictionary in Latine and English* (1575).[30] *Libertus* is defined as "he, or shee that is made free of a bonde seruaunt, one infranchised," while *libertas* is rendered as "freedome, libertie to speake, and liue as one listeth." Liberty is specifically understood as the freedom to speak; the *libertus*, who has *served* as a free man, should surely also hold the right to *speak* as a free man.[31]

But even though Simo notes that Sosia has served "like a freeman," he does not shy away from recalling Sosia's vendibility. He explicitly notes that he bought Sosia (*Ego postquam te emi . . .*) and claims that in emancipating him, "[he] payed [him] the highest price that [he] had" (*Quod habui summum pretium, persolui tibi*). This "payment" is figurative—Sosia's departure represents an affective loss for Simo—but it is also literal: Roman slaves could represent a significant component of personal property and could consequently fetch a high price. By manumitting Sosia, Simo is losing a portion of his assets. *Persolui*, however, contains a double meaning. It signifies not only "to pay truely," but also "to requite" or "to release."[32] While Simo does release Sosia, his freedom, like his original enslavement, is calibrated in economic terms. *Tibi*, meanwhile, signifies both "to you" and "for you." Thus, even as Simo frees his slave, he also pays *for* him; the economics of liberation recall those of captivity, refiguring Sosia as a slave at the very moment of his manumission by rhetorically resituating him within the economy of the traffic in slaves. Finally, *pretium* denotes both "rewarde" and "pryce."[33] And so, although Sosia is rewarded for his service—completing the exchange of *operae* and *obsequium* for *libertas* conventionally understood as the process of manumission—he is also both paid for his service (in a fiscal transaction) and symbolically "bought" once more.

The semantic difficulties in this exchange, which signal broader political and economic concerns, are registered by the differences in Renaissance translations of this passage. Maurice Kyffin's 1588 translation, for instance, renders *Propterea quod seruiebas liberaliter / Quod habui summum pretium, persolui tibi* as "by cause thou didst thy seruice honestlie, and with good will, lo, of a Bondslaue I made thee my free man, so as I rewarded thee with the very best thing I had."[34] Like Thomas Cooper, Kyffin underscores the sense of "honestie" in *liberaliter*; but his translation also emphasizes that Sosia was a slave with "with good *will*" (emphasis added), suggesting not only that Sosia performed his servitude courteously and affably, but also that he exercised his personal "will" in so doing. Kyffin elects to read *pretium* as "reward," rather than "price," but, tellingly, his translation also notes that Sosia remains "*my* free man" (emphasis added), the word "my" signaling that this manumitted slave remains, paradoxically, still possessed. Meanwhile, Thomas Newman's 1627 translation seems to gloss over most of the semantic difficulties in this passage: "and for I found thee carefull / In thy imployments, the best good I had / To answer it, I gaue thee; libertie."[35] We see here that "libertie" is a gift "g[i]u[e]n" in return for the "carefull" performance of the slave's duties, with *pretium* simply denoting a "good" thing. In Newman's translation, liberty comprises part of a clear transaction, a monetary as well as a gift return in exchange for "careful employment," with the deserving service characterized by "care" rather than consent.

The language of price and payment, gift and gratitude here also evokes the more murky and unsettled language of the gift.[36] But perhaps the more pressing point here is that in the case of Sosia as well as of Ariel, the exchange is fundamentally incomplete. The irony of Simo's and Prospero's boasts of freeing their servants is that neither Sosia nor Ariel is, of course, truly free; free service has *not*, in fact, been rewarded with liberty. I have already noted that both Sosia and Ariel remain compelled to gratitude, bound to remember their captivity, but both must also perform real acts of continued service to their former masters. Indeed, Prospero repeatedly refers to Ariel, even after his emancipation from Sycorax's imprisonment, as "[his] slave" (1.2.270), echoing the terms in which he speaks of Caliban ("Caliban, my slave" [1.2.308], "poisonous slave" [1.2.319]). If Caliban, famously, is called a "*thing* of darkness" (5.1.278), Ariel, too, is a "Dull *thing*" (1.2.285) and a "malignant *thing*" (1.2.257, all emphases added), imagined as a possessed "thing" even if he negotiates the impulse to resist such possession and to be "malignant."

Virginia Mason Vaughan and Alden T. Vaughan have addressed precisely this question of Ariel's "slavery," reading Prospero's assertion that "Thou, my slave, / As thou report'st thyself, was then her [Sycorax's] servant" (1.2.270–71) thus: "Ariel's apparent protest that he is Prospero's *slave* echoes a common complaint of servants in Shakespeare's time; Prospero mocks the contention."[37] This is a persuasive reading; but what Prospero does here is also to argue that Ariel failed in his duty to Sycorax. Her "commands" may have been "earthy and abhorred," but Ariel was nonetheless "a spirit too delicate / To act" them; it was "Refusing her grand hests" that led to his captivity in the "cloven pine" (1.2.272–77). In other words, Ariel is an unexpected analogue for Kent, resistant to the kind of service to bad ends that he is expected to render. Yet, if Prospero is to be believed, it was Ariel's refusal to serve as he should that led to his enslavement; his slavery, then, appears oddly warranted.

But Prospero also demonstrates here the slippage between the words "servant" and "slave." Although, as I have noted, Vaughan and Vaughan argue that early modern servants frequently levied complaints of slavery, Ariel himself never explicitly argues that he is a slave.[38] What he claims, rather, is breach of contract or promise on Prospero's part. Using the language of "liberty" and "bat[ing]," he suggests that Prospero is not only tyrannical but also uncreditable, a man who reneges on his promises and violates contracts.[39]

The ramifications of such violation of contract, and its implications for structures of credit, have been well established.[40] Victoria Kahn, for instance, has addressed the ways in which structures of language comprised or compromised the provenance of consent: "Seventeenth-century men and women wondered whether a verbal promise was legally binding, and if so, whether because of conscience or because of some material evidence—some 'consideration' or benefit—which established the secular validity of a contract."[41] In other words, to what extent does Prospero's promise to "bate" Ariel constitute a binding contract? Part of the perplexing confusion around Prospero's promise is that we never hear him articulate it. All we receive instead is Ariel's verbal iteration of Prospero's prior pledge. Prospero's refusal to repeat or reiterate it himself might demonstrate the power of aural contract—to speak may be to contract—but is notable in light of the fact that Prospero *does* repeat much else, those narratives called ever more into question by the very fact of their reiteration. Indeed, the fact that Prospero must repeat his words suggests that he cannot be taken *at* his word. To repeat is also to revivify, so that Prospero's reiteration of Ariel's purported ingratitude comprises a speech act that threatens to bring again into being Ariel's imprisonment. After all, as Lewis Carroll reminds us, "It's a poor sort of memory that only works backward."[42]

But what really compels Ariel's subjection? If the condition of captivity assumes the teleology not only of manumission (a teleology I have suggested is fictive) but also of escape, what is perplexing about Ariel is his simultaneous spatial unboundedness and his bondage to Prospero. Why, in other words, can't Ariel escape? In contemporary and later slavery narratives, captivity seems spatially delimited; the question in some ways is of *which* land, sea, or ocean one must cross in order to escape the tyranny of bondage. Thus, the condition of slavery might register temporal but usually not spatial unboundedness. But Ariel's situation does not conform to this pattern. He has almost unlimited spatial mobility and yet still chooses to return to Prospero. Caliban, conversely, cannot leave the island of his own volition, and so appears to fit more readily the understanding of an enslaved person. When Miranda claims, "therefore wast thou / Deservedly confined into this rock" (1.2.359–60), the "rock" might refer to a cave, as the Arden editors suggest, but it might also plausibly allude to the island itself. Spatially bound, Caliban cannot escape his servitude. Whereas Ariel is ethereal, Caliban is (sub)terranean; the former is released to the air, the other bound to the earth.[43] His service, then, is of a different order to Ariel's; because he does not serve under the conditions of (at least physical) freedom, he cannot demonstrate good service. Constrained by compulsion, Caliban may more closely resemble a slave simply because he cannot enact the same degree of volition as Ariel can, if we understand a slave to be someone who cannot be a servant, who cannot serve as servants must: freely.

But there is something resonant and poignant about the fact that it is Miranda, with whom Caliban once shared a "cell," who remarks on Caliban's "deserved confine[ment]" on his "rock." Prospero describes himself to

Miranda as "master of a full poor *cell* / And thy no greater father" (1.2.20–21); later, he tells Caliban that he has "used thee, / Filth as thou art, with humane care, and lodged thee / In mine own *cell* till thou didst seek to violate / The honor of my child" (1.2.345–48, emphasis added). Both Miranda and Caliban, we see, are inhabitants of this "cell" and therefore structurally if not consanguinally members of the same household—and by extension, the same family. When Prospero calls himself "master" of the cell as well as Miranda's "father," he plays on the multiple meanings of the Latin *magister* as master, teacher, and father, as I have suggested earlier; these resonances are only reinforced when he later refers to himself as Miranda's "schoolmaster" (1.2.172).[44] This, of course, might account for why Miranda's pedagogical relationship with Caliban was so frequently reassigned by editors of the text to Prospero. But Miranda herself not only employs the language of the teacher, claiming that she "taught thee each hour / One thing or other" (1.2.353–54); she also explicitly recalls the Renaissance grammar schoolmaster, who teaches his pupils the *ars rhetorica* and who must educate his charges in the art of persuasion. Like him, Miranda "Took pains to make [Caliban] speak" (1.2.353), arguing:

> When thou didst not, savage,
> Know thine own meaning but wouldst gabble like
> A thing most brutish, I endowed thy purposes
> With words that made them known. (1.2.354–57)

I therefore suggest that we may read Miranda as the humanist schoolmaster who (purportedly) shepherds his charges from "brutish" "gabbl[ing]" to the discourses "that made them known." And as we know, one of the pedagogical vectors by which he attempted this civilizing move was the language of Terence, of whom Maurice Kyffin gushed in his translation of *Andria*: "Among all the Romane writers, there is none (by the iudgement of the learned) so much auailable to bee read and studied, for the true knowledge and puritie of the Latin tong."[45] Small wonder, then, that Terence, as T. W. Baldwin noted in his magisterial study of Shakespeare's sources, comprised a cornerstone of the grammar school education.[46]

If Miranda and Caliban are articulated as part of the same household and family even as Miranda assumes the role of pedagogue and humanist *magister*, Victoria Kahn persuasively suggests that what we see at this early modern moment is a shift in the organization and understanding of political authority: "In the Tudor and Stuart periods, the family was a far more common analogy for political order than was contract. The affective bonds presupposed by such putatively natural relations were a mainstay of contemporary arguments for political authority."[47] *The Tempest* may manifest a turning point in these different conceptions of political authority. But the end of the play nonetheless demonstrates the uncertain logics of authority and obligation, contract and consent, servitude and slavery in its refusal of trajectories of manumission and teleologies of liberty.

The fate of both Caliban and Ariel at the end of *The Tempest* reaffirms the tenuousness of such a teleology. As we revisit the conclusion of the play, we remember that conventional wisdom would have it that Caliban learns the error of his ways and reenters Prospero's service, while Ariel is assured his freedom after just one more errand.

> *Prospero*: I'll deliver all,
> And promise you calm seas, auspicious gales,
> And sail so expeditious that shall catch
> Your royal fleet far off.—My Ariel, chick,
> That is thy charge. Then to the elements
> Be free, and fare thou well. (5.1.315–20)

At the end of the play, Prospero "promises" to "deliver" the island's visitors—but then immediately hands this task off to Ariel: "That is *thy* charge" (emphasis added). In other words, the promise he articulates will be upheld by his servant, suggesting the lack of distinction between master and servant. But Prospero also relies on Ariel to fulfill his promises, the latter's labor rendered so easily that Prospero can, quite literally, speak for him. Yet this is, in theory, his last charge. "*Then* to the elements / Be free," he says, the long-promised moment of emancipation again deferred—now, finally, beyond the temporal scope of the play.

But what is also odd here is the language of the almost-manumission: "*Then* to the elements / Be free." Hasn't Ariel "been free" to the elements over the course of the play already? Ariel has consistently been described as airy, unconstrained; as I have discussed, he is spatially unrestrained, making his bondage to Prospero all the more perplexing (unlike Caliban, he can leave the island; why, then, does he stay with his master?). For Ariel to be free "to the elements" surely doesn't allow him more freedom than that which he has already been exercising. In asking what has, after all, kept him bound for the duration of the play, we are compelled to grapple not only with the fictions of consent that undergird the performance of happy service, but also the "stain" of servitude, which is no less persistent for being invisible. My aim here is not to conclude that Ariel "actually" remains enslaved, or that he emerges as a "proto-slave" in the terms of an Atlantic chattel economy. Nor do I wish to retroactively conflate Ariel's status with the specific conditions of Caliban's labor and bondage. Rather, I want to underscore that the fungibility and transportability of these categories—of freedom, bondage, and manumission, not to mention the "stain of slavery" itself—denotes a calculated contingency, and to emphasize that such a strategic availability of Roman conceptual frameworks for early modern authors and audiences alike not only authorizes but also comes to render legible both the discursive underpinnings of perpetual indebtedness and, as I will suggest, the somatic markers of enslavement.

These somatic implications were marked in multiple ways. As Miles Grier brilliantly argues in his concept of "inkface," even the technologies of ink and paper are themselves central to the early modern and early Atlantic formations of racialized slavery and blackness; Grier traces the "racial character"—in all senses of "character"—made manifest through "inkface" to achieve its racialized effects.[48] But as he notes, the affinities between tattoo, print, and the stigma of slavery are key to this strategy: "this cultural project entailed *remembering* British peoples who were tattooed and enslaved but *transferring* their literally stigmatized appearance to Amerindian and African peoples, marking them as subjects of British cultural and political hegemony."[49] I have argued that the *macula servitutis* staged and negotiated here mobilizes the perpetual indebtedness of the Roman freedman, rehearsing its invidious slippage from metaphor to manifestation; Grier demonstrates how the somatic inscription of such a "stain" was recalled—and reaffirmed—by the very technologies of print that invoked them.

And so we must turn, finally, to Caliban, and to the notoriously vexed ending of the play which this figure generates. I argue that Caliban's classical antecedents, once unearthed, must also trouble the teleology of manumission, revealing the pernicious tenacity of the *macula servitutis*. In the final moments in which we see Caliban, Prospero lays claim to him with the words "this thing of darkness I / Acknowledge mine" (5.1.278–79). It has, of course, long been a critical commonplace that the words "thing of darkness" mobilize the play's postcolonial readings, and that they do so in language that is at once racialized and intimate. Ania Loomba, for instance, locates Prospero as the patriarchal successor to Sycorax: "unlike the fair Moorish women who can be converted and assimilated into European families, this 'hag' from Algiers must be eliminated and detached from her child, who can then be adopted as the white man's burden, acknowledged by Prospero as a 'thing of darkness' who is both alien and 'mine.'"[50]

This reading situates Caliban as not only a familial but also a colonial adoptee, the "white man's burden" who also occupies, albeit temporarily, the status of a child housed in his colonizer's "own cell." Kim Hall, meanwhile, crucially argues that Prospero's description constructs a binary of light and dark while also firmly situating Caliban on one side of the dyad: "Caliban functions as a 'thing of darkness' against which a European social order is tested and proved."[51] And as Patricia Akhimie reveals, Caliban's status as an uncultivatable servant is registered by the epidermal and ontological sign of the "pinch," a "pinch" that simultaneously denotes—and authorizes—his privation.[52]

In other words, as Paul Brown's now-classic essay demonstrates, the lines "this thing of darkness I / Acknowledge mine" (which also serve as Brown's title) open richly onto the play's postcolonial readings, including the nexus of "masterlessness" and "savagism" that Brown so carefully delineates.[53] But I also want to draw attention to how the classical antecedents of this moment, which have so far remained critically understudied, undergird the nexus of manumission and mastery, of a bound past and an enslaved future, which frames this articulation of a personal, affective, or familial "acknowledgment" of Prospero's "thing of darkness." That is, to understand fully the racialized foundations and postcolonial futures of this moment, we must also excavate its classical past.

In Roman law, the ceremony of *mancipatio* authorized the transfer of property; that property included *mancipia*, or slaves. (*Mancipium* itself is a neuter noun, signaling the "thing"-ness of the *mancipium*). Both *mancipium* and *mancipatio* find a root in *manus*, and indeed the *mancipium* denoted a slave who had been transferred by "corporeal apprehension" and had been taken possession of by the hand.[54] The ceremony required the presence of no fewer than five witnesses who were Roman citizens, as well as another citizen holding a pair of scales; it was formalized by the utterance of a certain sequence of words, beginning with "I affirm that this slave is mine."[55]

For Prospero to "acknowledge" his "thing of darkness" in the terms of possession, as "mine," is, I argue, to evoke explicitly the language and the form of the *mancipatio*. These words, then, not only reaffirm the affective or familial dynamics between Prospero and Caliban but also ratify the larger structures and specters of servitude that inform it. These words carry the force of an enacting clause that constitutes (not just conveys) a legal, public transfer of property. The word "acknowledge," moreover, not only suggests "to auowe" in early modern dictionaries, but also to "knowe againe" or to "*Confesse*."[56] To confess—that is, to affirm in the presence of witnesses—signals a site of ontological resistance, but also denotes a legal register; Prospero's "acknowledgment" thus evokes the juridical language of confession which also recalls that other legal ceremony, the *mancipatio*. Indeed, to "acknowledge" is also to claim, to "own" in the sense of assertion or admission—but also in the legal sense of holding property, taking us back to the operation of *mancipatio*. In these last moments of the play, Prospero simultaneously recalls Caliban's previous place in his household, as an adopted son, "acknowledges" him in the language of consanguineal descent, as "mine," and registers him as a *mancipium*.

Prospero's quasi-familial formulations at the close of the play should not surprise us, for originally the category of *res mancipi* also included the children of Roman parents. Although they likely would not be conveyed by *mancipium/mancipatio*, that the category of *res mancipi* could include both slaves and Roman children underscores the tension of the word "mine," and indeed of Caliban's earlier home in Prospero's own "cell."[57] But as we know, freedmen were also framed in a familial register; *liberti* may have embodied a kind of fiction of freedom, but they also performed affective functions in the affiliative household spaces they supplied and occupied. Thus, "The former slave became a son 'sine natura', while the owner took the place of the (absent) father."[58] Caliban's tenuous status as both adoptee and bondman precisely renders the contradictions of the *libertus*'s manumission, ending *The Tempest* on a note of deliberate ambiguity that mimics the narrative and trajectory of manumission to affirm the persistence of the *macula servitutis*. Caliban, I have proposed, is a slave because he cannot serve freely; by gesturing toward him as a *mancipium*, the play ends by retroactively reinscribing him as a slave, affirming him as a son, and ensuring his continued bondage. But, suspended between the performance of the *mancipatio* and the possibility of familial manumission as he is, Caliban's status as a "thing of darkness," I suggest, also encodes the ineradicable tenacity of the *macula servitutis*, so implacable as an absent presence yet so easily recalled to life. If *The Tempest* ends with an uncanny forecast of its postcolonial futures, it does so only by unveiling its impossible, immovable Roman forebears, revealing the centrality of classical slavery to incipient early modern racial discourses and formations both of "darkness" and, more chillingly, of what—or who—could come to constitute a "thing."

The "Negromantick Summons" of "An Honest True and Faithfull Servant": The Case of Adam

The Tempest, I have suggested, stages the problem of manumission tainted by the *macula servitutis*, and of liberty dependent on the fictions of consent that frame the performance of servitude. But if the contingencies of consent and coercion, bondage and unboundedness are both iterated and mediated by the different relationships of *The Tempest*, they also acquire particular resonance in the social and legal context of the New World. In this section, I discuss the case of the indentured servant Adam Saffin—to whom I will refer as an enslaved person, although his precise status is, as I shall demonstrate, unclear—which, I argue, simultaneously illuminates and pressures the imperative for a particular manner of "cheerful" bondage, reveals the role of recompense in the performance of such service, interrogates the teleology of manumission, and underscores the peculiar problematics of racialized servitude.[59]

In 1694, John Saffin of Bristol, Massachusetts, contracted to emancipate his "negro man Adam" upon the completed performance of faithful service:

> Bee it known unto all men by these presents That I John Saffin of Bristol in the Province of the Massachusetts Bay in New England out of meer kindness to and for the Encouragem[en]t of my negro man Adam to go on chearfully in his Business & Imploym[en]t by me now putt into, the Custody Service and command of Thomas Shepherd my Tenant on boundfield Farm in Bristol afores[ai]d for and During the Terme of Seaven years from the Twenty fifth day of March last past 1694—fully to be compleat and Ended or as I may otherwise See cause to Imploy him. I say I doe by these presents of my own free & Voluntary Will & pleasure from and after the full end & Expiration of Seven years beginning on the Twenty fifth day of March last past and from thenceforth fully to be compleat and Ended, Enfranchise clear and make free my s[ai]d negro man named Adam to be fully at his own Dispose and Liberty as other free men are or ought to be according to all true Intents & purposes whatsoever. Allways provided that the s[ai]d Adam my Servant do in the mean time go on chearfully quietly and Industriously in the Lawfull Business that either my Self or my Assigns shall from time to time reasonably Sett him about or imploy him in and doe behave and abear himself as an Honest true and faithfull Servant ought to doe during the Tearm of Seven years as aforesaid.[60]

The question of Adam's status is already complicated in this initial contract.[61] Adam is Saffin's ("my") "negro man," a piece of transferable property inasmuch as he is leased along with Boundfield Farm to Saffin's tenant, Thomas Shepherd.[62] Yet Saffin also calls Adam a "Servant"—quite possibly a euphemism for "slave," but probably not exclusively so, since in other documents relating to the case Adam is explicitly designated a "slave." Indeed, Saffin later calls himself "a meer Vassall to his slave [Adam]," rhetorically inverting the hierarchy between slave and master while situating both himself and his servant as slaves, even as he contests Adam's position of subordination by describing himself as Adam's "Vassall."[63] The length of Adam's indentured servitude—seven years—also recalls that of an early modern apprenticeship, and in fact the possibilities for Adam's liberty or consent, much like those of an English apprentice, remain vexed.[64] Adam's lack of freedom as an indentured servant is clear: Saffin's promise to release Adam at the end of his servitude "to be fully at his own Dispose and Liberty as other free men are or ought to be according to all true Intents & purposes whatsoever" underscores the fact that Adam's legal status is *not* that of "other free men" (irrespective, apparently, of race), even as he acknowledges that the condition of "Dispose and Liberty" accruing to the status of a free man is not always as complete as it "ought to be." But Adam's emancipation is crucially contingent on a particular *manner*, not merely a term, of service: Saffin will free him "Allways provided that ... Adam ... go on *chearfully quietly and Industriously* in the Lawfull Business that either my Self or my Assigns shall from time to time reasonably ... imploy him in and doe behave and *abear himself as an Honest true and faithfull Servant ought to doe*" (emphasis mine). In a remarkable echo of Ariel's servitude, in order to earn his freedom Adam must perform his service not only competently and "Industriously" but also "chearfully": he must be not only "Honest" but also "faithfull." He must, in other words, "tell ... no lies" and "[serve] / Without or grudge or grumblings."[65] Yet Saffin fails to articulate exactly what constitutes such "cheerful" and "faithfull" service; he merely insists that Adam "behave" as an ideal "Honest true and faithfull Servant *ought* to do" (emphasis mine). The condition of "cheerful" service, like the nature of a free man's liberty, is muddied in Saffin's contract by the presumption that the parties to and readers of the contract understand what "ought" to be the case in both instances.

Yet the contract contains a peculiar contradiction. Although Saffin pledges to "Enfranchise clear and make free" his servant of his own "free & Voluntary Will & pleasure" (the last word one that later recurs to describe Adam's *violation* of the contract), Adam must, oddly, also be *persuaded* to his service. Saffin's promise is undertaken not simply out of "meer kindness to" Adam, but also, as Saffin himself discloses, as a means of "Encouragem[en]t" to Adam "to go on chearfully in his Business & Imploym[en]t." In a peculiarly paradoxical articulation, in order to be freed, Adam must serve "chearfully."[66] But in order to "encourage" his slave to serve, in effect, like a free man, Saffin must promise him liberty, even as he casts this gesture as "voluntary." Both the service and the promise of emancipation, then, are at once volitional and compelled.[67]

Adam violates the contract, Saffin will allege, in a number of ways. At the conclusion of the term of seven years, having returned to Saffin's household, Adam asserts his freedom: "he took his Cloaths out of the house by stealth, and went about the Town at his pleasure; which said actions of his," according to Saffin, "had there been no other, was enough to forfeit his freedom."[68] Adam's "pleasure" and his newfound physical and geographical freedom are implicitly opposed to Saffin's "pleasure" in granting Adam or withholding from him such liberty. Significantly, it is Adam's removal of his *clothes* that particularly irks Saffin, even though on several occasions Saffin includes "Cloaths" in his accounting of the expenses he has been put to on Adam's behalf—"Cloaths, Bedding food and Phisick"—which suggests that these garments may comprise something in the way of wages. But if clothes mediate their function as both gifts and livery, for Adam to take his clothes to use for his own "pleasure" is not only to destabilize the economy of clothing as gift (rather than as something to be "taken") but also to sever the affective ties between master and servant through the medium of clothing as the "material mnemonic" of their mutual obligation.[69]

But Saffin further accuses Adam of failing to perform, during the term of his servitude, the conditions of his emancipation. Far from being "Industrious," Adam was, Saffin argues, "very Lazie and Remiss, would favour himself, and (when he could) would sliely make others bear the weight of the work."[70] More troubling, Adam grew "intollerably insolent, quarrelsome and outragious," and even violent toward Thomas Shepherd and his family. These accusations were supported by Shepherd but refuted by several other witnesses, including another man to whom Adam was "bound out," Wilkins, who testified to Adam's "sobriety and fidelity" according to the terms of the contract.[71] Saffin, in fact, now emphasizes the *necessity* of promising Adam his freedom, in order to compel in a man of such "Turbulent humour" a sense of obligation to serve decorously: "knowing him to be a Desperate Dangerous Villaine, and of a Turbulent humour I Endeavored to Oblige him to his

Duty, and thereupon promised his freedome under my hand att the End of the Terme upon the Conditions . . ."⁷² Adam, moreover, has committed these acts of violence against his master and his family despite the fact that they have reportedly treated him with kindness: "His Master *Shepard* like wise for his encouragement let him have a piece of rich ground to plant Tobacco in, by which he said Negro made (as I am informed) above *Three Pounds* a year, besides his own use: his said Master also set him at his Table to eat with himself, his Wife & Children, (for which indeed I have blam'd him.) Notwithstanding for all this kindness and indulgence towards this wretched Negro, he grew so intollerably insolent, quarrelsome and outragious."⁷³ Saffin's disapproval of Adam's place at Shepherd's own "Table" underscores that such familiarity between enslaved and enslaver was uncommon, and was already seen as potentially breeding complacency or ingratitude in the enslaved person.⁷⁴ If Caliban, housed "in [Prospero's] own cell," betrays the affective bonds between master and servant by his attempt upon Miranda, Adam, too, behaves in so "vexatious and grievous" a manner that Shepherd claims that he "dare no longer keep him in [his] house."⁷⁵

Yet Adam's negotiation of his position of simultaneous intimacy and subordination in his master's household, like Ariel's, troubles his status as an enslaved person. If Adam is indentured to and dependent upon Saffin for "Cloaths, Bedding food and Phisick," he also has a measure of *in*dependence, earning "above *Three Pounds* a year" from his small-scale tobacco farming. Referred to variously as a "man," a "Servant," and a "slave" in the documents pertaining to the case, his status is at times also indistinguishable from that of English indentured servants; he "eat[s] of the same as the English Servants" when he is in Saffin's household.⁷⁶ And his position is further vexed by being imbricated within a peculiar, often multiplied and shifting, relationship of landlord to tenant which renders obscure who, exactly, Adam's master actually is.

Yet Adam's lack of agency is also evident in the reason for the urgency of his petition: "the s[ai]d Adam dayly pursues yo[u]r subscriber for the Tryall of his s[ai]d liberty the s[ai]d Adam being dayly threatned by the s[ai]d M[aste]r Saffin, to be sent out of this province into forreigne, parts to remaine a slave during his life."⁷⁷ If Adam's status as chattel is troubled by his gestures toward financial and affective independence, it is reaffirmed by Saffin's authority to consign Adam to a more permanent, and harsher, form of slavery. Like Ariel, Adam occupies a liminal position predicated on both servitude and intimate service and bolstered by the threat of "remaine[ing]" an enslaved person far beyond the allotted time.

The case of Adam crucially pressures the idea of manumission as a gift, and the teleological end of bondage. If one "serves like a free man," is one contractually *due* one's freedom, or must it still be granted as a reward? And can liberty be prescribed or proscribed through contract, or does it always comprise a form of gift?[78] For the primary adjudicators of Adam's case, liberty is a crucially valuable concept, "a thing of great value, even next to life," and so freedom must be liberally construed, even—or perhaps especially—for racially differentiated slaves, since "there was much to be allowed to the behaviour of Negroes, who are so ignorant, rude and bruitish."[79] There is of course a pun on the word "bruitish," which suggests "uncivilized" or "violent" as well as "noisy." Although Saffin has mandated that Adam serve "quietly," the magistrates' decision argues that Adam perhaps "naturally" inclines toward both loudness and rudeness and therefore cannot be strictly held to that part of the contract. Saffin, indeed, claims that Adam has issued him a "Negromantick Summons" to attend a meeting with Samuel Sewall, whereupon he is "very gravely admonish[ed]" that "since [he] had given such a thing [the promise of manumission] under [his] Hand and Seal, [he] ought to stand to it, and perform it."[80] There is still, however, much disagreement about this; to a jury's initial view, "the s[ai]d Adam negro hath not performed the condition for which he was to be Enfranchized & therefore is to continue a servant to his s[ai]d Master."[81] This decision once again distinguishes the fact of service from the condition for emancipation. And of course it reverses the emancipation which Adam has claimed for himself. The instability of Adam's "freedom" is evident in the court's ruling, after it is disclosed that Saffin attempted to send Adam out of the country in direct opposition to the court's orders, that "Adam negro be in peace untill by due process of Law he be found to be a Slave."[82] The teleology of freedom is never more in doubt than here, when Adam's legally mandated "peace" may be broken by a reinstatement of his previous slavery. And although Adam is eventually allowed his freedom—his name appears in a later record of the town's free men—like the Roman freedman, he retains the stamp of his prior servitude: the name he is given by some record keepers, Adam Saffin, announces his past status as Saffin's property.[83]

* * *

I want to end this chapter by thinking about Adam's suit in the larger context of colonial complaints by servants whom we assume to be vulnerable, marginal, and oppressed, and of extant hierarchies of nation, race, and labor. In a discussion of servant complaints in seventeenth- and eighteenth-century Maryland, Christine Daniels argues against what she reads as anachronistic understandings of early American indentured servants' victimization, instead illuminating the legal recourse available to, and frequently made use of by, servants when their masters failed in their duties or responsibilities to them or attempted to exploit them.[84] Indeed, Daniels contends that servants were overwhelmingly successful in their suits against their masters and that consent was seen as a touchstone for the enforceability of servants' contracts. Thus, in the case of the servant Edward Hotchkiss, who wished to leave at the end of his term of indenture but whose master wanted to punish him as a runaway, Justice Michael Brooks ruled that "hee had liberty to complain w[i]th out being tearmed a Runaway."[85] Daniels goes on to observe:

> Brooks's phrase—"liberty to complain"—is significant; it reveals his cognizance of a British jurisprudential culture open to English indentured servants but closed to African and African-American slaves. English servants had assented, through contracts, to their condition and to certain requisites inherent in it. Their contracts, however, did not demand that they accede to unreasonable treatment or give up the protection the law provided against cruel masters. Servants, like other Englishmen, could "not be subjected to any law or power amonge themselves *without their consent*: Whatsoever is more than this, is neither lawful nor durable." It was, instead, "bondage or licentiousnesse" that would "invariably lead to slavery."[86]

Central to Brooks's judgment is the distinction between service and slavery.[87] Given the number of petitions by English servants in the New World who claimed that they had been wrongfully detained beyond the period of their contracted indenture, the case of Adam seems exemplary in some ways and extraordinary in others. On the one hand, Adam's argument that he, too, had been wrongly denied his promised freedom was eventually upheld by the court to which he petitioned. On the other hand, the documents of this case fail to establish whether he is "really" an indentured servant or an enslaved person; Adam, furthermore, is not English, although he appears at the "Court of *Bristol* . . . that he might have all benefits of Law as an English man."[88] The fact that Adam exercises his "liberty to complaine," and that this liberty is legally upheld, at first seems to complicate the distinction that Daniels herself makes about legal redress being the province of primarily English servants.

Yet the case of Adam also underscores—and presages—what Saidiya Hartman refers to as "indebted servitude": a post-emancipation form of freedom that imposed "forms of discipline" which relied not on corporal punishment but on strategies of indebtedness, guilt, and obligation.[89] Hartman's suggestion that "emancipation instituted indebtedness" invokes the *macula servitutis* which I have been discussing in this chapter; but it also echoes Simo's, Ariel's, and Adam's obligation to serve after a particular "manner" in order to receive a tenuous, revocable, and paradoxically bound manumission which is structured as a "gift," with all the obligations, as this book has discussed, that that entails.[90] My aim here is not to collapse the historical and material distinctions between Roman, early modern, and nineteenth-century contexts of servitude and manumission. Rather, I want to underscore the conceptual genealogies of bondage that undergird and make legible to early modern readers and audiences the semiotics of Ariel's and Adam's "fictions of consent," and in turn construct a hermeneutics of manumission founded on contingency, revocability, and indeed servitude, even as they press the strategies of epidermal race into their own service.

For we remember that on being confronted by Sewall regarding his breach of promise, Saffin defensively asserts: "as for small faults I should have winkt at them, but he having behaved himself so diametrically contrary to those Conditions, it was intollerable and not to be born with: and I would ask any indifferent person what obligation lay upon me to give him his Freedom, if it were not for the consideration aforesaid, and all the men in the Country are as much obliged to set their Negroes free as I am: and if he (as you say) acts but as a Negro, he must be a Negro still for ought I know, &c."[91] In return for being "kindly used," Saffin alleges, and "eat[ing] of the same as the English Servants did," Adam fails to "in any wise [perform] the Condition" of his contracted manumission. Pointing out that a defense founded on his "Negro nature" in fact authorizes differential social, political, and judicial treatment rather than excusing Adam's behavior, Saffin argues that if he is obligated to release his servant, so too are other masters of "Negroes," raising the alarming prospect that Adam's suit will upend the fiction that underwrites contracts, and which paradoxically mandates willing service: that "Honest true and faithfull" service is volitional, not enforced. Adam's liberty is (eventually, and on appeal) upheld, with the court insisting that "the s[ai]d Adam & his heirs be at peace & quiet & free with all their Chattles from the s[ai]d John Saffin Esqr and his heirs for Ever."[92] But Saffin's description of Adam's invocation of proper judicial process as "Negromantick"—collapsing the outlandish, devilish practice of the "blacke art" of "necromancie" with the person of the "Negro"[93]—and his assertion that Adam's "ignorant, rude and bruitish" behavior simply confirms that "he must be a Negro still" anticipate the ways in which the politics of an "honest, true and faithful" servitude performed "chearfully, quietly and industriously" not only pave the way for the structures of racialized slavery.[94] They also, as I have argued in this chapter, are framed from the outset by the specter of somatic difference, of a strange, insistent "stain" of slavery.

EPILOGUE

Fictions of Consent in the Atlantic World

Fictions of Consent has argued that slavery is a fundamentally English phenomenon, its architecture built on the everyday relations of early modern England, and its foundations rooted in England's universal fiction of free service. As it has traced the complex dynamics of servitude and bondage in the quotidian yet deeply compromised theaters of service—the early modern family, the household, the classroom, and the stage, for instance—this book has sought to demonstrate how the fictions of consent constructed across networks of amity, obligation, mutuality, obedience, protection, contract, and consanguinity are neither innocent nor neutral, but rather strategic. It is these strategies—these fictions—that, I have argued, prepare the rhetorical and ideological ground for the frameworks of slavery. Through the rehearsal and reiteration of these fictions of consent, the accretion and dispersal of discourses and contexts, slavery becomes not just possible, but palatable. *Fictions of Consent* thus strives to hold early modern England to account for the discourses of race and slavery that it authorized and amplified, and that would take such powerful ideological hold in the Atlantic world.

And yet, the literary and documentary texts explored in this book engage the contemporary contexts of English captivity and bondage in order to underscore that that stain of slavery, going forward from early modern England, can *only* be inscribed on the bodies of black persons. For early modern English writers, the futures of slavery must be secured with the prospect of hereditability written on and through the figures and bodies of children, and the "true" family must simultaneously be bound by blood. I want to end, then, by thinking briefly about the fictions of family in the Atlantic world, fictions that were propagated in the name of white "benevolence," but which operated in the clear interest of white supremacy. These fictions, and the languages and logics that sustained them, were seeded in the pedagogical contexts of the schoolroom.

The preceding chapters have sought to excavate the genealogies of slavery in the everyday circumstances of early modern England in which they are so deeply implicated; I conclude now by turning briefly to the afterlives and aftershocks of the early modern texts and discourses of "free service" and servitude which structured the rhetorical frameworks of slavery so successfully. The long and insidious history of American slavery, and the ways in which discourses of affection and mutuality were weaponized in its service, are of course beyond the scope of this book. But by looking to the persistent echoes of Terentian fictions of consent in the Atlantic world, and by returning to the classroom and its pedagogy of "happy slavery," now in the much later context of nineteenth-century Britain and America, I propose that we may discern how the fictions of "free service" and of family devised in and through the space of the schoolroom were vital to the operations of race and slavery in the Atlantic world.

Terentian Echoes in the British Atlantic World

In Morgan Godwyn's famous polemic arguing for the conversion of slaves to Christianity, *The Negro's & Indians Advocate* (1680), a key definition of slavery in a paratextual note relies on an unexpected source: the words of Simo to his faithful freedman Sosia at the opening of Terence's *Andria*.[1] Arguing for the humane treatment of slaves, Godwyn quotes Cicero (Figure 20):

> We must take notice that there is a *Right belonging unto Slaves,** whom they that advise us to treat as hired Servants, in exacting their Labour, but allowing them their DUE, do not advise amiss.
>
> *That by Servus *is meant a Slave, this in* Terence, (Ego postquam te emi a parvulo, feci e servo, ut esses libertus mihi) *doth plainly shew* . . .[2]

Godwyn, however, truncates the full exchange between Simo and Sosia in the first scene of *Andria* in order to stress both that Simo purchased Sosia as a child, and that Simo transformed Sosia from a slave into a freedman. Although Godwyn emphasizes the rights of slaves, this paratextual comment instead not only precisely underscores the lifelong abjection which slaves frequently experienced, but also draws on a passage which specifically celebrates not the "Right belonging unto Slaves," but rather the perpetual contingency to which slaves and freedmen are subject.

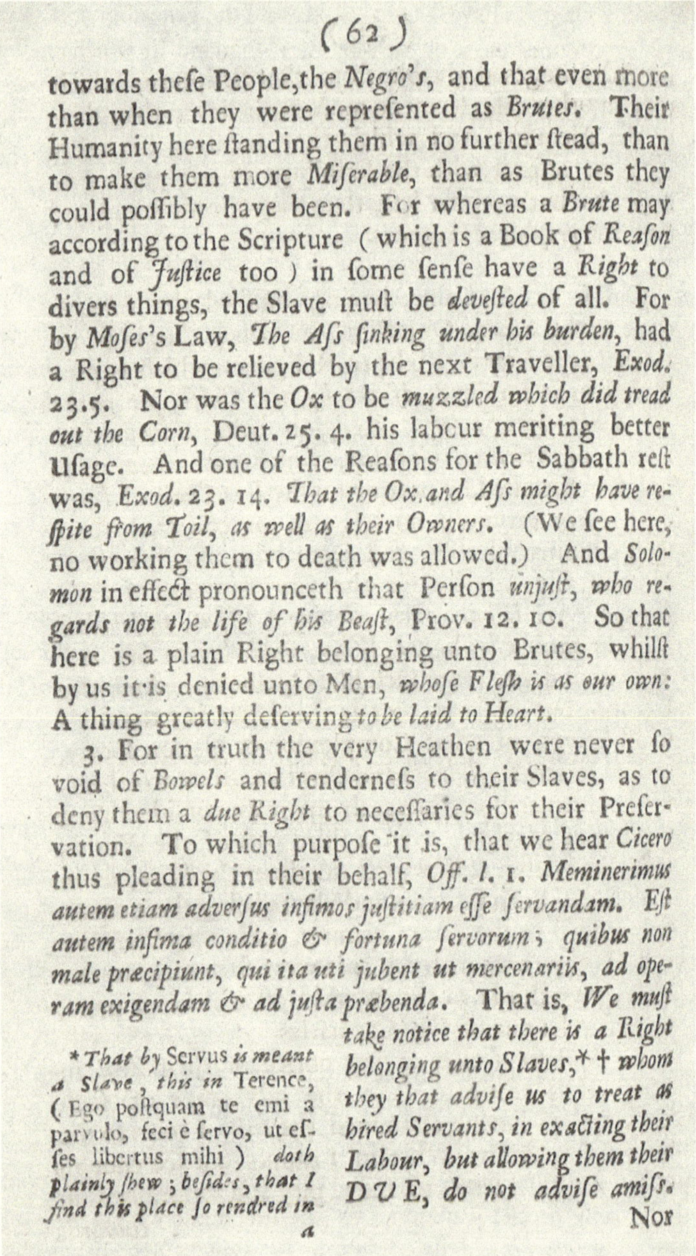

(62)

towards these People, the *Negro's*, and that even more than when they were represented as *Brutes*. Their Humanity here standing them in no further stead, than to make them more *Miserable*, than as Brutes they could possibly have been. For whereas a *Brute* may according to the Scripture (which is a Book of *Reason* and of *Justice* too) in some sense have a *Right* to divers things, the Slave must be *devested* of all. For by *Moses*'s Law, *The Ass sinking under his burden*, had a Right to be relieved by the next Traveller, *Exod.* 23.5. Nor was the *Ox* to be *muzzled which did tread out the Corn*, Deut. 25. 4. his labour meriting better Usage. And one of the Reasons for the Sabbath rest was, *Exod.* 23. 14. *That the Ox and Ass might have respite from Toil, as well as their Owners.* (We see here, no working them to death was allowed.) And *Solomon* in effect pronounceth that Person *unjust, who regards not the life of his Beast*, Prov. 12. 10. So that here is a plain Right belonging unto Brutes, whilst by us it is denied unto Men, *whose Flesh is as our own:* A thing greatly deserving *to be laid to Heart.*

3. For in truth the very Heathen were never so void of *Bowels* and tenderness to their Slaves, as to deny them a *due Right* to necessaries for their Preservation. To which purpose it is, that we hear *Cicero* thus pleading in their behalf, *Off. l.* 1. *Meminerimus autem etiam adversus infimos justitiam esse servandam. Est autem infima conditio & fortuna servorum; quibus non male præcipiunt, qui ita uti jubent ut mercenariis, ad operam exigendam & ad justa præbenda.* That is, *We must take notice that there is a Right belonging unto Slaves,** † *whom they that advise us to treat as hired Servants, in exacting their Labour, but allowing them their DUE, do not advise amiss.*

* *That by* Servus *is meant a Slave, this in* Terence, (Ego postquam te emi a parvulo, feci è servo, ut esses libertus mihi) *doth plainly shew; besides, that I find this place so rendred in a*

Nor

Figure 20. Morgan Godwyn, *The Negro's & Indians Advocate* (London, 1680), 62. RB 16628, The Huntington Library, San Marino, California.

Nearly fifty years later, the title page of Robert Dodsley's notable work *Servitude: A Poem* would feature an epigraph excerpted from the same moment in *Andria* (Figure 21). This time, the quoted section is more extensive:

———*Feci è Servo ut esses Libertus mihi,*
Proptereà quòd serviebas liberaliter
Quod habui Summum Pretium, persolvi tibi.
—————————————*Gaudeo,*
Si tibi quid feci aut facio, quod placeat Domine.[3]

For Dodsley, the "footman poet" whose work describes the obligations of a dutiful servant, this epigraph anticipates the poem's discourse on benevolent authority and grateful service. Yet the epigraph contains a short but crucial omission: the blank space before "Gaudeo" which is scored through replaces Sosia's critical admission that he remembers Simo's munificence (*in memoria habeo*) and Simo's affirmation in response that he does not regret his generosity (*haud muto factum*). The implicit coercion in Sosia's remembrance and the implied threat in Simo's declaration are both absent here. What remains is merely the depiction of liberty in return for "free" service, for which the freedman remains perpetually grateful. It is on this basis that Dodsley, in his short "Introduction" to "All Noblemen, Gentlemen, and Ladies, who keep many Servants," argues that "nothing procures a more faithful Service from a grateful Temper, than the Liberality of a Master," even as he literally erases the Terentian fiction of consent that underwrites this exchange, fundamentally *mis*reading—and altering—this moment in *Andria*.[4] Yet the freedman's allusion to his master as "Domine" rather than "Simo" and the title of the poem itself—"Servitude"—gesture to a more unsettling possibility: that Terence is being used to authorize the master's imperative to compel the performance of "faithful" service.[5]

The (mis)appropriation of Terence by both Godwyn and Dodsley is, perhaps, unsurprising; after all, Godwyn, an Oxford-educated Church of England clergyman, and Dodsley, whose father was master of a free school, had more than likely received Terence at an early age. Yet their (perhaps strategic) misreading of Terence suggestively gestures to the way in which the fictions of consent disseminated by the early modern reception of classical slave comedy had quickly become naturalized throughout the early modern British Atlantic world.

Fifty years after the publication of Dodsley's work, however, the cultural place of Terence would be both invoked and questioned by a very different

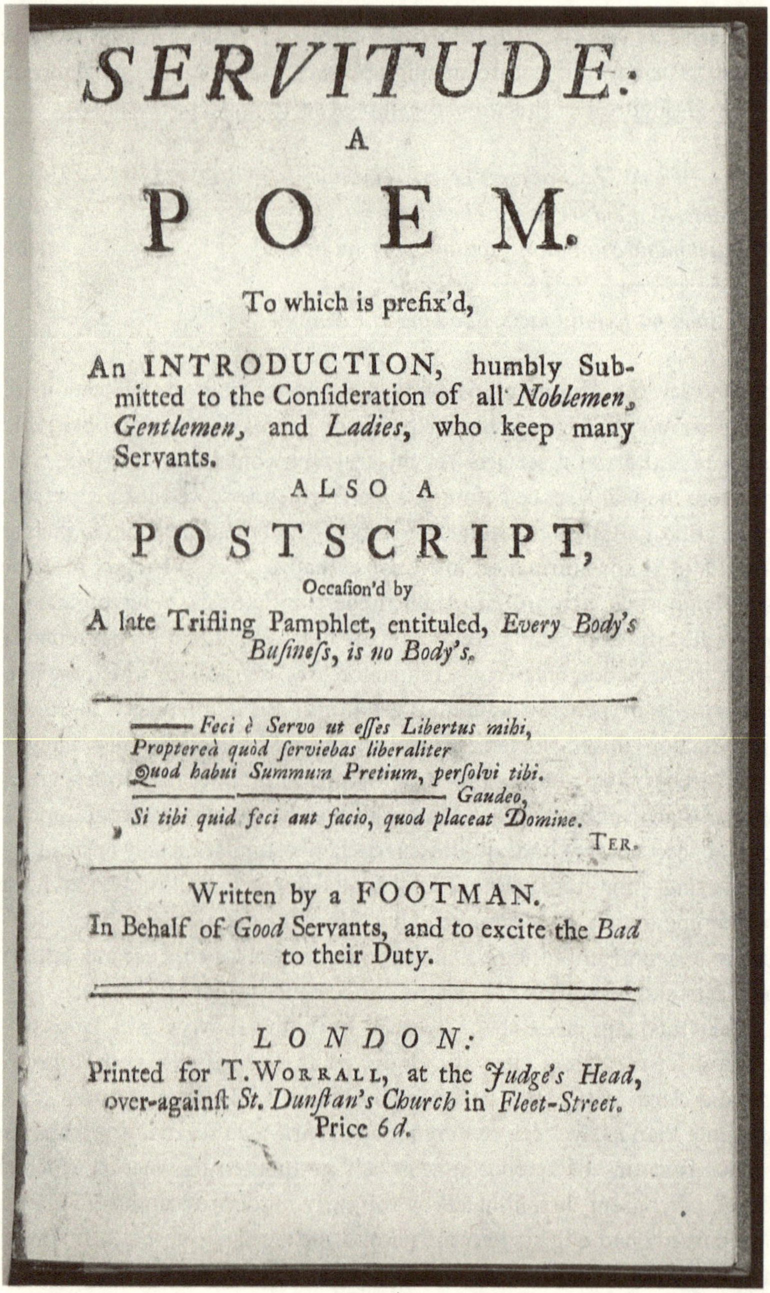

SERVITUDE:
A
POEM.

To which is prefix'd,

An INTRODUCTION, humbly Submitted to the Consideration of all *Noblemen, Gentlemen,* and *Ladies,* who keep many Servants.

ALSO A

POSTSCRIPT,

Occasion'd by

A late Trifling Pamphlet, entituled, *Every Body's Business, is no Body's.*

―― *Feci è Servo ut esses Libertus mihi,*
Proptereà quòd serviebas liberaliter
Quod habui Summum Pretium, persolvi tibi.
―――――――― *Gaudeo.*
Si tibi quid feci aut facio, quod placeat Domine.
TER.

Written by a FOOTMAN.
In Behalf of *Good* Servants, and to excite the *Bad* to their Duty.

LONDON:
Printed for T. WORRALL, at the *Judge's Head,* over-against *St. Dunstan's Church* in *Fleet-Street.*
Price 6 d.

Figure 21. Robert Dodsley, *Servitude: A Poem* (London, 1729), title page. Case Y 185 .D3626, Newberry Library, Chicago.

kind of classically educated writer, the enslaved American poet Phillis Wheatley, who in "To Maecenas" gestures both to Terence's prominence and to his unusual history of bondage:

> The happier *Terence** all the choir inspir'd,
> His soul replenish'd, and his bosom fir'd;
> But say, ye *Muses*, why this partial grace,
> To one alone of *Afric*'s sable race;
> From age to age transmitting thus his name
> With the first glory in the rolls of fame?
>
> *He was an *African* by birth.⁶

Terence had, of course, himself been a slave, while Wheatley would be manumitted shortly after the publication of these poems. Terence and Wheatley were both educated by their masters (and in Wheatley's case, by her master and mistress's children as well). But in addressing her poem to "Maecenas," Wheatley acknowledges the "patron" of her art, the Wheatley family, framing herself—like Terence—as the recipient of both personal and pedagogical generosity from her master.⁷ As "To Maecenas" ends with the request to "grant, *Maecenas*, thy paternal rays, / Hear me propitious, and defend my lays," Wheatley explicitly evokes the slippage between patronage and "paternal rays," strategically deploying the framing of the slave master as a father figure in order to argue (successfully, as it transpired) both for her art and for her manumission.⁸ And as I shall discuss in the next section by means of some brief but (I hope) illuminating examples, Wheatley's evocation of "Maecenas"—and, tacitly, the Wheatley family—as both a parent and a patron invokes the slippage between the master and the father not only in Renaissance editions and cribs of slave comedies designed for early modern schoolchildren, but also in juvenile slave literature and pedagogical material in the eighteenth and nineteenth centuries, on both sides of the Atlantic.

Happy Slaves: Fictions of Consent in Nineteenth-Century Juvenile Literature

In 1763, the pseudonymous author Tommy Tagg published his *Collection of Pretty Poems for the Amusement of Children Three Foot High*. This tiny book (its small footprint visually reflects the children "three foot high" for whom it was intended) contained, among other narratives, "The Story of Inkle and Yarico." The tale, which appears in multiple versions, features a young sailor who is stranded in a strange land and is rescued and kept safe by a beautiful woman, Yarico, who (depending on the version in question) is either black or Indian. Although Inkle makes promises of love and fidelity to Yarico, he does not hesitate later to sell her into slavery.

The story of Inkle and Yarico first appears in Richard Ligon's 1657 *A True & Exact History Of the Island of Barbados*; in Ligon's version, Inkle lands in America, and Yarico is described as an "Indian Maid."[9] The story proved popular and was adapted widely; in George Colman's 1787 opera based on the story, for instance, Inkle lands in the West Indies.[10] In Tagg's version, however, Inkle lands on a "barb'rous Coast . . . / Possess'd by Men who thirst for human Blood," descriptions which, in their evocations of both barbarousness and cannibalism, might recall early modern tales of travel in America and Africa.[11] Later, Yarico herself is described as a "Negro Virgin," and depicted as a black woman in an accompanying woodcut (Figure 22).[12] The lovers Inkle and Yarico board a ship travelling to Barbados, where

> The Planters thick'ning on the Key appear,
> To purchase Negro Slaves if any there;
> When the false Youth by cursed Avarice sway'd,
> Horrid to mention; sells his faithful Maid.[13]

Although Yarico begs Inkle to "let the Infant in my Womb I bear, / The Blessing taste of your paternal Care," Inkle "thrust her from him with remorseless Hand."[14]

The sale by enslavers of their own enslaved children was nothing new, but what is striking about this moment in "The Story of Inkle and Yarico" is its deviation from a familiar trope in eighteenth- and early nineteenth-century American children's literature: the articulation of the slave master as a father (figure), which echoes—and distorts—the play on *magister* in Terence's *Andria*.[15] Thus, Eliza Farrar's *The Adventures of Congo in Search of his Master*, for instance, explicitly renders cheerful bondage in terms of the slippage between master and father. Published in London in 1823 and republished in Boston between 1824 and 1834, *The Adventures of Congo* announces in its preface that it is "written for children from ten to twelve years of age," and its publication history suggests its transatlantic appeal.[16] In this "American Tale,"

80   *A Collection of*

The Story of INKLE *and* YARICO.

YE Virgin Train, an artless Dame inspire
  Unlearnt in Schools, unblest with natal Fire,
To save this Story from devouring Fate,
And the dire Arts of faithless Men relate.
A Youth I sing, in Face and Form divine,
In whom both Art and Nature did combine;
                                      With

Figure 22. Tommy Tagg, *A Collection Of Pretty Poems For the Amusement of Children Three Foot High* (London, between 1758 and 1800), 80. DXP A0188, American Antiquarian Society. Courtesy, American Antiquarian Society.

a reluctant enslaver and planter turned abolitionist and merchant, Mr. Stewart, rescues the enslaved Congo from an unscrupulous trader and binds him to serve for three years. But when Stewart attempts to release him at the end of that term, Congo is distraught; the text, indeed, devotes one of its engraved illustrations to a visual depiction of Congo's anxiety at the agonizing prospect of being separated from his master. In his distress, Congo suggestively points out that he has no father or mother—that his filial allegiance, in other words, belongs entirely to his master. Congo's anguish is only finally quieted when Mr. Stewart "allow[s]" Congo "the pleasure of believing himself inseparably connected with the family of his benefactor."[17] This is an important line: we remember that the word "family" derives in part from the Latin for a household slave, *famulus*; that the word "family" in one of its earliest senses refers to "the servants of a particular household or establishment."[18] But Congo only *believes* himself part of the family, a crucial component of the affective fiction that obtains here.

This imbrication of kinship and servitude generates a larger network of bondage organized by relational rhetorics in this narrative: Mr. Stewart's and Congo's respective sons also enter into a relationship of master and servant. In the story, the younger Stewart sails for England, and although he hesitates to separate his servant, the younger Congo, from his father, Congo senior is delighted at what he views as the opportunity to cement the relationship between his master and surrogate father, Stewart senior, and his own biological son, Congo junior. By accompanying his master, Stewart junior, the younger Congo will perform the roles of guardian, chaperone, and servant to the younger Stewart, who will himself quite literally take the place of Congo junior's father. The affective dynamics between master and servant, proxy father and son, are thus replicated and secured through the generations, ratified and strengthened by the sanguinal succession from father to son. Although Congo junior does become separated from his master in the course of the narrative—in the process traveling alone to Ireland and Wales, where he is initially welcomed as an exotic black servant—the story eventually ends in a joyful (and quasi-familial) reunification of master and servant: "The alternate tears and smiles, sobs and cries of joy, uttered by Congo ... kept the spectators in silent wonder for some minutes. Mr. Stewart, however, soon became more composed; and once convinced of the reality of the scene before him, he darted towards Congo, and *allowed his faithful servant to bury his face in the bosom of his long lost master*" (emphasis added).[19] Despite the mutual delight at their reunion, Stewart's more contained response reaffirms the difference between them, a distinction underscored by the fact that Congo's display of "faithful" fealty must be *allowed* by his master.

Although *The Adventures of Congo* is an antislavery narrative centered on the possibilities for loyal service *after* manumission, the nexus of servitude and kinship, family and bondage, consent and coercion is so firmly inscribed, so utterly legible, that even texts that articulate the *problem* of slavery deploy the fictions of happy servitude. This precise tension also emerges in *Cuffy the Negro's Doggrel Description of the Progress of Sugar*, which charts the production of sugar from cane to consumption and comprises part of a series intended for British children (Figure 23).[20] The poem explicitly identifies the provenance of the sweetmeats and cakes which English children enjoy—that source, of course, being black labor:

And when little massas suck the lollypop,
When they buy nice cake too at the pastry-shop,
When the luscious sweetmeat make them feast like kings,
Think, poor negro's labour all this comfort brings![21]

This text also identifies the human cost of that pleasure, even as it demands an appropriate affective response: "O pity the poor Negro," it begins, enjoining its juvenile readers to provide "kind relief to poor black" and insisting that "White and black [are] all one."[22] "To make sugar white," *Cuffy* suggests, requires not just labor but *blood*: "Blood, and nasty someting, baker now put in-ee."[23] The "whitening" of sugar is thus a racial process that simultaneously erases the true cost of its production. Yet the text's "doggerel" form parodies Cuffy's voice even as it also invites its reader to inhabit it, effectively to embody him, echoing the early modern grammar schoolboys who performed, enacted, and ventriloquized the classical slaves they encountered. At the same time, this text emphasizes that its readers are "little massas" who not only relish the products of black labor but may eventually become themselves the "masters" of enslaved peoples.

Moreover, despite the ways in which this children's text provides a suggestively abolitionist message, it also enjoys a kind of nostalgia for a time when "Cuffy's massa doctor'd him when sick, / Gave him food in plenty, clothes too, warm and thick."[24] "Happy so lived Cuffy—slave," the poem insists, before

2   CUFFY THE NEGRO'S

O PITY the poor Negro—cold the wind does blow!
No warm clothes defend him from the frost and
    snow.
Born in burning Afric', Cuffy loves the sun;
Shiv'ring, cold, and barefoot, Cuffy think no fun!
Once poor Cuffy's massa doctor'd him when sick,
Gave him food in plenty, clothes too, warm and
    thick.
Sometimes Cuffy idle, then he catch fum-fum;*
Sometimes Cuffy work hard, then he drink good
    rum!

                * A flogging.

Figure 23. *Cuffy The Negro's Doggrel Description Of The Progress of Sugar* (London, 1823), 2. D823 C965, John Carter Brown Library. Courtesy, John Carter Brown Library.

Cunning captain coax'd him to walk across de sea,
"Come," he said, "to England, land of liberty."
Cuffy ran away—went on board the ship,
Cat-o'nine-tails there made him hop and skip.
Now discharged in England, hunger make him die.[25]

England appears a "land of liberty," but the freedom Cuffy seeks has instead reduced him to privation and a true form of dependency ("Beg he must or perish!"); *Cuffy* may insist that the "white man" "pity the poor negro boy," but it simultaneously reinforces the trope of the "happy" slave, of a bondage undertaken—to quote the case of Adam Saffin—"chearfully quietly and Industriously."[26] Thus, beneath an image of careful and industrious planting, the reader receives a useful but insidious aphorism: "Never will you see black man sulky pouting."[27] In its idealized depiction of cheerful black servitude, and even as it gestures to the problems of slavery, *Cuffy* thus continues to propound the fictions of consent that underwrite the exploitation of black labor.

If both *Cuffy* and *The Adventures of Congo* are directed at white children, the crucial role of these fictions becomes readily apparent when we turn to a text written specifically for black schoolchildren: the images and accompanying large-print narratives of *Post-Emancipation Life* (in the Caribbean) published between 1833 and 1837 by the Ladies' Society for Promoting the Early Education of Negro Children.[28] Intended for beginning readers, the subject of these narratives are the former enslaved people in the British West Indies who were "emancipated" by the Slavery Abolition Act of 1833 but were nonetheless compelled to continue serving their masters as apprentices. According to the text, "These people were once slaves, but now they are apprenticed to their master for six years, after which they will be free."[29] As they depict and describe the process of sugar production in Antigua, these texts serve a dual pedagogical purpose for their schoolroom readers, teaching both literacy and the naturalization of submission, advising their juvenile readers: "I hope you always try to do everything properly, and whether you are set to lay the cuttings in the Cane-holes, to pick grass for the cattle, or to mend a hole in your clothes, you should always try to do it in the best manner."[30]

As these texts celebrate the newly manumitted yet indentured slave, we hear chilling echoes of the *Book of Common Prayer*; for these laborers, freedom is (nothing *but*) perfect service. Thus, in the lesson accompanying the idealized image of a benevolent master addressing his former slave, the

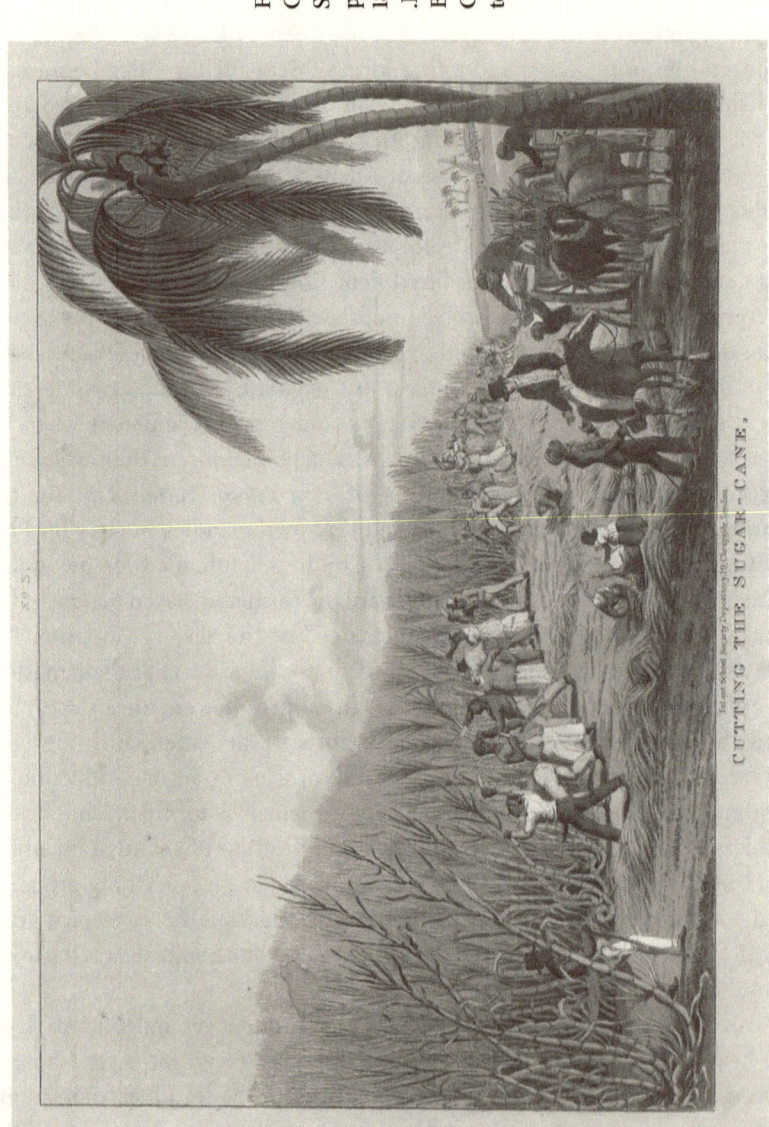

Figure 24. William Clark, "Cutting the Sugar-Cane" (first printed London, 1823). 3-Size D833 .L155p, John Carter Brown Library. Courtesy, John Carter Brown Library.

Figure 25. David Claypoole Johnston, *A Proslavery Incantation Scene. Or Shakspeare Improved* (U.S., not before 1856). ART File S528m1 no. 86 (size L). Used by permission of the Folger Shakespeare Library under a Creative Commons Attribution-ShareAlike 4.0 International License.

indentured servant is enjoined to a form of faithful service which has been divinely ordained (Figure 24): "These are all good people; they love their *Massa*, who has had them taught to read and love God's holy Word. They are very thankful to God, that He has blessed their dear *Massa*. He has come on horseback to see how his Negroes get on. How kindly he seems to speak to poor Cadjoe, whose eyes sparkle with joy. But though Cadjoe is no longer a slave, he does not forget that he is a servant. He remembers that God has said, 'Servants, be subject to your masters in all things.'"[31] In a didactic book such as *The Instructive Alphabet* (1809), which is bound together with William Cowper's "The Negro's Complaint," an antislavery poem commissioned by the Committee for the Abolition of the Slave Trade, the latter work is literally framed as a pedagogical text alongside the most rudimentary knowledge of the alphabet.[32] For the readers of *Post-Emancipation Life*, however, to be literate is to be naturalized into the fictions of consent that obtain from apprenticeship to indenture to slavery, and back again.

* * *

In *Fictions of Consent*, I have argued that the field of early modern English literature, more than we might perhaps have acknowledged or imagined, both intervenes in and is interpellated by the structures of slavery. I close now with a later, perhaps anachronistic, coda, to offer a final reflection on the ways in which nineteenth-century American arguments around slavery and abolition turned to this earlier moment—and to the literary canon their authors doubtless learned in the classroom—to make and mobilize their claims. In an antebellum cartoon by David Claypoole Johnston, proslavery advocates bearing slave bills of sale, notices of runaway slaves, whips, and shackles burn abolitionist documents in a witches' cauldron (Figure 25).[33] Mimicking the witches of *Macbeth*, these figures comically echo the meter and the magic of their spell: "Double double Free Soil trouble, / Till Slavery crush the Free Soil bubble." The alternate title for this cartoon, we note, is "Shak[e]speare Improved," denoting an early modern literary canon strategically appropriated in the service of a satire on slavery. As this book has sought to recover the literary histories of early modern England's genealogies of servitude, my hope is that it has also begun to reveal the *longue durée* of its futures of slavery, a future which is still very much present, and to excavate—and refuse—the fictions that sustain it, that were forged in early modern England and that have persisted for far too long.

NOTES

Introduction

1. John Rushworth, *Historical Collections. The Second Part* (London, 1680), 468; see also John Lilburne, *A true relation of the materiall passages of Lieut. Col. Iohn Lilburnes sufferings* (London, 1646), 6. For a longer discussion of Cartwright's case and the legal status of English slavery, see George Van Cleve, "*Somerset's Case* and Its Antecedents in Imperial Perspective," *Law and History Review* 24, no. 3 (2006): 601–46.

2. The significance of Cartwright's case—and of the phrase "too pure an Air for Slaves to breath in"—was such that, nearly 140 years later, it would be invoked to argue for the freedom of the enslaved man James Somerset in the famous English case of *Somerset v. Stewart* (1772). This case would in turn often be misinterpreted as signaling "the emancipation of black slaves in England," whereas in fact "Long after the Somerset case, advertisements for the sale of black slaves continued to appear in English newspapers." See Peter Fryer, *Staying Power: The History of Black People in Britain* (London: Pluto Press, 2010; first published 1984), 120–26, at 125–26. See also Van Cleve, "*Somerset's Case* and Its Antecedents," and David Olusoga, *Black and British: A Forgotten History* (London: Macmillan, 2016), chapter 4, for further discussion of *Somerset v. Stewart*. In *Butts v. Penny* (1677), "The earliest reported English case on the legal status of slaves in England (after *Cartwright's Case*)," it was decided that Africans could be property; but in *Chamberlaine v. Harvey* (1696) and *Smith v. Browne and Cooper* (1701), Lord Chief Justice Holt challenged this ruling, famously stating in the latter case that "As soon as a negro comes into England, he becomes free. One may be a villein in England but not a slave." (See Van Cleve, "*Somerset's Case*," 614, 616–18; and Olusoga, 119–20.)

3. William Harrison, *The description of England*, in Raphael Holinshed, *The First and second volumes of Chronicles* [*Chronicles of England, Scotlande, and Irelande*] (London, 1587), 163 [sig. P3r].

4. See David Olusoga's tweet and response to this message (@DavidOlusoga), "It looks like HM Treasury have now deleted this tweet. The real question is why anyone thought this was ok? I really do think we're getting better at accepting the UK's role in slavery and the slave trade, but things like this make me question my optimism," Twitter, February 10, 2018, https://twitter.com/davidolusoga/status/962252398273224705?lang=en.

5. Throughout, I use "service" to refer to the kinds of labor—domestic and otherwise—that would have registered as free, and as part of the service society to which everyone in early modern England belonged. I use "servitude," conversely, to refer principally to forms of bound or "unfree" labor, even as I discuss the extent to which "bound" labor relies on the adoption of frameworks of consent. The term "servitude," as this book will discuss, is a fraught term in early modern England, where it comes to both denote and deny more explicit modes of enslavement.

6. Michael Guasco's important recent study of the scope of bondage in the Mediterranean and Atlantic worlds, *Slaves and Englishmen: Human Bondage in the Early Modern Atlantic World* (Philadelphia: University of Pennsylvania Press, 2014) underscores early modern English knowledges of and contemporary familiarity with forms of slavery. Guasco crucially discusses how slavery comprised "an integral part of [England's] national story" (14), against and in relation to which ideas of "Englishness" and of "essential" English liberty could take shape. The title of this introduction may recall that of Guasco's concluding chapter ("Slavery Before 'Slavery' in Pre-Plantation America"), though I use similar phrasing to very different ends.

7. *The Several Declarations Of The Company Of Royal Adventurers Of England Trading Into Africa* (London, 1667).

8. This work builds on recent discussions of early modern pedagogy and the Latin curricula of English grammar schools in Lynn Enterline's *Shakespeare's Schoolroom: Rhetoric, Discipline, Emotion* (Philadelphia: University of Pennsylvania Press, 2012); Robert S. Miola's *Shakespeare's Reading* (Oxford: Oxford University Press, 2000) and *Shakespeare and Classical Comedy: The Influence of Plautus and Terence* (Oxford: Oxford University Press, 1994); and Colin Burrow's *Shakespeare and Classical Antiquity* (Oxford: Oxford University Press, 2013).

9. *The booke of the common prayer* (London, 1549), sig. A4r.

10. The 1547 Vagrancy Act was, perhaps unsurprisingly, repealed after two years on account of its harshness. Nonetheless, the stipulations of this Act illuminate the legal and discursive apparatus by which slavery was, however temporarily, legally authorized and indeed compelled. For further discussion of the 1547 Vagrancy Act, particularly in relation to English practices of villeinage and the rhetoric of slavery, see C. S. L. Davies, "Slavery and Protector Somerset: The Vagrancy Act of 1547," *Economic History Review* 19, no. 3 (1966): 533–49; and Mary Nyquist, "Base Slavery and Roman Yoke" in *The Oxford Handbook of English Law and Literature, 1500–1700*, ed. Lorna Hutson (Oxford: Oxford University Press 2017), esp. 631–32.

11. *Anno primo Edwardi Sexti Statvtes made in the Parliament* (London, 1548), sig. A5v.

12. Ibid., sig. A5v–B1r.

13. Ibid., sig. A5v–A6r.

14. For a discussion of the use of ink tattooing as a way of marking servitude somatically, see Miles P. Grier, "Inkface: The Slave Stigma in England's Early Imperial Imagination," in *Scripturalizing the Human: The Written as the Political*, ed. Vincent L. Wimbush (New York: Routledge, 2015), 193–220. The "legibility" of racialized slavery would of course come to be complicated by the precise *illegibility* of complexions and characteristics which could register as "white." Indeed, American abolitionists would later rely on the visual spectacle of light-skinned enslaved children to appeal to the sympathies of their audience, whose sense of shame, they calculated, would more readily be activated by the sight of enslaved people who appeared to be "white," even as such images troublingly raised the possibility of invisible forms of racial mixture and "passing." See Mary Niall Mitchell, *Raising Freedom's Child: Black Children and Visions of the Future After Slavery* (New York: New York University Press, 2008), 1–7. The "one-drop rule" precisely registered the hereditability of slavery within a system which sought to resolve the instability of epidermal markers alone.

15. John Bullokar, *An English Expositor* (London, 1616), sig. G6v; and Robert Cawdrey, *A Table Alphabeticall* (London, 1604), sig. E1v.

16. Claudius Hollyband, *A Dictionarie French and English* (London, 1593), sig. O4v (translating the French "Fiction & controuvement"); and Edward Phillips, *The New World of English Words: Or, a General Dictionary* (London, 1658), sig. P2v.

17. In speaking of race as a "fiction," I think in particular of Karen E. Fields and Barbara J. Fields's concept of "racecraft" in *Racecraft: The Soul of Inequality in American Life* (London: Verso, 2012) as well as Henry Louis Gates, Jr.'s formulation of race in "Editor's Introduction: Writing 'Race' and the Difference It Makes," in *"Race," Writing, and Difference*, ed. Gates, 1–20 (Chicago: University of Chicago Press, 1986). Ian Smith emphasizes that race "is an oppressive, aggregate *fiction*," one that "confuses the material or corporal human being – in the broadest phenomenal sense not limited to color—with a discursive fiction that is invented to stratify and give permanent meaning to the dynamics of human interaction"; while Dennis Austin Britton and Kimberly Anne Coles remind us that "Race has always been more about fiction than fact, and we do not expect our fictions to be stable, even if they are governed by generic conventions." See Smith, *Race and Rhetoric in the Renaissance: Barbarian Errors* (New York: Palgrave Macmillan, 2009), 21, 95–96; and Britton and Coles, "Spenser and Race: An Introduction," *Spenser Studies* 35 (2021): 3.

18. Geraldine Heng, *The Invention of Race in the European Middle Ages* (Cambridge, UK: Cambridge University Press, 2018), 3 (original text in italics). Britton and Coles powerfully describe race as "a strategy" ("Spenser and Race," 10).

19. Imtiaz Habib, *Black Lives in the English Archives, 1500–1677: Imprints of the Invisible* (Aldershot, UK: Ashgate, 2008), 56.

20. The most notable exceptions are Imtiaz Habib, whose magisterial study of black lives in early modern England (ibid.) addresses the coarticulation of blackness and slavery (see also pp. 55–56 for a discussion of the Vagrancy Act); Gustav Ungerer, whose book *The Mediterranean Apprenticeship of British Slavery* (Madrid: Editorial Verbum, 2008) traces the involvement of English merchants in the slave trade as early as the late fifteenth century; and Michael Guasco's *Slaves and Englishmen*. I concur firmly with Guasco's central assertion that slavery informed both English "self-fashioning" and its practices in the Atlantic world. I depart from Guasco's suggestion, however, that "early English impressions of slavery as it existed beyond England's borders were not determined by racial—or even proto-racial—conceits" (6); rather, I work to demonstrate how the fictions of slavery and those of race are coarticulated and coextensive in this period. Finally, and most recently, Emily Weissbourd has explored the possibility of English involvement in an emergent slave trade in "'Those in Their Possession': Race, Slavery, and Queen Elizabeth's 'Edicts of Expulsion,'" *Huntington Library Quarterly* 78, no. 1 (2015): 1–19.

21. See, for instance, Ungerer, *The Mediterranean Apprenticeship of British Slavery*, 93–95; and Weissbourd, "'Those in Their Possession,'" 16–17.

22. On Renaissance service, please see David Schalkwyk, *Shakespeare, Love and Service* (Cambridge, UK: Cambridge University Press, 2008); Judith Weil, *Service and Dependency in Shakespeare's Plays* (Cambridge, UK: Cambridge University Press, 2005); David Evett, *Discourses of Service in Shakespeare's England* (New York: Palgrave Macmillan, 2005); Mark Thornton Burnett, *Masters and Servants in English Renaissance Drama and Culture: Authority and Obedience* (New York: St. Martin's Press, 1997); and Elizabeth Rivlin, *The Aesthetics of Service in Early Modern England* (Evanston, IL: Northwestern University Press, 2012). See also Richard Strier's essay "Faithful Servants: Shakespeare's Praise of Disobedience" in *The Historical Renaissance: New Essays on Tudor and Stuart Literature and Culture*, ed. Heather Dubrow and Richard Strier (Chicago: University of Chicago Press, 1988), 104–33. Recent works theorizing early modern bondage include Amanda Bailey, *Of Bondage: Debt, Property, and Personhood in Early Modern England* (Philadelphia: University of Pennsylvania Press, 2013); Melissa E. Sanchez, *Erotic*

Subjects: The Sexuality of Politics in Early Modern English Literature (Oxford: Oxford University Press, 2011); and Mary Nyquist, *Arbitrary Rule: Slavery, Tyranny, and the Power of Life and Death* (Chicago: University of Chicago Press, 2013).

23. Recent discussions of the nexus of race, intimacy, and proximity include Kim F. Hall, *Things of Darkness: Economies of Race and Gender in Early Modern England* (Ithaca, NY: Cornell University Press, 1995); Emily C. Bartels, *Speaking of the Moor: From "Alcazar" to "Othello"* (Philadelphia: University of Pennsylvania Press, 2008); Jean E. Feerick, *Strangers in Blood: Relocating Race in the Renaissance* (Toronto: University of Toronto Press, 2010); and Marjorie Rubright, *Doppelgänger Dilemmas: Anglo-Dutch Relations in Early Modern English Literature and Culture* (Philadelphia: University of Pennsylvania Press, 2014).

24. Throughout this book, I use "natality" to refer to a (seemingly naturalized) reproductive imperative. For recent work on children, consent, and early modern political life, meanwhile, see Holly Brewer, *By Birth or Consent: Children, Law, and the Anglo-American Revolution in Authority* (Chapel Hill: University of North Carolina Press, 2005); Blaine Greteman, *The Poetics and Politics of Youth in Milton's England* (Cambridge, UK: Cambridge University Press, 2013); and Michael Witmore, *Pretty Creatures: Children and Fiction in the English Renaissance* (Ithaca, NY: Cornell University Press, 2007).

Chapter 1

1. MS Aubrey 13, fols. 252–53, Bodleian Library, Oxford (at fol. 252r). The story, Williamson notes, has been retold by his mother several times; indeed, he has received the tale from her, suggesting that this anecdote has assumed a quasi-mythical quality.

2. Amanda Bailey, *Flaunting: Style and the Subversive Male Body in Renaissance England* (Toronto: University of Toronto Press, 2007), 6.

3. Mateo Alemán, *The Rogve: Or The Life Of Gvzman De Alfarache* (London, 1622), sig. V6v. A "picaro," according to Richard Perceval's *A Dictionarie In Spanish and English* (London, 1599), is "a simple base fellowe, a poore labourer, a porter" (sig. R1v).

4. MS EL 2578, The Huntington Library, San Marino, California.

5. As Frances E. Dolan usefully observes, "While identifying something as a legal fiction sometimes works to explain why we should stop talking about it, it might instead open a new conversation about what a fiction means, what it enables or constrains, and how 'fictions' can outlast the original conditions of their production." See *True Relations: Reading, Literature, and Evidence in Seventeenth-Century England* (Philadelphia: University of Pennsylvania Press, 2013), 148. See also Lorna Hutson's discussion of the early modern dramatic fictions that legal narratives allowed in *The Invention of Suspicion: Law and Mimesis in Shakespeare and Renaissance Drama* (Oxford: Oxford University Press, 2007).

6. Ian Smith, "Othello's Black Handkerchief," *Shakespeare Quarterly* 64, no. 1 (2013): 4.

7. Steve Hindle, "Technologies of Identification Under the Old Poor Law," *The Local Historian: Journal of the British Association for Local History* 36, no. 4 (2006): 220–36.

8. Geraldine Heng, *The Invention of Race in the European Middle Ages* (Cambridge, UK: Cambridge University Press, 2018), 15. I discuss the use and circulation of livery badges later in this chapter.

9. John Cowell, *The Interpreter: Or Booke Containing the Signification of Words* (Cambridge, 1607), sig. 2S2v; *Oxford English Dictionary, Second Edition* (1989), s.v. "livery, n.," 2.a.

10. Thomas Overbury, *A Wife Now The Widdow of Sir Thomas Overbvrye . . .* (London, 1614), sig. F2v.

11. The *OED* also defines livery as "the dispensing of food, provisions, or clothing ... to retainers or servants; hence *gen.* provision, allowance." *Oxford English Dictionary, Second Edition* (1989), s.v. "livery, *n.*," 1.a.

12. Lancelot Andrewes, *Apospasmatia Sacra* (London, 1657), 330–33. This passage provides a commentary on Genesis 3:21.

13. For a discussion of the affordances of household and guild livery, see also Peter Stallybrass, "Worn Worlds: Clothes and Identity on the Renaissance Stage," in *Subject and Object in Renaissance Culture*, ed. Margreta de Grazia, Maureen Quilligan, and Peter Stallybrass (Cambridge, UK: Cambridge University Press, 1996), 289–93.

14. See Lawrence Stone, *The Crisis of the Aristocracy, 1558–1641* (Oxford: Clarendon Press, 1965), 201–3.

15. See Steve Rappaport, *Worlds Within Worlds: Structures of Life in Sixteenth-Century London* (Cambridge, UK: Cambridge University Press, 1989), 218. See also Chapter 2 for a discussion of the intersections of livery and slavery in public processions.

16. For further discussion of the structure and operations of the livery companies, see Ian W. Archer, *The Pursuit of Stability: Social Relations in Elizabethan London* (Cambridge, UK: Cambridge University Press, 1991), 100–148.

17. In Thomas Dekker's *The Shoemakers' Holiday* (1600), for instance, Hodge refers to the shoemaker Rafe as "a *brother* of our trade, a good workman" (10.75–76, emphasis mine). All citations from *The Shoemakers' Holiday* refer to *Renaissance Drama: An Anthology of Plays and Entertainments*, 2nd ed., ed. Arthur F. Kinney (Malden, MA: Blackwell, 2005), 365–408.

18. Ann Rosalind Jones and Peter Stallybrass, *Renaissance Clothing and the Materials of Memory* (Cambridge, UK: Cambridge University Press, 2000), 11.

19. Leeds Barroll, *Politics, Plague, and Shakespeare's Theater: The Stuart Years* (Ithaca, NY: Cornell University Press, 1991), 9–10, 49. As I shall argue, the professional actors' designation as liveried servants certainly paved the way to "bed, board, pay" when they toured.

20. Scott McMillin and Sally-Beth MacLean, *The Queen's Men and their Plays* (Cambridge, UK: Cambridge University Press, 1998), 28.

21. The Act "ranked players lacking a patron with peddlers, tinkers, and petty chapmen as 'Rogues, Vacaboundes, and Sturdy Beggers ... havinge not Land or Maister, nor using any lawfull Marchaundize Crafte or Mysterye'" (E. K. Chambers, *The Elizabethan Stage* [Oxford: Clarendon Press, 1923], IV, 269–71, qtd. in Peter H. Greenfield, "Touring," in *A New History of Early English Drama*, ed. John D. Cox and David Scott Kastan [New York: Columbia University Press, 1997], 259).

22. Greenfield notes that performing troupes with royal or noble patronage were rewarded on tour "as early as 1277 at Canterbury, 1307 at Leicester, [and] 1377 at Worcester." See "Touring," 252.

23. *Records of Early English Drama: Sussex*, ed. Cameron Louis (Toronto: University of Toronto Press, 2000), 118–20.

24. Greenfield, "Touring," 257. For a longer discussion of the acting companies' practices and conditions of touring, see Siobhan Keenan, *Travelling Players in Shakespeare's England* (Basingstoke, UK: Palgrave Macmillan, 2002).

25. There seems also to be something of an elision of the bodies of the players themselves here. It is their feudal inscriptions—their liveries—that are recognized, not the players themselves. At the same time, their bodies are constituted by their clothing; it is their liveries, not their persons, that are legible.

26. Greenfield, "Touring," 256–57.

27. *Letter from John Hatcher vc to Lord Burghley, Chancellor,* in *Records of Early English Drama: Cambridge,* ed. Alan H. Nelson (Toronto: University of Toronto Press, 1989), 1.290–91 (at 291).

28. Paul Whitfield White also notes that often on tour players were lodged in noble households and given food, shelter, and payment. The players' circulation between noble *households,* quite apart from the way in which rewards and payments are dispensed, seems to underscore the way in which, in livery and on tour, they function and are seen as household servants of a noble patron. See White, *Theatre and Reformation: Protestantism, Patronage, and Playing in Tudor England* (Cambridge, UK: Cambridge University Press, 1993), 26, qtd. in Kathleen E. McLuskie and Felicity Dunsworth, "Patronage and the Economics of Theater," in *A New History of Early English Drama,* 427.

29. Stone, *Crisis of the Aristocracy,* 203.

30. Qtd. in Stone, 212.

31. Chambers, *Elizabethan Stage,* II, 86, qtd. in Greenfield, "Touring," 252.

32. *English Gilds. The Original Ordinances of more than one hundred Early English Gilds,* ed. Toulmin Smith (London, 1870), 388.

33. *The Merchant of Venice,* 2.2.94–101. All references follow *The Norton Shakespeare,* 3rd ed., gen. ed. Stephen Greenblatt (New York: W. W. Norton, 2016). Further references will be cited parenthetically within the text. I also follow this edition in rendering the name as "Lancelet." As Patricia Parker argues, this name (and this spelling) recalls a "lancet" or surgical knife, thereby invoking an association with cutting, bloodletting, and castration which seems particularly resonant in terms of Lancelet's joke—or fear—that "I am a Jew if I serve the Jew any longer" (2.2.100–101). See Parker, "Cutting Both Ways: Bloodletting, Castration/Circumcision, and the 'Lancelet' of *The Merchant of Venice,*" in *Alternative Shakespeares 3,* ed. Diana E. Henderson (Abingdon, UK: Routledge, 2008), 95–118.

34. Cowell, *The Interpreter,* sig. S3r: "In the other signification, it betokeneth a deliuery of possession vnto those tenents, which hould of the king in *capite,* or in knights seruice: for the king by his prerogatiue hath *primier seysini* (or the first possession) of all lands and tenements so houlden of him."

35. I return to a discussion of the gift in Chapter 3. In Chapter 5, meanwhile, I explore the kinds of obligation implicitly created by the "gift" of deliverance from a former master, with particular regard to *The Tempest* and to early American contexts, and to the forms of servitude enabled by obligation.

36. James Shapiro, *Shakespeare and the Jews* (New York: Columbia University Press, 1996), 8.

37. Ian Smith notes that Lancelet's desired change of livery, "the outward badge of service and affiliation," also "involves lateral racial and religious attachments (from Jew to Christian)." See "The Textile Black Body: Race and 'Shadowed Livery' in *The Merchant of Venice,*" in *The Oxford Handbook of Shakespeare and Embodiment: Gender, Sexuality, and Race,* ed. Valerie Traub (Oxford: Oxford University Press, 2016), 181.

38. See Steven R. Mentz, "The Fiend Gives Friendly Counsel: Launcelot Gobbo and Polyglot Economics in *The Merchant of Venice,*" in *Money and the Age of Shakespeare: Essays in New Economic Criticism,* ed. Linda Woodbridge (New York: Palgrave Macmillan, 2003), 177–87.

39. For readings of Antonio and Bassanio as investors, "hazarding" current wealth to gain greater returns, see Scott Cutler Shershow's "Shakespeare Beyond Shakespeare" in *Marxist Shakespeares,* ed. Jean E. Howard and Scott Cutler Shershow (New York: Routledge, 2001), 258–60.

40. Jones and Stallybrass, *Renaissance Clothing*, 28.

41. Margreta de Grazia, "The Ideology of Superfluous Things: *King Lear* as Period Piece," in *Subject and Object in Renaissance Culture*, ed. de Grazia, Quilligan, and Stallybrass, 17–42.

42. Stone, *Crisis of the Aristocracy*, 212.

43. Craig Muldrew, *The Economy of Obligation: The Culture of Credit and Social Relations in Early Modern England* (Basingstoke, UK: Palgrave, 1998).

44. Ibid., 3.

45. Ibid., 157–58.

46. See Janet Adelman, "Her Father's Blood: Race, Conversion, and Nation in *The Merchant of Venice*," *Representations* 81, no. 1 (2003): 4–30. Adelman's essay usefully unfolds the contingencies of Jewish conversion and assimilation by tracing the play's racialization of Jewishness in somatic and even epidermal terms. See also M. Lindsay Kaplan, "Jessica's Mother: Medieval Constructions of Jewish Race and Gender in *The Merchant of Venice*," *Shakespeare Quarterly* 58, no. 1 (2007): 1–30 as well as Dennis Austin Britton, *Becoming Christian: Race, Reformation, and Early Modern English Romance* (New York: Fordham University Press, 2014), esp. 145–50, for an important discussion of race, religion, and conversion in *The Merchant of Venice*.

47. The quotation in the heading is from Thomas Dekker, *The Owles Almanacke. Prognosticating many strange accidents which shall happen to this Kingdome of Great Britaine this yeere, 1618* (London, 1618), 36 [sig. F1v].

48. Unmarked blue coats are more commonly represented on the early modern stage than coats with badges that declare a specific master, although G. K. Hunter notes that "it seems probable that the stage offered its audiences, daily accustomed to seeing men in livery, some simplified indicators of genealogy and heraldry, attached to the most famous peerages" (see "Flatcaps and Bluecoats: Visual Signals on the Elizabethan Stage," *Essays and Studies* 33 [1980]: 32 n. 1).

49. For a useful account of the significance of credit and clothing in the play, see Jean E. Howard, *Theater of a City: The Places of London Comedy, 1598–1642* (Philadelphia: University of Pennsylvania Press, 2007), 105–10.

50. John Cooke, *Greenes Tu quoque, Or, The Cittie Gallant* (London, 1614), sig. D3r. Subsequent references will be cited parenthetically within the text. The play was "performed by the Queen Anne's Men at court and at the Red Bull in 1611 and printed in 1614" (Howard, 106).

51. See Howard, 112, on this point: "Thrust by his prodigality into a life of servitude, [Staines] recoups his fortunes by cleverly assuming various sartorial disguises and performing his way back into economic and social respectability."

52. Thomas Dekker, *The Second Part Of The Honest Whore* (London, 1630), sig. B4r.

53. Ben Jonson, *A Pleasant Comedy, Called: The Case is Alterd* (London, 1609), sig. B3r.

54. Jean MacIntyre and Garrett P. J. Epp make the point that character is in effect the costume, so Orlando must exchange clothes on stage both because it is more economical dramatically and to signal that the character remains the same despite the change in costume (see "'Cloathes worth all the rest': Costumes and Properties," in *A New History of Early English Drama*, ed. Cox and Kastan, 269–86).

55. Thomas Nashe, *Haue with you to Saffron-walden. Or, Gabriell Harueys hunt is vp.* (London, 1596), sig. P2v. Further references will be cited parenthetically in the text.

56. This sense of the word "livery" connoting an authorizing provenance more generally seems to have been quite commonplace. In *Another Letter Of Mr. A. C. To His Dis-Iesuited Kinseman* (London, 1602), Anthony Copley refers to "sundrie bookes . . . which from time to time

haue come forth without anie name or knowne liuerie at all" (sig. G1r). The lack of "liuerie," here, alludes to the origins of the book and how it is unknown whence exactly it comes, while livery itself denotes an authorized origin.

57. A "trencher" literally means "a flat piece of wood, square or circular, on which meat was served and cut up; a plate or platter of wood, metal, or earthenware" (*Oxford English Dictionary*, s.v. "trencher, *n. 1*," 2.). Hence, a "trencher-carrier" is a servingman.

58. See Gervase Markham's *A Health to the Gentlemanly profession of Seruingmen; or, The Seruingmans Comfort* (London, 1598) for several instances of plowmen failing to enact the role of servingmen properly; Markham also articulates larger concerns about the deteriorating position of servingmen. References will be cited parenthetically in the text.

59. William Shakespeare, *The Tragicall Historie of Hamlet Prince of Denmarke* (London, 1603), sig. F2v.

60. Jonson, *A Pleasant Comedy, Called: The Case is Alterd*, sig. G4r.

61. A "scutcheon" or "scutheon" refers to an "escutcheon," or cognizance.

62. Please see Chapter 5 for a longer discussion of the ways in which, in certain frameworks and discourses of slavery, bondage persists after manumission.

63. Dekker, *The Second Part Of The Honest Whore*, sig. D1r; Cooke, *Greenes Tu quoque*, sig. D2r.

64. Markham, *A Health to the Gentlemanly profession of Seruingmen*.

65. Richard Crimsal, *A pleasant new Dialogue: Or, The discourse between the Serving-man and the Husband-man* (London, 1640).

66. A point also noted by the plowman in *A pleasant new Dialogue*: "The Proverbe of a Serving-man, / as alwayes I doe understand. / In prime of yeeres hee'l roare and swagger, / and being growne old he turnes a begger."

67. References to *Love's Labor's Lost* follow *The Norton Shakespeare*, 3rd ed.

68. See Jones and Stallybrass, *Renaissance Clothing*, 242–44.

69. Richard Huloet, *Abcedarivm Anglico Latinvm* (London, 1552), sig. C5r. The class connotations of "botcher" are evident when in *Arden of Faversham*, for instance, Arden accuses Mosby of being "A botcher, and no better at the first, / Who, by base brokerage getting some small stock, / Crept into service of a nobleman, / And, by his servile flattery and fawning, / Is now become the steward of his house, / And bravely jets it in his silken gown." *Arden of Faversham*, in *Renaissance Drama*, ed. Kinney, 227–69, 1.1.25–30. The problem here is that Mosby's upward mobility is obtained through "base brokerage" and "flattery and fawning," which is framed rhetorically in terms of the move from ragged clothes (such as a "botcher" would handle) to "fine silks."

70. For one instance of such derogatory usage, see the phrase "A moste lousie caste sute of his," in *The First Part of The Return from Parnassus* (3.1.944), in *The Three Parnassus Plays (1598–1601)*, ed. J. B. Leishman (London: Ivor Nicholson & Watson, 1949).

71. Jones and Stallybrass, *Renaissance Clothing*, 11.

72. Dekker, *The Shoemakers' Holiday*, 2.64–77.

73. Livery is of course often given in addition to or in lieu of wages. Consider, for example, that in *The Diary of Ralph Josselin 1616–1683*, ed. Alan Macfarlane (London: Oxford University Press for the British Academy, 1976), Josselin, a clergyman, records payment in wages and clothing to his servant Peter in 1669: "Peter hired for another yeare, which is to end the day after Halsted faire. and to have 4 li. 10s. and paire of shoes" (549). The following year, while Josselin still allows the use of his mare, there is no payment in clothing, and the wages themselves, which

are only now explicitly named as such, have increased: "Peters yeare is to come out Octob. 31. 1671. he is to have 5 li. wages and his mare going untill. candlemas day" (556).

74. Kate Mertes, *The English Noble Household, 1250–1600: Good Governance and Politic Rule* (New York: Basil Blackwell, 1988), 132; Bailey, *Flaunting*, 52.

75. There is another problem here; the gentleman is attended by "onely one man," underscoring the way in which large numbers of servants are giving way to fewer retainers and servants.

76. George Chapman, *Bussy D'Ambois: A Tragedie* (London, 1607), sig. B3v.

77. See Jones and Stallybrass, *Renaissance Clothing*, 242–44; and above in this chapter.

78. See Stephen Orgel, *Impersonations: The Performance of Gender in Shakespeare's England* (Cambridge, UK: Cambridge University Press, 1996), 67. For an important discussion of the significance of apprenticeship in the livery companies to the early modern theater, see David Kathman, "Grocers, Goldsmiths, and Drapers: Freemen and Apprentices in the Elizabethan Theater," *Shakespeare Quarterly* 55, no. 1 (2004): 1–49.

79. Steve Hindle discusses the use of certificates, passports, and badges as "technologies of identification to distinguish between the worthy settled poor and the unworthy unsettled idle" in "Technologies of Identification Under the Old Poor Law," 221. The "passporting" function of livery, badges, and other material markers, I suggest, would come to anticipate the constraints on the ability of poor or disenfranchised populations in the Atlantic world to exercise rights of mobility, including, eventually, the use of "freedom papers" to announce and nominally safeguard the free status of black travelers in eighteenth- and nineteenth-century America.

80. See Smith, "Othello's Black Handkerchief."

81. For a foundational reading of the economic implications of the Moorish woman, see Kim F. Hall, "Guess Who's Coming to Dinner? Colonization and Miscegenation in 'The Merchant of Venice,'" *Renaissance Drama* 23 (1992): 87–111.

82. Smith, "The Textile Black Body," 181. See also Patricia Akhimie's discussion of Morocco's "indelible" blackness in *Shakespeare and the Cultivation of Difference: Race and Conduct in the Early Modern World* (New York: Routledge, 2018), 1–5. For a discussion of Morocco in relation to networks of trade and slavery, see Gustav Ungerer, "Portia and the Prince of Morocco," *Shakespeare Studies* 31 (2003): 89–126.

83. Smith, "The Textile Black Body," 184.

Chapter 2

1. An account of this visit was published as *The Arrivall and Intertainements of the Embassador, Alkaid Jaurar Ben Abdella, with his Associate, Mr. Robert Blake. From the High and Mighty Prince, Mulley Mahamed Sheque, Emperor of Morocco, King of Fesse, and Suss. With . . . our Kings especiall grace and favour manifested in the happy Redemption of three hundred and two of his Majesties poore subjects, who had beene long in miserable slavery at Salley in Barbary* (London, 1637).

2. Ibid., 9.

3. Ibid., 12–13.

4. The red cloth of the blackamoors' clothing echoes the color of crown servants' livery. As Anthony Gerard Barthelemy notes, spectators may also have seen representations of black figures in the Lord Mayor's pageants of London, which were produced by the livery companies, in the late sixteenth and seventeenth centuries; see *Black Face, Maligned Race: The Representation of Blacks in English Drama from Shakespeare to Southerne* (Baton Rouge: Louisiana

State University Press, 1987). These characters "serve[d] as visible reminders of British success in trade and exploration" (47) and in the late seventeenth century also trafficked in the trope of the "happy slave" (52–59).

5. As Chapter 1 suggests, the redeemed captives' new clothing raises significant questions about the implications of the material mnemonic of their "former" master which they still wear on their bodies. I discuss the contingent nature of the manumitted slave at greater length in Chapter 5. Although some scholars distinguish between the status of "slaves" and "captives," particularly in light of the longer history of chattel slavery, my usage of both terms here reflects the conflation of these categories in *The Arrivall and Intertainements*: "they were the *Emperors Slaves or Captives*" (emphasis mine).

6. *The Arrivall and Intertainements of the Embassador*, 4–5 (italics in original; please see the Note on Transcription). For a discussion of the circulation of abducted boys in English and Ottoman contexts, and its racial and sexual implications, see Abdulhamit Arvas, "Leander in the Ottoman Mediterranean: The Homoerotics of Abduction in the Global Renaissance," *English Literary Renaissance* 51, no. 1 (2021): 31–62, as well as other work in progress by Arvas.

7. *The Arrivall and Intertainements of the Embassador*, 9.

8. I focus in particular on Terence due to this author's well-established and foundational place in the early stages of the grammar school curriculum. As T. W. Baldwin notes in his magisterial study of classical pedagogy, "Terence is . . . almost universally a lower school author." See Baldwin, *William Shakspere's Small Latine and Lesse Greeke* (Urbana: University of Illinois Press, 1944), 641. Not only, then, did Shakespeare almost certainly know Terence quite well; any former grammar schoolboy would have recognized references to the dramatist through whom he had learned his Latin, assumed codes of comportment, and practiced becoming a gentleman. And Terence's African heritage was also most likely rendered legible; as Misha Teramura has recently argued, early modern readers represented and registered Terence as black. See Teramura, "Black Comedy: Shakespeare, Terence, and *Titus Andronicus*," *English Literary History* 85, no. 4 (2018): 877–908.

9. *The Taming of the Shrew*, 1.1.158. All references follow *The Norton Shakespeare*, 3rd ed., gen. ed. Stephen Greenblatt (New York: W. W. Norton, 2016). Further references will be cited parenthetically within the text.

10. See *The Second Comedie Of Pvb. Terentivs, Called Evnvchvs, Or, The Eunuche, English and Latine . . . after the Method of Dr. Webbe* (London, 1629), 15–16. The Latin reads as follows: "Quid agas? Nisi [ut] te redimas captum, quam queas minimo: si nequeas paululo, at quanti queas."

11. Ibid., 16. The Latin reads: "Itane suades?"

12. *Servus* was thought to derive from *servāre*, to save. Adrian Pârvulescu notes that "Some late Roman sources interpreted *servus* as 'saved' from *servāre* 'to save' because the slaves were believed to be originally prisoners of war whose lives had been spared." See Pârvulescu, "Lat. *servus*," *Indogermanische Forschungen* 115 (2010): 190–97. As I discuss later in this chapter, the seventeenth-century theologian Thomas Jackson derives the same etymology in speaking of the *servus*.

13. I discuss representations of the freedman and his complicated, revocable freedom at greater length in Chapter 5.

14. John Véron, *A Dictionary in Latine and English, heretofore set foorth by Master Iohn Veron, and now newly corrected and enlarged, For the vtilitie and profite of all young students in*

the Latine tongue, as by further search therin they shall finde. By R.W. (London, 1575). A shorter version had earlier appeared in Robert Estienne's *Dictionariolum Puerorum* (1552).

15. Véron, *A Dictionary in Latine and English*, sig. ¶2r (italics original).

16. Ibid., sig. 2L8v.

17. Ibid., sig. 2P8r.

18. Joseph Webbe, *The First Comedy Of Pvb. Terentivs, Called Andria, Or, The Woman of Andros, English and Latine* (London, 1629), sig. A4v–B1r.

19. Indeed, in Terence's *Eunuchus*, the repeated emphasis on the younger son Chaerea's youth, which enables him to pass for a eunuch, also underscores his tragic inability to navigate the liberty he claims when he runs away from military service.

20. Paul Sullivan, "Playing the Lord: Tudor *Vulgaria* and the Rehearsal of Ambition," *English Literary History* 75, no. 1 (2008): 179–96. Sullivan suggests that "many *vulgaria* glamorize schoolroom punishment, and others ventriloquize devotion to learning Latin as a way to rise in the world. Many others, however, express delight in delinquency, triumph in play, and frustration with the constraints of rank and privilege" (182), also noting that "the strangest of the *vulgaria* lay bare the power of schoolroom violence to exact the worship of the oppressed on the one hand, and to stimulate dreams of armed resistance on the other" (187). Once "homegrown vulgars" were replaced with "dialogue culled directly from Terence" by John Anwykyll in the late fifteenth century and Nicholas Udall in the early sixteenth century, "schoolboys practiced the cheeky rhetoric of Terence's clever slaves, greedy parasites, randy old men, and scapegrace sons [and] the phrasebooks had the ironic effect of wielding the authority of classical Latin for potentially transgressive ends. Though most of the sentences from Terence provided phrases for ordinary daily communication, many took the boys beyond their own experience, social circumstances, and conventions of morality" (188).

21. *Manus* means "hand" (as well as "force"), and the ritual of *mancipatio*, which was "required for recognition of conveyance to 'title' of legal ownership to a thing" (in other words, to something in the category of *res mancipi*, discussed below), also derives its name from the sense of "taking in hand." Indeed, Adolf Berger notes that the act of grasping by the hand was one of the "decisive gestures" performed during *mancipatio*. (See the "Encyclopedic Dictionary of Roman Law," *Transactions of the American Philosophical Society* 43, no. 2 [1953], 573.) This emphasis on "taking in hand" was particularly important in light of the *mancipium*'s ties to agriculture. If the ritual of *mancipatio* enabled the transaction of property, it also underscored the way that slaves were the only *human* element of the category of *res mancipi*. *Res mancipi* comprised a class of physical property that included "land and any other forms of property associated with its cultivation, such as slaves, livestock, and servitudes," a "servitude" being a "[right] over another's property," such as "a right of way or the right to draw water," while "The ownership of *res mancipi* could only be transferred through a formal public act of conveyance." See Dennis Kehoe, "Dominium," in *The Encyclopedia of Ancient History*, eds. R. S. Bagnall et al. (2012). https://onlinelibrary-wiley-com.myaccess.library.utoronto.ca/doi/abs/10.1002/9781444338386.wbeah13087. The word *mancipium* denoted both the slave and the ritual of *mancipatio*. And the *mancipatio* not only involved the transfer of "things" (human or otherwise) and the ritual possession of an "object" by "taking it in hand," it also crucially comprised a financial transaction. I discuss the *mancipatio* further in Chapter 5, with regard to *The Tempest*'s Caliban.

22. See Michael Guasco, *Slaves and Englishmen: Human Bondage in the Early Modern Atlantic World* (Philadelphia: University of Pennsylvania Press, 2014), 33–36 and 244 n. 61. For a longer

discussion of More's *Utopia* in relation to the 1547 Vagrancy Act, see Matthew Ritger, "Reading *Utopia* in the Reformation of Punishment," *Renaissance Quarterly* 72, no. 4 (2019): 1225–68.

23. Although Sosia is "Simo's *Steward*," the slave Davus is described as a "*Servant to* Pamphilus; *a saucy, cunning, intriguing Fellow, always helping his Master out in his Amours, and putting Tricks upon* Simo" (italics in original). See *Terence's Comedies: Made English. With his Life; and some Remarks at the End. By Several Hands* (London, 1694; the translator Laurence Echard's name is omitted), sig. A12v. We note that here Davus is Pamphilus's servant, not Simo's, obscuring the fact that in the Latin original, Davus owes allegiance to Simo himself. In Thomas Newman's 1627 translation of *Andria*, conversely, Davus is a "Seruant of the family." See *The Two First Comedies Of Terence called Andria, and the Eunuch newly Englished by Thomas Newman* (London, 1627), sig, A8r.

24. *Oxford English Dictionary*, s.v. "slave, *n.1* (and *adj.*)," 1.a.

25. *Oxford English Dictionary*, s.v. "servant, *n.*," 1.

26. Randle Cotgrave defines the French "Servant" in his *Dictionarie Of The French And English Tongves* (London, 1611) as "Seruing, attending, waiting on, obseruing, obseruant, obsequious vnto; also, helping, steadding, auailing" whereas "Servage" is "Seruitude, slauerie, bondage, thralldome" (sig. 4D2r). The word "bondman," which Maurice Kyffin uses in his 1588 translation of *Andria* to describe the *libertus* Sosia's former condition, falls into the semantic category of slavery: Thomas Elyot's 1538 *Dictionary* entry for "Seruiliter" defines it as "lyke a bondman or slaue" (*The Dictionary of syr Thomas Eliot knyght* [London, 1538], sig. Z4r); while in 1569 Richard Grafton argues that "before the commyng of the sayde William [the Conqueror] there were no slaues or bondmen" (*A Chronicle at large and meere History of the affayres of Englande* [London, 1569], "This seconde Volume," 2). And as I have already noted, Véron's dictionary renders *servus* as a "bondman." But while "bondman" implied slavery, in the early modern period it was also being inflected by the more contractual sense of "bondsman."

27. Thomas Cooper, *Thesavrvs Lingvae Romanae & Britannicae* (London, 1565), sig. L5v; Cotgrave, *A Dictionarie Of The French And English Tongves*, sig. 3M1v; *Oxford English Dictionary*, s.v. "page, *n.1*," I.2.a.

28. Cotgrave, *A Dictionarie Of The French And English Tongves*, sig. 3M1v–3M2r.

29. Keith Bradley notes that although it might seem as though "no occupation in Roman society was closed to slaves," "the only exception . . . was military service, from which slaves were legally, and uniquely, barred." *Slavery and Society at Rome* (Cambridge, UK: Cambridge University Press, 1994), 65.

30. *Oxford English Dictionary*, s.v. "page, *n.1*," I.1.

31. See Lynn Enterline, "Schooling in the English Renaissance," *Oxford Handbooks Online* (2016, not paginated). As Enterline notes, drawing on Bourdieu's theory of *habitus* in a reading of imitation in the grammar school classroom, "sixteenth-century pedagogy forged an early, strong link between classical eloquence and the vocal and bodily social scripts that enabled a boy to find a place first in the grammar school environment and later, beyond its walls, among groups of similarly educated men." Enterline also underlines the theatrical and metatheatrical implications of the schoolroom, as school theatricals "offered excellent instruction in the rhetorical techniques of *actio*," and such training in *actio* itself revealed the performative nature of social and behavioral scripts. For an influential discussion of the ideological interventions of humanist pedagogy, see Richard Halpern, *The Poetics of Primitive Accumulation: English Renaissance Culture and the Genealogy of Capital* (Ithaca, NY: Cornell University Press, 1991). Other important treatments

of early modern humanist education include Rebecca W. Bushnell, *A Culture of Teaching: Early Modern Humanism in Theory and Practice* (Ithaca, NY: Cornell University Press, 1996) and Anthony Grafton and Lisa Jardine, *From Humanism to the Humanities: Education and the Liberal Arts in Fifteenth- and Sixteenth-Century Europe* (London: Duckworth, 1986).

32. Roger Ascham, *The Scholemaster: or plaine and perfite waye of teachyng children, to vnderstand, write, and speake, the Latin tong, but specially purposed for the priuate brynging vp of youth in Ientlemen and Noble mens houses* (London, 1570), sig. C4r (missigned C3r), sig. D2r. Ascham was not himself a schoolmaster but a tutor.

33. *A pretie and Mery new Enterlude: called the Disobedient Child. Compiled by Thomas Ingelend late Student in Cambridge* (London, 1570), sig. G4v. Further references will be cited parenthetically.

34. See Freyja Cox Jensen, Dana L. Key, and Emma Whipday, "*The Disobedient Child*: A Tudor Interlude in Performance," *Shakespeare* 16, no. 1 (2020): 60–67, esp. 64. The schoolmaster's discipline, according to Halpern, also "assumed and reinforced the sovereign authority of the monarch or magistrate," even as humanist learning "intervened" in early modern class formation (*The Poetics of Primitive Accumulation*, 25–26).

35. William Cartwright, *The Royall Slave. A Tragi-Comedy.* (Oxford, 1639). The title page notes that the play was "presented" on "August 30 1636." References will be cited parenthetically within the text. For a reading of the pre-Islamic Persian contexts of the play, see Chloë Houston, "Persia and Kingship in William Cartwright's *The Royall Slave* (1636)," *Studies in English Literature, 1500–1900* 54, no. 2 (2014): 455–73. Nedda Mehdizadeh's work in progress, meanwhile, significantly deepens our understanding of the importance of early modern Persia to contemporary English literary and cultural production.

36. See Houston, "Persia and Kingship," 460.

37. As Lynn Enterline has demonstrated, schoolroom beatings situated teachers as quasi-parental and yet quasi-erotic figures. For a rich discussion of the networks of pedagogy, affect, and discipline in early modern schoolrooms, see Enterline, *Shakespeare's Schoolroom: Rhetoric, Discipline, Emotion* (Philadelphia: University of Pennsylvania Press, 2012).

38. See Noémie Ndiaye, "Aaron's Roots: Spaniards, Englishmen, and Blackamoors in *Titus Andronicus*," *Early Theatre* 19, no. 2 (2016): 59–80; Gustav Ungerer, *The Mediterranean Apprenticeship of British Slavery* (Madrid: Editorial Verbum, 2008); and Emily Weissbourd, "'Those in Their Possession': Race, Slavery, and Queen Elizabeth's 'Edicts of Expulsion,'" *Huntington Library Quarterly* 78, no. 1 (2015): 1–19.

39. We note that the "ignobility" of enslaving others necessitates the creation of alternative narratives of conquest. "Friend" is a particularly telling descriptor here since it denotes not only affective intimacy but also, as Henry Cockeram's *English Dictionarie* (London, 1623) suggests, the sense of a "benefactor" (sig. B8v). Cratander may not be a patron, but he certainly inhabits the role of "one that doth one good" in providing useful cover for Persia's complete political access to Ephesus.

40. Enterline, *Shakespeare's Schoolroom*, 144.

41. *An Exact Collection Of The Works Of Doctor Iackson, P. of C. C. C. Oxon, Such as were not Published before* (London, 1654), 3042.

42. Ibid. As I have noted, *puer* signified both a "childe" and a "seruant." I will return to the problem of the "heire," another kind of legal fiction, in Chapter 4.

43. Webbe, *The First Comedy of Pvb. Terentivs, Called Andria*, sig. B1r.

44. I discuss definitions of the "family" in early modern England, which included servants as well as children, at greater length later in this chapter. For a discussion of the ways in which enslaved people were analogized to children in later American contexts, see Holly Brewer, *By Birth or Consent: Children, Law, and the Anglo-American Revolution in Authority* (Chapel Hill: University of North Carolina Press, 2005), 355–59. Brewer discusses the capacity for children's consent to labor contracts on pp. 242–45, arguing that "it was rank, and rank alone, that determined whether one could be forced to sign a labor contract" (243).

45. *An Exact Collection Of The Works Of Doctor Iackson*, 3043.

46. See my discussion of the relationship between livery and liberty in Chapter 1. Jackson also understands the "hired servant" as a *famulus* rather than a *servus*, while "meer servants" seem to encompass *mancipia* as well as *servi*: "*Meer Servants* (or *servants absolutely* or in whole) were such as the Latines called *Mancipia*, such as we call in English *Slaves* or *Bondmen*. . . . Unto this state or Condition of life, that is, of being a *Slave* or *Bondman*, no man is bound or subject by *Nature*; No Man will willingly or voluntarily subject himself. Such as heretofore have been, and in divers Countries yet are, Servants in this sense, were made such by others from a pretended right or Title of Conquest, and were called *Mancipia, quasi manu Capti*, because they had been taken in War, and might by rigour of Justice, at least by rigour of *Hostile Law*, be put to Death, as men convicted of Rebellion by taking Armes. Now the price of their Redemption from death, was losse of *Civil Liberty* as well for themselves as their posterity. These were truly and properly called *Servi*, according to the native *Etymologie* of this name in Latin, *Servi quasi Servati*; They were again wholly and meerly *Servants*, according to the utmost extent of the Nature, and of the Real Conditions or properties of Civil *Servitude*: that is, Their Lords or *Masters* had an *absolute Right* or Interest not only in their *Bodily Actions* or Imployments, but over their very *Persons*, their Bodies, their Children, and whasoever by any Title did belong unto them. The Interest, Power or Dominion which Masters by the Civil Law or Law of Nations, had over their *Servi* or *Mancipia*, their *Slaves* or *Bondmen*, was altogether such, and as absolute, as a *Free-holder* hath over his own Inheritance or *Fee simple*; that is, a power or Right not only to reap or take the Annual Fruits or Commodities of it, but full Right to *Let* or *Sett* for *Term* of years, or to alienate or sell the Propertie: For so were *Bondmen* and their Children bought and sold, as Lands and Goods or Cattle are with us." Ibid., 3043.

47. Ibid., 3044, 3043.

48. Michael Witmore notes that "in some instances, masters of children's companies had the power to impress boys from grammar schools whom they thought apt performers," while Matthew Kendrick draws our attention to the "controversy" surrounding the "Merchant Taylors' school when several boys were kidnapped and impressed into service with the Children of the Revels." See Michael Witmore, *Pretty Creatures: Children and Fiction in the English Renaissance* (Ithaca, NY: Cornell University Press, 2007), 98–99; and Matthew Kendrick, *At Work in the Early Modern English Theatre: Valuing Labor* (Madison, NJ: Fairleigh Dickinson University Press, 2015), 80. For a discussion of the notorious case of Thomas Clifton, who was kidnapped and forced to appear on stage, see Bart van Es, *Shakespeare in Company* (Oxford: Oxford University Press, 2013), 256–57. We note also that in the Vagrancy Act of 1547, children could be taken "from any suche begger beinge the mother therof, nourisher or keper, whether they bee willing or not," as could a child who was "without any suche norice, mother or keper by himselfe wanderinge." Although anyone "claiming" such a child in this way must "promisse to bring the same childe up in some honest labor or occupatio[n] til he or she come to the age of xx. yeares the woman childe, or xxiiii the man childe," the child in question must undergo "what labour, occupation, or seruice

soeuer the sayd Master shal appoynt him, or her, during the sayde time." The punishment for not doing so is severe: should the child "runne away at any time, once, or motimes ... then it shalbe lawful for euerie suche Maister, to take the saide childe again, and to kepe and punish the said childe, *in cheynes or otherwise, and vse him or her as hys slaue* in all pointes, for the time before rehearsed, of the age of such childe, that is to say, till xx. the woman childe, and the man childe xxiiii." (*Anno primo Edwardi Sexti Statvtes made in the Parliament* [London, 1548]; sig. A6v–B1r, emphasis added). The children taken in as "seruauntes or apprentices," in other words, must submit to their labor, or potentially be taken into slavery in "cheynes."

49. *A Diamonde most Precious, worthy to be marked: Instructing all Maysters and Seruauntes, how they ought to leade their lyues* ... (London, 1577). STC 10929, Folger Shakespeare Library.

50. Ibid., 47 [sig. F4r].

51. Ibid., 48 [sig. F4v]. Chapter 5 will discuss in more detail the ways in which manumission is frequently contingent on "free service."

52. Chapter 4 turns to indentured servants to discuss in greater detail the problematization of consent in the indenture contract.

53. See Steve Hindle, *On the Parish?: The Micro-Politics of Poor Relief in Rural England c. 1550–1750* (Oxford: Oxford University Press, 2004), 192 (italics in original). For a longer discussion of pauper apprenticeship, see *On The Parish?*, 191–223.

54. Hindle notes, too, that "the advantages of apprenticing children 'timely,' when they were pedagogically malleable, were frequently stressed. [The 1601 text] *An Ease for Overseers* urged that poor children, like 'a twigge that will best bende when it is greene,' were 'fittest to be bound when they are young.'" This in turn meant that "judges repeatedly emphasized that children might be apprenticed from the age of 7." See *On the Parish?*, 213–14.

55. See Chapter 4 for a longer discussion of lacunae in indenture contracts.

56. Colin Burrow, *Shakespeare and Classical Antiquity* (Oxford: Oxford University Press, 2013), 139. Burrow underscores "the structural and foundational role of Terence within early-modern educational and theatrical practice" (142). See also Martine van Elk, "'Thou shalt present me as an eunuch to him': Terence in Early Modern England," in *A Companion to Terence*, ed. Anthony Augoustakis and Ariana Traill (Malden, MA: Wiley-Blackwell, 2013), 410–28, for a useful discussion of the place of Terence in early modern England.

57. The class makeup of the grammar schoolroom was not uniformly elite, and indeed could be quite varied, as Ursula Potter has demonstrated in "Performing Arts in the Tudor Classroom," in *Tudor Drama Before Shakespeare, 1485–1590: New Directions for Research, Criticism, and Pedagogy*, ed. Lloyd Kermode, Jason Scott-Warren, and Martine van Elk (New York: Palgrave Macmillan, 2004), 143–65, esp. 145. Potter's essay usefully explores the place of performative and dramatic techniques in the early modern classroom.

58. Although some critics have argued that England did not become fully involved in the slave trade until the mid-seventeenth century, the enslaver John Hawkins had undertaken slave voyages as early as the 1560s, and there is evidence both of English slaving practices and of enslaved Africans being brought to England before that time. Peter Fryer's *Staying Power: The History of Black People in Britain* (London: Pluto Press, 2010), first published in 1984, provides a key account (see esp. 4–12), and in a vital discussion of early English involvement in slavery, Kim F. Hall notes that "African voyages were truly the nursery to English seamen" (see *Things of Darkness : Economies of Race and Gender in Early Modern England* [Ithaca, NY: Cornell University Press, 1995], 19–22, at 19). Meanwhile, other European countries such as Portugal were, of course, participating fully in the slave economy at this time, and as scholars such as Imtiaz Habib,

Gustav Ungerer, and Emily Weissbourd have suggested, English merchants may have been engaging with them in forms of chattel slavery. See Habib, *Black Lives in the English Archives, 1500-1677: Imprints of the Invisible* (Aldershot, UK: Ashgate, 2008); Ungerer, *The Mediterranean Apprenticeship of British Slavery*; and Weissbourd, "'Those in Their Possession.'" For an important discussion of Hawkins's travel narratives, see Matthieu Chapman, *Anti-Black Racism in Early Modern English Drama: The Other "Other"* (New York: Routledge, 2017), Chapter 4; as well as Sujata Iyengar, *Shades of Difference: Mythologies of Skin Color in Early Modern England* (Philadelphia: University of Pennsylvania Press, 2005), chapter 8.

59. Virginia Mason Vaughan notes that while slave markets are depicted in sixteenth- and seventeenth-century plays, the slaves bought and sold are principally Europeans and Turks, and suggests that blackness did not come to be associated specifically with slavery until the 1670s. See Vaughan, *Performing Blackness on English Stages, 1500-1800* (Cambridge, UK: Cambridge University Press, 2005), 141. However, there were certainly black servants in early modern England, and, as I shall argue, Latin dictionaries and cribs both cemented and contested the association between complexion and captivity. Imtiaz Habib's *Black Lives in the English Archives*, provides a longer, and vital, discussion of the archives of black servants in England. Emily Weissbourd, meanwhile, has persuasively read *Othello* in terms of the networks of Iberian slavery; see "'I Have Done the State Some Service': Reading Slavery in *Othello* through *Juan Latino*," *Comparative Drama* 47, no. 4 (2013): 529-51. See also Camille Wells Slights, "Slaves and Subjects in *Othello*," *Shakespeare Quarterly* 48, no. 4 (1997: 377-90) for an earlier discussion of slavery in *Othello*. Ambereen Dadabhoy discusses technologies of race, migration, and enslavement in "Barbarian Moors: Documenting Racial Formation in Early Modern England," in *The Cambridge Companion to Shakespeare and Race*, ed. Ayanna Thompson (Cambridge, UK: Cambridge University Press, 2021), 30-46. References to *Othello* follow *The Norton Shakespeare*, 3rd ed., and are cited parenthetically in the text.

60. See Daniel J. Vitkus, ed., *Piracy, Slavery, and Redemption: Barbary Captivity Narratives from Early Modern England* (New York: Columbia University Press, 2001).

61. If some narratives of early modern English slavery seem to challenge critical associations between race and slavery, so too do accounts of classical slaves, who, Emily Wilson argues, were marked by their foreignness ("Ave Jeeves!," *London Review of Books* 30, no. 4 [2008]: 2). And like early modern captives, they often became enslaved by being captured by pirates, as well as in war. Anne Duncan also notes that while not all classical actors were slaves, during the Republic most actors were foreigners, from either Greece or other eastern lands as well as Italy. See Duncan's *Performance and Identity in the Classical World* (Cambridge, UK: Cambridge University Press, 2006), 162-63.

62. See Hall, *Things of Darkness*, 18-19 on the associations forged between "aristocratic white bodies, black servitude, and foreign wealth" by portraits and other depictions of "black people with badges of slavery." I suggest that these "badges of slavery," as in Hawkins's coat of arms, also secure entry for white, English people to a kind of newfound and specifically English status.

63. MS X.d.566, Folger Shakespeare Library.

64. Ibid.

65. We note that here, as in *The Arrivall and Intertainements of the Embassador* (1637), captivity and slavery are interchangeable terms.

66. MS Rawlinson Letters 59, fol. 408, Bodleian Library, Oxford.

67. Sir Thomas Overbury, *A True and Perfect Account of the Examination, Confession, Tryal, Condemnation, and Execution of Joan Perry, and her two Sons, John & Richard Perry, For*

the Supposed Murder of William Harrison, Gent. Being One of the most Remarkable Occurrences which hath happened in the memory of Man . . . Likewise Mr. Harrison's own Account, how he was Conveyed into Turkey, and there made a Slave for above two years; and then his Master which Bought him there, Dying, how he made his Escape, and what hardship he endured, who at last (through the Providence of God) returned to England, while he was supposed to be Murder'd; here having been his Man-Servant Arraigned (who falsly Impeached his own Mother and Brother as Guilty of the Murder of his Master) they were all three Arraign'd, Convicted, and Executed on Broad-way-Hills in Glocester-shier (London, 1676). I include the full title of this account to underscore the ways in which Harrison's slave narrative is knitted into discourses of familial disorder on the one hand (significant precisely because the household is an uncertain affective and relational structure, as I discuss more fully in Chapter 3) and to structures of household service and stewardship on the other. For a discussion of "legal 'truth'" in this text, see Judith Hudson, "Seventeenth-Century Legal Fictions: The Case of John Perry," *The Seventeenth Century* 32, no. 3 (2017): 297–320.

68. Overbury, *A True and Perfect Account*, 5.
69. Ibid., 12.
70. Ibid., 17.
71. Ibid., 18.
72. For a longer discussion of the trope of, and tensions within, "turning Turk," see Daniel Vitkus, *Turning Turk: English Theater and the Multicultural Mediterranean, 1570–1630* (New York: Palgrave Macmillan, 2003). Harrison, conversely, is untouched by the real and religious threat of the stabbing "Steletto," which also threatens castration and conversion.
73. Overbury, *A True and Perfect Account*, 20.
74. Ibid., 22.
75. Even Harrison's labor during his captivity varies. "Employed" to keep his master's "Still house," he must on occasion also "gather Cotton-Wool," moving uneasily between trades and occupations; manual labor and oversight; bondage and "employment."
76. *An Exact Collection Of The Works Of Doctor Iackson*, 3041–42. The phrase *"whosoever committeth Sin is the servant of Sin"* is underlined by hand in the Folger Library's copy of this text. See J89 (folio), Folger Shakespeare Library.
77. *The booke of the common prayer* (London, 1549), sig. A4r.
78. This was not just a formal component of captivity narratives. Michael Guasco suggests that it was also "the accidental, or criminal, nature of English enslavement [that] buttressed the conventional wisdom that Englishmen were, in a pure state of nature, free"; Englishmen were, in these accounts, frequently stolen into slavery through no fault of their own. See Guasco, *Slaves and Englishmen*, 128.
79. MS Rawlinson Letters 100, fol. 397, Bodleian Library, Oxford.
80. Amanda Bailey discusses the debt bond and its relationship to corporeal seizure more fully in *Of Bondage: Debt, Property, and Personhood in Early Modern England* (Philadelphia: University of Pennsylvania Press, 2013).
81. See this chapter's discussion of pauper indentures; I will discuss more fully the potential for corporeal vulnerability in relation to the use of indentures in Chapter 4.
82. Stowe MS 176, fol. 138, British Library, London.
83. Webbe, *The Second Comedie Of Pvb. Terentivs, Called Evnvchvs*, sig. C4r. Further references will be cited parenthetically within the text.

84. The fact that Pamphila never speaks during the play means that in later, eighteenth century translations, Pamphila's name is often included in the list of characters under the rubric "mute characters." But if Pamphila is omitted in the early modern period due to her lack of speech, this could suggest that these translations saw themselves not only as faithful, formal school texts but also as adaptive playtexts (in which a play is understood as performance as well as ludic subversion). Even in the *Dramatis Personae* of "The Fair *Andrian*" (1694), however, which includes the category of "Mutes," the Ethiopian maid for her part does not appear, not even as a "mute." See *Terence's Comedies* (London, 1694), sig. A12v.

85. See the early modern translator Thomas Newman's version of the same moment: "Procure her me by force stelth, or intreatie; / I weigh not which way, so I may enioy her." Chaerea earlier argues that "this wench is nothing like our *Citie* Mammals." See Newman, *The Two First Comedies Of Terence called Andria, and the Eunuch*, 72, 71 (emphasis mine). The fact that, as the title page affirms, this translation is "*Fitted for scholler Priuate acction in their schooles*" underscores the reception of this text, and its depiction of slavery and difference, by schoolchildren.

86. Ibid., 63.

87. *Pericles*, 5.0.3. *The Norton Shakespeare*, 3rd ed.

88. *Three Turk Plays from Early Modern England: Selimus, Emperor of the Turks; A Christian Turned Turk; and The Renegado*, ed. Daniel J. Vitkus (New York: Columbia University Press, 2000). As Vitkus notes, the sources for Massinger's play range from Cervantes's *Don Quixote* to early modern travel narratives and accounts of Islamic culture; critics have discussed *The Renegado* principally as a "Turk play." See the Introduction to *Three Turk Plays*, 40–41. But the echoes of Terence's *Eunuchus* are unmistakable: the captured noblewoman Paulina recalls the beautiful slave Pamphila, and the frequent verbal play on circumcision and castration not only evinces English curiosity about (and fear of) the rites of conversion and the physical markers of "turning Turk"; it also evokes the central disguise plot of *Eunuchus* and—aptly, in terms of enacting the play—the problem of *performing* the eunuch. The eunuch's proximity—and hence potential sexual access—to his female cohabitants is parodied in *Eunuchus*. The danger of sexual contact between the eunuch and his "bedfellow" is violently realized by Chaerea, who grotesquely perverts both the form and the function of a eunuch: he is not castrated, and far from being a protector, he is a violator. It is precisely his sexual access, however, that Gazet longs for in *The Renegado*. Although Eastern eunuchs are sexualized objects of curiosity to English readers, as *The Renegado* attests, the rampant sexuality attributed to the eunuch has much deeper theatrical roots in Terence's enormously popular, and troubling, play, especially in the figure of Chaerea. Anston Bosman explores the affordances between the figure of the eunuch and the "blackamoor" in Terence's *Eunuchus* and early modern plays including *The Renegado* in "'Best Play with Mardian': Eunuch and Blackamoor as Imperial Culturegram," *Shakespeare Studies* 34 (2006): 123–57.

89. Véron, *A Dictionary in Latine and English*, sig. 2E2r.

90. We note that in Véron's lexicon, the catalogue of terms for blackness is bookended by *nihil*, a strikingly dour note, if also an unintentional one.

91. Véron, *A Dictionary in Latine and English*, sig. G1r.

92. Cooper, *Thesavrvs Lingvae Romanae & Brittanicae*, sig. F6r.

93. John Conybeare, *Miscellany of John Conybeare* (ca. 1575–1595), fol. 14r. V.a.467, Folger Shakespeare Library.

94. Ibid., fol. 21v.

95. Stephen Orgel, *Impersonations: The Performance of Gender in Shakespeare's England* (Cambridge, UK: Cambridge University Press, 1996), 1.

96. In John Florio's *Qveen Anna's New World of Words* (London, 1611), "Ethiópa" is rendered as "an Ethiopian, a Black-more" (sig. P4r), while by the 1668 publication of John Wilkins's *An Essay Towards a Real Character And a Philosophical Language* (London, 1668), "Ethiopian" is defined as "[adj. Black (person.]" (sig. 3F2r).

97. Newman, *The Two First Comedies Of Terence called Andria, and the Eunuch*, 62. The Latin follows Webbe, *The Second Comedie Of Pvb. Terentivs, Called Evnvchvs*, sig. E1v.

98. The word "minas" reflects the Greek provenance and setting of the play.

99. Newman, *The Two First Comedies Of Terence*, 79.

100. See Vaughan, *Performing Blackness on English Stages*, 75–76, as well as Emily C. Bartels, "Too Many Blackamoors: Deportation, Discrimination, and Elizabeth I," *Studies in English Literature, 1500–1900* 46, no. 2 (2006): 305–22.

101. Susan E. Phillips, "Schoolmasters, Seduction, and Slavery: Polyglot Dictionaries in Pre-Modern England," in *Medievalia et Humanistica: Studies in Medieval and Renaissance Culture*, n.s. 34, ed. Paul Maurice Clogan (Lanham: Rowman and Littlefield, 2008), 129–58.

102. For further discussion and different readings of these "expulsion edicts," see Miranda Kaufmann, "Caspar Van Senden, Sir Thomas Sherley and the 'Blackamoor' Project," *Historical Research* 81, no. 212 (2008): 366–71; and Weissbourd, "'Those in Their Possession.'" Weissbourd persuasively argues that these so-called expulsion edicts may actually signal early English attempts to traffic, like Spain, in the bodies of its black denizens.

103. I propose that we might also view *ethiopissa* in terms of the unnamed and enslaved Venus in the archives and afterlives of Atlantic slavery; see Saidiya Hartman's "Venus in Two Acts," *Small Axe* 12, no. 2 (2008): 1–14. Hartman's essay pushes against the limits of the archive to render its absences legible, particularly in the case of enslaved black women. But Hartman also notes the imbrication of slavery and Latinity (and, implicitly, the early modern pedagogy and learning of Latin—and slavery *through* Latin—that this chapter discusses) when she notes that "The Jamaican overseer Thomas Thistlewood *recorded in Latin* his sexual exploits with enslaved women" (1 n.1; emphasis mine). Jennifer L. Morgan, meanwhile, observes that the Latin phrase "partus sequitur ventrem" that was inserted into the text of the 1662 Virginia code regulating the hereditability of slavery "served to connect English slave law to Roman antecedents," and explores its implications; see "*Partus sequitur ventrem*: Law, Race, and Reproduction in Colonial Slavery," *Small Axe* 22, no. 1 (2018): 1–17, at 4. Here, again, Latinity underwrites slavery.

104. *Terenti[us] cu[m] directorio vocabuloru[m] sententiaru[m] artis comice glosa i[n]terlineali come[n]tarijs Donato Guidone Ascensio* (Strasbourg, 1496), fol. 39v. RB 31147, The Huntington Library, San Marino, California. All the characters are in early modern dress in the woodcuts.

105. *Terenti[us] cum directorio vocabuloru[m], sententiaru[m] artis comice, glosa i[n]terlineali, come[n]tarijs Donato, Gvidone Ascensio* (Strasbourg, 1496), fol. 28v. Folio Inc. 473, Newberry Library, Chicago.

106. *Terenti[us] cu[m] directorio vocabuloru[m] sententiaru[m] artis comice glosa i[n]terlineali come[n]tarijs Donato Guidone Ascensio* (Strasbourg, 1496), fol. 28v. RB 31147, The Huntington Library, San Marino, California.

107. As Arthur L. Little, Jr. notes in a vital essay on "the relationship of whites to the unmarked property of whiteness," in texts such as William Harrison's "Of the General Constitution of the Bodies of the Britons" (1577), which asserted that "As for slaves and bondmen

we have none," English writers receive from Roman sources "a classically derived and historically fixed whiteness deeply embedded in human freedom" to secure a fundamental association between whiteness and freedom. See Little, "Re-Historicizing Race, White Melancholia, and the Shakespearean Property," *Shakespeare Quarterly* 67, no. 1 (2016): 84–103, esp. 92, 102–03. See also Chapter 3 of Ian Smith's *Race and Rhetoric in the Renaissance: Barbarian Errors* (New York: Palgrave Macmillan, 2009) for an important reading of the reception of classical "Ethiopians" in light of their "origins of whiteness" (55); Smith's book advances an essential account of language as a crucial technology of race-making and of "Humanism's role in the discursive history of race" (71).

108. Elyot, *The Dictionary of syr Thomas Eliot knyght*, sig. N1r.

109. Thomas Thomas, *Dictionarivm Lingvae Latinae Et Anglicanae* (Cambridge, 1587), sig. 2M3v.

110. Ibid., sig. 3H5v.

111. Elyot, *The Dictionary of syr Thomas Eliot knyght*, sig. H3r; Charles Hoole, *An easie Entrance To The Latine Tongue* (London, 1649), sig. S4r. In Thomas's *Dictionarivm Lingvae Latinae Et Anglicanae*, "famulus" is glossed as "a manseruant, a household seruant" (sig. Z2v).

112. *Oxford English Dictionary*, s.v. "family, *n.*," A.I.1.a; 2.b.

113. Ellesmere MS 2515, *The Comons . . . Complaine of the Multitude of straungers that are setled amongst vs*, Huntington Library, San Marino, CA.

114. Bartels, "Too Many Blackamoors," 307–8. Bartels suggests that Elizabeth's second letter is "written with an eye to English 'masters' who would rather hold 'Negroes' as servants than employ the English (presumably at a cost or greater cost) in their stead" (314).

115. Habib, *Black Lives in the English Archives*, 49.

116. London Metropolitan Archives Digital Collection (formerly Guildhall Library Manuscripts Section). See St Botolph Aldgate: 27 August 1587, GL MS 9221/2; 8 August 1593, GL MS 9222/1; October 1593, GL MS 9223/2 in the Appendix to Habib's *Black Lives in the English Archives*.

117. Habib, *Black Lives in the English Archives*, 107.

118. Ibid., 144.

119. *Othello*, ed. Michael Neill (Oxford: Oxford University Press, 2006), 357 n. 24.

120. Emily C. Bartels suggests that "Desdemona . . . claims . . . the Moor . . . as a part of her own heritage and identity. . . . To comprehend [the] crisis [of her 'strangely deteriorating marriage'], she remembers that her 'mother had a maid called Barbary' . . . Desdemona takes on Barbary's voice and story as her own . . . Barbary's identity as lover overshadows her cultural or racial features to the point that her unspecified identity, as or as not Moorish, matters less to Desdemona than the maid's resemblance to herself . . . Desdemona's history, thus, takes the idea of cultural exchange to another level, pressing it beyond the bounds of character, geography, and history, raising the possibility that before there was in Venice a Moor, there was a maid called Barbary, 'the name of the Moor' written indelibly and indistinguishably onto the body of Venice." *Speaking of the Moor: From "Alcazar" to "Othello"* (Philadelphia: University of Pennsylvania Press, 2008), 188–89.

Chapter 3

1. Miranda Kaufmann, "Blanke, John (fl. 1507–1512), royal trumpeter," *Oxford Dictionary of National Biography*, 25 Sept. 2014; accessed 1 May 2021. https://www.oxforddnb.com/view/10.1093/ref:odnb/9780198614128.001.0001/odnb-9780198614128-e-107145. Scholars have

surmised that John Blanke may have arrived in England with Catherine of Aragon. For a longer discussion of John Blanke, see Imtiaz Habib, *Black Lives in the English Archives, 1500–1677: Imprints of the Invisible* (Aldershot, UK: Ashgate, 2008), 39–49, which also situates Blanke within a larger nexus of black denizens in early modern England; and Miranda Kaufmann, "John Blanke, the Trumpeter," chapter 1 in *Black Tudors: The Untold Story* (London: Oneworld, 2017), 7–31.

2. We might also read Blanke's cap as a turban, an item which carries particular valences in this context. Since the turban in early modern England is closely associated with Islam, Turks, and Persians, Blanke's "turban" might invoke an early modern association between blackness and otherness, Turk and blackamoor.

3. This is one of two instances in which Blanke is represented in the Westminster Tournament Roll. See also Kaufmann, "John Blanke," *Oxford Dictionary of National Biography*.

4. MS Wood F. 43, fols. 154–58, Bodleian Library, Oxford.

5. I discuss the status of slavery in early modern England at greater length in the Introduction. For a very brief overview of the English legal context, see Miranda Kaufmann, "English Common Law, Slavery and," in *Encyclopedia of Blacks in European History and Culture*, ed. Eric Martone, vol. 1 (Westport, CT: Greenwood Press, 2008), 200–203; as well as Michael Guasco, *Slaves and Englishmen: Human Bondage in the Early Modern Atlantic World* (Philadelphia: University of Pennsylvania Press, 2014), 11–40. For a discussion of the early modern archives of English slavery and their contingencies, see Habib, *Black Lives in the English Archives*, esp. 54–57.

6. Patricia Parker, "Black *Hamlet*: Battening on the Moor," *Shakespeare Studies* 31 (2003), 144.

7. Geffrey Whitney, *A Choice of Emblemes, and Other Devises* (Leiden, 1586), 57.

8. Parker, "Black *Hamlet*," 145.

9. See Kim F. Hall, "Reading What Isn't There: 'Black' Studies in Early Modern England," *Stanford Humanities Review* 3, no. 1 (1993): 23–33.

10. This question has been taken up vigorously by several scholars of early modern race; however, the historical work of recovering the archival traces of early modern black people has in recent years been undertaken most fulsomely by Imtiaz Habib in *Black Lives in the English Archives*.

11. Ibid., 12. Habib addresses his usage of "black" to refer to "non-white, non-English" at the very beginning of his study, "in conformity with the endemically loose way an early modern English cultural consciousness sees them" (1 n. 1).

12. MS EL 2514, Huntington Library, San Marino, California. See Figure 8.

13. "Inmates," meanwhile, alludes to "Maried men," "men not maried, wherof some are Jorneymen" and "widowes and maidens which doe lodge in other mens houses."

14. Z/PROJECT/BAL/C/P69/BEN1/A/010/MS04098/1, Z/PROJECT/BAL/C/P69/KAT1/A/002/MS17833, and P69/KAT1/A/012/MS17837A. "Switching the Lens: Rediscovering Londoners of African, Caribbean, Asian and Indigenous Heritage 1561–1840," London Metropolitan Archives Data Collections. https://search.lma.gov.uk/scripts/mwimain.dll?logon&application=UNION_VIEW&language=144&file=[lma]through-the-lens.html.

15. See also my discussion of the role of property in the practice of *mancipatio* in relation to *The Tempest* (Chapter 5).

16. See, for instance, Emily C. Bartels's *Speaking of the Moor: From "Alcazar" to "Othello"* (Philadelphia: University of Pennsylvania Press, 2008) and Jean E. Feerick's *Strangers in Blood: Relocating Race in the Renaissance* (Toronto: University of Toronto Press, 2010). Bartels suggests that, rather than writing "against" the "other," current critical scholarship might benefit from

"review and revision" of the "limited axes of difference" in "speaking of the Moor" (10). Feerick, meanwhile, underscores the importance of lineage and blood to conceptions of race, illuminating the ways in which differences and contiguities (of blood, of rank, and of provenance) become harder to sustain as discourses of colonial degeneration take hold. An important recent critical study of proximity in early modern race studies is Marjorie Rubright's *Doppelgänger Dilemmas: Anglo-Dutch Relations in Early Modern English Literature and Culture* (Philadelphia: University of Pennsylvania Press, 2014), although Rubright's focus is the early modern Dutch community in England. On race, "sameness," service, and kinship, see also my essay "'More Than Kin, Less Than Kind': Similitude, Strangeness, and Early Modern English Homonationalisms," *Shakespeare Quarterly* 67, no. 1 (2016): 14–29.

17. Bartels argues that "the impulse behind [the introduction of Moors on the English stage] was . . . the desire to come to terms with a more reaching and emergent globalization," although she reads that against specifically imperial or colonial desire, suggesting instead that it represented a "[need] to figure out the politics and parameters of a new globally oriented environment" (*Speaking of the Moor*, 17). Rubright's work, meanwhile, addresses the relative lack of critical attention to "how correspondences and likenesses between the English and their near neighbors might also have threatened, disrupted, ruptured, or coalesced ideas of Englishness" (*Doppelgänger Dilemmas*, 22). In illuminating the visual and linguistic approximations between the English and the Dutch, Rubright demonstrates how racial formation could be predicated not on seeming distinction but on apparent similitude.

18. Kim F. Hall, *Things of Darkness: Economies of Race and Gender in Early Modern England* (Ithaca, NY: Cornell University Press, 1995), esp. 4–6.

19. "The Blackamore wench to the boy," Sloane MS 1792, fol. 115v, British Library, London. Kim F. Hall argues that "though they propose the overcoming of difference through the joining of black and white, these poems posit that joining as the loss of white identity and ultimately affirm the black/white binary." See *Things of Darkness*, 118. In his brief discussion of these paired poems, Ian Frederick Moulton notes the textual variants in manuscript transmission: "In at least one manuscript from the 1630s, the genders of the speakers in this pair of poems are reversed." See "The Manuscript Circulation of Erotic Poetry in Early Modern England," in *The Cambridge Companion to Erotic Literature*, ed. Bradford K. Mudge (Cambridge, UK: Cambridge University Press, 2017), 72. The title of the poem in Sloane MS 1792 ("The Blackamore wench to the boy") alters "maid" to "wench," thereby echoing the "blackamore wench" of Newman's translation of Terence which I discuss in Chapter 2 and inserting the suggestion of servitude that attaches to "wench." In so doing, it also prefigures the centrality of slavery to the white body writ large: the body politic, the family, and, as here, the corporeal body.

20. The substitution of "shades" for "shadowes" in line 4 seems significant in this regard. The author distinguishes the natural "shades" of night from the "shadowes" which the "faire boy" will himself cast later in the poem, reinforcing the depiction of the darkness as incorporate within the white body.

21. In closing one's eyes, one also views the world as dark. Thus the "blackamore wench" casts her complexion as an effect of nature, extending the metaphorical comparison to night to the whole world.

22. "A Riddle upon Coals" (Add MS 78762, fols. 10v–11r, British Library, London) begins with the line, "A negro I tho' sprung from Northern Climes," drawing on the paradox of darkness emerging from fair "Northern Climes."

23. "Reply," Sloane MS 1792, fol. 116r, British Library, London.

24. I think here of Dympna Callaghan's influential argument regarding early modern racial impersonation that "Blackness, whether actual or cosmetic, was defined by an anterior whiteness ... as an overlay of whiteness" and consequently that "Miscegenation ... consists precisely of 'black over white,' ... and has its parallel in the techniques of Renaissance theatricality." See *Shakespeare Without Women: Representing Gender and Race on the Renaissance Stage* (Abingdon, UK: Routledge, 2000), 79, 86.

25. This seems to illustrate precisely some of the contradictions of the heir that Luke Wilson discusses in "*Macbeth* and the Contingency of Future Persons," *Shakespeare Studies* 40 (2012): 53–62. See also Chapter 4.

26. See Kim F. Hall, "'These Bastard Signs of Fair': Literary Whiteness in Shakespeare's Sonnets," in *Post-Colonial Shakespeares*, ed. Ania Loomba and Martin Orkin (New York: Routledge, 1998), 64–83. I follow Cheryl I. Harris's foundational argument about the property rights which accrue to whiteness in "Whiteness as Property," *Harvard Law Review* 106, no. 8 (1993): 1707–91.

27. Chapter 4 discusses in greater detail the politics of natality and family.

28. The earliest meaning of the "family" registered "the servants of a particular household or establishment, considered collectively." By the fifteenth century, it also came to mean "a group of people living as a household, traditionally consisting of parents and their children, and also (chiefly in early use) any servants, boarders, etc.," but also came to be inflected by the sense of consanguinity and a common blood lineage. Thus, "family" also denoted "any group of people connected by blood, marriage, adoption, etc." as well as "those descended or claiming descent from a common ancestor; a lineage." See *Oxford English Dictionary*, s.v. "family, *n.* and *adj.*," A.I. 1.a; 2.a; 2.b; and 3.a.

29. Ben Jonson, *Volpone*, in *The Alchemist and Other Plays*, ed. Gordon Campbell (Oxford: Oxford University Press, 1995), 1.1.64–66. Subsequent references will be cited parenthetically within the text.

30. The *Oxford English Dictionary* notes the provenance of "fable" in *fabula*, "the plot or story of a play or poem," as well as its archaic usage as "the subject of common talk." See 3; 4.b. As *fabula*, the rumor receives narrative heft.

31. See Michael Neill's "'In Everything Illegitimate': Imagining the Bastard in Renaissance Drama," *Yearbook of English Studies* 23 (1993): 270–92.

32. See Howard Marchitello's "Desire and Domination in *Volpone*," *Studies in English Literature, 1500–1900* 31, no. 2 (1991): 293.

33. *Oxford English Dictionary*, s.v. "parasite, *n.*," 2.a; Robert Cawdrey, *A Table Alphabeticall* (London, 1604), sig. G4r; John Bullokar, *An English Expositor* (London, 1616), sig. L7v.

34. In Plautus's *Captivi*, for instance, the parasite Ergasilus conveys the joyful news of Hegio's son's return to him—but not before asking for a feast in his honor.

35. Thomas Thomas, *Dictionarivm Lingvae Latinae Et Anglicanae* (London, 1587), sig. 2B8r.

36. Thomas Newman, *The Two First Comedies Of Terence called Andria, and the Eunuch newly Englished by Thomas Newman. Fitted for scholler Priuate acction in their Schooles* (London, 1627), 55.

37. We remember that Mosca claims only to repeat—that is, to echo—the rumor that his master is the "true father of his family." We may recall, too, the use of imitation and mimesis as a pedagogical strategy in the early modern grammar schoolroom.

38. *Oxford English Dictionary*, s.v. "observe, *v.*," 4; II; I. 1. b.; II. 6. a.; II. 6. c.; II. 6. d.

39. The prefix "ob-" signifies a contrary manner or meaning, or inverse direction (see *Oxford English Dictionary*, s.v. "ob-, *prefix*").

40. Joseph Webbe, *The Second Comedie Of Pvb. Terentivs, Called Evnvchvs, Or, The Eunuche, English and Latine* (London, 1629), sig. 2F3r (square brackets in the original text denote English words without corresponding Latin terms).

41. Ibid., sig. 2F4v–2G2r.

42. Ibid., sig. 2G2v.

43. References to *Othello* follow *The Norton Shakespeare*, 3rd ed. gen. ed. Stephen Greenblatt (New York: W. W. Norton, 2016), and are cited parenthetically within the text.

44. M. B., *The Triall of true Friendship; Or perfit mirror, wherby to discerne a trustie friend from a flattering Parasite. Otherwise, A knacke to know a knaue from an honest man: By a perfit mirrour of both: Soothly to say; Trie ere you trust; Beleeue no man rashly*. (London, 1596), sig. B1r–B1v, sig. B2v.

45. Ibid., sig. B2r.

46. This also recalls to us recent scholarship on early modern racialization as proximity (see above in this chapter), as well as the "blackamore wench's" pleas for nearness, which adopt the rhetorical trope of the (frequently masculine) friend as "another selfe." The language of the friend as "another selfe" also echoes the long history of scholarship in queer studies which attends to the figure of the "friend." See, for instance, Alan Bray's foundational work in "Homosexuality and the Signs of Male Friendship in Elizabethan England," in *Queering the Renaissance*, ed. Jonathan Goldberg (Durham, NC: Duke University Press, 1994), 40–61, and *The Friend* (Chicago: University of Chicago Press, 2003).

47. This model of intimacy is echoed in the figure of the secretary, as I discuss later in the chapter. The "unfained consent" which characterizes the opposite of a parasitical dynamic, "true friendship," is complicated by the nexus of payment, debt, and gratitude contained within the structures of service.

48. Parasitism is, in M.B.'s pamphlet, opposed to friendship, not to service. But as David Schalkwyk has remarked, the lines between service, love, and friendship remain indistinct. See *Shakespeare, Love and Service* (Cambridge: Cambridge University Press, 2008). *Othello*'s Emilia, indeed, in many respects exemplifies the friend into whom one "may transport his affections, repose his secrets, and commit his enterprises" (M.B., *The Triall of true Friendship*, sig. B1v); she is, in Othello's words, "a closet, lock, and key of villainous secrets" (4.2.21).

49. *Oxford English Dictionary*, s.v. "strange, *adj.*, and *n.*" 3; 1.a.

50. *Oxford English Dictionary*, s.v. "native, *adj.*," II. 5.a.

51. Thomas Middleton and William Rowley, *The Changeling*, in *Renaissance Drama: An Anthology of Plays and Entertainments*, 2nd ed., ed. Arthur F. Kinney (Malden, MA: Blackwell, 2005), 2.2.119. Subsequent references will be noted parenthetically within the text.

52. *Oxford English Dictionary*, s.v. "precious, *adj.*, *adv.*, and *n.*," 2. "Of great monetary value; expensive, costly."

53. *Oxford English Dictionary*, s.v. "precious, *adj.*, *adv.*, and *n.*," 1.a. "Of great moral, spiritual, or other non-material value; beloved, held in high esteem."

54. *Oxford English Dictionary*, s.v. "recompense, *v.*,": 1.a. "To reward, requite, or repay (a person) for something done or given"; 1.b. "To compensate, or make amends to (a person) for a loss or injury sustained"; 2.a. "To compensate or make up for (a loss, injury, defect, etc.)"; 2.b.

"To make compensation or atonement for (a misdeed or wrong committed)"; 2.c. "To make a repayment or requital for (something done or given)"; 3. "To make repayment, return, or amends"; 4. "To give in repayment or return; to mete out in requital."

55. For a longer discussion of the sexual resonances of women's "rings," see Karen Newman, "Portia's Ring: Unruly Women and Structures of Exchange in *The Merchant of Venice*," *Shakespeare Quarterly* 38, no. 1 (1987): 19–33.

56. In *Twelfth Night*, for instance, Olivia sends Cesario a ring to signal her desire for him, under the pretense that it is in fact the Count Orsino's ring that she rejects along with his romantic overtures.

57. For livery as a "material mnemonic," see Ann Rosalind Jones and Peter Stallybrass, *Renaissance Clothing and the Materials of Memory* (Cambridge, UK: Cambridge University Press, 2000), at 11. See Chapter 1 for a longer discussion of livery.

58. Laurence Nowell, *Vocabularium Saxonicum* (ca. 1567), s.v. "Gnedre," in *Lexicons of Early Modern English*, ed. Ian Lancashire (Toronto: University of Toronto Press, 2018). http://leme.library.utoronto.ca.

59. The *Oxford English Dictionary* notes this shift in meaning, defining "wage" as "A payment to a person for service rendered. Formerly used widely, e.g. for the salary or fee paid to persons of official or professional status [although we note that in early modern lexicons, wages and salary are repeatedly defined as a stipend given to a servant, reinforcing the way in which wages and salary are rhetorically linked to service]. Now (except in rhetorical language) restricted to mean: The amount paid periodically, esp. by the day or week or month, for the labour or service of an employee, worker, or servant" (s.v. "wage, *n.*," 2.). Thomas Blount's *Glossographia: or A Dictionary* (London, 1656) defines "salary" as a "recompence or consideration made to any man for his pains or industry bestowed on another mans business; wages given to servants, a stipend" (sig. 2L8r). See also "hyre, wages, or salary" in Richard Huloet's *Abcedarivm Anglico Latinvm* (London, 1552), sig P6v.

60. De Flores is also described as wearing a "black mask," and, as Lara Bovilsky notes, the play's descriptions of his appearance in the language of ugliness and deformity might also be understood in racialized terms and may portend the fear of miscegenation. See Bovilsky, *Barbarous Play: Race on the English Renaissance Stage* (Minneapolis: University of Minnesota Press, 2008), 139–54. See also Katherine Schaap Williams's discussion of the "black mask" in relation to discourses of disability in *Unfixable Forms: Disability, Performance, and the Early Modern English Theater* (Ithaca, NY: Cornell University Press, 2021), 139.

61. Marcel Mauss, *The Gift: The Form and Reason for Exchange in Archaic Societies*, trans. W. D. Halls (New York: Norton, 1990). See also chapter 5, "The Principle of Reciprocity," in Claude Lévi-Strauss's *The Elementary Structures of Kinship*, rev. ed., trans. James Harle Bell, John Richard von Sturmer, and ed. Rodney Needham (Boston: Beacon Press, 1969).

62. Mauss, *The Gift*, 16.

63. "The first gift of a *vaygu'a* bears the name of *vaga*, 'opening gift'. It is the starting point, one that irrevocably commits the recipient to make a reciprocating gift. . . . It is obligatory; it is expected, and it must be equivalent to the first gift. Occasionally it may be seized by force or by surprise. For a *yotile* that is an insufficient return gift, revenge may be taken . . . at the very least by insult. . . . If one is not able to reciprocate, at the very least one may offer a *basi*. . . . It is a kind of advance present, whose purpose is to delay. It appeases the former donor, now the creditor; but does not free the debtor, the future donor." Ibid., 26.

64. The play, of course, confirms that money is *not* an accurate measure of value; Beatrice-Joanna is prepared to pay De Flores handsomely even though she would "fain be rid of him" (3.4.72).

65. See Thomas Elyot's definition of "creatura" in *The Dictionary of syr Thomas Eliot knyght* (London, 1538) as "a creature or thinge made of nothynge" (sig. E3r).

66. *A Letter sent by the Maydens of London, to the vertuous Matrones & Mistresses of the same, in the defense of their lawfull Libertie. Answering the Mery Meeting* . . . (London, 1567), sig. B6r.

67. Ibid., A3v–A4r.

68. Ibid., A4r–A4v. The "poore maidens" go on to compare their condition explicitly to that of bondage, arguing that "it were to much against reason, to intreate euill, when they haue done their dueties to vse *as slaues or bondewomen, being free borne*" (sig. A4v, emphasis added). The maidservants here affirm a natural and natal condition of essential freedom, and express a form of corporeal unity in order to underscore their treatment as "slaues or bondewomen" as a violation of their natural rights, even as their rhetoric strategically wields an affective register, as I will discuss.

69. Ibid., A5r–A5v.

70. The phonological affinities between care, *caritas*, and *carus* are striking. Raymond Williams traces "charity" from both *caritas* and "*carus*—dear," adding that "Forms of the Latin word had taken on the sense of dearness of price as well as affection." See *Keywords: A Vocabulary of Culture and Society*, rev. ed. (New York: Oxford University Press, 1985), 54. The discourse of reciprocity in these letters is animated by these slippages between care, *caritas*, *carus*, and charity. "Care," as I will demonstrate, suggests both provision and solicitude, while *caritas* suggests (Christian) love and charity: "Greek *agape* had been distinguished into *dilectio* and *caritas* in the Vulgate, and Wyclif translated these as love and charity. Tyndale rendered *caritas* as love." See Williams, 54.

71. M.B., *The Triall of true Friendship*, sig. B2r. The inseparability of maidservant and mistress recalls both M.B.'s reading of a "trustie friend" as "another selfe" and, more strikingly, the metaphors of bodily incorporation that I have been discussing in this chapter, whether racialized, parasitical, political, or familial.

72. Critics have suggested that the *Letter* was not written by maidservants at all, but rather by someone trained in marshalling arguments. Ann Rosalind Jones argues that "Fehrenbach takes the specialized legal vocabulary of the pamphlet as proof that it must have been composed by a man. . . . Its homely humor and command of domestic detail, however, convince me that a collaboration of women servants with a sympathetic man writing from the Inns of Court is equally plausible." See "Maidservants of London: Sisterhoods of Kinship and Labor" in *Maids and Mistresses, Cousins and Queens: Women's Alliances in Early Modern England*, ed. Susan Frye and Karen Robertson (Oxford: Oxford University Press, 1999), 28. See Jones's essay for a longer discussion of the *Letter*'s portrayal and construction of female alliance and networks of labor.

73. MS EL 6425, The Huntington Library, San Marino, California.

74. "Governesses" are mentioned infrequently in early modern literature, especially in the later (and current) sense of "A female teacher or instructor, esp. one employed in a private household." Rather, in the early modern period a "governess" signified either "A woman who holds or exercises authority over a place, institution, or group of people; a female ruler" or "A woman responsible for the care, supervision, or direction of a person, typically a child or young

lady." See the *Oxford English Dictionary,* s.v. "governess, *n.*," 2.c.; 1.b.; 2.b. The position of the governess, of course, is ultimately belied by her name: although she "governs" her charge—just as Elizabeth I is the "governess" of her realm—she is also dependent upon her employer or master.

75. MS EL 6426, The Huntington Library, San Marino, California.

76. For Derrida, not only reciprocation but even the very *memory* of the gift annuls the fact of the gift: "'the gift not only must not be repaid but not be kept in memory, retained as symbol of a sacrifice, as symbolic in general.... From the moment the gift would appear as gift, as such, as what it is, in its phenomenon, its sense and its essence, it would be engaged in a symbolic, sacrificial, or economic structure that would annul the gift' (23). Therefore, the gift is the 'very figure of the impossible' (7)." Jacques Derrida, *Given Time: I. Counterfeit Money,* trans. Peggy Kamuf (Chicago: University of Chicago Press, 1992), qtd. in Scott Cutler Shershow, *The Work and the Gift* (Chicago: University of Chicago Press, 2005), 87–88. See also Ilana Krausman Ben-Amos, *The Culture of Giving: Informal Support and Gift-Exchange in Early Modern England* (Cambridge, UK: Cambridge University Press, 2008), and Felicity Heal, *The Power of Gifts: Gift Exchange in Early Modern England* (Oxford: Oxford University Press, 2014), for more sustained discussions of early modern gift-giving.

77. MS EL 2694, The Huntington Library, San Marino, California. For a longer discussion of this case and of Daniell's declaration, see Andrew Gordon, "Material Fictions: Counterfeit Correspondence and the Culture of Copying in Early Modern England," in *Cultures of Correspondence in Early Modern Britain,* ed. James Daybell and Andrew Gordon (Philadelphia: University of Pennsylvania Press, 2016), 85–109, esp. 102–9. Jonathan Goldberg discusses the extent to which early modern secretaries were expected to engage in "authorized" forgery of their masters' writing and signatures. See *Writing Matter: From the Hands of the English Renaissance* (Stanford, CA: Stanford University Press, 1990), 248. While acknowledging the very public nature of letters, James Daybell discusses the fear of forgery surrounding letters: "handwriting is not necessarily a singular possession or identity of a person, but rather a commodity that can be faked, an identity assumed. Fear of such treachery contributed to the insecurity associated with letters; many distrusted the post as a medium to communicate matters they wished to keep secret." See *Women Letter-Writers in Tudor England* (Oxford: Oxford University Press, 2006), 71. And yet precisely the ability to assume a different identity, another self, in order to incorporate the body of one's employer's message or meaning in a letter cemented the mutual relationship of master and secretary at the same time as it remained vulnerable to the intimate revealing himself as a potentially dangerous interloper, traitor, or forger, as a "stranger within."

78. Angel Day, *The English Secretary, Or Methode of writing of Epistles and Letters: With A declaration of such Tropes, Figures, and Schemes, as either vsvally or for ornament sake are therein required* (London, 1599), sig. 2N2r.

79. On account of "the greate treachery and Cosenage of the said Daniell being a servaunte to the said late Earle," Daniell eventually received "an extraordinary and exemplary punishment": the court ordered him to pay a fine and "be committed to the prison of the Fleet and there to remaine all the daies of his life."

80. I return to the politics of memory in Chapter 5, and in particular to the ways in which the condition of manumission is contingent upon the rehearsal of gratitude. Remembrance, it repeatedly emerges, frames the dynamics of recompense to strategic ends. As I shall discuss, remembrance can be mandated in order not only to enforce the memory of slavery, inscribing enslavement in perpetuity, but to threaten the possibility of *re*-enslavement.

81. See *The Perticular Dewtie of Everie Severall officer: The Stewarde*, MS EL 1180, The Huntington Library, San Marino, California, which contains an early modern account of the office of the steward. For a detailed discussion of the role of the "estate steward" in seventeenth-century England, see D. R. Hainsworth, *Stewards, Lords and People: The Estate Steward and his World in Later Stuart England* (Cambridge, UK: Cambridge University Press, 1992).

82. *Twelfth Night*, 2.3.68–69. All references follow *The Norton Shakespeare*, 3rd ed. Further references will be cited parenthetically within the text.

83. "My lady" works as a pun, evoking Petrachan formulations of servitude and love. But Maria has also referred to Olivia as "my lady" (1.3.4), fixing the reference within the register of service.

84. Although the field of early modern studies has attended to the role of male secretaries in early modern England, there has been much less work on female secretaries, particularly in terms of the secretary's specifically lexical function; an exception is Julie Crawford's essay "Women's Secretaries," in *Queer Renaissance Historiography: Backward Gaze*, ed. Vin Nardizzi, Stephen Guy-Bray, and Will Stockton (New York: Routledge, 2009), 111–34. Maria, as we have seen and as Crawford notes, inhabits the secretary's role as both an intimate and an amanuensis to a striking degree.

85. When at the end of the play Olivia finally sets eyes on the letter, however, she immediately recognizes the handwriting as Maria's: although it is "much like the character" of her own writing, she concedes, "out of question, 'tis Maria's hand" (5.1.334–35). Olivia's clarification reinstates the lexical and hierarchical difference between mistress and maidservant, but also contains the worst of Maria's secretarial abuses, which for all their comic effects also illustrate the danger of the rogue secretary. The pun here, of course, falls on "hand"; it is Maria's hand*writing*, but also her hand, which imitates her mistress's "character."

86. Day, *The English Secretary*, sig. 2N2r.

87. For a discussion of female homosociality in the play, see Jessica Tvordi, "Female Alliance and the Construction of Homoeroticism in *As You Like It* and *Twelfth Night*," in *Maids and Mistresses, Cousins and Queens: Women's Alliances in Early Modern England*, ed. Frye and Robertson, 123. Camille Slights argues that "even [Toby] realizes that 'pleasure will be paid, one time or another', and he marries Maria 'in recompense' (5.1.364) for her part in the gulling of Malvolio." See "The Principle of Recompense in *Twelfth Night*," *Modern Language Review* 77, no. 3 (1982), 543. David Schalkwyk, however, notes that "Sir Toby bestows an aristocratic reward for service with his marriage to Olivia's lady-in-waiting," suggesting that Maria's actions comprise good "service," not to her mistress, but to Sir Toby. See "Love and Service in *Twelfth Night* and the Sonnets," *Shakespeare Quarterly* 56, no. 1 (2005), 90. For a discussion of Maria's imitative letter-writing in terms of hierarchy and social mobility, see Michelle M. Dowd, *Women's Work in Early Modern English Literature and Culture* (New York: Palgrave Macmillan, 2009), 37–46.

88. We might think, for instance, of Massinger's *The Renegado* (1630), in which the servant Gazet is nearly persuaded to become a eunuch on the promise of sexual access to women.

89. William Heminge, *The Fatal Contract, A French Tragedy* (London, 1653), sigs. B4r, B4v. Subsequent references will be cited parenthetically within the text. The first performance of the play was probably in 1638–1639.

90. See Andrea Stevens, "'The Eunuch Much Sears Her Breast': Remedying Adulteration in William Heminge's *The Fatal Contract*," in *Thunder at a Playhouse: Essaying Shakespeare and the Early Modern Stage*, ed. Peter Kanelos and Matt Kozusko (Selinsgrove, PA: Susquehanna

University Press, 2010), 212–33, at 215, emphasis added. This illuminating essay explores the significance of gendered personation in the play, suggesting that "In this play of racial masquerade 'unmasking' has nothing, in short, to do with demonstrating a character's underlying whiteness. Instead, to unmask is to assert the enduring presence of something like 'natural' femininity" (226). I would suggest, however, that the two are intertwined; it is specifically Chrotilda's *white* femininity that prompts and authorizes her to mobilize this performance. As Stevens notes in the introduction to her edition of *The Fatal Contract*, following Arthur L. Little, Jr., "The threat of rape . . . is central to this character's performance of black masculinity." See *The Fatal Contract*, ed. Stevens, in *The Routledge Anthology of Early Modern Drama*, ed. Jeremy Lopez (Abingdon, UK: Routledge, 2020), 136–94, at 137. What Chrotilda, in disguise, narrates is of course the threatened rape of a white woman. And Arthur Little argues that although Chrotilda has previously been raped by a white nobleman, her disguise turns her "into her own, nevertheless black, rapist." See *Shakespeare Jungle Fever: National-Imperial Re-Visions of Race, Rape, and Sacrifice* (Stanford, CA: Stanford University Press, 2000), 61. In writing of "the idea of miscegenational rape," Little "insist[s] on a critical foregrounding of the textualizing, and, indeed, the fleshy—fetishistic, scopic, imaginary—incorporation of blackness into the white rape narrative." Ibid., 5. On the play's staging of blackface disguise, see also Virginia Mason Vaughan, *Performing Blackness on English Stages, 1500–1800* (Cambridge, UK: Cambridge University Press, 2005), 121–29. We must remember that, as Ayanna Thompson argues, "a racialized epistemology is . . . constructed through the codification, empowerment, and normalization of the *white/right gaze* of the English audience," and that Castrato/Chrotilda's performance of blackface *colludes* with this gaze. See Thompson, *Performing Race and Torture on the Early Modern Stage* (New York: Routledge, 2008), 4, emphasis added.

91. I am aware that in speaking of this character, my language has shifted here to speaking of Chrotilda rather than "the eunuch/Eunuch/Castrato," even though "she" does not appear at this point—or indeed any point—in the play. I have retained this sense of a dual nomenclature in order to expose and—hopefully—to challenge our persistent desire to secure the "body beneath," but also to underscore the fact that the eunuch/Eunuch is indeed *always* Chrotilda, and to keep in view the agent and aims of this performance of blackface and the operations of whiteness that enact it.

92. See the *Oxford English Dictionary*, s.v. "slave, *n. 1* (and *adj.*)," 1.b. For a discussion of the pejorative valences of "slave," see Mary Nyquist, "Base Slavery and Roman Yoke," in *The Oxford Handbook of English Law and Literature 1500–1700*, ed. Lorna Hutson (Oxford: Oxford University Press, 2017), 624–48. This play, indeed, does seem to gesture toward a rhetorical and conceptual economy in slavery. Although slaves are not listed in "The Persons of the Play" (sig. A4v)—which include "Six of the Guard" and "A Lackey," among other figures—when Clovis attempts to set his men upon Clotair ("Upon him slaves"), the Queen intercedes: "O set not on thy slaves, if he must die, / Let thy sacrifice not butcher him" (sig. D3r). This exchange suggests the uncertain nature of the discourse of slavery at this moment—and indeed Clotair's instruction for the murder of his brother reveals this uncertainty again: "Where's our guard / That lets a traytor pull me by the berd? / Upon him slaves" (sig. D3v). Yet, when Lanove—a "Noble [man] of *France*" and friend to Lamot and Dumain—expresses his reluctance to invade the Palace it is on account of the fact that "it's no base act / We undertake, but our whole Countries freedom / From slaverie and bondage; men of worth stand bare / To pages and gilt Butterflies?" (sig. E3r). Here, the imperative for deference to "pages and gilt Butterflies" is what registers as "slaverie"; if such "pages" are addressed in the contemptuous terms of slavery earlier in the play, the problem here seems to lie in the fact that to

submit to such "slaves" is what, ironically, comprises "bondage." And when Aphelia laments her husband's treatment of her, she suggests that domestic unrest approximates the condition of bondage. Thus, she suggests to her waiting-women that "I am fitter to attend on you; / I am become a servant and a slave / To every moodie passion of my Lord" (sig. F4v).

93. Namely, that "They fear you will accept her as the Queen, / Of whom you may beget a hopefull issue / And frustrate their intents, who but expect / Your hop'd-for death, and perhaps plotted too" (sig. E2r).

94. Thus, when Clotair, reeling from the news that the eunuch delivers to him of Aphelia's supposed infidelity, requests his silence with the words, "Peace slave, / Thou that infects all peace" (sig. G1v), he adopts the term "slave" as a rebuke, even as he suggests that the eunuch is a corrupting, infecting force. The reference to the slave's "shadow" recalls the "blackamore wench" of Henry Rainolds's "A Black-Moor Maid wooing a Fair Boy"; in both instances, the blackamoor's complexion is rhetorically imagined as a prosthetic and agential darkening force.

95. A "Vagabond" suggests not only "A rogue, one that wanders to and fro," according to Henry Cockeram's *The English Dictionarie* (London, 1623), sig. L2r, but also a "roamer, faitour, earth-planet, wandering idlesbie, ranging or gadding rogue" (see Randle Cotgrave's *A Dictionarie Of The French And English Tongves* [London, 1611], sig. 4K2v). What is curious here is that the so-called "vagabond," whose name itself suggests wandering and the problem of illegible origins, is here quite clearly traced to "Aethiope." Nonetheless, the "vagabond" here also appears to be provisionally racialized as "sun-burnt." "Vagabond" also invokes the sense of the "runnagate, one that will stay no where," according to Robert Cawdrey's 1604 *A Table Alphabeticall* (sig. I6r), and also recalls the vagrants who could be beaten and branded under the auspices of the 1547 Vagrancy Act; see the Introduction. That occasional brand of slavery is now reimagined as a "sun-burnt" somatic marker of the "Ethiop" who reemerges as the "blackamoor."

96. Both Chrotilda and Chaerea are characters in disguise (the former is a victim of rape; the latter is himself a rapist), and both adopt the disguise of a eunuch in order to gain privileged access within a household economy and to forge close affective ties with a female member of that household.

97. *A Midsummer Night's Dream*, 5.1.389–92. All references follow *The Norton Shakespeare*, 3rd ed. Further references will be cited parenthetically within the text.

98. For a brief discussion of this moment as a "fantas[y] of racial whiteness," see Arthur L. Little, Jr., "Re-Historicizing Race, White Melancholia, and the Shakespearean Property," *Shakespeare Quarterly* 67, no. 1 (2016): 94.

99. Edmund Coote, *The English Schoole-maister* (London, 1596), sig. N1r.

100. Cawdrey, *A Table Alphabeticall*, sig. G8v.

101. Miles P. Grier, "Inkface: The Slave Stigma in England's Early Imperial Imagination," in *Scripturalizing the Human: The Written as the Political*, ed. Vincent L. Wimbush (New York: Routledge, 2015), 193–220; and Patricia Akhimie, "Bruised with Adversity: Reading Race in *The Comedy of Errors*," in *The Oxford Handbook of Shakespeare and Embodiment : Gender, Sexuality, and Race*, ed. Valerie Traub (Oxford: Oxford University Press, 2016), 195. For a vital discussion of the importance of critical race studies to book and print history more broadly, see B. K. Adams, "Fair/Foul," in *Shakespeare/Text: Contemporary Readings in Textual Studies, Editing and Performance*, ed. Claire M. L. Bourne (London: Bloomsbury Arden Shakespeare, 2021), 29–49.

102. Akhimie, "Bruised with Adversity," 190.

103. *The Comedy of Errors*, 1.2.46 and 4.4.30–31. All references follow *The Norton Shakespeare*, 3rd ed. Further references will be cited parenthetically within the text.

104. See W.W.'s translation, the title of which attests to the early modern status of the play: *Menaecmi: A pleasant and fine Conceited Comaedie, taken out of the most excellent wittie Poet Plautus: Chosen purposely from out the rest, as least harmefull, and yet most delightfull* (London, 1595); on the identity of W.W., see Katharine A. Craik, who suggests that W.W. is probably not, as is often thought, Willam Warner, but rather William Webbe. Craik, "Warner, William (1558/9–1609), poet and lawyer," *Oxford Dictionary of National Biography*. 23 Sep. 2004; Accessed 1 May 2021. https://www.oxforddnb.com/view/10.1093/ref:odnb/9780198614128.001.0001/odnb-9780198614128-e-28770. See also Maurice Hunt, "Slavery, English Servitude, and *The Comedy of Errors*," *English Literary Renaissance* 27, no. 1 (1997): 31–56, esp. 49–50. Hunt reminds us that the violence of Shakespeare's adaptation also constitutes a departure from its source: "The slave Messenio is never beaten in Plautus' *Menaechmi*" (ibid., 35).

105. See, for instance, L.H.'s *A Dictionarie French and English* (London, 1571), where "La Famille & race" is rendered as "the house, kinred, the familie" (sig. O1v), while "Vn Race" is glossed as "a race, an ofspring, a kindred" (sig. 2B1v).

106. See Joyce Green MacDonald, *Women and Race in Early Modern Texts* (Cambridge, UK: Cambridge University Press, 2002), 94. For further discussion of indenture, servitude, and interracial unions, see Kathleen M. Brown, *Good Wives, Nasty Wenches, and Anxious Patriarchs: Gender, Race, and Power in Colonial Virginia* (Chapel Hill: University of North Carolina Press, 1996), 131–35.

Chapter 4

1. Robert Evelyn, *A Direction for Adventvrers With small stock to get two for one, and good land freely: And for Gentlemen, and all Servants, Labourers, and Artificers to live plentifully. And the true Description of the healthiest, pleasantest, and richest plantation of new Albion, in North Virginia, proved by thirteen witnesses. Together With, A Letter from Master Robert Evelin, that lived there many yeares, shewing the particularities, and excellency thereof* (London, 1641).

2. Ibid., sig. A4v.

3. Ibid.

4. Ibid., sig. A1r.

5. Ibid., sig. A4v.

6. *The Several Declarations Of The Company Of Royal Adventurers Of England Trading Into Africa* (London, 1667). For a discussion of the organization and aims of the Company of Royal Adventurers, particularly before its re-formation as the Royal African Company, see William A. Pettigrew, *Freedom's Debt: The Royal African Company and the Politics of the Atlantic Slave Trade, 1672-1752* (Chapel Hill: University of North Carolina Press, 2013), esp. 22–24.

7. Evelyn, *A Direction for Adventvrers*, sig. A4v. Amanda Bailey discusses more fully the ways in which debt bonds assumed the body as surety, leading to the seizure of the body at the moment of default. See Amanda Bailey, *Of Bondage: Debt, Property, and Personhood in Early Modern England* (Philadelphia: University of Pennsylvania Press, 2013). See also the case of Henry Raines, who escaped seven years of captivity in Barbary only to be arrested for debt on his return to England (Chapter 2).

8. Addressing the relatively low numbers of apprentices who actually went on to receive the freedom of the city, Ilana Krausman Ben-Amos notes that "In 1662 the mayor of Bristol complained that many of those transported to the plantations were 'children and apprentices run away from their parents and masters.'" See "Failure to Become Freemen: Urban Apprentices in Early Modern England," *Social History* 16, no. 2 (1991), 169. The plantations might

also, then, have comprised—or have been seen to comprise—a release from the "bondage" of apprenticeship.

9. Amanda Bailey distinguishes the vendibility of the bodies of indentured servants from their contemporary counterparts, English apprentices: "The selling off of a servant's contract was not entirely unknown in seventeenth-century England, since, for example, with the permission of guild members, a master could sell his apprentice to another company member. But ... the binding of an apprentice with the intent to sell him was considered a gross abuse of authority. The colonial market in servants, however, explicitly identified servants as saleable goods...." See Bailey, *Of Bondage*, 112–13.

10. Ibid., 5–6.

11. For further discussion of the *mancipium*, see also Chapter 2 and Chapter 5.

12. The question of the extent to which indentured servitude is seen as an analogue to or an alternate form of slavery is one that has been taken up at length by historians. The term "Barbadosing," for instance, reflects the practice of enforced kidnap and transport to Barbados, and several historians have noted a decline in voluntary migration to North America in the latter half of the seventeenth century, and the concomitant rise in coerced migration. Scholars such as Hilary McD. Beckles, John Donoghue, and Simon P. Newman, meanwhile, have argued for the affordances between more extreme forms of white servitude and the conditions of African enslavement. Beckles has extensively discussed white bound servitude in Barbados and the violence that accompanied it, suggesting that "All workers in the colony were enslaved to a degree. This view runs contrary to the assertion that white indentured servants were not enslaved and that only Africans experienced slavery. This hypothesis has been misunderstood precisely because of a refusal to recognize the elasticity of bondage as a category: it included white indentured servants, enslaved and indentured Indian captives and chattelized imported Africans." See *The First Black Slave Society: Britain's "Barbarity Time" in Barbados, 1636–1876* (Kingston, Jamaica: University of the West Indies Press, 2016), 38. John Donoghue, meanwhile, suggests that "we can recast mid-seventeenth-century 'indentured servitude' in the English Atlantic as a form of slavery that existed alongside the perpetual enslavement of Native Americans and people of African heritage," and argues that the term "indentured servitude" perpetuates the "concealment" of the chattel status it registers: "'Indentured servant' is hardly an objective signifier, as those who employ it unwittingly follow the lead of the slaveholders themselves, who concealed the slavery they imposed on the people they bought and sold from Britain and Ireland under the rhetorical cloak of the tradition of English service, partly as a way to shield themselves from well-informed contemporary criticism that they had made 'slaves' out of Christians. Despite the entrenched place the term holds in the lexicon of early American and English Atlantic studies, it is unsatisfactory for this particular period. A more apt term is 'bond slave.'" See "'Out of the Land of Bondage': The English Revolution and the Atlantic Origins of Abolition," *American Historical Review* 115, no. 4 (2010): 945, 948–49. Although Donoghue argues for a discourse of multiple "slaveries," Susan Dwyer Amussen reminds us of the political register of discourses of slavery in the period, as well as the reluctance of contemporary writers to use the term "servitude"; see *Caribbean Exchanges: Slavery and the Transformation of English Society, 1640–1700* (Chapel Hill: University of North Carolina Press, 2007), 127–29. Simon P. Newman, however, in keeping with Beckles and Donoghue, suggests that "British understandings of bound labor thus existed on a continuum and encompassed white vagrants, convicts, and prisoners of war, bound Scots, Irishmen, and Englishmen, as well as African slaves and pawns in West Africa, and African slaves in Barbados" and "locate[s] slavery within a broad spectrum of

other systems of labor, highlighting the shared working experiences of the enslaved and other workers. It is my contention that slavery and race may not have been so intrinsically interconnected as previous scholars have assumed." See *A New World of Labor: The Development of Plantation Slavery in the British Atlantic* (Philadelphia: University of Pennsylvania Press, 2013), 2, 13. In a useful discussion, Jenny Shaw reads *Englands Slavery, or Barbados Merchandize*, the 1659 petition of Marcellus Rivers and Oxenbridge Foyle, two royalists who had been expelled to Barbados; this petition explicitly framed their experiences and those of their fellow Englishmen within the scope of slavery. Shaw argues that the petition explicitly draws on the experiences of enslaved Africans, histories that the authors may have received, and assumed, from those alongside whom they worked; as Shaw notes, the petition rests on the naturalized distinction between Englishness and slavery, and the already naturalized association between enslavement and Africanness. The appropriation of these experiences is, Shaw suggests, problematic, but it also registers a rhetorical and material commodification of African experiences of enslavement. See *Everyday Life in the Early English Caribbean: Irish, Africans, and the Construction of Difference* (Athens: University of Georgia Press, 2013), esp. 19–24. For a useful discussion of the larger historical narrative of "white slavery" and its implications, see Jerome S. Handler and Matthew C. Reilly, "Contesting 'White Slavery' in the Caribbean: Enslaved Africans and European Indentured Servants in Seventeenth-Century Barbados," *New West Indian Guide* 91, no. 1–2 (2017): 30–55.

13. *A Booke Of Presidents, With Additions of diuers necessarie Instruments, meete for all such as desire to learne the manner and forme how to make Euidences and Instruments, &c.* (London, 1607), 53r–53v.

14. Ibid., 53v.

15. Z.c.22 (38), Folger Shakespeare Library; G. A. Oxon. b. 111 (13), Bodleian Library, Oxford.

16. X.d.734 and X.d.735, Folger Shakespeare Library. Although the former is a printed form, the latter, unusually, is an engraved document, significantly raising the cost of this legal instrument.

17. According to the records of Magdalen College, one Henry Holden, son of Humphrey Holden of Erdington in the county of Warwick, appears as a Demy in 1682 and a Fellow in 1686. This evidence suggests that while Holden's elder son went up to Oxford as a scholar, his younger sons were placed in city apprenticeships. See *Magdalen College and King James II 1686–1688: A Series of Documents*, ed. J. R. Bloxam (Oxford: Clarendon Press, 1886), 123.

18. X.d.734, Folger Shakespeare Library.

19. For a longer discussion of the tensions in the word "fiction," please see the Introduction.

20. As Chapter 1 discusses, "livery" comprises the textile clothing that (often) marks its wearer as a servant and (sometimes) as affiliated with a particular household; but it also signals a larger sense of provision, including room and board.

21. For a longer discussion of the implications of and slippages between service and servitude in late seventeenth-century England, see Amussen, *Caribbean Exchanges*, esp. chapter 4.

22. See Joel Norton's Apprenticeship to Ebenezer Talman (1765). Talman Family Papers, MS 662, Series I, Box 1, Folder 6, Sterling Memorial Library, Yale University. The apprentice, Norton, does not, however, sign the indenture, and, tellingly, he is bound out only until the age of sixteen. This, as well as the fact that Norton is contracted as a "Minor Son" of a deceased father by his "Guardian," Ephraim Norton, suggests that Norton may be a pauper apprentice. Like William

Redman, who must provide to his poor apprentice Jeremie Feere at the end of his term of service "double Apparel of all sorts, good and new" (see Chapter 2), Talman must "deliver" to Norton "at the Expiration of said Term ... two Suits of Cloaths fitting for all Parts of his Body one of them to be good & new fit to be worn on Sabbaths & other publick Occations. the other fit to be worn on every Day and also an English Bible." In addition, this apprenticeship includes a particular pedagogical dimension: "the said Ebenezer Tallman Doth hereby covenant to teach & instruct said Apprentice to write & read English also four Rules in Arithmatick." This reflects the nominal pedagogical justification for apprenticeship I have earlier discussed, but also perhaps a distinction between English and American apprenticeship contracts. In their transatlantic study of pauper apprenticeship, Steve Hindle and Ruth Wallis Herndon note "the preference for literacy clauses in America," and suggest that "American pauper apprenticeship was less like typical English parish apprenticeship and more like the formal craft apprenticeships that had governed entry to trade guilds in England." See "Recreating Proper Families in England and North America: Pauper Apprenticeship in Transatlantic Context," in *Children Bound to Labor: The Pauper Apprentice System in Early America*, ed. Ruth Wallis Herndon and John E. Murray (Ithaca, NY: Cornell University Press, 2009), 32, 20. For further discussion of pauper apprenticeship in early America, see the introduction to and other essays in *Children Bound to Labor*.

23. Indeed, noting that "serious differences made servitude in Virginia more onerous than servitude in England," Edmund S. Morgan even suggests that "Almost all [Virginian] servants were therefore in a condition resembling that of the least privileged type of English servant, the parish apprentice." See *American Slavery, American Freedom: The Ordeal of Colonial Virginia* (New York: W. W. Norton, 1975), 126.

24. Indentured servant contracts for Barbados, Maryland, Virginia, and Pennsylvania. V.b.16 (1–66), Folger Shakespeare Library. The collection consists of sixty-six indenture contracts, part of a larger extant collection of over eight hundred; most of the remainder of the indentures are contained in the Middlesex Sessions Records. This collection is unusual in its capaciousness; surprisingly few collections of indenture contracts remain, and since a pair of indentures would be separated, with one indenture held by the traveling servant, many of these copies have since been lost. The indentures in this collection are preserved only, we surmise, due to legislation issued in 1682 (and renewed in 1686), the "Order to Prevent Abuses in Transporting Servants," ostensibly addressing the problem of spiriting, and because a "merchant" identified in these indentures, William Haveland, and a Justice of the Peace, Abraham Bayly, were tried and convicted for spiriting. I give relevant dates of indentures as "1682/3." For a more detailed discussion of this case, see John Wareing, *Indentured Migration and the Servant Trade from London to America, 1618–1718: "There Is Great Want of Servants"* (Oxford: Oxford University Press, 2017), esp. 123, 212–15. Sonia Tycko notes that the 1682 order meant that the indenture previously held by the servant would now be retained in a registry; as a result, "The 1682 order in effect removed one layer of protection from servants—namely, possession of a counterpart contract" while "middlemen and masters had better protection from accusations of spiriting." See "Bound and Filed: A Seventeenth-Century Service Indenture from a Scattered Archive," *Early American Studies: An Interdisciplinary Journal* 19, no. 1 (2021): 166–90, at 188; this essay convincingly argues for the location of another indenture in this collection at The Huntington Library, San Marino, California. For an overview of this collection as well as the larger "London Record" of which it is a part, see Wareing, *Indentured Migration and the Servant Trade*, 262–67.

25. V.b.16 (6), Folger Shakespeare Library.

26. See, for instance, V.b.16 (2), Folger Shakespeare Library.

27. See, respectively, V.b.16 (9); V.b.16 (12); and V.b.16 (62); Folger Shakespeare Library.

28. See V.b.16 (11) and V.b.16 (13), Folger Shakespeare Library.

29. V.b.16 (16); V.b.16 (12); Folger Shakespeare Library. I think here of Jean E. Feerick's work on blood-based understandings of race in *Strangers in Blood: Relocating Race in the Renaissance* (Toronto: University of Toronto Press, 2010). See also Shaw, *Everyday Life in the Early English Caribbean*, for a fuller discussion of the place of Irish Catholics in the English Caribbean.

30. See V.b.16 (1), V.b.16 (32), V.b.16 (49), and V.b.16 (53), Folger Shakespeare Library, for some instances of indentured female servants; see V.b.16 (20) for the contract of "Edmond Smyth aged 38 years brick^layer^."

31. See V.b.16 (64) and V.b.16 (52), Folger Shakespeare Library, respectively. The requisite "age of consent" to bind oneself into servitude appears to be twenty-one (see below in this chapter).

32. See, respectively, V.b.16 (19), V.b.16 (27), V.b.16 (64), and V.b.16 (66), Folger Shakespeare Library.

33. V.b.16 (35), Folger Shakespeare Library.

34. V.b.16 (8), Folger Shakespeare Library. The italicized text represents manuscript annotations within the blank spaces in the documents.

35. In Chapter 5, I discuss in more detail the imperative for "faithful" service and the potential revocability of manumission from servitude.

36. See V.b.16 (10), V.b.16 (11), and V.b.16 (12), Folger Shakespeare Library, for examples of different marks.

37. While it is important not to privilege literacy in early modern England too much at the expense of aurality, the unsigned contract (and the unread contract) fundamentally trouble the narratives of consent on which the contract is based. That is, the indenture contract is premised on the legible materiality of consent. Moreover, Abbot Emerson Smith notes that although some indentured servants "made verbal agreements with the merchants who shipped them," these were "of no legal validity and would not be enforced in the colony." See *Colonists in Bondage: White Servitude and Convict Labor in America, 1607–1776* (Chapel Hill: University of North Carolina Press, 1947), 19; this is an important early history of indentured servitude.

38. See Smith, *Colonists in Bondage*, 19–20; and Wareing, *Indentured Migration and the Servant Trade*, 46–50. Wareing suggests that while one category of servants, consigned servants, was contracted and transported to a particular master or mistress across the Atlantic, another category of exchanged servants "migrated in much less favourable circumstances in a two-stage commodity exchange. They were recruited and bound in England to be sold, and then resold as human cargo in the colonies" (47).

39. See V.b.16 (14), Folger Shakespeare Library.

40. See V.b.16 (51), Folger Shakespeare Library.

41. See V.b.16 (65), Folger Shakespeare Library.

42. See V.b.16 (59), Folger Shakespeare Library.

43. My aim here, again, is not to conclude that we should conflate the categories of service and enslavement or necessarily view these forms of indenture as "other slaveries," as Donoghue proposes. Rather, I hope to demonstrate the strategic coarticulation of these categories, which lays the groundwork on which heritable forms of slavery are established. This heritability, I will argue later in this chapter, is central to the representation of natality and the place of children in systems of servitude.

44. For a brief account of the 1682 order and its renewal, see Smith, *Colonists in Bondage*, 78–79.

45. *At the Court at Whitehall, December the Thirteenth, 1682 . . . Whereas it has been Represented to His Majesty, That by reason of the frequent Abuses of a lewd sort of People called Spirits, in Seducing many of His Majesties Subjects to go on Shipboard, where they have been Seized and Carried by Force to His Majesties Plantations in America* (London, 1682).

46. See Chapter 2.

47. *At the Court at Whitehall, December the Thirteenth, 1682*.

48. Hugh Jones, *The Present State of Virginia. Giving A particular and short Account of the Indian, English, and Negroe Inhabitants Of that Colony* (London, 1724), sig. H3r. Jones simultaneously raises and dismisses the idea that the condition of the last sort of "white Servants," "those Convicts or Felons that are transported," might constitute a form of slavery: "Their being sent thither to work as Slaves for Punishment, is but a mere Notion, for few of them ever lived so well and so easy before, especially if they are good for any thing. These are to serve seven, and sometimes fourteen Years, and they and Servants by Indentures have an Allowance of Corn and Cloaths, when they are out of their Time, that they may be therewith supported, till they can be provided with Services, or otherwise settled" (sig. H3r–H3v). The fact that these "Convicts or Felons" are bound for a specific period of time and recompensed "when they are out of their Time" underscores their distinction from "Slaves."

49. *Oxford English Dictionary*, s.v. "kid, *n.1*," 5.c.; 5.a.

50. B. E., *A New Dictionary of the Terms Ancient and Modern of the Canting Crew* (London, 1699), sig. G6r.

51. Indenture between Pentecost Teague, John Popel, and Robert Quary (1709). Y.d.554, Folger Shakespeare Library. See Chapter 2 for a discussion of the *mancipium*.

52. Gen MSS Misc, Grp 1223, Item F-1. Deed of sale for a slave, 1738/9. Beinecke Library, Yale University.

53. See, for instance, J. Martin Evans, *Milton's Imperial Epic: "Paradise Lost" and the Discourse of Colonialism* (Ithaca, NY: Cornell University Press, 1996); and Paul Stevens, "*Paradise Lost* and the Colonial Imperative," *Milton Studies* 34 (1996): 3–21.

54. As Jennifer L. Morgan reminds us in "*Partus sequitur ventrem*: Law, Race, and Reproduction in Colonial Slavery," *Small Axe* 22, no. 1 (2018), "Atlantic slavery rested upon a notion of heritability" (1). Morgan notes that the paradigms that reimagined European notions of descent into the logics of heritable slavery organized around racialization represented a profound shift in the early modern Atlantic world: "If a child fathered by a free white man with an enslaved African woman became a slave, that child was transformed from kin to property. Thus, in essence, slaveowners and slaveowning legislators enacted the legal and material substitution of a thing for a child: no white man's *child* could be enslaved, while all black women's *issue* could. This happens as though it were common sense, when, in fact, it was a profound reversal of European notions of heredity in the service of a relatively new notion of difference and bondage" (5). Reading the case of Maria, an enslaved woman captured by Sir Francis Drake, Morgan argues that it reveals "a new way of understanding the world—one in which reproduction became commodity-production under the logics of colonial possessions" (8). For a foundational discussion of the nexus of race, gender, and labor in relation to slavery and reproduction, see Jennifer L. Morgan, *Laboring Women: Reproduction and Gender in New World Slavery* (Philadelphia: University of Pennsylvania Press, 2004).

55. All references follow *Paradise Lost*, ed. Barbara K. Lewalski (Malden, MA: Blackwell, 2007).

56. References to Sonnet 19 follow *Paradise Regained, Samson Agonistes, and the Complete Shorter Poems*, ed. William Kerrigan, John Rumrich, and Stephen M. Fallon (New York: Modern Library, 2012), 157–58.

57. In a New World context, this of course complicates the idea that planters and other transplants find respite from debt bondage—a particularly ironic argument given that indentured servants precisely bind their bodies as collateral for the debt (of their passage to the New World) that they incur.

58. David Hawkes, "Milton and Usury," *English Literary Renaissance* 41, no. 3 (2011): 517.

59. *The booke of the common prayer* (London, 1549), sig. A4r.

60. Ibid.

61. Evans, *Milton's Imperial Epic*, 80.

62. By the 1680s, the promise of land at the end of their contracts was fading for English men and women who made the journey to the plantations. But for Adam and Eve, the liberty of their servitude and the willingness of their indenture is intended to lead to *greater* dominion; in essence, Adam and Eve offer the individuated fantasy of imperial expansion at the same time as they gesture to the horror of Sisyphean work, deferred redemption, and correct, faithful, and willing discourses and enactments of servitude.

63. Luke Wilson, "*Macbeth* and the Contingency of Future Persons," *Shakespeare Studies* 40 (2012): 53.

64. Ibid., 57.

65. *Oxford English Dictionary*, s.v. "grandparent, *n.*"

66. Timothie Bright, *Characterie An Arte of shorte, swifte, and secrete writing by Character* (London, 1588), sig. I9v.

67. See *The Riverside Milton*, ed. Roy Flannagan (Boston: Houghton Mifflin, 1998), 365 n.128.

68. Both "travail" and "labour," of course, evoke childbirth as well as manual toil.

69. In speaking of the "Child," I refer both to the category of the child writ large as well as to the idealized "Child" who secures the future; see Lee Edelman's *No Future: Queer Theory and the Death Drive* (Durham, NC: Duke University Press, 2004).

70. David Benatar, *Better Never to Have Been: The Harm of Coming into Existence* (New York: Oxford University Press, 2006). In this way, Adam and Eve's anti-natalism marries Lee Edelman's invocation to "insist that the future stop here" with José Esteban Muñoz's theory of a queer utopia, the childless utopia on the horizon. See Edelman, *No Future*, 31; and José Esteban Muñoz, *Cruising Utopia: The Then and There of Queer Futurity* (New York: New York University Press, 2009).

71. We note that while David Benatar, for instance, argues against natality for all sentient beings, the Voluntary Human Extinction Movement currently advocates for anti-natalism in part on ecological and humanitarian grounds, to preserve other life forms as well as the planet as a whole.

72. Nathan Bailey, *An Universal Etymological English Dictionary* (London, 1721), sig. 6B4r.

73. See Margo Hendricks, "Race: A Renaissance Category?" in *A New Companion to English Renaissance Literature and Culture*, ed. Michael Hattaway (Malden, MA: Blackwell, 2010), 535–44 on the meanings of "race"; and Feerick, *Strangers in Blood*.

74. Feerick, *Strangers in Blood*, 9.

75. Ibid., 16.

76. Ibid., 20.

77. "Colonization—in Ireland, Virginia, and the West Indies—collided with these theories of identity rooted in land and soil, catalyzing profound revaluations of the period's dominant account of blood. Efforts to reproduce the social body of England in new soils, that is, had the effect of unsettling the system of race then dominantly constituting England's social structure." Ibid., 18.

78. For an examination of the premodern "architectures of racial formation" that often coarticulated sin and blackness, see Geraldine Heng, *The Invention of Race in the European Middle Ages* (Cambridge, UK: Cambridge University Press, 2018). For an extended discussion of the nexus of blackness, bondage, and biblical provenance, see David M. Goldenberg, *The Curse of Ham: Race and Slavery in Early Judaism, Christianity, and Islam* (Princeton, NJ: Princeton University Press, 2003).

79. For further discussion of the implications of slavery in *Paradise Lost*, see Maureen Quilligan, "Freedom, Service, and the Trade in Slaves: The Problem of Labor in *Paradise Lost*," in *Subject and Object in Renaissance Culture*, ed. Margreta de Grazia, Maureen Quilligan, and Peter Stallybrass (Cambridge, UK: Cambridge University Press, 1996), 213–34; Steven Jablonski, "Ham's Vicious Race: Slavery and John Milton," *Studies in English Literature, 1500–1900* 37, no. 1 (1997): 173–90; and Mary Nyquist, *Arbitrary Rule: Slavery, Tyranny, and the Power of Life and Death* (Chicago: University of Chicago Press, 2013). Jablonski "conclude[s] that Milton, for all his hatred of tyranny and love of liberty, was opposed to the enslavement of the wrong people rather than to slavery per se. . . . the idea of slavery was part of his idea of liberty. Implicit in his every reference to 'rational liberty' was a reference to irrational slavery, for by his grim logic, not to be worthy of freedom was to be worthy of slavery" (186). Nyquist, meanwhile, parses *Paradise Lost*'s treatment of freedom and slavery, particularly in relation to the "curse of Ham" and allusions to his "vicious race" that Jablonski's essay also unfolds, arguing that "At the time Milton writes, Western Europeans associate the Hamitic curse with sub-Saharan Africans, an identification *Paradise Lost* may assume its readers will make and certainly does nothing to counteract" and suggesting that *Paradise Lost*'s depiction of penal slavery "also legitimizes colonial conquest" (146). Daniel Shore argues that "the penal conception of slavery is also subtly encapsulated in the double sense of the Latinate 'vicious' current in Milton's English: at once outwardly cruel or wicked (as in present-day 'vicious') and inwardly flawed or debased (as in present-day 'vitiated')." See "Was Milton White?" *Milton Studies* 62, no. 2 (2020): 256; this essay vitally argues that Milton "engaged in the project of remaking white identity into a racially unmarked conception of universal liberal personhood" (253).

Chapter 5

1. Maurice Kyffin, *Andria The first Comoedie of Terence, in English. A furtherance for the attainment vnto the right knowledge, & true proprietie, of the Latin Tong. And also a commodious meane of help, to such as haue forgotten Latin, for their speedy recouering of habilitie, to vnderstand, write, and speake the same. Carefully translated out of Latin, by Maurice Kyffin* (London, 1588), sig. B4r. See Chapter 2 for more discussion of *Andria*.

2. Thomas Elyot, *The Dictionary of syr Thomas Eliot knyght* (London, 1538), sig M3r; Thomas Thomas, *Dictionarivm Lingvae Latinae Et Anglicanae* (Cambridge, 1587), sig. 2K6v.

3. This chapter is careful to distinguish between "freemen" and "freedmen," not least because a "freeman" also denoted, at this time, one who had the freedom of the city. Thus, William Stepney, in *The Spanish Schoole-master* (London, 1591), chooses to render into Spanish the stock phrases "I am a freeman of London" (sig. Q7v) and "he is a free man of London" (sig. R1v), while Thomas Thomas glosses "*Civis*" as "A citizen, both the man and woman, of the same citie or countrie: our Countrieman, a Burgesse, a freeman" (sig. L4r). For a longer discussion of the early modern language of freemen and citizenship, see John Michael Archer, *Citizen Shakespeare: Freemen and Aliens in the Language of the Plays* (New York: Palgrave Macmillan, 2005). In a discussion of "the prehistory of modern citizenship" via Balibar, Archer notes that "Balibar locates the first stirrings of citizenship-as-subjectivity much later than Aristotle, in the intersection of Roman law with a Christianized empire.... Although subject to the emperor, the citizen was classified as a *subditus* rather than a *servus* or slave" (2).

4. See Henrik Mouritsen, *The Freedman in the Roman World* (Cambridge, UK: Cambridge University Press, 2011). Tellingly, the *macula servitutis* attaches itself not only to the mind but also to the body of the slave, so that the dead bodies of slaves were required to be removed from the city limits earlier than the dead bodies of free men, on account of the slaves' greater essential "pollution." See Mouritsen, 20. The word *macula* itself registers both as a "stain" and as "dishonor," with several early modern lexicons emphasizing its sense of a "blemish." Thomas Thomas's *Dictionarivm*, for instance, glosses *macula* as "A spot, a blemish, a naturall marke or token whereby a thing is knowne: *also* an infamie, reproch, dishonour, staine, disworship, discredit" (sig. 2L8v). We might recall the "blots of Nature's hand" discussed in Chapter 3; these "blots" register as somatic and hereditable markers.

5. I discuss the provisions of the 1547 Vagrancy Act in the Introduction; this edict stipulated that "masterless men" could be taken into slavery if they refused to enter service.

6. Abner C. Goodell, Jr., "John Saffin and His Slave Adam," *Publications of the Colonial Society of Massachusetts* I (1892–1894), 85–112.

7. *The Tragedy of King Lear*, 1.1.136–39. All references follow *The Norton Shakespeare*, 3rd ed., gen. ed. Stephen Greenblatt (New York: W. W. Norton, 2016). Further references will be cited parenthetically within the text.

8. For a longer discussion of the figure of the *magister*, see Chapter 2.

9. Richard Strier, "Faithful Servants: Shakespeare's Praise of Disobedience," in *The Historical Renaissance: New Essays on Tudor and Stuart Literature and Culture*, ed. Heather Dubrow and Richard Strier (Chicago: University of Chicago Press, 1988), 104–33.

10. Scholars such as David Schalkwyk and Michael Neill follow this reading; in a generative recent essay, Amrita Dhar has explored the ramifications of "faithful service" in the play for our understanding of affect and disability in *Lear*. As I have recently suggested, the project of searching for or parsing "faithful service" also participates in a larger project of white supremacy, drawing on a nostalgia for the fictions of the happy "family" (writ large) to shore up the investments in white supremacy that underwrite them. See Schalkwyk, *Shakespeare, Love and Service* (Cambridge, UK: Cambridge University Press, 2008); Neill, *Putting History to the Question: Power, Politics, and Society in English Renaissance Drama* (New York: Columbia University Press, 2000); Dhar, "Seeing Feelingly: Sight and Service in *King Lear*," in *Disability, Health, and Happiness in the Shakespearean Body*, ed. Sujata Iyengar (New York: Routledge, 2015), 76–92; and Chakravarty, "Race, Labor, and the Future of the Past: *King Lear*'s 'True Blank,'" *postmedieval* 11, no. 2–3 (2020): 204–11.

11. For a longer discussion of the uses of consent to authorize early modern political structures, see Melissa E. Sanchez, *Erotic Subjects: The Sexuality of Politics in Early Modern English*

Literature (Oxford: Oxford University Press, 2011). Sanchez reminds us that "what is experienced as ennobling love may in fact be debasing infatuation. In its political dimension this signifies the erotic enslavement and self-deceit that, according to writers from la Boétie to Milton to Algernon Sidney, is the true prop of tyranny," adding in a footnote that "Algernon Sidney attributes tyranny not to force but to deluded consent" (151).

12. *An Exact Collection Of The Works Of Doctor Iackson, P. of C.C.C. Oxon, Such as were not Published before* (London, 1654), 3048, 3050. The next part of the title reflects Jackson's thesis regarding satanic servitude and divine freedom: "Christ exercising his Everlasting Priesthood. Mans Freedom from Servitude to Sin, effected by Christ sitting at the Right Hand of God, and there Officiating as a most Compassionate High-priest in behalf of Sinners." The epigraph on the title page pithily sums up Jackson's directive: "*Verily! Verily! He that committeth Sin is the Servant of Sin: / If the Son make you Free, then ye shall be Free indeed."*

13. *The booke of the common prayer* (London, 1549), sig. A4r.

14. *An Exact Collection Of The Works Of Doctor Iackson*, 3050.

15. Ibid.

16. David Evett discusses iterations of freedom and service in this period as they originate in the *Book of Common Prayer* in *Discourses of Service in Shakespeare's England* (New York: Palgrave Macmillan, 2005).

17. Joseph Webbe, *The First Comedy Of Pvb. Terentivs, Called Andria, Or, The Woman of Andros, English and Latine* (London, 1629), sig. A3v–A4r. Unless otherwise noted, all passages from *Andria* are taken from this translation.

18. We note, too, that even on manumission a *libertus* did not attain the status of an *ingenuus*, or free-born individual. The *macula servitutis* or "stain of slavery" therefore made it impossible ever to attain the legal or social status of a freeman (as opposed to merely a *freed*man). As I have noted, this chapter distinguishes between "freeman" and "freedman" to refer, respectively, to the *ingenuus* and the *libertus*.

19. *P. Terentii Afri Poetae Lepidissimi Comoediae* (Paris, 1552), 68 (sig. f4v). We may contrast this with the straightforward—and less editorialized—translation of *in memoria habeo* in other contemporary works. Nicholas Udall, for instance, renders this phrase as "I remember it well, or I beare it well in mynde" in his *Flovres for Latine Spekynge Selected and gathered oute of Terence, and the same translated in to Englysshe* (London, 1534), sig. A1r.

20. *P. Terentii Afri Poetae Lepidissimi Comoediae*, 68 (sig. f4v).

21. As I shall discuss at greater length at the end of this chapter, Saidiya V. Hartman reminds us in her discussion of "The burden of debt, duty, and gratitude foisted onto the newly emancipated in exchange or repayment for their freedom" that this form of obligation would later also comprise part of the structural "debt of emancipation" for the American slave. See Hartman, *Scenes of Subjection: Terror, Slavery, and Self-Making in Nineteenth-Century America* (New York: Oxford University Press, 1997), 130. I am grateful to Miles Grier for drawing my attention to this point.

22. The adaptation of *Andria* in *The Tempest* has not, to my knowledge, been critically discussed hitherto.

23. *The Tempest*, 1.2.242–50. All references to the play follow *The Norton Shakespeare*, 3rd ed. Further references will be cited parenthetically within the text.

24. At the same time, the directive "Let me remember thee" adopts a posture of confidence, the words "let me" claiming authority while purportedly seeking authorization. For more on

representations of memory and forgetting in early modern England, see Hester Lees-Jeffries, *Shakespeare and Memory* (Oxford: Oxford University Press, 2013) and Garrett A. Sullivan, Jr., *Memory and Forgetting in English Renaissance Drama: Shakespeare, Marlowe, Webster* (Cambridge, UK: Cambridge University Press, 2005). I also discuss the discourse of memory in affective economies of service in Chapter 3.

25. *P. Terentii Afri Poetae Lepidissimi Comoediae*, 61 (sig. f1r).

26. I shall return to this point later with regard to Ariel, who notably cannot speak freely (see below in this chapter), and to the mandate of gratitude to which enslaved persons in America were subject.

27. The idea of the "perfect," in early modern England, encompassed the sense of not only the exquisite, or even God-like, but also something full, complete, absolute. See, for instance, Timothie Bright's *Characterie An Arte of shorte, swifte, and secrete writing by Character* (London, 1588), which renders "Absolute" as "*Perfect*" (sig. A1r) and "Entire" as "*All, or perfect*" (sig. C7r).

28. Terence, *Guidonis Iuuenalis natione Cenomani in Terentium* . . . (Lyon, 1493), sig. a8v. T79, Folger Shakespeare Library. The manuscript marginalia include a notation of "*fides*," with an additional manicule drawing attention to the discussion of this exchange in the commentary.

29. Thomas Cooper, *Thesavrvs Lingvae Romanae & Britannicae* (London, 1565), sig. 5I2v.

30. John Véron, *A Dictionary in Latine and English, heretofore set foorth by Master Iohn Veron, and now newly corrected and enlarged, For the vtilitie and profite of all young students in the Latine tongue, as by further search therin they shall finde. By R. W.* (London, 1575), sig. 2A8r.

31. The imperative to articulate gratitude constitutes, I suggest, another iteration of the *macula servitutis*: the oral performance of the very gratitude that reinforces one's essential servility. The material metaphor of the *macula servitutis* lends itself easily, I propose, to the discursive register of a rhetorical performance.

32. Cooper, *Thesavrvs Lingvae Romanae & Britannicae*, sig. 4Z3r.

33. Elyot, *The Dictionary of syr Thomas Eliot knyght*, sig. S6v.

34. Kyffin, *Andria The first Comoedie of Terence, in English*, sig. B4r.

35. Thomas Newman, *The Two First Comedies Of Terence called Andria, and the Eunuch newly Englished by Thomas Newman* (London, 1627), sig. B1r.

36. For two very different models of the gift, see Marcel Mauss's classic *The Gift: The Form and Reason for Exchange in Archaic Societies*, trans. W. D. Halls (New York: Norton, 1990) and Jacques Derrida's *Given Time: I. Counterfeit Money*, trans. Peggy Kamuf (Chicago: University of Chicago Press, 1992). I discuss gift practices in networks of service in Chapter 3.

37. William Shakespeare, *The Tempest*, ed. Virginia Mason Vaughan and Alden T. Vaughan, The Arden Shakespeare, 3rd ser. (New York: Bloomsbury, 2011), 190–91.

38. In her essay "Base Slavery and Roman Yoke," in *The Oxford Handbook of English Law and Literature, 1500–1700*, ed. Lorna Hutson (Oxford: Oxford University Press, 2017), 624–45, Mary Nyquist reflects on the rhetorical (and rhetorically pejorative) force of slavery; see also Chapter 3. If the distinction between service and slavery was absolute for English servants (to articulate oneself as a slave was to situate one's master as a tyrant; to call oneself a slave, however, was also to call into question the fundamental association between Englishness and liberty), that distinction was a luxury not afforded outside England's borders. And, as I have discussed in this book, such slavery was certainly well known to English audiences through travel narratives as well as English accounts of slavery and redemption. For a recent discussion of early modern

England's experiences of and encounters with bondage in a global context and a pre-plantation moment, see Michael Guasco's *Slaves and Englishmen: Human Bondage in the Early Modern Atlantic World* (Philadelphia: University of Pennsylvania Press, 2014).

39. For a discussion of Ariel in relation to the terms of apprenticeship, see Andrew Gurr, "Industrious Ariel and Idle Caliban," in *Travel and Drama in Shakespeare's Time*, ed. Jean-Pierre Maquerlot and Michèle Willems (Cambridge, UK: Cambridge University Press, 1996), 193–208. Reading the play in the context of theatrical labor, Daniel Vitkus analogizes Ariel's servitude to the labor of the "bound" boy actor who would have played him; see "'Meaner Ministers': Mastery, Bondage, and Theatrical Labor in *The Tempest*," in *A Companion to Shakespeare's Works, Volume IV: The Poems, Problem Comedies, Late Plays*, ed. Richard Dutton and Jean E. Howard (Malden, MA: Blackwell, 2003), 408–26, esp. 415–16.

40. See Craig Muldrew, *The Economy of Obligation: The Culture of Credit and Social Relations in Early Modern England* (Basingstoke, UK: Palgrave, 1998), and Amanda Bailey, *Of Bondage: Debt, Property, and Personhood in Early Modern England* (Philadelphia: University of Pennsylvania Press, 2013).

41. Victoria Kahn, *Wayward Contracts: The Crisis of Political Obligation in England, 1640–1674* (Princeton, NJ: Princeton University Press, 2004), 4.

42. Lewis Carroll, *Through the Looking-Glass* (New York: M. F. Mansfield and A. Wessels, 1899), 64.

43. Indeed, many productions stage these two characters in terms of the visual, sartorial, and corporeal dialectics of weightlessness and weightiness; air and earth; light and dark; physical unboundedness and corporeal confinement.

44. Hiewon Shin reads pedagogy in *The Tempest* in terms of early modern adoption and women's knowledge and education in "Single Parenting, Homeschooling: Prospero, Caliban, Miranda," *Studies in English Literature 1500–1900* 48, no. 2 (2008): 373–93. Tom Lindsay argues for Caliban's pedagogical disillusionment in "'Which first was mine own king': Caliban and the Politics of Service and Education in *The Tempest*," *Studies in Philology* 113, no. 2 (2016): 397–423. Melissa E. Sanchez discusses the erotic valences of Caliban's subjection to Prospero in "Seduction and Service in *The Tempest*," *Studies in Philology* 105, no. 1 (2008): 50–82.

45. Kyffin, *Andria The first Comoedie of Terence, in English*, sig. A1r. For a useful overview of the significance of Terence to Shakespeare's work, see the chapter on "Roman Comedy" in Colin Burrow's *Shakespeare and Classical Antiquity* (Oxford: Oxford University Press, 2013), esp. 138–43.

46. "For an understanding of how all sixteenth century drama grew, not merely nor chiefly in England, the study of Terence in the grammar schools and out is fundamental." See T. W. Baldwin, *William Shakespere's Small Latine and Lesse Greeke*, vol. 1 (Urbana: University of Illinois Press, 1944), 642. Burrow, however, cautions readers that "Baldwin is prone to overestimate the quality of Shakespeare's education" (*Shakespeare and Classical Antiquity*, 269).

47. Kahn, *Wayward Contracts*, 10. See also Su Fang Ng, *Literature and the Politics of Family in Seventeenth-Century England* (Cambridge, UK: Cambridge University Press, 2007), for a useful study of the family and political authority in early modern England.

48. Miles P. Grier, "Inkface: The Slave Stigma in England's Early Imperial Imagination," in *Scripturalizing the Human: The Written as the Political*, ed. Vincent L. Wimbush (New York: Routledge, 2015), 206.

49. Ibid., 196.

50. Ania Loomba, *Shakespeare, Race, and Colonialism* (Oxford: Oxford University Press, 2002), 166–67.

51. Kim F. Hall, *Things of Darkness: Economies of Race and Gender in Early Modern England* (Ithaca, NY: Cornell University Press, 1995), 142.

52. See Patricia Akhimie, *Shakespeare and the Cultivation of Difference: Race and Conduct in the Early Modern World* (New York: Routledge, 2018), esp. Chapter 4. As Akhimie crucially argues, "Marking some groups as unimprovable is achieved by withholding or restricting access to the very kinds of nurturing that conduct books maintain are necessary to grow a better subject: to 'pinch' is to injure by withholding opportunities for advancement through education or other kinds of cultivation, by punishing ambition or attempts at advancement, and by restricting mobility and freedom of thought. Members of this abject group, slave-like, would then be incapable of making competing claims to the land, without access to education or advancement by any means, and deprived of their histories of lineage (meaning family and blood, as well as structures of inheritance such as primogeniture). The lack of civility, humanity, urbanity, even will, that results from such sustained withholding, can then seem or be made to seem inherent. Over time such groups may come to seem inhuman when they are merely bereft" (180–81).

53. Paul Brown, "'This Thing of Darkness I Acknowledge Mine': *The Tempest* and the Discourse of Colonialism," in *Political Shakespeare: New Essays in Cultural Materialism*, ed. Jonathan Dollimore and Alan Sinfield (Ithaca, NY: Cornell University Press, 1985), 48–71.

54. *A Dictionary of Greek and Roman Antiquities*, 3rd ed., Volume II, ed. William Smith, William Wayte, and G. E. Marindin (London: John Murray, 1891), 118.

55. Ibid. There are in fact several "witnesses" to Prospero's statement in this scene: Ferdinand, Miranda, Gonzalo, the Boatswain, Sebastian, Alonso, Stefano, Trinculo, and Ariel himself. Thus, I want to suggest that this apparent discursive marker ("I acknowledge mine") of possible familial transformation also evokes and stages precisely the Roman ceremony that would legally affirm and ratify Caliban's enslavement.

56. John Baret, *An Alvearie or Triple Dictionarie, in Englishe, Latin, and French* (London, 1574), sig. C5r; Bright, *Characterie*, sig. A1v.

57. See *A Dictionary of Greek and Roman Antiquities*, ed. Smith et al., 117. The framing of Caliban as a *mancipium* opens suggestively onto a range of questions. The form of the *mancipatio* suggests that the *mancipium*'s status as slave precedes the *mancipatio*; is Caliban already a *mancipium*? Neither his treatment nor his actions, over the course of the play, indicate this in any uncomplicated way. Rather, Caliban has offered to transfer his fealty to Trinculo and Stephano, indicating, for many readers, his "essential" servitude, but also suggesting that he considers himself able to vend his services, to authorize his own labor.

58. Mouritsen, *The Freedman in the Roman World*, 147.

59. There has been a considerable amount of excellent scholarly work undertaken on the legal and political role of indentured servants in the early modern Atlantic world; for some recent examples, see Christopher Tomlins, *Freedom Bound: Law, Labor, and Civic Identity in Colonizing English America, 1580–1865* (Cambridge, UK: Cambridge University Press, 2010); Simon P. Newman, *A New World of Labor: The Development of Plantation Slavery in the British Atlantic* (Philadelphia: University of Pennsylvania Press, 2013); and John Wareing, *Indentured Migration and the Servant Trade from London to America, 1618–1718: "There Is Great Want of Servants"* (Oxford: Oxford University Press, 2017).

60. See Goodell, "John Saffin and His Slave Adam," 88.

61. The case of Adam was the subject of a vigorous debate between John Saffin and the judge and printer Samuel Sewall. Sewall penned an antislavery tract titled *The Selling of Joseph* (Boston, 1700); in response, Saffin published *A Brief and Candid Answer to a Late Printed Sheet, Entitled, The Selling of Joseph* (Boston, 1701). Until recently, there had been relatively little critical attention paid to this case; these discussions included Lawrence W. Towner's article "The Sewall-Saffin Dialogue on Slavery," *William and Mary Quarterly* 21, no. 1 (1964): 40–52, and Albert J. Von Frank's situating of this case within a wider context of slavery and race in "John Saffin: Slavery and Racism in Colonial Massachusetts," *Early American Literature* 29, no. 3 (1994): 254–72. James J. Allegro briefly discusses the case in his article "'Increasing and Strengthening the Country': Law, Politics, and the Antislavery Movement in Early-Eighteenth-Century Massachusetts Bay," *New England Quarterly* 75, no. 1 (2002): 5–23; and Jeannine Marie DeLombard touches on the case in *Slavery on Trial: Law, Abolitionism, and Print Culture* (Chapel Hill: University of North Carolina Press, 2007), 3–4. More recent critical interventions, however, include Heather Miyano Kopelson's *Faithful Bodies: Performing Religion and Race in the Puritan Atlantic* (New York: New York University Press, 2014), esp. 101–11; and David Kazanjian's essay "'To see the Issue of these his Exorbitant Practices': A Response to 'The Dispossessed Eighteenth Century,'" *The Eighteenth Century* 55, no. 2/3 (2014): 273–82. Kopelson offers the important reminder that although Sewall's treatise *The Selling of Joseph* (1701) was an antislavery tract, it "critiqued slavery partly based on the idea that Africans were unchangeably inferior. . . . one of his arguments against slavery was that it would bring in increasing numbers of Africans who had 'such a disparity in their Conditions, Colour and Hair, that they can never embody with us, and *grow into orderly Families*, to the Peopling of the Land.' Those individuals would 'still remain in our Body Politick as a kind of extravasat Blood,' that is, blood forced from its proper vehicle of veins and arteries into other bodily tissue, causing problems. The vague solution Sewall proposed was to stop the practice of enslaving Africans and to bring no more into New England, filling labor needs with white servants who could marry masters' daughters" (*Faithful Bodies*, 110, emphasis added). The rhetoric here, then, rehearses the dangers of and distinctions between slavery and family discussed in Chapter 3 as well as the contingencies of blood: white servants have the capacity to join "orderly" sanguinal families while the blood of black enslaved people threatens a sanguinal (and racial) excess.

62. In a declaration regarding Adam's character, Shepherd (also referred to as Shepard) describes his servant by characterizing him as a kind of chattel. Shepherd recalls that he "had with the Stock of cattle and Sheep a certain negro man named Adam to Serve [him] into the bargain during the Lease" (qtd. in Goodell, "John Saffin and His Slave Adam," 90); Adam, in this articulation, comprises part of a "bargain" along with "cattle and Sheep." Shepherd sent Adam back to Saffin, however, before the expiration of the contract.

63. Petition of John Saffin dated 26th May 1703, in Goodell, 96–97, at 96.

64. See Chapter 4 for a longer discussion of the affinities between English apprenticeship indentures and Atlantic contracts for indentured servants.

65. *The Tempest*, 1.2.248–49.

66. The echoes of English apprenticeship indentures are particularly resonant here; we remember that such contracts also enjoin the apprentice to serve "faithfully," his master's "lawful Commandments every where gladly do." See, for instance, Folger X.d.734, discussed in Chapter 4.

67. Kazanjian argues that "Saffin . . . did not simply seek to dispossess Adam of something that was essentially his, such as his labor. He sought to *possess* Adam with a certain being: the desire for, or love of, quiet industry on behalf of his master." See "'To see the Issue of these his Exorbitant Practices,'" 280.

68. John Saffin, *A Brief and Candid Answer to a late Printed Sheet, Entituled, The Selling of Joseph Whereunto is annexed, A True and Particular Narrative by way of Vindication of the Author's Dealing with and Prosecution of his Negro Man servant for his vile and exorbitant Behaviour towards his Master, and his Tenant Thomas Shepard; which hath been wrongfully Represented to their P[r]ejudice and Defamation.* . . . Reprinted in Goodell, "John Saffin and His Slave Adam," 103–12; at 105. Goodell gives the title page and the "annexed" narrative. The first part of the pamphlet is reprinted in George Henry Moore, *Notes on the History of Slavery in Massachusetts* (New York: D. Appleton & Co., 1866), 251–56.

69. Ann Rosalind Jones and Peter Stallybrass, *Renaissance Clothing and the Materials of Memory* (Cambridge, UK: Cambridge University Press, 2000), 11. See also Chapter 1 for a longer discussion of livery and its mnemonic function in early modern England.

70. Saffin, *A Brief and Candid Answer*, in Goodell, 104.

71. Goodell, 91.

72. Petition of John Saffin dated 15 November 1703, Massachusetts Archives ix. 153, reprinted in Goodell, 100–101, at 101.

73. Saffin, *A Brief and Candid Answer*, in Goodell, 104.

74. For a discussion of the "grateful slave trope" in a later literary context, see George Boulukos, *The Grateful Slave: The Emergence of Race in Eighteenth-Century British and American Culture* (Cambridge, UK: Cambridge University Press, 2008).

75. Saffin, *A Brief and Candid Answer*, in Goodell, 104, 108. Saffin also obliquely alludes to a threat of sexual violence when he claims that Adam has "call[ed] the Maids vile names, and threatn[ed] them (as they said) that they were sometimes afraid to be in the Room with him." Ibid., 105.

76. Ibid., 105.

77. Petition by Adam's attorney, Thomas Newton, 8th May 1703, in Goodell, 94–95, at 95.

78. The language of debt and obligation is explicitly evoked in this case: Adam and Thomas Newton argue that "[Adam] *oweth* the s[ai]d John Saffin no Service but is free by Vertue of an Instrum[en]t under the hand and Seal of the s[ai]d John Saffin" (Adam's plea qtd. in Goodell, 97, emphasis mine).

79. Qtd. in Goodell, 89.

80. Saffin, *A Brief and Candid Answer*, in Goodell, 105.

81. Record of "a Court of General Sessions of the Peace held at Boston for the County of Suffolke on the third day of August *Anno Domini* One Thousand Seven hundred and three," in Goodell, 98.

82. Records of the Superior Court of Judicature, 1700–1714, fol. 100, in Goodell, 95.

83. We note, too, that the formerly enslaved person in America, as well as their descendants, carries through their nomenclature what Hortense J. Spillers calls "the captor father's mocking presence." See "Mama's Baby, Papa's Maybe: An American Grammar Book," *Diacritics* 17, no. 2 (1987), 80; qtd. in Hartman, *Scenes of Subjection*, 155. Hartman also notes "the paradox of emancipation and the dispossession that acquires the status of a legacy" (155) in bearing the enslaver's name and passing it down.

84. See Christine Daniels, "'Liberty to Complaine': Servant Petitions in Maryland, 1652–1797," in *The Many Legalities of Early America*, ed. Christopher L. Tomlins and Bruce H. Mann (Chapel Hill: University of North Carolina Press, 2001), 219–49.

85. William Hand Browne et al., eds., *The Archives of Maryland* (Baltimore, 1887–), XLI, 179–80, qtd. in Daniels, 229.

86. Daniels, 229.

87. Daniels argues that even the term "servitude" was used interchangeably with "apprenticeship" by court clerks until 1690 (ibid., 222).

88. Saffin, *A Brief and Candid Answer*, in Goodell, "John Saffin and His Slave Adam," 106.

89. Hartman, *Scenes of Subjection*, 126, 139.

90. Ibid., 131. As Hartman notes, "to be free was to be a debtor—that is, obliged and dutybound to others. Thus the inaugural gestures that opened these texts announced the advent of freedom and at the same time attested to the impossibility of escaping slavery.... Despite the invocation of the natural rights of man, the emphasis on the 'gift' of freedom and the accompanying duties, to the contrary, implied not only that one had to labor in exchange for what were deemed natural and inalienable rights but also that the failure to do so might result in their revocation" (131–32).

91. Saffin, *A Brief and Candid Answer*, in Goodell, "John Saffin and His Slave Adam," 106.

92. Records of the Superior Court of Judicature, 1700–1714, fol. 114, in Goodell, 100.

93. Robert Cawdrey, *A Table Alphabeticall, conteyning and teaching the true writing, and vnderstanding of hard vsuall English wordes, borrowed from the Hebrew, Greeke, Latine, or French, &c.* (London, 1604), sig. F7v.

94. Saffin, *A Brief and Candid Answer*, in Goodell, 107.

Epilogue

1. See Chapter 5.

2. Morgan Godwyn, *The Negro's & Indians Advocate, Suing for their Admission into the Church: Or A Persuasive to the Instructing and Baptizing of the Negro's and Indians in our Plantations* (London, 1680), 62. For a more detailed discussion of the nexus of race and conversion in this text, see Rebecca Anne Goetz, *The Baptism of Early Virginia: How Christianity Created Race* (Baltimore: Johns Hopkins University Press, 2012), esp. 106–8.

3. Robert Dodsley, *Servitude: A Poem* (London, 1729).

4. Ibid., 4, 7.

5. Dodsley indeed repeatedly refers to the servant's "servitude" in order to distinguish it both from slavery and from the "service" into which it is transformed by the happy exchange of the master's liberality for the servant's "faithful" duty ("With what Humanity then ought a Master to treat that Man whom Fortune has subjected to be his Servant? How ought he to endeavour to mollify and alleviate the Irksomeness of his Servitude?" See *Servitude*, 6). Yet "servitude" clearly registered the sense of bondage in contemporary lexicons. John Kersey's *A New English Dictionary* (London, 1702) defines the word as "*slavery*" (sig. 2C1r), and Benjamin Norton Defoe's *A New English Dictionary* of 1737 also glosses "servitude" as "Bondage, Slavery" (sig. 2D3r). It is perhaps suggestive that in both lexicons the entry for "servitude" is immediately preceded by that for "servitour," which Defoe defines as a "serving Man, or Waiter" but which, in the context of the university, signals "a Scholar who waits upon others for his Maintenance" (sig. 2D3r) or, in Kersey's words, "*a poor University Scholar, that attends upon others*" (sig. 2C1r). In both instances, the "servitour" underscores an uneasy association between servitude and education, recalling and reinforcing its early modern resonances.

6. *Poems On Various Subjects, Religious And Moral. By Phillis Wheatley, Negro Servant to Mr. John Wheatley, of Boston, in New England* (London, 1773), 11. Wheatley's poems were published in London due to the difficulty in finding an American printer willing to publish the work of an enslaved author.

7. We recall that the Roman freedman's former master was also known as his "patron."
8. Wheatley, *Poems On Various Subjects*, 12.
9. Richard Ligon, *A Trve & Exact History Of the Island of Barbados* (London, 1657), 55 (sig. P2r).
10. Colman's father, George Colman the Elder, was a renowned translator of Terence.
11. Tommy Tagg, *A Collection Of Pretty Poems For the Amusement of Children Three Foot High* (London, 1763), 81.
12. Ibid., 82. The image is located on p. 80. Figure 22 is reproduced from the American Antiquarian Society's copy of this work (London, between 1758 and 1800; edition uncertain).
13. Tommy Tagg, *A Collection Of Pretty Poems For the Amusement of Children Three Foot High* (London, 1763), 86.
14. Ibid., 88.
15. Paula T. Connolly notes that "Slave narratives would denounce the proslavery conflation of 'master/mistress' and 'father/mother,' exposing the proslavery metaphor of benevolent paternalism as a literal expression of sexual exploitation. In plantation novels, however, the conflation of master/parent carries no suggestion of miscegenation, but only the assurance of kind masters who provide for slaves in the most selfless of ways." See *Slavery in American Children's Literature, 1790–2010* (Iowa City: University of Iowa Press, 2013), 59–60.
16. Eliza Farrar, *The Adventures Of Congo In Search Of His Master; An American Tale. Containing A True Account Of A Shipwreck, And Interspersed with Anecdotes founded on Facts* (London, 1823; Boston, between 1824 and 1834). Citations are to the latter edition. For readings of *The Adventures of Congo* in the larger context of the place of slavery in nineteenth-century juvenile fiction, see Holly Keller, "Juvenile Antislavery Narrative and Notions of Childhood," *Children's Literature* 24 (1996): 86–100; and Sarah N. Roth, "The Mind of a Child: Images of African Americans in Early Juvenile Fiction," *Journal of the Early Republic* 25, no. 1 (2005): 79–109.
17. Farrar, *The Adventures Of Congo*, 18.
18. See Chapter 2.
19. Farrar, *The Adventures Of Congo*, 162.
20. *Cuffy The Negro's Doggrel Description Of The Progress Of Sugar* (London, 1823).
21. Ibid., 3.
22. Ibid., 2, 17, 16.
23. Ibid., 15.
24. Ibid., 2.
25. Ibid., 3.
26. Ibid., 3. See also Chapter 5.
27. *Cuffy The Negro's Doggrel Description Of The Progress Of Sugar*, 6.
28. Ladies' Society for Promoting the Early Education of Negro Children, *Post-Emancipation Life* (London, between 1833 and 1837). John Carter Brown Library, Providence, RI. The images accompanying the print narratives are taken from William Clark's *Ten Views of the Island of Antigua* (London, 1823).
29. "No. I: Holeing the Cane-Piece," in *Post-Emancipation Life*. These "apprenticeships" were, of course, compulsory, in a significant departure from the semblance of contractual consent that framed apprenticeship in England. But post-emancipation "apprenticeship" was also frequently experienced as a harsher and more violent condition than the slavery which had preceded it. Since masters were anticipating the departure of the people they had enslaved, many no longer saw the need to treat them even as useful "investments" for the future. Thus, as James

Williams, an "Apprenticed Labourer in Jamaica," notes in his *Narrative of Events Since the First of August, 1834* (London, 1837), "Apprentices get a great deal more punishment now than they did when they was slaves; the master take spite, and do all he can to hurt them before the free come" (1).

30. "No. II: Planting the Sugar-Cane," in *Post-Emancipation Life*.
31. "No. III: Cutting the Canes," in *Post-Emancipation Life*.
32. *The Instructive Alphabet* (New York, 1809).
33. David Claypoole Johnston, *A Proslavery Incantation Scene. Or Shakspeare Improved* (U.S., not before 1856). ART File S528m1 no. 86 (size L), Folger Shakespeare Library. See also Heather S. Nathans, "'Blood Will Have Blood': Violence, Slavery, and *Macbeth* in the Antebellum American Imagination," in *Weyward Macbeth: Intersections of Race and Performance*, ed. Scott L. Newstok and Ayanna Thompson (New York: Palgrave Macmillan, 2010), 23–33.

BIBLIOGRAPHY

Manuscripts

Beinecke Rare Book and Manuscript Library, Yale University
Gen. MSS Misc., Grp 1223, Item F-1

Bodleian Library, Oxford
MS Aubrey 13
MS Rawlinson Letters 59
MS Rawlinson Letters 100
MS Wood F. 43

British Library, London
Add. MS 78762
Sloane MS 1792
Stowe MS 176

Folger Shakespeare Library, Washington DC
MS V.a.467
MSS V.b.16 (1–66)
MS X.d.566
MS X.d.734
MS X.d.735
MS Y.d.554
MS Z.c.22 (38)

Huntington Library, San Marino, California
MS EL 1180
MS EL 2514
MS EL 2515
MS EL 2578
MS EL 2694
MS EL 6425
MS EL 6426

Manuscripts and Archives, Sterling Memorial Library, Yale University
Talman Family Papers, MS 662, Series I, Box 1, Folder 6

Electronic Resources

Lexicons of Early Modern English, ed. Ian Lancashire. Toronto: University of Toronto Press, 2018. http:/leme.library.utoronto.ca.

Middle English Dictionary Online, ed. Frances McSparran, et al. Ann Arbor: University of Michigan Library, 2000–2018. https://quod.lib.umich.edu/m/middle-english-dictionary/dictionary.

Oxford English Dictionary Online. Oxford University Press, 2021. https://www-oed-com.myaccess.library.utoronto.ca/.

"Switching the Lens: Rediscovering Londoners of African, Caribbean, Asian and Indigenous Heritage, 1561 to 1840," London Metropolitan Archives Collections Catalogue. https://search.lma.gov.uk/scripts/mwimain.dll?logon&application=UNION_VIEW&language=144&file=[lma]through-the-lens.html.

Published Sources

Adams, B. K. "Fair/Foul." In *Shakespeare/Text: Contemporary Readings in Textual Studies, Editing and Performance*, ed. Claire M. L. Bourne, 29–49. London: Bloomsbury Arden Shakespeare, 2021.

Adelman, Janet. "Her Father's Blood: Race, Conversion, and Nation in *The Merchant of Venice*," *Representations* 81, no. 1 (2003): 4–30.

Akhimie, Patricia. "Bruised with Adversity: Reading Race in *The Comedy of Errors*." In *The Oxford Handbook of Shakespeare and Embodiment: Gender, Sexuality, and Race*, ed. Valerie Traub, 186–96. Oxford: Oxford University Press, 2016.

———. *Shakespeare and the Cultivation of Difference: Race and Conduct in the Early Modern World*. New York: Routledge, 2018.

Alemán, Mateo. *The Rogve: Or The Life of Gvzman De Alfarache*. London, 1622.

Allegro, James J. "'Increasing and Strengthening the Country': Law, Politics, and the Antislavery Movement in Early-Eighteenth-Century Massachusetts Bay," *New England Quarterly* 75, no. 1 (2002): 5–23.

Amussen, Susan Dwyer. *Caribbean Exchanges: Slavery and the Transformation of English Society, 1640–1700*. Chapel Hill: University of North Carolina Press, 2007.

Andrewes, Lancelot. *Apospasmatia Sacra*. London, 1657.

Anno primo Edwardi Sexti Statvtes made in the Parliament. London, 1548.

Archer, Ian W. *The Pursuit of Stability: Social Relations in Elizabethan London*. Cambridge, UK: Cambridge University Press, 1991.

Archer, John Michael. *Citizen Shakespeare: Freemen and Aliens in the Language of the Plays*. New York: Palgrave Macmillan, 2005.

The Arrivall and Intertainements of the Embassador, Alkaid Jaurar Ben Abdella, with his Associate, Mr. Robert Blake. From the High and Mighty Prince, Mulley Mahamed Sheque, Emperor of Morocco, King of Fesse, and Suss. London, 1637.

Arvas, Abdulhamit. "Leander in the Ottoman Mediterranean: The Homoerotics of Abduction in the Global Renaissance," *English Literary Renaissance* 51, no. 1 (2021): 31–62.

Ascham, Roger. *The Scholemaster: or plaine and perfite waye of teachyng children, to vnderstand, write, and speake, the Latin tong, but specially purposed for the priuate brynging vp of youth in Ientlemen and Noble mens houses*. London, 1570.

At the Court at Whitehall, December the Thirteenth, 1682 . . . Whereas it has been Represented to His Majesty, That by reason of the frequent Abuses of a lewd sort of People called Spirits, in Seducing many of His Majesties Subjects to go on Shipboard, where they have been Seized and Carried by Force to His Majesties Plantations in America. London, 1682.

B., M. *The Triall of true Friendship; Or perfit mirror, wherby to discerne a trustie friend from a flattering Parasite*. London, 1596.

Bailey, Amanda. *Flaunting: Style and the Subversive Male Body in Renaissance England*. Toronto: University of Toronto Press, 2007.

———. *Of Bondage: Debt, Property, and Personhood in Early Modern England*. Philadelphia: University of Pennsylvania Press, 2013.

Bailey, Nathan. *An Universal Etymological English Dictionary*. London, 1721.

Baldwin, T. W. *William Shakespere's Small Latine and Lesse Greeke*, vol. 1. Urbana: University of Illinois Press, 1944.

Baret, John. *An Alvearie or Triple Dictionarie, in Englishe, Latin, and French*. London, 1574.

Barroll, Leeds. *Politics, Plague, and Shakespeare's Theater: The Stuart Years*. Ithaca, NY: Cornell University Press, 1991.

Bartels, Emily C. *Speaking of the Moor: From "Alcazar" to "Othello"*. Philadelphia: University of Pennsylvania Press, 2008.

———. "Too Many Blackamoors: Deportation, Discrimination, and Elizabeth I," *Studies in English Literature, 1500–1900* 46, no. 2 (2006): 305–22.

Barthelemy, Anthony Gerard. *Black Face, Maligned Race: The Representation of Blacks in English Drama from Shakespeare to Southerne*. Baton Rouge: Louisiana State University Press, 1987.

Beckles, Hilary McD. *The First Black Slave Society: Britain's "Barbarity Time" in Barbados, 1636–1876*. Kingston, Jamaica: University of the West Indies Press, 2016.

Ben-Amos, Ilana Krausman. *The Culture of Giving: Informal Support and Gift-Exchange in Early Modern England*. Cambridge, UK: Cambridge University Press, 2008.

———. "Failure to Become Freemen: Urban Apprentices in Early Modern England," *Social History* 16, no. 2 (1991): 155–72.

Benatar, David. *Better Never to Have Been: The Harm of Coming into Existence*. Oxford: Oxford University Press, 2006.

Berger, Adolf. "Encyclopedic Dictionary of Roman Law," *Transactions of the American Philosophical Society* 43, no. 2 (1953): 333–808.

Blount, Thomas. *Glossographia: or A Dictionary*. London, 1656.

Bloxam, J. R., ed. *Magdalen College and King James II 1686–1688: A Series of Documents*. Oxford: Clarendon Press, 1886.

A Booke Of Presidents, With Additions of diuers necessarie Instruments, meete for all such as desire to learne the manner and forme how to make Euidences and Instruments, &c. London, 1607.

The booke of the common prayer and administracion of the Sacramentes, and other rites and Ceremonies of the Churche: after the vse of the Churche of England. London, 1549.

Bosman, Anston. "'Best Play with Mardian': Eunuch and Blackamoor as Imperial Culturegram," *Shakespeare Studies* 34 (2006): 123–57.

Boulukos, George. *The Grateful Slave: The Emergence of Race in Eighteenth-Century British and American Culture*. Cambridge, UK: Cambridge University Press, 2008.

Bovilsky, Lara. *Barbarous Play: Race on the English Renaissance Stage*. Minneapolis: University of Minnesota Press, 2008.

Bradley, Keith. *Slavery and Society at Rome*. Cambridge, UK: Cambridge University Press, 1994.

Bray, Alan. *The Friend*. Chicago: University of Chicago Press, 2003.

———. "Homosexuality and the Signs of Male Friendship in Elizabethan England." In *Queering the Renaissance*, ed. Jonathan Goldberg, 40–61. Durham, NC: Duke University Press, 1994.

Brewer, Holly. *By Birth or Consent: Children, Law, and the Anglo-American Revolution in Authority*. Chapel Hill: University of North Carolina Press, 2005.

Bright, Timothie. *Characterie An Arte of shorte, swifte, and secrete writing by Character*. London, 1588.

Britton, Dennis Austin. *Becoming Christian: Race, Reformation, and Early Modern English Romance*. New York: Fordham University Press, 2014.

———, and Kimberly Anne Coles. "Spenser and Race: An Introduction," *Spenser Studies* 35 (2021): 1–19.

Brown, Kathleen M. *Good Wives, Nasty Wenches, and Anxious Patriarchs: Gender, Race, and Power in Colonial Virginia*. Chapel Hill: University of North Carolina Press, 1996.

Brown, Paul. "'This Thing of Darkness I Acknowledge Mine': *The Tempest* and the Discourse of Colonialism." In *Political Shakespeare: New Essays in Cultural Materialism*, ed. Jonathan Dollimore and Alan Sinfield, 48–71. Ithaca, NY: Cornell University Press, 1985.

Bullokar, John. *An English Expositor: Teaching The Interpretation of the hardest words vsed in our Language*. London, 1616.

Burnett, Mark Thornton. *Masters and Servants in English Renaissance Drama and Culture: Authority and Obedience*. New York: St. Martin's Press, 1997.

Burrow, Colin. *Shakespeare and Classical Antiquity*. Oxford: Oxford University Press, 2013.

Bushnell, Rebecca W. *A Culture of Teaching: Early Modern Humanism in Theory and Practice*. Ithaca, NY: Cornell University Press, 1996.

Callaghan, Dympna. *Shakespeare Without Women: Representing Gender and Race on the Renaissance Stage*. Abingdon, UK: Routledge, 2000.

Carroll, Lewis. *Through the Looking-Glass*. 1871. New York: M. F. Mansfield and A. Wessels, 1899.

Cartwright, William. *The Royall Slave. A Tragi-Comedy*. Oxford, 1639.

Cawdrey, Robert. *A Table Alphabeticall, conteyning and teaching the true writing, and vnderstanding of hard vsuall English wordes, borrowed from the Hebrew, Greeke, Latine, or French. &c.* London, 1604.

Chakravarty, Urvashi. "'More Than Kin, Less Than Kind': Similitude, Strangeness, and Early Modern English Homonationalisms," *Shakespeare Quarterly* 67, no. 1 (2016): 14–29.

———. "Race, Labor, and the Future of the Past: *King Lear*'s 'True Blank,'" *postmedieval* 11, no. 2–3 (2020): 204–11.

Chapman, George. *Bussy D'Ambois: A Tragedie*. London, 1607.

Chapman, Matthieu. *Anti-Black Racism in Early Modern English Drama: The Other "Other"*. New York: Routledge, 2017.

Cockeram, Henry. *The English Dictionarie: Or, An Interpreter of hard English Words*. London, 1623.

Connolly, Paula T. *Slavery in American Children's Literature, 1790–2010*. Iowa City: University of Iowa Press, 2013.

Cooke, John. *Greenes Tu quoque, Or, The Cittie Gallant*. London, 1614.

Cooper, Thomas. *Thesavrvs Lingvae Romanae & Britannicae*. London, 1565.

Coote, Edmund. *The English Schoole-maister*. London, 1596.

Copley, Anthony. *Another Letter Of Mr. A. C. To His Dis-Iesuited Kinseman, Concerning The Appeale, State, Iesvites*. London, 1602.

Cotgrave, Randle. *A Dictionarie Of The French And English Tongves*. London, 1611.

Cowell, John. *The Interpreter: Or Booke Containing the Signification of Words*. Cambridge, 1607.

Cox Jensen, Freyja, Dana L. Key, and Emma Whipday. "*The Disobedient Child*: A Tudor Interlude in Performance," *Shakespeare* 16, no. 1 (2020): 60–67.

Craik, Katharine A. "Warner, William (1558/9–1609), poet and lawyer," *Oxford Dictionary of National Biography*. 23 Sept. 2004; Accessed 1 May 2021. https://www.oxforddnb.com/view/10.1093/ref:odnb/9780198614128.001.0001/odnb-9780198614128-e-28770.

Crawford, Julie. "Women's Secretaries." In *Queer Renaissance Historiography: Backward Gaze*, ed. Vin Nardizzi, Stephen Guy-Bray, and Will Stockton, 111–34. New York: Routledge, 2009.

Crimsal, Richard. *A pleasant new Dialogue: Or, The discourse between the Serving-man and the Husband-man*. London, 1640.

Cuffy The Negro's Doggrel Description Of The Progress Of Sugar. London, 1823.

Dadabhoy, Ambereen. "Barbarian Moors: Documenting Racial Formation in Early Modern England." In *The Cambridge Companion to Shakespeare and Race*, ed. Ayanna Thompson, 30–46. Cambridge, UK: Cambridge University Press, 2021.

Daniels, Christine. "'Liberty to Complaine': Servant Petitions in Maryland, 1652–1797." In *The Many Legalities of Early America*, ed. Christopher L. Tomlins and Bruce H. Mann, 219–49. Chapel Hill: University of North Carolina Press, 2001.

Davies, C. S. L. "Slavery and Protector Somerset: The Vagrancy Act of 1547," *Economic History Review* 19, no. 3 (1966): 533–49.

Day, Angel. *The English Secretary, Or Methode of writing of Epistles and Letters: With A declaration of such Tropes, Figures, and Schemes, as either vsvally or for ornament sake are therein required*. London, 1599.

Daybell, James. *Women Letter-Writers in Tudor England*. Oxford: Oxford University Press, 2006.

De Grazia, Margreta. "The Ideology of Superfluous Things: *King Lear* as Period Piece." In *Subject and Object in Renaissance Culture*, ed. Margreta de Grazia, Maureen Quilligan, and Peter Stallybrass, 17–42. Cambridge, UK: Cambridge University Press, 1996.

Defoe, Benjamin Norton. *A New English Dictionary, Containing a Large and almost Compleat Collection of Useful English Words*. London, 1737.

Dekker, Thomas. *The Owles Almanacke. Prognosticating many strange accidents which shall happen to this Kingdome of Great Britaine this yeere, 1618*. London, 1618.

———. *The Second Part Of The Honest Whore*. London, 1630.

DeLombard, Jeannine Marie. *Slavery on Trial: Law, Abolitionism, and Print Culture*. Chapel Hill: University of North Carolina Press, 2007.

Derrida, Jacques. *Given Time: I. Counterfeit Money*, trans. Peggy Kamuf. Chicago: University of Chicago Press, 1992.

Dhar, Amrita. "Seeing Feelingly: Sight and Service in *King Lear*." In *Disability, Health, and Happiness in the Shakespearean Body*, ed. Sujata Iyengar, 76–92. New York: Routledge, 2015.

Dodsley, Robert. *Servitude: A Poem*. London, 1729.

Dolan, Frances E. *True Relations: Reading, Literature, and Evidence in Seventeenth-Century England*. Philadelphia: University of Pennsylvania Press, 2013.

Donoghue, John. "'Out of the Land of Bondage': The English Revolution and the Atlantic Origins of Abolition," *American Historical Review* 115, no. 4 (2010): 943–74.

Dowd, Michelle M. *Women's Work in Early Modern English Literature and Culture*. New York: Palgrave Macmillan, 2009.

Duncan, Anne. *Performance and Identity in the Classical World*. Cambridge, UK: Cambridge University Press, 2006.

E., B. *A New Dictionary of the Terms Ancient and Modern of the Canting Crew*. London, 1699.

Edelman, Lee. *No Future: Queer Theory and the Death Drive.* Durham, NC: Duke University Press, 2004.
Elyot, Thomas. *The Dictionary of syr Thomas Eliot knyght.* London, 1538.
Enterline, Lynn. "Schooling in the English Renaissance." *Oxford Handbooks Online,* 2016.
———. *Shakespeare's Schoolroom: Rhetoric, Discipline, Emotion.* Philadelphia: University of Pennsylvania Press, 2012.
Evans, J. Martin. *Milton's Imperial Epic: "Paradise Lost" and the Discourse of Colonialism.* Ithaca, NY: Cornell University Press, 1996.
Evelyn, Robert. *A Direction for Adventvrers With small stock to get two for one, and good land freely: And for Gentlemen, and all Servants, Labourers, and Artificers to live plentifully.* London, 1641.
Evett, David. *Discourses of Service in Shakespeare's England.* New York: Palgrave Macmillan, 2005.
Farrar, Eliza. *The Adventures of Congo In Search Of His Master; An American Tale.* London, 1823; Boston, between 1824 and 1834.
Feerick, Jean E. *Strangers in Blood: Relocating Race in the Renaissance.* Toronto: University of Toronto Press, 2010.
Fields, Karen E., and Barbara J. Fields. *Racecraft: The Soul of Inequality in American Life.* London: Verso, 2012.
Fit John, John. *A Diamonde most Precious, worthy to be marked: Instructing all Maysters and Seruauntes, how they ought to leade their lyues . . .* London, 1577. STC 10929, Folger Shakespeare Library.
Florio, John. *Qveen Anna's New World of Words.* London, 1611.
Fryer, Peter. *Staying Power: The History of Black People in Britain.* London: Pluto Press, 2010.
Gates, Henry Louis, Jr. "Editor's Introduction: Writing 'Race' and the Difference It Makes," in *"Race," Writing, and Difference,* ed. Henry Louis Gates, Jr., 1–20. Chicago: University of Chicago Press, 1986.
Godwyn, Morgan. *The Negro's & Indians Advocate, Suing for their Admission into the Church: Or A Persuasive to the Instructing and Baptizing of the Negro's and Indians in our Plantations.* London, 1680.
Goetz, Rebecca Anne. *The Baptism of Early Virginia: How Christianity Created Race.* Baltimore: Johns Hopkins University Press, 2012.
Goldberg, Jonathan. *Writing Matter: From the Hands of the English Renaissance.* Stanford, CA: Stanford University Press, 1990.
Goldenberg, David M. *The Curse of Ham: Race and Slavery in Early Judaism, Christianity, and Islam.* Princeton, NJ: Princeton University Press, 2003.
Goodell, Abner C., Jr. "John Saffin and His Slave Adam," *Publications of the Colonial Society of Massachusetts* I (1892–1894): 85–112.
Gordon, Andrew. "Material Fictions: Counterfeit Correspondence and the Culture of Copying in Early Modern England." In *Cultures of Correspondence in Early Modern Britain,* ed. James Daybell and Andrew Gordon, 85–109. Philadelphia: University of Pennsylvania Press, 2016.
Grafton, Anthony, and Lisa Jardine. *From Humanism to the Humanities: Education and the Liberal Arts in Fifteenth- and Sixteenth-Century Europe.* London: Duckworth, 1986.
Grafton, Richard. *A Chronicle at large and meere History of the affayres of Englande.* London, 1569.
Greenblatt, Stephen, gen. ed. *The Norton Shakespeare.* 3rd ed. New York: W. W. Norton, 2016.

Greenfield, Peter H. "Touring." In *A New History of Early English Drama*, ed. John D. Cox and David Scott Kastan, 251–68. New York: Columbia University Press, 1997.

Greteman, Blaine. *The Poetics and Politics of Youth in Milton's England*. Cambridge, UK: Cambridge University Press, 2013.

Grier, Miles P. "Inkface: The Slave Stigma in England's Early Imperial Imagination." In *Scripturalizing the Human: The Written as the Political*, ed. Vincent L. Wimbush, 193–220. New York: Routledge, 2015.

Guasco, Michael. *Slaves and Englishmen: Human Bondage in the Early Modern Atlantic World*. Philadelphia: University of Pennsylvania Press, 2014.

Gurr, Andrew. "Industrious Ariel and Idle Caliban." In *Travel and Drama in Shakespeare's Time*, ed. Jean-Pierre Maquerlot and Michèle Willems, 193–208. Cambridge, UK: Cambridge University Press, 1996.

H., L. *A Dictionarie French and English*. London, 1571.

Habib, Imtiaz. *Black Lives in the English Archives, 1500–1677: Imprints of the Invisible*. Aldershot, UK: Ashgate, 2008.

Hainsworth, D. R. *Stewards, Lords and People: The Estate Steward and his World in Later Stuart England*. Cambridge, UK: Cambridge University Press, 1992.

Hall, Kim F. "Guess Who's Coming to Dinner? Colonization and Miscegenation in 'The Merchant of Venice,'" *Renaissance Drama* 23 (1992): 87–111.

———. "Reading What Isn't There: 'Black' Studies in Early Modern England," *Stanford Humanities Review* 3, no. 1 (1993): 23–33.

———. "'These Bastard Signs of Fair': Literary Whiteness in Shakespeare's Sonnets." In *Post-Colonial Shakespeares*, ed. Ania Loomba and Martin Orkin, 64–83. New York: Routledge, 1998.

———. *Things of Darkness: Economies of Race and Gender in Early Modern England*. Ithaca, NY: Cornell University Press, 1995.

Halpern, Richard. *The Poetics of Primitive Accumulation: English Renaissance Culture and the Genealogy of Capital*. Ithaca, NY: Cornell University Press, 1991.

Handler, Jerome S., and Matthew C. Reilly. "Contesting 'White Slavery' in the Caribbean: Enslaved Africans and European Indentured Servants in Seventeenth-Century Barbados." *New West Indian Guide* 91, nos. 1–2 (2017): 30–55.

Harris, Cheryl I. "Whiteness as Property," *Harvard Law Review* 106, no. 8 (1993): 1707–91.

Hartman, Saidiya. *Scenes of Subjection: Terror, Slavery, and Self-Making in Nineteenth-Century America*. New York: Oxford University Press, 1997.

———. "Venus in Two Acts," *Small Axe* 12, no. 2 (2008): 1–14.

Hawkes, David. "Milton and Usury," *English Literary Renaissance* 41, no. 3 (2011): 503–28.

Heal, Felicity. *The Power of Gifts: Gift Exchange in Early Modern England*. Oxford: Oxford University Press, 2014.

Heminge, William. *The Fatal Contract, A French Tragedy*. London, 1653.

Hendricks, Margo. "Race: A Renaissance Category?" In *A New Companion to English Renaissance Literature and Culture*, ed. Michael Hattaway, 535–44. Malden, MA: Blackwell, 2010.

Heng, Geraldine. *The Invention of Race in the European Middle Ages*. Cambridge, UK: Cambridge University Press, 2018.

Herndon, Ruth Wallis, and John E. Murray, eds. *Children Bound to Labor: The Pauper Apprentice System in Early America*. Ithaca, NY: Cornell University Press, 2009.

Hindle, Steve. *On the Parish?: The Micro-Politics of Poor Relief in Rural England c. 1550–1750*. Oxford: Oxford University Press, 2004.

———. "Technologies of Identification Under the Old Poor Law," *Local Historian: Journal of the British Association for Local History* 36, no. 4 (2006): 220–36.

———, and Ruth Wallis Herndon. "Recreating Proper Families in England and North America: Pauper Apprenticeship in Transatlantic Context." In *Children Bound to Labor: The Pauper Apprentice System in Early America*, ed. Ruth Wallis Herndon and John E. Murray, 19–36. Ithaca, NY: Cornell University Press, 2009.

Holinshed, Raphael. *The First and second volumes of Chronicles* [*Chronicles of England, Scotlande, and Irelande*]. London, 1587.

Hollyband, Claudius. *A Dictionarie French and English*. London, 1593.

Hoole, Charles. *An easie Entrance To The Latine Tongue*. London, 1649.

Houston, Chloë. "Persia and Kingship in William Cartwright's *The Royall Slave* (1636)," *Studies in English Literature, 1500–1900* 54, no. 2 (2014): 455–73.

Howard, Jean E. *Theater of a City: The Places of London Comedy, 1598–1642*. Philadelphia: University of Pennsylvania Press, 2007.

Hudson, Judith. "Seventeenth-Century Legal Fictions: The Case of John Perry," *The Seventeenth Century* 32, no. 3 (2017): 297–320.

Huloet, Richard. *Abcedarivm Anglico Latinvm*. London, 1552.

Hunt, Maurice. "Slavery, English Servitude, and *The Comedy of Errors*," *English Literary Renaissance* 27, no. 1 (1997): 31–56.

Hunter, G. K. "Flatcaps and Bluecoats: Visual Signals on the Elizabethan Stage," *Essays and Studies* 33 (1980): 16–47.

Hutson, Lorna. *The Invention of Suspicion: Law and Mimesis in Shakespeare and Renaissance Drama*. Oxford: Oxford University Press, 2007.

This Indenture made, Witnesseth that ____ Son of ____ hath put himselfe Apprentice, to ____ of the University of Oxon. G. A. Oxon. b. 111 fol. 13r, Bodleian Libraries, University of Oxford.

Ingelend, Thomas. *A pretie and Mery new Enterlude: called the Disobedient Child*. London, 1570.

The Instructive Alphabet. New York, 1809.

Iyengar, Sujata. *Shades of Difference: Mythologies of Skin Color in Early Modern England*. Philadelphia: University of Pennsylvania Press, 2005.

Jablonski, Steven. "Ham's Vicious Race: Slavery and John Milton," *Studies in English Literature, 1500–1900* 37, no. 1 (1997): 173–90.

Jackson, Thomas. *An Exact Collection Of The Works Of Doctor Iackson, P. of C. C. C. Oxon, Such as were not Published before*. London, 1654. J89 (folio), Folger Shakespeare Library.

Johnston, David Claypoole. *A Proslavery Incantation Scene. Or Shakspeare Improved*. U.S., not before 1856.

Jones, Ann Rosalind. "Maidservants of London: Sisterhoods of Kinship and Labor." In *Maids and Mistresses, Cousins and Queens: Women's Alliances in Early Modern England*, ed. Susan Frye and Karen Robertson, 21–32. Oxford: Oxford University Press, 1999.

———, and Peter Stallybrass. *Renaissance Clothing and the Materials of Memory*. Cambridge, UK: Cambridge University Press, 2000.

Jones, Hugh. *The Present State Of Virginia. Giving A particular and short Account of the Indian, English, and Negroe Inhabitants of that Colony*. London, 1724.

Jonson, Ben. *A Pleasant Comedy, Called: The Case is Alterd. As it hath beene sundry times acted by the children of the Black-friers*. London, 1609.

———. *Volpone*. In *The Alchemist and Other Plays*, ed. Gordon Campbell. Oxford: Oxford University Press, 1995.

Kahn, Victoria. *Wayward Contracts: The Crisis of Political Obligation in England, 1640–1674*. Princeton, NJ: Princeton University Press, 2004.

Kaplan, M. Lindsay. "Jessica's Mother: Medieval Constructions of Jewish Race and Gender in *The Merchant of Venice*," *Shakespeare Quarterly* 58, no. 1 (2007): 1–30.

Kathman, David. "Grocers, Goldsmiths, and Drapers: Freemen and Apprentices in the Elizabethan Theater," *Shakespeare Quarterly* 55, no. 1 (2004): 1–49.

Kaufmann, Miranda. *Black Tudors: The Untold Story*. London: Oneworld, 2017.

———. "Blanke, John (fl. 1507–1512), royal trumpeter." *Oxford Dictionary of National Biography*. 25 Sep. 2014; Accessed 1 May 2021. https://www.oxforddnb.com/view/10.1093/ref:odnb/9780198614128.001.0001/odnb-9780198614128-e-107145.

———. "Caspar Van Senden, Sir Thomas Sherley and the 'Blackamoor' Project," *Historical Research* 81, no. 212 (2008): 366–71.

———. "English Common Law, Slavery and." In *Encyclopedia of Blacks in European History and Culture*, ed. Eric Martone, vol. 1, 200–203. Westport, CT: Greenwood Press, 2008.

Kazanjian, David. "'To see the Issue of these his Exorbitant Practices': A Response to 'The Dispossessed Eighteenth Century,'" *The Eighteenth Century* 55, no. 2/3 (2014): 273–82.

Keenan, Siobhan. *Travelling Players in Shakespeare's England*. Basingstoke, UK: Palgrave Macmillan, 2002.

Kehoe, Dennis. "Dominium." In *The Encyclopedia of Ancient History*, ed. R. S. Bagnall et al. (2012). https://onlinelibrary-wiley-com.myaccess.library.utoronto.ca/doi/abs/10.1002/9781444338386.wbeah13087.

Keller, Holly. "Juvenile Antislavery Narrative and Notions of Childhood," *Children's Literature* 24 (1996): 86–100.

Kendrick, Matthew. *At Work in the Early Modern English Theater: Valuing Labor*. Madison, NJ: Fairleigh Dickinson University Press, 2015.

Kersey, John. *A New English Dictionary: Or, a Compleat Collection of the Most Proper and Significant Words, Commonly used in the Language*. London, 1702.

Kinney, Arthur F., ed. *Renaissance Drama: An Anthology of Plays and Entertainments*. 2nd ed. Malden, MA: Blackwell, 2005.

Kopelson, Heather Miyano. *Faithful Bodies: Performing Religion and Race in the Puritan Atlantic*. New York: New York University Press, 2014.

Kyffin, Maurice. *Andria The first Comoedie of Terence, in English. A furtherance for the attainment vnto the right knowledge, & true proprietie, of the Latin Tong. And also a commodious meane of help, to such as haue forgotten Latin, for their speedy recouering of habilitie, to vnderstand, write, and speake the same. Carefully translated out of Latin, by Maurice Kyffin*. London, 1588.

Ladies' Society for Promoting the Early Education of Negro Children. *Post-Emancipation Life*. London, between 1833 and 1837. 3-Size D833 .L155p, John Carter Brown Library.

Lees-Jeffries, Hester. *Shakespeare and Memory*. Oxford: Oxford University Press, 2013.

Leishman, J. B., ed. *The Three Parnassus Plays (1598–1601)*. London: Ivor Nicholson & Watson, 1949.

A Letter sent by the Maydens of London, to the vertuous Matrones & Mistresses of the same, in the defense of their lawfull Libertie. London, 1567.

Lévi-Strauss, Claude. *The Elementary Structures of Kinship*, rev. ed., trans. James Harle Bell, John Richard von Sturmer, and ed. Rodney Needham. Boston: Beacon Press, 1969.

Ligon, Richard. *A Trve & Exact History Of the Island of Barbados*. London, 1657.

Lilburne, John. *A true relation of the materiall passages of Lieut. Col. Iohn Lilburnes sufferings.* London, 1646.

Lindsay, Tom. "'Which first was mine own king': Caliban and the Politics of Service and Education in *The Tempest*," *Studies in Philology* 113, no. 2 (2016): 397–423.

Little, Arthur L., Jr. "Re-Historicizing Race, White Melancholia, and the Shakespearean Property," *Shakespeare Quarterly* 67, no. 1 (2016): 84–103.

———. *Shakespeare Jungle Fever: National-Imperial Re-Visions of Race, Rape, and Sacrifice.* Stanford, CA: Stanford University Press, 2000.

Loomba, Ania. *Shakespeare, Race, and Colonialism.* Oxford: Oxford University Press, 2002.

Lopez, Jeremy, ed. *The Routledge Anthology of Early Modern Drama.* Abingdon, UK: Routledge, 2020.

Louis, Cameron, ed. *Records of Early English Drama: Sussex.* Toronto: University of Toronto Press, 2000.

MacDonald, Joyce Green. *Women and Race in Early Modern Texts.* Cambridge, UK: Cambridge University Press, 2002.

Macfarlane, Alan, ed. *The Diary of Ralph Josselin 1616–1683.* London: Oxford University Press for the British Academy, 1976.

MacIntyre, Jean, and Garrett P. J. Epp. "'Cloathes worth all the rest': Costumes and Properties." In *A New History of Early English Drama*, ed. John D. Cox and David Scott Kastan, 269–86. New York: Columbia University Press, 1997.

McLuskie, Kathleen E., and Felicity Dunsworth. "Patronage and the Economics of Theater." In *A New History of Early English Drama*, ed. John D. Cox and David Scott Kastan, 423–40. New York: Columbia University Press, 1997.

McMillin, Scott, and Sally-Beth MacLean. *The Queen's Men and Their Plays.* Cambridge, UK: Cambridge University Press, 1998.

Marchitello, Howard. "Desire and Domination in *Volpone*," *Studies in English Literature, 1500–1900* 31, no. 2 (1991): 287–308.

Markham, Gervase. *A Health to the Gentlemanly profession of Seruingmen; or, The Seruingmans Comfort.* London, 1598.

Mauss, Marcel. *The Gift: The Form and Reason for Exchange in Archaic Societies*, trans. W. D. Halls. New York: Norton, 1990.

Mentz, Steven R. "The Fiend Gives Friendly Counsel: Launcelot Gobbo and Polyglot Economics in *The Merchant of Venice*." In *Money and the Age of Shakespeare: Essays in New Economic Criticism*, ed. Linda Woodbridge, 177–87. New York: Palgrave Macmillan, 2003.

Mertes, Kate. *The English Noble Household, 1250–1600: Good Governance and Politic Rule.* New York: Basil Blackwell, 1988.

Milton, John. *The Complete Poems*, ed. John Leonard. New York: Penguin, 1998.

———. *Paradise Lost*, ed. Barbara K. Lewalski. Malden, MA: Blackwell, 2007.

———. *Paradise Regained, Samson Agonistes, and the Complete Shorter Poems*, ed. William Kerrigan, John Rumrich, and Stephen M. Fallon. New York: Modern Library, 2012.

———. *The Riverside Milton*, ed. Roy Flannagan. Boston: Houghton Mifflin, 1998.

Miola, Robert S. *Shakespeare and Classical Comedy: The Influence of Plautus and Terence.* Oxford: Oxford University Press, 1994.

———. *Shakespeare's Reading.* Oxford: Oxford University Press, 2000.

Mitchell, Mary Niall. *Raising Freedom's Child: Black Children and Visions of the Future After Slavery.* New York: New York University Press, 2008.

Moore, George Henry, ed. *Notes on the History of Slavery in Massachusetts*. New York: D. Appleton & Co., 1866.

Morgan, Edmund S. *American Slavery, American Freedom: The Ordeal of Colonial Virginia*. New York: W. W. Norton, 1975.

Morgan, Jennifer L. *Laboring Women: Reproduction and Gender in New World Slavery*. Philadelphia: University of Pennsylvania Press, 2004.

———. "*Partus sequitur ventrem*: Law, Race, and Reproduction in Colonial Slavery," *Small Axe* 22, no. 1 (2018): 1–17.

Moulton, Ian Frederick. "The Manuscript Circulation of Erotic Poetry in Early Modern England." In *The Cambridge Companion to Erotic Literature*, ed. Bradford K. Mudge, 64–84. Cambridge, UK: Cambridge University Press, 2017.

Mouritsen, Henrik. *The Freedman in the Roman World*. Cambridge, UK: Cambridge University Press, 2011.

Muldrew, Craig. *The Economy of Obligation: The Culture of Credit and Social Relations in Early Modern England*. Basingstoke, UK: Palgrave, 1998.

Muñoz, José Esteban. *Cruising Utopia: The Then and There of Queer Futurity*. New York: New York University Press, 2009.

Nashe, Thomas. *Haue with you to Saffron-walden. Or, Gabriell Harueys hunt is vp*. London, 1596.

Nathans, Heather S. "'Blood Will Have Blood': Violence, Slavery, and *Macbeth* in the Antebellum American Imagination." In *Weyward Macbeth: Intersections of Race and Performance*, ed. Scott L. Newstok and Ayanna Thompson, 23–33. New York: Palgrave Macmillan, 2010.

Ndiaye, Noémie. "Aaron's Roots: Spaniards, Englishmen, and Blackamoors in *Titus Andronicus*," *Early Theatre* 19, no. 2 (2016): 59–80.

Neill, Michael. "'In Everything Illegitimate': Imagining the Bastard in Renaissance Drama," *Yearbook of English Studies* 23 (1993): 270–92.

———. *Putting History to the Question: Power, Politics, and Society in English Renaissance Drama*. New York: Columbia University Press, 2000.

Nelson, Alan H., ed. *Records of Early English Drama: Cambridge*, Volume 1. Toronto: University of Toronto Press, 1989.

Newman, Karen. "Portia's Ring: Unruly Women and Structures of Exchange in *The Merchant of Venice*," *Shakespeare Quarterly* 38, no. 1 (1987): 19–33.

Newman, Simon P. *A New World of Labor: The Development of Plantation Slavery in the British Atlantic*. Philadelphia: University of Pennsylvania Press, 2013.

Newman, Thomas. *The Two First Comedies Of Terence called Andria, and the Eunuch newly Englished by Thomas Newman*. London, 1627.

Ng, Su Fang. *Literature and the Politics of Family in Seventeenth-Century England*. Cambridge, UK: Cambridge University Press, 2007.

Nowell, Laurence. *Vocabularium Saxonicum*. London, ca. 1567.

Nyquist, Mary. *Arbitrary Rule: Slavery, Tyranny, and the Power of Life and Death*. Chicago: University of Chicago Press, 2013.

———. "Base Slavery and Roman Yoke." In *The Oxford Handbook of English Law and Literature, 1500–1700*, ed. Lorna Hutson, 624–48. Oxford: Oxford University Press, 2017.

Olusoga, David. *Black and British: A Forgotten History*. London: Macmillan, 2016.

Orgel, Stephen. *Impersonations: The Performance of Gender in Shakespeare's England*. Cambridge, UK: Cambridge University Press, 1996.

Overbury, Thomas (1581–1613). *A Wife Now The Widdow of Sir Thomas Overbvrye* . . . London, 1614.

Overbury, Thomas (d. 1684). *A True and Perfect Account of the Examination, Confession, Tryal, Condemnation, and Execution of Joan Perry, and her two Sons, John & Richard Perry, For the Supposed Murder of William Harrison, Gent.* London, 1676. Wing 0614.

Parker, Patricia. "Black *Hamlet*: Battening on the Moor," *Shakespeare Studies* 31 (2003): 127–64.

———. "Cutting Both Ways: Bloodletting, Castration/Circumcision, and the 'Lancelet' of *The Merchant of Venice*." In *Alternative Shakespeares 3*, ed. Diana E. Henderson, 95–118. Abingdon, UK: Routledge, 2008.

Pârvulescu, Adrian. "Lat. *servus*," *Indogermanische Forschungen* 115 (2010): 190–97.

Perceval, Richard. *A Dictionarie In Spanish and English*. London, 1599.

Pettigrew, William A. *Freedom's Debt: The Royal African Company and the Politics of the Atlantic Slave Trade, 1672–1752*. Chapel Hill: University of North Carolina Press, 2013.

Phillips, Edward. *The New World of English Words: Or, a General Dictionary*. London, 1658.

Phillips, Susan E. "Schoolmasters, Seduction, and Slavery: Polyglot Dictionaries in Pre-Modern England." In *Medievalia et Humanistica: Studies in Medieval and Renaissance Culture*, n.s. 34, ed. Paul Maurice Clogan, 129–58. Lanham: Rowman and Littlefield, 2008.

Potter, Ursula. "Performing Arts in the Tudor Classroom." In *Tudor Drama Before Shakespeare, 1485–1590: New Directions for Research, Criticism, and Pedagogy*, ed. Lloyd Kermode, Jason Scott-Warren, and Martine van Elk, 143–65. New York: Palgrave Macmillan, 2004.

Quilligan, Maureen. "Freedom, Service, and the Trade in Slaves: The Problem of Labor in *Paradise Lost*." In *Subject and Object in Renaissance Culture*, ed. Margreta de Grazia, Maureen Quilligan, and Peter Stallybrass, 213–34. Cambridge, UK: Cambridge University Press, 1996.

Rappaport, Steve. *Worlds Within Worlds: Structures of Life in Sixteenth-Century London*. Cambridge, UK: Cambridge University Press, 1989.

Ritger, Matthew. "Reading *Utopia* in the Reformation of Punishment," *Renaissance Quarterly* 72, no. 4 (2019): 1225–68.

Rivers, Marcellus, and Oxenbridge Foyle. *Englands Slavery, or Barbados Merchandize*. London, 1659.

Rivlin, Elizabeth. *The Aesthetics of Service in Early Modern England*. Evanston, IL: Northwestern University Press, 2012.

Roth, Sarah N. "The Mind of a Child: Images of African Americans in Early Juvenile Fiction," *Journal of the Early Republic* 25, no. 1 (2005): 79–109.

Rubright, Marjorie. *Doppelgänger Dilemmas: Anglo-Dutch Relations in Early Modern English Literature and Culture*. Philadelphia: University of Pennsylvania Press, 2014.

Rushworth, John. *Historical Collections. The Second Part*. London, 1680.

Saffin, John. *A Brief and Candid Answer to a Late Printed Sheet, Entitled, The Selling of Joseph*. Boston, 1701.

Sanchez, Melissa E. *Erotic Subjects: The Sexuality of Politics in Early Modern English Literature*. Oxford: Oxford University Press, 2011.

———. "Seduction and Service in *The Tempest*," *Studies in Philology* 105, no. 1 (2008): 50–82.

Schalkwyk, David. "Love and Service in *Twelfth Night* and the Sonnets," *Shakespeare Quarterly* 56, no. 1 (2005): 76–100.

———. *Shakespeare, Love and Service*. Cambridge, UK: Cambridge University Press, 2008.

The Several Declarations Of The Company Of Royal Adventurers Of England Trading Into Africa. London, 1667.
Sewall, Samuel. *The Selling of Joseph: A Memorial.* Boston, 1700.
Shakespeare, William. *Othello*, ed. Michael Neill. Oxford: Oxford University Press, 2006.
———. *The Tempest*, ed. Virginia Mason Vaughan and Alden T. Vaughan. New York: Bloomsbury, 2011.
———. *The Tragicall Historie of Hamlet Prince of Denmarke.* London, 1603.
Shapiro, James. *Shakespeare and the Jews.* New York: Columbia University Press, 1996.
Shaw, Jenny. *Everyday Life in the Early English Caribbean: Irish, Africans, and the Construction of Difference.* Athens: University of Georgia Press, 2013.
Shershow, Scott Cutler. "Shakespeare Beyond Shakespeare." In *Marxist Shakespeares*, ed. Jean E. Howard and Scott Cutler Shershow, 245–64. New York: Routledge, 2001.
———. *The Work and the Gift.* Chicago: University of Chicago Press, 2005.
Shin, Hiewon. "Single Parenting, Homeschooling: Prospero, Caliban, Miranda," *Studies in English Literature 1500–1900* 48, no. 2 (2008): 373–93.
Shore, Daniel. "Was Milton White?," *Milton Studies* 62, no. 2 (2020): 252–65.
Slights, Camille Wells. "The Principle of Recompense in *Twelfth Night*," *Modern Language Review* 77, no. 3 (1982): 537–46.
———. "Slaves and Subjects in *Othello*," *Shakespeare Quarterly* 48, no. 4 (1997): 377–90.
Smith, Abbot Emerson. *Colonists in Bondage: White Servitude and Convict Labor in America, 1607–1776.* Chapel Hill: University of North Carolina Press, 1947.
Smith, Ian. "Othello's Black Handkerchief," *Shakespeare Quarterly* 64, no. 1 (2013): 1–25.
———. *Race and Rhetoric in the Renaissance: Barbarian Errors.* New York: Palgrave Macmillan, 2009.
———. "The Textile Black Body: Race and 'Shadowed Livery' in *The Merchant of Venice*." In *The Oxford Handbook of Shakespeare and Embodiment: Gender, Sexuality, and Race*, ed. Valerie Traub, 170–85. Oxford: Oxford University Press, 2016.
Smith, Toulmin, ed. *English Gilds: The Original Ordinances of more than one hundred Early English Gilds.* London, 1870.
Smith, William, William Wayte, and G. E. Marindin, eds. *A Dictionary of Greek and Roman Antiquities*, 3rd ed., Volume 2. London: John Murray, 1891.
Stallybrass, Peter. "Worn Worlds: Clothes and Identity on the Renaissance Stage." In *Subject and Object in Renaissance Culture*, ed. Margreta de Grazia, Maureen Quilligan, and Peter Stallybrass, 289–320. Cambridge, UK: Cambridge University Press, 1996.
Stepney, William. *The Spanish Schoole-master.* London, 1591.
Stevens, Andrea. "'The Eunuch Much Sears Her Breast': Remedying Adulteration in William Heminge's *The Fatal Contract*." In *Thunder at a Playhouse: Essaying Shakespeare and the Early Modern Stage*, ed. Peter Kanelos and Matt Kozusko, 212–33. Selinsgrove, PA: Susquehanna University Press, 2010.
———. Introduction to "The Fatal Contract." In *The Routledge Anthology of Early Modern Drama*, ed. Jeremy Lopez, 136–38. Abingdon, UK: Routledge, 2020.
Stevens, Paul. "*Paradise Lost* and the Colonial Imperative," *Milton Studies* 34 (1996): 3–21.
Stone, Lawrence. *The Crisis of the Aristocracy, 1558–1641.* Oxford: Clarendon Press, 1965.
Strier, Richard. "Faithful Servants: Shakespeare's Praise of Disobedience." In *The Historical Renaissance: New Essays on Tudor and Stuart Literature and Culture*, ed. Heather Dubrow and Richard Strier, 104–33. Chicago: University of Chicago Press, 1988.

Sullivan, Jr., Garrett A. *Memory and Forgetting in English Renaissance Drama: Shakespeare, Marlowe, Webster.* Cambridge, UK: Cambridge University Press, 2005.

Sullivan, Paul. "Playing the Lord: Tudor *Vulgaria* and the Rehearsal of Ambition," *English Literary History* 75, no. 1 (2008): 179–96.

Tagg, Tommy. *A Collection Of Pretty Poems For the Amusement of Children Three Foot High.* London, 1763.

Teramura, Misha. "Black Comedy: Shakespeare, Terence, and *Titus Andronicus*," *English Literary History* 85, no. 4 (2018): 877–908.

Terence. *Guidonis Iuuenalis natione Cenomani in Terentium* ... Lyon, 1493. T79, Folger Shakespeare Library.

———. *P. Terentii Afri Poetae Lepidissimi Comoediae.* Paris, 1552. RB 137922, The Huntington Library, San Marino.

———. *Terenti[us] cum directorio vocabuloru[m], sententiaru[m] artis comice, glosa i[n]terlineali, come[n]tarijs Donato, Gvidone Ascensio.* Strasbourg, 1496. Folio Inc. 473, Newberry Library, Chicago. RB 31147, The Huntington Library, San Marino, California.

Terence's Comedies: Made English. With his Life; and some Remarks at the End. By Several Hands. London, 1694.

Thomas, Thomas. *Dictionarivm Lingvae Latinae Et Anglicanae.* Cambridge, 1587.

Thompson, Ayanna. *Performing Race and Torture on the Early Modern Stage.* New York: Routledge, 2008.

Tomlins, Christopher. *Freedom Bound: Law, Labor, and Civic Identity in Colonizing English America, 1580–1865.* Cambridge, UK: Cambridge University Press, 2010.

Towner, Lawrence W. "The Sewall-Saffin Dialogue on Slavery," *William and Mary Quarterly* 21, no. 1 (1964): 40–52.

Tvordi, Jessica. "Female Alliance and the Construction of Homoeroticism in *As You Like It* and *Twelfth Night.*" In *Maids and Mistresses, Cousins and Queens: Women's Alliances in Early Modern England,* ed. Susan Frye and Karen Robertson, 114–30. Oxford: Oxford University Press, 1999.

Tycko, Sonia. "Bound and Filed: A Seventeenth-Century Service Indenture from a Scattered Archive." *Early American Studies: An Interdisciplinary Journal* 19, no. 1 (2021): 166–90.

Udall, Nicholas. *Flovres for Latine Spekynge Selected and gathered oute of Terence, and the same translated in to Englysshe.* London, 1534.

Ungerer, Gustav. *The Mediterranean Apprenticeship of British Slavery.* Madrid: Editorial Verbum, 2008.

———. "Portia and the Prince of Morocco," *Shakespeare Studies* 31 (2003): 89–126.

Van Cleve, George. "*Somerset's Case* and Its Antecedents in Imperial Perspective," *Law and History Review* 24, no. 3 (2006): 601–46.

Van Elk, Martine. "'Thou shalt present me as an eunuch to him': Terence in Early Modern England." In *A Companion to Terence,* ed. Anthony Augoustakis and Ariana Traill, 410–28. Malden, MA: Wiley-Blackwell, 2013.

Van Es, Bart. *Shakespeare in Company.* Oxford: Oxford University Press, 2013.

Vaughan, Virginia Mason. *Performing Blackness on English Stages, 1500–1800.* Cambridge, UK: Cambridge University Press, 2005.

Véron, John. *A Dictionary in Latine and English, heretofore set foorth by Master Iohn Veron, and now newly corrected and enlarged, For the vtilitie and profite of all young students in the*

Latine tongue, as by further search therin they shall finde. By R. W. London, 1575. RB 69723, The Huntington Library, San Marino, California.

Vitkus, Daniel J. "'Meaner Ministers': Mastery, Bondage, and Theatrical Labor in *The Tempest*." In *A Companion to Shakespeare's Works, Volume IV: The Poems, Problem Comedies, Late Plays*, ed. Richard Dutton and Jean E. Howard, 408–26. Malden, MA: Blackwell, 2003.

———, ed. *Piracy, Slavery, and Redemption: Barbary Captivity Narratives from Early Modern England*. New York: Columbia University Press, 2001.

———, ed. *Three Turk Plays from Early Modern England: Selimus, Emperor of the Turks; A Christian Turned Turk; and The Renegado*. New York: Columbia University Press, 2000.

———. *Turning Turk: English Theater and the Multicultural Mediterranean, 1570–1630*. New York: Palgrave Macmillan, 2003.

Von Frank, Albert J. "John Saffin: Slavery and Racism in Colonial Massachusetts," *Early American Literature* 29, no. 3 (1994): 254–72.

W., W. *Menaecmi: A pleasant and fine Conceited Comaedie, taken out of the most excellent wittie Poet Plautus*. London, 1595.

Wareing, John. *Indentured Migration and the Servant Trade from London to America, 1618–1718: "There is Great Want of Servants."* Oxford: Oxford University Press, 2017.

Webbe, Joseph. *The First Comedy Of Pvb. Terentivs, Called Andria, Or, The Woman of Andros, English and Latine*. London, 1629.

———. *The Second Comedie Of Pvb. Terentivs, Called Evnvchvs, Or, The Eunuche, English and Latine*. London, 1629.

Weil, Judith. *Service and Dependency in Shakespeare's Plays*. Cambridge, UK: Cambridge University Press, 2005.

Weissbourd, Emily. "'I Have Done the State Some Service': Reading Slavery in *Othello* Through Juan Latino," *Comparative Drama* 47, no. 4 (2013): 529–51.

———. "'Those in Their Possession': Race, Slavery, and Queen Elizabeth's 'Edicts of Expulsion,'" *Huntington Library Quarterly* 78, no. 1 (2015): 1–19.

Wheatley, Phillis. *Poems On Various Subjects, Religious and Moral. By Phillis Wheatley, Negro Servant to Mr. John Wheatley, of Boston, in New England*. London, 1773.

White, Paul Whitfield. *Theatre and Reformation: Protestantism, Patronage, and Playing in Tudor England*. Cambridge, UK: Cambridge University Press, 1993.

Whitney, Geffrey. *A Choice of Emblemes, and Other Devises*. Leiden, 1586.

Wilkins, John. *An Essay Towards a Real Character and a Philosophical Language*. London, 1668.

Williams, James. *A Narrative of Events Since the First of August, 1834, By James Williams, An Apprenticed Labourer in Jamaica*. London, 1837.

Williams, Katherine Schaap. *Unfixable Forms: Disability, Performance, and the Early Modern English Theater*. Ithaca, NY: Cornell University Press, 2021.

Williams, Raymond. *Keywords: A Vocabulary of Culture and Society*, rev. ed. New York: Oxford University Press, 1985.

Wilson, Emily. "Ave Jeeves!," *London Review of Books* 30, no. 4 (February 2008).

Wilson, Luke. "*Macbeth* and the Contingency of Future Persons," *Shakespeare Studies* 40 (2012): 53–62.

Witmore, Michael. *Pretty Creatures: Children and Fiction in the English Renaissance*. Ithaca, NY: Cornell University Press, 2007.

INDEX

Abdella, Alkaid Jaurar Ben, 47–48
abolition, 2, 207–11, 214 n. 14
actors, 21, 23–25, 41–42, 60, 217 nn. 19, 21–22, 25, 218 n. 28; child, 3, 63, 226 n. 48, 254 n. 39; classical, 228 n. 61. *See also* theater
Adams, B. K., 242 n. 101
Adelman, Janet, 28, 219 n. 46
adoption, 188–89, 235 n. 28, 254 n. 44
"Aethiops." *See* Ethiopians
affective bondage, 8, 41, 60, 71, 97, 159, 169, 177, 180, 188–89, 192–93, 199
affective fictions, 11–12, 92, 153, 206, 225 n. 39
affective ties, 66, 72, 97, 108–22, 137, 186, 206, 229 n. 67, 238 n. 68, 242 n. 96
Africans, 7, 83, 87, 93, 187, 222 n. 8, 250 n. 79; enslaved, 8, 49, 67, 195, 203, 213 n. 2, 227 n. 58, 244 n. 12, 248 n. 54, 256 n. 61
Akhimie, Patricia, 129, 188, 255 n. 52
albus, 79–80
Alemán, Mateo: *The Rogue: or The Life of Guzman de Alfarache*, 16, 17
America, 3, 9, 12, 131–32, 139–40, 150, 199, 244 n. 12. *See also* Atlantic world; New World
Amerindian people, 187, 204, 244 n. 12
Amussen, Susan Dwyer, 244 n. 12
ancilla/ancillula, 54, 75, 82
Andrewes, Lancelot, 20
antislavery literature, 207–9, 212, 256 n. 61
Anwykyll, John, 223 n. 20
apprenticeship, 6, 21, 63–64, 95, 147, 191, 227 nn. 48, 54, 243 n. 8, 244 n. 9, 246 n. 23, 258 n. 87; indentures, 11, 46, 64–66, 133–40, 145, 245 n. 22, 256 n. 66; post-emancipation, 209–11, 259 n. 29
Archer, John Michael, 251 n. 3
Arden of Faversham, 220 n. 69
Ascham, Roger, 225 n. 32; *The Schoolmaster*, 56
ater, 79–80

Atlantic world, 6, 130, 198–99
authority: political, 185–86

B., M.: *The Triall of true Friendship*, 106, 236 n. 48, 238 n. 71
badges, 17–22, 29–30, 33–36, 38, 219 n. 48, 221 n. 79; of slavery, 67, 228 n. 62; of servitude, 10, 38
Bailey, Amanda, 14–15, 40, 133, 229 n. 80, 243 n. 7, 244 n. 9
Bailey, Nathan: *An Universal Etymological English Dictionary*, 166
Baldwin, T. W., 185, 222 n. 8, 254 n. 46
Bales, Peter, 117–18
"Barbadosing," 244 n. 12
barbarousness, 11, 161, 204
"Barbary" (as name), 87
Barlandus, Adrianus: commentary on *Andria*, 177
Barroll, Leeds, 23
Bartels, Emily C., 87, 232 nn. 114, 120, 233 n. 16, 234 n. 17
Barthelemy, Anthony Gerard, 221 n. 4
Bayly, Abraham, 246 n. 24
Beckles, Hilary McD., 244 n. 12
Benatar, David, 165, 249 n. 71
bill of sale (for a child), 150–51, 152 (fig.)
"blackamoor"/"blackamore," 7, 78, 82, 85–87, 93, 127, 242 n. 95
blackface, 241 nn. 90–91
blackness, 2, 7, 13, 43–44, 48, 67, 68, 80–87, 92–93, 95, 168, 187–89, 198, 228 nn. 59, 62, 233 n.10, 241 n. 90; incorporated/inscribed in white body, 94, 97–100, 125–27, 234 nn. 19–22, 235 n. 24; language of, 47, 77–78, 80, 82, 92–93, 230 n. 90, 233 n. 11. *See also* slavery: and bodily and somatic markers; slavery: and race
black servants, 83, 87, 92, 95–97, 123, 126–27, 130, 228 n. 59, 232 n. 114

Blake, Robert, 47–48
Blanke, John, 89, 90 (fig.), 92–93, 95, 232 n. 1, 233 nn. 2–3
blood, 9, 101–2, 107, 108, 111–13, 122, 124, 129–30, 159, 166–67, 207, 234 n. 16, 235 n. 28, 250 n. 77, 256 n. 61. *See also* family; heredity/hereditability
"blot," 128–29, 168, 251 n. 4. *See also* branding; heredity; "inkface"; *macula servitutis*; stain of slavery
blue coats, 17–18, 22, 28–38, 219 n. 48
bodies/the body, 16, 19, 42–44, 62–63, 98–100, 166, 198, 234 n. 19, 251 n. 4; conjoined between master and servant, 114–15, 118, 127; as vendible, 64, 74, 133, 243 n. 7, 244 n. 9
bondage. *See* captivity; consent; indentured service/servitude; slavery
"bondman," 52, 54, 86, 171, 176, 224 n. 26, 226 n. 46
A Booke of Presidents, 134, 137
Book of Common Prayer, 4, 72, 156–57, 175, 209
"botcher," 38, 220 n. 69
Bovilsky, Lara, 237 n. 60
branding, 4–6, 42, 242 n. 95
Brewer, Holly, 226 n. 44
Bridgewater, Earl of, 115–17, 118
Bright, Timothie: *Characterie An Art of Short, Swift, and Secret Writing by Character*, 160, 253 n. 27
Britton, Dennis Austin, 215 nn. 17–18
Brown, Paul, 188
Bullokar, John: *An English Expositor*, 6
Burghe, Mathew, 73–74
Burr, John, 150, 152 (fig.)
Burrow, Colin, 227 n. 56, 254 n. 46
Butts v. Penny, 213 n. 2

Callaghan, Dympna, 235 n. 24
candidus, 78
capitalism: crypto-, 122; nascent, 18, 28, 32, 36, 42, 43; racial, 168
captives, 56–58, 180, 222 n. 5, 228 n. 61, 244 n. 12; English, 3, 47–50, 58, 67–69, 131
captivity, 45–51, 54, 56–58, 61, 67–77, 88, 131–32, 179–84, 198, 228 nn. 59, 65, 229 n. 75; narratives, 3, 45–46, 51, 68, 70–74, 76, 229 n. 78
care/*carus*, 36–37, 115, 117–18, 120, 182, 238 n. 70

Carew, Sir Thomas, 68
caritas. *See* charity
Carroll, Lewis, 184
Cartwright, William: *The Royall Slave*, 56–60, 225 nn. 35, 39
Cartwright's case, 1, 2, 213 n. 2
cast clothing. *See* clothing: cast
Catherine of Aragon, 89, 232 n. 1
Cawdrey, Robert: *A Table Alphabeticall*, 6, 242 n. 95
census. *See* Return of Strangers
Chamberlaine v. Harvey, 213 n. 2
Chapman, George: *Bussy D'Ambois*, 40
charity/*caritas*, 117–18, 238 n. 70
Cheffhere, Richard, 147
Chettle, Henry, Thomas Dekker, and William Haughton: *The Pleasant Comodie of Patient Grissill*, 37–38, 40
childbirth, 162–63, 249 n. 68
childlessness, 164–65, 249 n. 70. *See also* natality: and anti-natalism
children/childhood, 9, 46, 55, 61–63, 226 nn. 44, 48, 243 n. 8, 249 n. 69; and apprenticeship, 64–66, 227 n. 54; enslaved, 48, 150–51, 176, 199, 204, 214 n. 14; and family, 86, 235 n. 28; of foreigners, 95; and heredity/futures of slavery, 45, 128–30, 134, 159, 198, 231 n. 103, 247 n. 43, 248 n. 54; miscegenated, 98; in *Paradise Lost*, 153, 158, 161–69; as *res mancipi*, 189, 226 n. 46; and servitude, 46, 88, 94, 147–52, 169, 170; in *The Tempest*, 188, 189; in *Volpone*, 101. *See also* heredity/hereditability; poor indentures; *puer*; school/the schoolroom: affinity with slaves in; slavery: and children
children's literature, 203–9
Christianity, 20, 72, 144, 174–75, 199, 212, 238 n. 70, 252 n. 12; in *The Merchant of Venice*, 26–28. *See also Book of Common Prayer*; Milton, John
Cicero, 79–80, 199
citizens/*cives*, 3, 42, 50, 61, 68, 72, 107, 188, 251 n. 3; captive, 50, 68, 75–76. *See also* freemen
Clark, William: *Ten Views of the Island of Antigua*, 210 (fig.), 259 n. 28
class, 29–30, 55, 125, 129, 167, 220 n. 69, 225 n. 34, 227 n. 57
classical slaves. *See* Plautus; Roman slave comedies; slavery: Roman; Terence

Clifton, Thomas, 3, 226 n. 48
clothing, 192; cast, 22–23, 26, 30–31, 38–41, 220 n. 70; circulation of, 22, 23, 30, 33–35, 38–39, 42–43; of redeemed captives, 48, 222 n. 5; as signifier, 22, 29–31, 33, 35, 38, 40–41, 43. *See also* badges; blue coats; livery; russet coats
Cockeram, Henry: *The English Dictionarie*, 225 n. 39, 242 n. 95
cognizances. *See* badges
Coke, Edward, 16–18
Coles, Kimberly Anne, 215 nn. 17–18
Colman, George the Elder, 259 n. 10
Colman, George the Younger: *Inkle and Yarico* (opera), 204
colonization, 157, 167–68, 250 n. 77
Committee for the Abolition of the Slave Trade, 212
commodification (of bodies/human life), 43–44, 54, 67, 83, 183, 189, 248 n. 54. *See also* property; *res mancipi*
Comons . . . Complaine of the Multitude of straungers that are setled amongst vs, The, 86–87
Company of Royal Adventurers of England Trading Into Africa, 132
complaints: of servants, 183, 194–95
complexion, 10, 19, 43–44, 48, 77, 80, 85, 89, 214 n. 14, 228 n. 59, 234 n. 21, 242 n. 94. *See also* blackness; race; whiteness
Connolly, Paula T., 259 n. 15
conquest, 58–59, 225 n. 39, 226 n. 46, 250 n. 79
consanguinity. *See* blood; family; heredity/hereditability
consent (and fictions thereof), 6–10, 15, 41, 49, 71, 74, 108, 113, 122, 137, 145, 149, 153, 172–76, 182–83, 186–87, 213 n. 5, 252 n. 11; and children, 46, 61–66, 140, 147–51, 247 n. 31; of freedmen, 51, 171; and indentured service, 130, 132–33, 137, 140–49, 151, 157–58, 167, 169, 247 n. 37; and livery, 16, 18–20, 41, 42; manipulated by native/English servants, 94, 106–13, 122; in the New/Atlantic World (for black servants/slaves), 190–91, 195–96, 198–99, 201, 207–11, 259 n. 29; parental, 64–66, 149; and the schoolroom, 46, 49, 58–59, 88. *See also* sexual exploitation
contract, 10, 11, 61–62, 108, 198; in *The Tempest*, 178, 183–84, 186. *See also* apprenticeship: indentures; indentured service/servitude: contracts for
convicts, 150, 244 n. 12, 248 n. 48. *See also* debt: bondage
Conybeare, John, 79–80, 85
Cooke, John: *Greene's Tu Quoque*, 29–31, 36, 41, 219 nn. 50–51
Cooper, Thomas: *Thesaurus Linguae Romanae & Brittanicae*, 78–80, 181, 182
Copley, Anthony, 219 n. 56
Cotgrave, Randle: *A Dictionarie of the French and English Tongues*, 55, 224 n. 26, 242 n. 95
Cowell, John: *The Interpreter*, 20, 26, 218 n. 34
Cowper, William: "The Negro's Complaint," 212
Cranmer, Thomas, 175
credit, 27–28, 33, 36, 41, 183
cribs, 46, 77, 228 n. 59
Crimsal, Richard: *A pleasant new Dialogue*, 36, 220 n. 66
Cuffy the Negro's Doggrel Description of the Progress of Sugar, 207, 208 (fig.), 209
cullison. *See* badges
"custom of the country," 91, 144

Dadabhoy, Ambereen, 228 n. 59
dangers: of servants to masters, 107, 108, 113, 118, 240 n. 85
Daniell, John, 94, 117–18, 120, 239 n. 79
debt, 22, 173, 187, 196, 236 n. 47, 252 n. 21, 257 n. 78, 258 n. 90; bondage, 73–74, 132–33, 243 n. 7, 249 n. 57; in *The Changeling*, 94, 108–13; in *The Merchant of Venice*, 27–28; in other literary sources, 29, 32, 35; in *Paradise Lost*, 12, 122, 153, 156–58
Defoe, Benjamin Norton: *A New English Dictionary*, 258 n. 5
"deformity," 161–62, 237 n. 60
degeneration, 125, 127, 166, 234 n. 16
Dekker, Thomas: *The Owles Almancke*, 219 n. 47; *The Second Part Of The Honest Whore*, 31–32, 36, 219 n. 54; *The Shoemakers' Holiday*, 38–41, 217 n. 17. *See also* Chettle, Henry, Thomas Dekker, and William Haughton: *The Pleasant Comodie of Patient Grissill*
Derrida, Jacques, 117, 122, 239 n. 76
Dhar, Amrita, 251 n. 10

dictionaries and lexicons, 6, 77–80, 228 n. 59. *See also* Bailey, Nathan; Bullokar, John; Cooper, Thomas; Cotgrave, Randle; Defoe, Benjamin Norton; E., B.; Elyot, Thomas; Florio, John; Hollyband, Claudius; Huloet, Richard; Kersey, John; Phillips, Edward; Stepney, William; Thomas, Thomas; Véron, John; Wilkins, John

difference, 9, 20, 47, 67–68, 74, 76, 85, 93–94, 97, 123, 127, 197, 234 nn. 16–19, 248 n. 54

disguise, 38; in *Eunuchus*, 75, 230 n. 88; in *The Fatal Contract*, 123–27, 241 n. 90, 242 n. 96; in *Greene's Tu Quoque*, 29, 219 n. 51; in *The Merchant of Venice*, 28

dismissal (of a servant), 32

Dodsley, Robert: *Servitude: A Poem*, 201, 202 (fig.), 258 n. 5

Dolan, Frances E., 216 n. 5

Donatus: gloss on *Andria*, 180

Donoghue, John, 244 n. 12, 247 n. 43

Drake, Francis, 3, 248 n. 54

Duncan, Anne, 228 n. 61

E., B.: *A New Dictionary of the Terms Ancient and Modern of the Canting Crew*, 150

economics, 18, 27–28, 32, 34–42

Edelman, Lee, 249 nn. 69–70

Edmondes, Sir Thomas, 73

education, 6, 49, 64, 185, 227 n. 56, 258 n. 5; of black children for submission, 209–11; withholding of, 255 n. 52. *See also* school/ the schoolroom

Edward IV, 25

Edward VI, 4

Egerton, Richard, 116

Elizabeth I, 21, 25; "expulsion edicts" of, 82–83, 86, 87, 95, 231 n. 102, 232 n. 114

Ellis, John, 147, 148 (fig.)

Elyot, Thomas: *Dictionary*, 171, 224 n. 26, 238 n. 65

emancipation. *See* abolition; apprenticeship: post-emancipation; manumission

Emberly, William, 147

encounter, 93, 98

English, the: as both masters and servants/ slaves, 50, 58, 67, 72–73. *See also* captives: English; English servants; slavery: of English subjects; slave trade

English (language), 52

English liberty/freedom. *See* freedom: English

Englishness, 67–68, 86, 214 n. 6, 228 n. 62, 234 n. 17, 245 n. 12, 253 n. 38. *See also* slavery: as constitutive of Englishness/ English subjects

English servants, 92, 94, 95, 130, 193, 195, 253 n. 38. *See also* white servants

English subjects (white), 11, 95, 97

enslaved people. *See* "slave"; slavery

Enterline, Lynn, 60, 214 n. 8, 224 n. 31, 225 n. 37

escape, 3, 70, 184

Essex, Earl and Countess of, 117–18

Ethiopians, 50, 75–76, 80–86, 93, 126, 231 n. 96, 232 n. 107, 242 n. 95

eunuchs, 48, 101, 126, 230 n. 88, 240 n. 88; in *Eunuchus*, 50, 75, 81–82, 126, 223 n. 19, 230 n. 88; in *The Fatal Contract*, 123–27, 242 nn. 94, 96

Evans, J. Martin, 157

Evelyn, Robert: *A Direction for Adventurers*, 131–32

expansion, 153, 163, 167, 249 n. 62

expulsion edicts. *See* Elizabeth I: "expulsion edicts" of

"fable," 101–2, 235 n. 30

"family," 8–9, 86, 235 n. 28, 243 n. 105

family, 2, 6–10, 11, 64, 86–88, 92, 94–97, 100, 116–18, 122–23, 130, 137, 198–99, 229 n. 67, 156 n. 61; and *The Adventures of Congo*, 206–7; and *The Changeling*, 108, 112–13; and *The Comedy of Errors*, 129–30; and *Eunuchus*, 107; and *The Fatal Contract*, 123, 126–27; and *The Merchant of Venice*, 26, 28; and *A Midsummer Night's Dream*, 128, 130; and *Othello*, 88, 107; and *Paradise Lost*, 12, 153, 158–63, 166–70; and *The Tempest*, 185, 188–89; and *Twelfth Night*, 119–23; and *Volpone*, 100–103, 107, 235 n. 37. *See also* slavery: and family

famulus, 9, 11, 54, 61–62, 64, 86–88, 92, 100, 126, 147, 167, 206, 226 n. 46, 232 n. 111

Farrar, Eliza: *The Adventures of Congo in Search of his Master*, 204, 206–7, 209

father, 66, 101–2, 158; *magister* as, 53, 60, 61, 173, 185; slave master as, 176, 189, 203–4, 206, 259 n. 15

Feere, Jeremie, 64, 65 (fig.), 66, 246 n. 22
Feerick, Jean E., 166–67, 234 n. 16, 250 n. 77
Feinande, Emanuell, 97
feudalism, 10, 18–19, 21, 24, 27–28, 32, 35–36, 42
fiction(s), 6–7, 14, 23, 49, 74, 112, 133, 137–38, 198–99, 212, 215 n. 17, 216 n. 5. *See also* affective fictions; consent (and fictions thereof); "fable"; freedom: fictions of; legal fictions
Fields, Karen E., and Barbara J., 215 n. 17
Fisher, Edward, 135
Fit John, John: *A Diamonde Most Precious*, 63–64
Florio, John: *Queen Anna's New World of Words*, 231 n. 96
"footman," 54
foreigners/foreignness, 42, 44, 55, 67, 76, 85–88, 92, 95, 103, 107, 228 n. 61
foreign familiar, 11, 100, 103, 107, 123, 126. *See also* parasite
forgery, 117–19, 121–22, 239 n. 77
Foyle, Oxenbridge, 245 n. 12
freedmen, 3, 9–10, 12, 51, 171–72, 175–78, 187, 189, 194, 251 n. 3, 252 n. 18, 259 n. 7; in Terence's *Andria*, 52, 54, 171, 176–78, 180–81, 199, 201
freedom, 63, 187, 133, 195, 238 n. 68; of body and mind, 64; conditions/contingency of, 12, 59, 88, 171–72, 176–77, 180–84, 186, 191–94, 196, 201, 258 n. 90; dangers of, 58, 209; English, 1, 46, 48, 58, 68, 91, 149, 214 n. 6, 229 n. 78, 232 n. 107, 253 n. 38; fictions of, 47, 59, 108, 189; and livery, 16, 18, 21, 26, 38, 42–44; and service/servitude, 4, 8–10, 17, 48, 51, 61, 71–72, 74, 132, 137, 153, 156, 158, 174–75, 180–81, 184, 209; to speak, 181. *See also* manumission; service: free
"freedom dues," 144
"freedom papers," 221 n. 79
freeholding, 132
freemen, 21, 42, 251 n. 3, 252 n. 18
friendship, 59–60, 103, 106–7, 115–16, 198, 225 n. 39, 236 nn. 46–48, 238 n. 71
futures. *See* slavery, futures of
futurity (familial/reproductive), 123, 125, 128, 158–60, 163–65, 169–70

Gates, Henry Louis, Jr., 215 n. 17
gender, 56, 100, 126, 127, 241 n. 90
generation. *See* childbirth; heredity/hereditability; natality; succession
gift(s), 22, 26, 32, 34, 38–40, 71–72, 109–10, 158, 168, 192; Derridean, 117, 122, 239 n. 76; liberty/manumission as, 71, 182, 194, 196, 258 n. 90; Maussian, 112–13, 118, 122, 237 n. 63; slaves as, 50, 75, 81
Gnatho. *See* Terence: *Eunuchus*
Godwyn, Morgan: *The Negro's & Indians Advocate*, 199, 200 (fig.), 201
Goldberg, Jonathan, 239 n. 77
governesses, 116, 238 n. 74
Grafton, Richard: *A Chronicle at large*, 224 n. 26
"grand parents," 160–61
gratitude, 12, 92, 110, 153, 156–58, 169, 172, 236 n. 47; clothing as mnemonic of, 39–40; lack of, 118, 177, 179, 184, 193; and manumission, 177, 180, 182–83, 239 n. 80, 252 n. 21, 253 n. 31; of master, 116
Gregory, Thaddeus, 150, 152 (fig.)
Grier, Miles, 129, 187, 252 n. 21
Grüninger, Johann: edition of Terence, 83–86
Guasco, Michael, 2, 214 n. 6, 215 n. 20, 229 n. 78
guilds, 244 n.9, 246 n. 22. *See also* livery companies

Habib, Imtiaz, 7, 87, 93, 215 n. 20, 227 n. 58, 228 n. 59, 233 nn. 10–11
Hainsley, Peter, 141 (fig.)
Hall, Kim F., 93, 97, 100, 188, 227 n. 58, 228 n. 62, 234 n. 19
Halpern, Richard, 225 n. 34
happy service/servitude/slavery, 12, 36, 72, 171, 187, 190–92, 199, 207–9, 222 n. 4
Harris, Cheryl I., 235 n. 26
Harrison, William: *The description of England*, 1, 231 n. 107
Harrison, William (captive), 70–73, 229 nn. 67, 72, 75
Hartman, Saidiya, 196, 231 n. 103, 252 n. 21, 257 n. 83, 258 n. 90
Harvey, Gabriel. *See* Nashe, Thomas: *Haue with you to Saffron-walden*
Haughton, William. *See* Chettle, Henry, Thomas Dekker, and William Haughton: *The Pleasant Comodie of Patient Grissill*
Haveland, William, 147, 246 n. 24

Hawkins, John, 3, 58, 67, 227 n. 58, 228 n. 62
heirs, 61, 100, 158–59, 162, 165, 170, 235 n. 25. *See also* heredity/hereditability; inheritance
Heminge, William: *The Fatal Contract*, 94, 123–27, 130, 240–42 nn. 89–96
Hendricks, Margo, 249 n. 73
Heng, Geraldine, 20, 250 n. 78
Henry VII, 25, 89
Henry VIII, 89, 95
heredity/hereditability, 9, 45, 63, 97–100, 102, 127–30, 169, 198, 214 n. 14, 231 n. 103, 247 n. 43, 248 n. 54, 251 n. 4. *See also* heirs; succession
Hindle, Steve, 19, 64, 221 n. 79, 227 n. 54, 246 n. 22
HM Treasury, 1–2, 213 n. 4
Holden, James and John, 136–39, 245 n. 17
Hollyband, Claudius: *A Dictionarie French and English*, 6
Holt, Lord Chief Justice, 213 n. 2
home, 9, 91–92, 123, 127, 130. *See also* household
homosocial alliance, 121–22
Hotchkiss, Edward, 195
household, 2, 10, 28, 41, 95, 103, 100, 198. *See also* family; home
Howard, Jean E., 219 n. 51
Huloet, Richard: *Abcedarium Anglico Latinum*, 38
Hunt, Maurice, 243 n. 104
Hunter, G. K., 219 n. 48
Huntingdon, Earl of, 17–18

identification: technologies of. *See* badges
"identity," 78
incorporation: racial difference as, 94, 97–100, 125, 174, 186, 238 n. 71; of servants into masters'/mistresses' bodies, 115, 118, 120, 122
indebtedness. *See* debt; slavery: and indebtedness
indentured service/servitude, 2, 64, 130, 132–34, 150, 153, 157–58, 167–70, 209–11, 244 nn. 9, 12, 247 nn. 38, 43, 249 n. 57; contracts of, 11, 91, 133, 140–51, 153, 170, 190–96, 246 n. 24, 247 n. 37, 257 n. 78. *See also* apprenticeship: indentures; poor indentures
information: known by servants of their masters, 92, 102–3, 137, 118

Ingelend, Thomas: *The Disobedient Child*, 56
inheritance, 100, 255 n. 52; in *Volpone*, 101–2. *See also* heirs; heredity/hereditability
"inkface" (Grier), 129, 187
The Instructive Alphabet, 212
interracial intimacy, 124. *See also* miscegenation
Irish people, 140, 150, 244 n. 12

Jablonski, Steven, 250 n. 79
Jackson, Thomas, 61–64, 72, 174–75, 222 n. 12, 226 n. 46, 229 n. 76, 252 n. 12
Jacob, 97
James VI and I, 21, 23, 25
Jewish people/Jewishness, 20, 26, 28, 218 n. 33, 37, 219 n. 46
Johnston, David Claypoole: *A Proslavery Incantation Scene. Or Shakspeare Improved*, 211 (fig.), 212
joint stock companies, 3, 132
Jones, Ann Rosalind, 238 n. 72
Jones, Hugh: *The Present State of Virginia*, 150, 248 n. 48
Jonson, Ben, 42; *The Case Is Altered*, 32, 34–35; *Volpone*, 94, 101–4, 107, 235 n. 37
Josselin, Ralph, 220 n. 73

Kahn, Victoria, 183, 185–86
Kehoe, Dennis, 223 n. 21
Kendrick, Matthew, 226 n. 48
Kersey, John: *A New English Dictionary*, 258 n. 5
Kichin, Nicholas, 142 (fig.)
kidnapping, 3, 63, 70–71, 226 n. 48. *See also* "Barbadosing"; captivity: narratives; spiriting
"kids," 150
King, Henry: "Reply," 99–100, 129, 234 n. 19. *See also* Rainolds, Henry: "A Black-Moor Maid wooing a Fair Boy"
King's Servants, 23
kinship, 52, 61, 81, 94, 119, 130, 159, 166, 170, 206–7. *See also* family
"knave," 83
Kopelson, Heather Miyano, 256 n. 61
Kyffin, Maurice: translation of *Andria*, 182, 185, 224 n. 26

labor, 8, 74, 83, 133, 194, 213 n. 5, 244 n. 12, 256 n. 67; Atlantic indentured, 131–34, 137;

black, 207–9; in *The Changeling*, 108–9, 113; child, 64, 66, 226 n. 48; domestic—problems, 86–87, 103, 114–15, 118; and livery, 18, 22, 26–27, 36–37, 39–40; in Milton, 153–59, 165–66, 168–69; in *The Tempest*, 186, 187, 255 n. 57
Ladies' Society for Promoting the Early Education of Negro Children, 209
land, 131–32, 168–69, 249 n. 62
Latin, 10–11, 49–53, 77–80, 222 n. 8, 223 n. 20, 228 n. 59, 231 n. 103
law, 189, 190, 195–96; against slavery in England, 1, 3–4, 8, 91, 213 n. 2. *See also* debt: bondage; vagrancy laws
legal fictions, 10, 18, 21, 23, 41, 88, 95, 151, 159, 216 n. 5
legibility, 6, 17–19, 40–41, 43, 44, 48, 123, 127–30, 214 n. 14
leisure: of servants, 114
Le Tourneur, Pierre: translation of *Othello*, 87
A Letter sent by the Maydens of London, 94, 113–15, 118–20, 238 nn. 68–72
letters of servant supplicants, 115–18
liberaliter, 12, 180–82, 201
libertas, 181–82
libertus/a (freed slave), 10, 12, 171–72, 175–77, 180–81, 189, 201, 252 n. 18. *See also* freedmen
liberty. *See* freedom
Ligon, Richard: *A True & Exact History Of the Island of Barbados*, 204
Lilburne, John, 1
Lily, William: *A Short Introduction of Grammar*, 50, 60, 68
lineage, 88, 101–2, 123, 125, 159–62, 166–68, 234 n. 16, 235 n. 28
literacy, 145, 209, 212, 246 n. 22, 247 n. 37
Little, Arthur L., Jr., 231 n. 107, 241 n. 90
livery, 14–22, 45, 47–48, 62–63, 89, 91, 134, 138, 145, 221 nn. 79, 4; and actors, 21, 23–25, 41–42, 217 nn. 19, 25, 218 n. 28; definition and etymology of, 10, 20–21, 38, 217 n. 11, 219 n. 56, 245 n. 20; and economics, 25–28, 32–43, 110, 113, 115, 192, 220 n. 73; and legibility, 7, 19, 28–31, 33–36, 38, 40–44; and race, 43–44. *See also* badges; blue coats; clothing: cast; livery companies
livery companies, 21–22, 41–42, 221 n. 4
London, 21–25, 42, 47, 63–64, 87, 95, 114, 140; outside of, 21, 23–25

Loomba, Ania, 187–88
loyalty, 59, 72, 173, 180, 207

MacDonald, Joyce Green, 130
MacIntyre, Jean, 219 n. 54
MacLean, Sally-Beth, 23
McMillin, Scott, 23
macula servitutis, 172, 177–81, 187–90, 196, 251 n. 4, 252 n. 18, 253 n. 31. *See also* stain of slavery
magister, 11, 53, 57, 60, 61, 88, 149, 171, 173, 180, 185, 204. *See also* schoolmasters
mancipatio, 12, 54, 133, 188–89, 223 n. 21, 255 nn. 55, 57
mancipium/a, 54, 64, 73, 75, 86, 133, 147, 150, 172, 188–89, 223 n. 21, 226 n. 46, 255 n. 57
manumission, 3, 12, 51, 60, 64, 68, 73, 171–73, 175–84, 186–96, 191–203, 207–11, 239 n. 80, 252 nn. 18, 21, 258 n. 90. *See also* redemption
March, John, 147
Markham, Gervase: *A Health to the Gentlemanly profession of Seruingmen*, 37, 40, 220 n. 58, 221 n. 75
marriage, 120–22, 126, 128, 130, 166, 235 n. 28, 240 n. 87
masterlessness, 4–5, 8, 172, 175, 188, 251 n. 5
Mauss, Marcel, 112–13, 118, 122, 237 n. 63
Mehdizadeh, Nedda, 225 n. 35
memory, 15, 35, 39, 116–18, 120, 177–80, 183–84, 239 n. 80, 252 nn. 19, 24; and Derridean gift, 122, 239 n. 76
Mertes, Kate, 40
Middleton, Thomas, and William Rowley: *The Changeling*, 94, 108–13, 118, 119, 122, 237 n. 60, 238 n. 64
Milton, John, 250 n. 79, 252 n. 11; *Paradise Lost*, 12, 122, 133–34, 153–70, 249 n. 62, 250 n. 79; Sonnet 19, 153–55, 158, 169
Miola, Robert S., 214 n. 8
miscegenation, 98–99, 101, 123, 125–27, 214 n. 14, 235 n. 24, 237 n. 60, 241 n. 90, 248 n. 54, 259 n. 15
"Moor," 80–81, 85, 93
Moore, Barbary, 87
Morgan, Edmund S., 246 n. 23
Morgan, Jennifer L., 231 n. 103, 248 n. 54

Moryson, Fynes, 25
mothers, 60, 226 n. 48, 259 n. 15
Mouritsen, Henrik, 172, 251 n. 4
Mudge, Hugh, 69–70
Muldrew, Craig, 27–28
Mulleneux, Richard, 89–91; his "negro boy," 91–92, 130
Munday, Anthony, 42
Muñoz, José Esteban, 249 n. 70
mutuality, 62, 94, 107, 115, 137, 144–47, 153, 171, 192, 198–99

names/naming, 87, 93, 194, 257 n. 83
Nashe, Thomas: *Haue with you to Saffron-walden*, 32–36
natality, 9, 122, 127–30, 151, 153, 158–69, 216 n. 24, 247 n. 43; and anti-natalism, 12, 159–60, 163–67, 169, 249 nn. 70–71. *See also* childbirth
Native American people. *See* Amerindian people
nativity, 107, 108, 123, 128–30
Ndiaye, Noémie, 58
Neill, Michael, 87, 251 n. 10
Newman, Simon P., 244 n. 12
Newman, Thomas: translation of *Andria*, 182, 224 n. 23; translation of *Eunuchus*, 82, 85, 103–4, 230 n. 85, 234 n. 19
New World, 2, 157, 168, 190, 195, 249 n. 57. *See also* America; Atlantic World
niger, 78
Norton, Joel, 139–40, 245 n. 22
Norton, Thomas, 144
nostalgia, 1, 15, 20, 22, 27, 29, 32, 35–36, 207, 251 n. 10
Nunes, Hector, 8
nurses, 60
Nyquist, Mary, 250 n. 79, 253 n. 38

obedience, 77, 155–58, 174–75, 198; refusal of, 173, 183
obligation, 19, 72, 92, 115–17, 192, 198, 201; in *The Changeling*, 94, 109–13; economies of, 26–27, 41, 117; and freedom/manumission, 177, 180, 186, 196, 218 n. 35, 252 n. 21, 257 n. 78; material mnemonics of, 39–40, 110, 192; in *Paradise Lost*, 122, 153, 158
"observe," 104, 236 n. 39
Olusoga, David, 213 n. 4
"one-drop rule," 159, 214 n. 14

"Order to Prevent Abuses in Transporting Servants," 147, 149, 246 n. 24
Overbury, Sir Thomas (1581–1613), 20
Overbury, Sir Thomas (d. 1684): *A True and Perfect Account*, 70–73

"page," 54, 55, 66
pages, 16, 28, 241 n. 92
parasite (figure of the), 94, 100–107, 123, 223 n. 20, 235 n. 34, 236 nn. 47–48
parents, 63, 149, 160–61, 259 n. 15. *See also* fathers; mothers
parish records, 87, 95, 97
Parker, Patricia, 92–93, 218 n. 33
pawnbrokers' shops, 29–31, 35
payment, 34, 89, 115, 145, 150, 236 n. 47, 237 n. 59; to actors, 24–25, 218 n. 28; in *The Changeling*, 108–13; and livery, 16, 22, 26, 37–40, 62, 115, 138, 145, 192, 220 n. 73; and manumission, 181–82
pedagogy. *See* education; school/the schoolroom
"perfect," the, 253 n. 27
Perry family (Joan, John, and Richard), 70, 72, 228 n. 67
Petrarch, 37, 100
Phillips, Edward: *The New World of English Words*, 6
Phillips, Susan, 83
"pinch," 188, 255 n. 52
plantation novels, 259 n. 15
Plautus, 3, 54, 68, 103, 104; *Captivi*, 235 n. 34; *Menaechmi*, 129, 243 n. 104
plowmen vs. servingmen, 36–37, 220 n. 58
poor indentures, 46, 64–66, 227 n. 54
Post-Emancipation Life, 209–11, 259 nn. 28–29
Potter, Ursula, 227 n. 57
poverty, 73–74, 209. *See also* poor indentures
print, 140, 150, 187
processions, 3, 21, 47–50
property: people as, 54, 76, 91, 97, 133, 150, 181, 183, 188–89, 191, 194, 213 n. 2, 223 n. 21, 248 n. 54; white —, 100, 235 n. 26
prosthetics, 19, 43–44, 242 n. 94
proximity (racial), 93, 97–100, 234 n. 16, 236 n. 46
puer, 52–53, 55
punishment and discipline: evaded by marriage, 75, 121; of the Fall, 163, 165–66, 169; of schoolboys, 46, 55–57, 223 n. 20,

225 nn. 34, 37; of servants/slaves, 1, 5, 57, 62–63, 196, 227 n. 48, 239 n. 79, 260 n. 29; servitude as, 248 n. 48
Purdue, John, 137, 139 (fig.)

Quary, Robert, 151 (fig.)
Queen's Men, 23–25
queer readings, 121, 159, 164, 236 n. 46, 249 n. 70

race, 26, 28, 42–44, 85, 95, 97, 127–30, 163–64, 166–68, 199, 228 n. 61, 243 n. 105, 250 n. 77; -making, 6–7, 9, 12, 26, 98, 166–67, 215 nn. 17, 20, 232 n. 107, 234 n. 17, 236 n. 46. *See also* blackness; whiteness
racialized bondage/slavery, 6–7, 9, 13, 19, 44–47, 50, 67–68, 74–77, 80, 85–86, 88, 92–94, 126–30, 150, 167, 171–73, 187–88, 196–97, 214 n. 14, 244 n. 12, 248 n. 54. *See also* slavery: and race
Raines, Henry, 73–74, 243 n. 7
Rainolds, Henry: "A Black-Moor Maid wooing a Fair Boy," 98–100, 234 nn. 19–21, 242 n. 94. *See also* King, Henry: "Reply"
rape. *See* sexual exploitation
recognizances. *See* badges
recompense, 92, 108–13, 117–18, 121–22, 179, 190, 236 n. 54, 239 n. 80
redemption (from bondage/captivity), 21, 48–51, 67–68, 71, 74, 132. *See also* manumission; redemption petitions; slavery: redemption from
redemption petitions, 3, 48, 51, 68–71, 73, 74, 245 n. 12
Redman, William, 64, 246 n. 22
religion. *See* Christianity; Jewish people/Jewishness
remembrance. *See* memory
res mancipi, 54, 133, 189, 223 n. 21
retainers: restricted in number, 21 25, 27, 221 n. 75
Return of Strangers, 95, 96 (fig.), 233 n. 13
"A Riddle upon Coals," 234 n. 22
Rivers, Marcellus, 245 n. 12
Robin (enslaved child), 150, 152 (fig.)
Robinson, Ralph: translations of *Utopia*, 54
Roman slave comedies, 45, 49–50, 53, 56, 81, 100, 172, 201. *See also* Plautus; Terence
Rowley, William. *See* Middleton, Thomas, and William Rowley: *The Changeling*

Rubright, Marjorie, 234 nn. 16–17
russet coats, 36–38

Saffin, Adam, 12, 173, 190–97, 209, 256 nn. 61–62, 67, 257 nn. 75, 78
Saffin, John, 173, 190–97, 256 nn. 61–62, 67, 257 nn. 75, 78
salary. *See* payment
Sanchez, Melissa E., 251 n. 11, 254 n. 44
Sancroft, William, 69, 73
Schalkwyk, David, 236 n. 48, 240 n. 87, 251 n. 10
school/the schoolroom, 3, 7–11, 45–47, 49–58, 74–75, 77–80, 88, 198–99, 209, 222 n. 8, 224 n. 31; affinity with slaves in, 46, 49, 51–56, 60–61, 66–67, 207. *See also* education; *magister*; *puer*; punishment and discipline: of schoolboys
schoolmasters, 56–58, 60, 79, 83, 185, 225 nn. 34, 37. See also *magister*
Scottish people, 140, 244 n. 12
secretaries, 92, 118, 121–22, 236 n. 47, 239 n. 77, 240 nn. 84–85
secrets. *See* information
self-abnegation, 174–75
"servage," 224 n. 26
"servant," 54–55, 62, 183, 191, 224 n. 26
servants, 61–63, 172, 226 n. 46, 247 n. 38. *See also* black servants; English servants; white servants
service, 2, 6–8, 213 n. 5; faithful, 71–72, 137, 144–45, 153–54, 170, 172–73, 181, 190–91, 196–97, 201, 212, 251 n. 10, 256 n. 66, 258 n. 5; free, 4, 6, 10, 12, 18, 41, 97, 108–9, 112, 118, 153, 157, 170, 172, 180–84, 189, 194, 198, 199, 201; language of, 10, 54–55, 62, 66, 91–92, 94, 129, 213 n. 5, 224 n. 26, 258 n. 5; manner of, 64, 137, 180–82, 190–92, 196–97, 209; and servitude/slavery, 2, 6–8, 46, 64–68, 70, 74, 97, 167, 132–33, 147, 195, 247 n. 43, 253 n. 38; — society, 3–4, 16, 19, 49, 66, 72–73, 102; voluntary, 134, 145, 151, 153–58, 191–92; willing, 4, 9, 64, 108–9, 118–19, 137, 144–47, 153, 158, 170, 172–73, 180, 182, 196. *See also* freedom: and service/servitude; happy service/servitude/slavery; indentured service/servitude; slavery: and coarticulation with service
serviliter, 224 n. 26
"servitour," 258 n. 5

"servitude," 66, 213 n. 5, 223 n. 21, 244 n. 12, 258 nn. 87, 5
servolus, 55
servus/i, 4, 9, 51–55, 61–62, 66, 75, 86, 88, 147, 180, 199, 222 n. 12, 224 n. 26, 226 n. 46
Sewall, Samuel, 194, 196, 256 n. 61
sexual exploitation, 75–77, 108–13, 124–27, 162, 241 n. 90, 242 n. 96, 257 n. 75, 259 n. 15
shadows, 98–99, 126, 234 n. 20, 242 n. 94
Shakespeare, William, 42, 222 n. 8; *The Comedy of Errors*, 94, 129, 130, 243 n. 104; *Hamlet*, 34; *King Lear*, 27, 173–75, 183, 251 n. 10; *Love's Labor's Lost*, 37; *Macbeth*, 158–59, 212; *The Merchant of Venice*, 25–28, 36, 41, 43–44, 218 nn. 33, 37; *A Midsummer Night's Dream*, 94, 128–30; *Othello*, 67–68, 87–88, 92, 103–7, 124, 232 n. 120, 236 n. 48; *Pericles*: Marina, 76–77; the sonnets, 100; *The Taming of the Shrew*, 50–51, 68; *The Tempest*, 12, 56, 172, 178–90, 193, 196, 252 nn. 22–24, 254 nn. 39, 43, 255 nn. 55, 57; *Titus Andronicus*, 93, 124; *Twelfth Night*, 94, 119–23, 237 n. 56, 240 nn. 83–85, 87
Shapiro, James, 26
Shaw, Jenny, 245 n. 12
Shore, Daniel, 250 n. 79
"slave," 54–55, 66, 108, 126, 183, 191, 193, 242 n. 94
slave literature, 12, 184, 203–11, 259 n. 15. *See also* captivity: narratives; Plautus; Roman slave comedies; Terence
slavery: and bound labor, 244–45 n. 12, 248 n. 48; and (English) captivity, 45–48, 58, 68–74, 88, 131–32, 229 n. 78; and bodily and somatic markers, 6, 9, 19, 42–44, 83, 85–86, 127–30, 168, 171–72, 187, 198–99, 214 n. 14, 251 n. 4, 242 n. 95; and children, 8–9, 52–53, 55, 60–61, 77, 88, 128–30, 150–51, 152 (fig.), 159–60, 166–70, 198–99, 203–11, 226 n. 44, 226–27 n. 48; and coarticulation with service, 8, 70, 74, 132–33, 183, 198, 213 n. 5, 238 n. 68, 247 n. 43; as constitutive of early modern England, 2, 48–49, 58, 67–68, 77, 83, 88, 91–92, 95, 97; as constitutive of Englishness/English subjects, 6, 11, 58, 67–68, 73–74, 94, 131–32, 213 n. 4, 214 n. 6, 228 n. 62; on the early modern stage, 123–30; and emancipation, 190–94, 209–11; of English subjects, 68–70, 77, 131;
and family, 6, 8–9, 11, 12, 86–89, 91–92, 123–30, 159–60, 166–70, 188–89, 198–99, 204–7, 229 n. 67, 248 n. 54, 256 n. 61; futures of, 9, 12–13, 88, 125, 127–30, 134, 159–60, 166–70, 188–89, 198–99, 212; genealogies of, 8–9, 13, 212; and indebtedness, 173, 177–78, 196, 252 n. 21; languages of, 49, 51, 54–55, 66–67, 77–83, 86, 92, 133, 171–72, 175, 189, 222 n. 12, 226 n. 46, 241 n. 92; legal status of in England, 1–2, 4–6, 8, 213 n. 2, 214 n. 10, 226–27 n. 48, 231 n. 103; and manumission, 171–72, 189; narratives of, 67, 70–72, 86, 107, 259 n. 15; pervasiveness of, 3, 47, 49, 67–68, 88, 198; and pedagogy, 11, 49, 51–54, 77–81, 88, 198, 258 n. 5; and performance, 49, 77, 123–30; and race, 6, 7, 47, 50, 67–68, 77–81, 83, 85–86, 93–95, 97, 123–30, 166–73, 187–89, 196–99, 203–11, 214 n. 14, 215 nn. 17, 20, 228 n. 62, 231–32 n. 107, 241 n. 90, 248 n. 54, 256 n. 61, 242 n. 95; redemption from, 67–71, 73–74, 107; and re-enslavement, 177–81, 188–89; Roman, 9–10, 12, 49, 51, 54, 74–77, 81–86, 171–72, 175–78, 187–89, 199–203, 222 n.12, 231 n. 103; in the schoolroom, 3, 11, 45–49, 51–54, 77, 88, 93–94, 198–99; and the transatlantic/Atlantic world, 12–13, 89, 91, 131–32, 150–51, 190–94, 198–212, 231 n. 103, 248 n. 54; ventriloquizing of, 51–54, 77, 86, 123–30; and whiteness, 67–68, 86, 124–25, 127, 206, 207, 209, 214 n. 14, 228 n. 62. *See also* Africans: enslaved; apprenticeship: post-emancipation; captives; captivity; children: and heredity/futures of slavery; commodification (of bodies/human life); futures: of slavery; happy service/servitude/slavery; indentured service/servitude; racialized bondage/slavery; service: and servitude/slavery; slave trade; stain of slavery
Slavery Abolition Act (1833), 2, 209
slave trade, 2, 3, 8, 46, 58, 67, 77, 82, 86, 91, 150, 152 (fig.), 182, 213 n. 4, 215 n. 20, 227 n. 58, 228 n. 59
Slights, Camille, 228 n. 59, 240 n. 87
Smith, Ian, 19, 26, 43–44, 215 n. 17, 218 n. 37, 232 n. 107
Smith v. Browne and Cooper, 213 n. 2
Smyth, Edmond, 247 n. 30

Index

Somerset v. Stewart, 213 n. 2
speech, 174, 181, 184, 185, 207; lack of, 75, 230 n. 84
Spencer, Thomas, 136, 138 (fig.)
Spillers, Hortense J., 257 n. 83
spiriting, 8, 132–33, 147, 157, 246 n. 24
stain of slavery, 9, 47, 68, 86, 97, 127, 130, 132, 168, 171–73, 197, 198. See also *macula servitutis*
Stepney, William: *The Spanish Schoolemaster*, 251 n. 3
Stevens, Andrea, 240 n. 90
stewards, 54, 72, 108, 119, 240 n. 81
strangeness/strangers, 9, 44, 49, 52, 71–72, 87, 95, 103, 107; the stranger within, 92, 94, 100, 107, 115, 239 n. 77. See also *Return of Strangers*
Strier, Richard, 173
succession, 9, 101–3, 134, 159, 161, 170, 206. See also heredity/heritability
sugar production, 207–10
Sullivan, Paul, 53, 223 n. 20
sumptuary laws, 25

Tagg, Tommy: "The Story of Inkle and Yarico," 203–4, 205 (fig.)
Talman, Ebenezer, 139–40, 245 n. 22
tattoo. *See* "inkface"
Teague, Pentecost, 151 (fig.)
Teramura, Misha, 222 n. 8
Terence, 3, 46, 49, 54, 66, 68, 88, 103, 185, 199, 203, 222 n. 8, 223 n. 20, 227 n. 56; *Andria*, 52–55, 149, 171, 175–78, 180–83, 199–201, 204, 224 nn. 23, 26, 230 n. 84, 252 nn. 19, 22; *Eunuchus*, 50–51, 74–77, 81–86, 103–7, 126, 128, 223 n. 19, 230 nn. 84–85, 88, 231 nn. 98, 103, 242 n. 96
Terry, Elizabeth and Abraham, 69–70
theater companies. *See* actors
theater, 10, 43, 235 n. 24. *See also* actors
Thomas, Thomas: *Dictionarium Linguae Latinae et Anglicanae*, 103, 171, 232 n. 111, 251 nn. 3, 4
Thompson, Ayanna, 241 n. 90
translation, 11, 46, 47, 49, 54–55, 66, 80–82, 85, 182
Turke, John, 135
Turner, William, 143 (fig.), 144
Tycko, Sonia, 246 n. 24

Udall, Nicholas, 223 n. 20, 252 n. 19
Ungerer, Gustav, 58, 215 n. 20, 227 n. 58

"vagabond," 126, 242 n. 95
vagrancy laws, 21, 24, 42, 217 n. 21; Vagrancy Act (1547), 4–7, 42, 66, 214 n. 10, 226 n. 48, 242 n. 95, 251 n. 5
vagrants, 19, 244 n. 12
Vaughan, Virginia Mason, 183, 228 n. 59
vendibility, 5, 37, 133, 150, 176, 181, 244 n. 9, 247 n. 38
Véron, John: *A Dictionary in Latine and English*, 51–52, 77–78, 79 (fig.), 181, 224 n. 26, 230 n. 90
Vitkus, Daniel J., 230 n. 88, 254 n. 39
Voluntary Human Extinction Movement, 249 n. 71

W., W., 243 n. 104
Waddington, Ralph, 51–52, 77
wages. *See* payment
Wareing, John, 247 n. 38
Warner, William, 243 n. 104
Webbe, Joseph: translation of *Andria*, 52–53, 55; translation of *Eunuchus*, 76, 82
Webbe, William, 243 n. 104
Weissbourd, Emily, 58, 215 n. 20, 227 n. 58, 228 n. 59, 231 n. 102
"wench," 54, 76, 127; "blackamore —," 82, 86, 98–99, 127, 234 n. 19, 236 n. 46
Westminster Tournament Roll, 89, 90 (fig.), 92–93, 95, 233 nn. 2–3
Wheatley, Phillis, 258 n. 6; "To Maecenas," 203
whiteness, 86, 92–94, 98, 125, 214 n. 14, 231 n. 107, 234 n. 19, 235 nn. 24, 26, 241 nn. 90–91; language of, 78–80, 92. *See also* blackness: incorporated/inscribed in white body; slavery: and whiteness
white servants, 150, 248 n. 48, 256 n. 61. *See also* English servants
white supremacy, 100, 198, 251 n. 10
Whitney, Geffrey: *A Choice of Emblemes*, 81 (fig.)
Wilkins, John: *An Essay Towards a Real Character*, 231 n. 96
Williams, James, 259 n. 29
Williams, John, 14–15, 216 n. 1

Williams, Raymond, 238 n. 70
Wilson, Emily, 228 n. 61
Wilson, Luke, 158–59, 235 n. 25
Winwood, Ralph, 73
Witmore, Michael, 226 n. 48

work. *See* labor
Worster, John, 146 (fig.)
Wylbram, Mary, 94, 115–17, 118, 119, 122

"yoke," 166

ACKNOWLEDGMENTS

This book, at its core, is about genealogies: the ones we know, the ones we must excavate, the ones that elide our grasp. So many years in the making, this book is indebted to a great many people and institutions, to networks of community and friendship without which this project would not have been possible at any stage, and to filiations and genealogies I am thrilled to finally be able to trace and acknowledge here. My thanks must first go to Peter Stallybrass, and to Zachary Lesser and David Wallace. I will always be immensely grateful for their feedback, support, and extraordinary generosity. Penn's English Department was a formative intellectual space, and I was fortunate to learn from the work and pedagogy of Heather Love, Michael Gamer, Suvir Kaul, Ania Loomba, Margreta de Grazia, Cary Mazer, Emily Steiner, Emily Wilson, and the participants and speakers of the Med-Ren seminar.

I was lucky to spend my first postdoctoral year in an extraordinarily welcoming and supportive intellectual community. The English department at Vanderbilt University took unusual care to mentor and nurture its postdoctoral and visiting faculty, and I am particularly grateful to Leah Marcus, Lynn Enterline, Jay Clayton, Mark Schoenfield, Janis May, Donna Caplan, Rebecca Chapman, Bethany Schneider, and Jane Wanninger for such a happy year in Nashville. Moving to Hawai'i for my first tenure-track position, at the University of Hawai'i at Mānoa, was an exhilarating intellectual and personal adventure, and I am indebted to my colleagues in the English Department and beyond who provided such a generous, exciting, and congenial place to think, learn, teach, and work: Frederika Bain, Ned Bertz, Kate Beutner, Steve Canham, Cindy Franklin, Candace Fujikane, Lisa King, Greta LaFleur, Chuck Lawrence, Laura Lyons, Brandy Nālani McDougall, Elizabeth McCutcheon, Gayle Nagasako, Cheryl Naruse, Rajam Raghunathan, Matthew Romaniello, Prasad Santhanam, Ayu Saraswati, S. Shankar, Valerie Wayne, and John Zuern. I am especially grateful to Laura Lyons and Valerie Wayne for their extraordinary intellectual generosity, friendship, and mentorship, to Chuck Lawrence for the Junior Faculty Seminar he so generously convened, and to the participants of the Early Modern Colloquium for their fellowship and scholarly conversation.

Moving to George Mason University in 2014, I was once again fortunate to join an extremely collegial and intellectually vibrant department. Tamara Harvey, Teresa Michals, and Stefan Wheelock offered invaluable feedback on portions of the project; with astonishing generosity, Eric Eisner read and provided comments on an earlier, incomplete version of the manuscript. Although Erika Lin left GMU shortly after I arrived, she has remained a colleague and friend ever since, and I am so very grateful for her advice, support, and kindness. I also wish to thank Denise Albanese, Jackie Burek, Samaine Lockwood, Michael Malouf, Robert Matz, Kristin Samuelian, Jessica Scarlata, and Debra Lattanzi Shutika.

My new colleagues in the English Department at the University of Toronto have already made it come to seem like home and have provided invaluable support as the book entered its final stages. I am especially grateful to my department chairs, Katherine Larson, Neil ten Kortenaar, and Paul Stevens, to Vice-Dean Maydianne Andrade, and to my official "department mentors," Mary Nyquist and Karina Vernon, for their unwavering support of junior faculty. I feel deeply fortunate to have the opportunity to think with, work closely alongside, and learn from so many extraordinary colleagues, and am especially grateful to Tania Aguila-Way, Kara Gaston, Marlene Goldman, Jeremy Lopez, Lynne Magnusson, Rijuta Mehta, Sonja Nikkila, SJ Sindu, Simon Stern, Misha Teramura, and Tamara Walker for their advice, conversation, and collaboration. In the final stages of revision, Liza Blake read and offered comments on the entire manuscript, allowing me to—finally—let it go. I am extraordinarily lucky to count Liza, along with Caylen Heckel, Avery Slater, Anna Thomas, and Katherine Schaap Williams, as dear friends as well as sterling colleagues and intellectual interlocutors. Finally, I deeply appreciate the kindness and administrative wizardry of Arthus Bihis, Susan Calanza, Gail Naraine, Ann-Marie Scott, and Banu Subramanian.

This project would not have been possible without the support of institutions and agencies which allowed precious time to think, write, reframe, and reimagine the project in addition to providing access to archives and materials and to invaluable intellectual communities. An ACLS/Mellon Dissertation Completion Fellowship supported the earliest version of this project; a few years later, a Barbara Thom Postdoctoral Fellowship allowed me to spend a transformative year in the beautiful environs of the Huntington Library, where I started to see, for the first time, what this book was truly about. I am indebted to Steve Hindle for his support and guidance and his sustaining belief in this project. I am also truly grateful to the amazing staff of the Huntington Library, especially Juan Gomez and Catherine Wehrey-Miller, and to an exceptionally generous cohort of fellows and researchers who helped me clarify the book's arguments, imparted much-needed wisdom, and provided welcome respite from work over meals and coffee, walks in the garden, and weekly yoga sessions. For their warmth, generosity, and fellowship, I particularly wish to thank Susan Barbour, Dympna Callaghan, Matthew Fisher, Catherine Franklin, Adria Imada, Susan Juster, Ann Little, Carla Mazzio, Marjorie Rubright, Jessica Rosenberg, and Kathleen Wilson.

A few years after that idyllic sojourn in San Marino, I was exceptionally fortunate to receive a Mellon Long-Term Fellowship at the Folger Shakespeare Library, where the book was revised anew. That time and support was, again, invaluable, and I am truly grateful to Caroline Duroselle-Melish, Amanda Herbert, Kathleen Lynch, Owen Williams, Michael Witmore, and the extraordinary Reading Room staff—including Meghan Carafano, Rachel Dankert, LuEllen DeHaven, Rosalind Larry, Camille Seerattan, and Abbie Weinberg—for their expert guidance and generative stewardship during that year. Another brilliant and generous group of fellow fellows and researchers—including James Bromley, Surekha Davies, Stephanie Koscak, Kat Lecky, Nedda Mehdizadeh, Nick Popper, Nigel Smith, Jessica Wolfe, and Julianne Werlin—comprised an exceptional community to think with and learn from. I will be forever indebted to Kat Lecky, who, at a crucial moment, and with extraordinary generosity and kindness, read and commented on the entire manuscript.

Several fellowships and grants supported travel to libraries and archives which shaped this project, its questions, and its contours in various and innumerable ways. A one-month Keck Foundation Fellowship at the Huntington Library and a Short-Term Fellowship at the Folger Shakespeare Library provided the foundations for later, year-long residencies, and I am very grateful to the Huntington and Folger Libraries for this support. A one-month Charles Montgomery Gray fellowship at the Newberry Library began my inquiry into the American afterlives of the early modern British texts I was exploring; a year later, a Paul W. McQuillen/Norman Fiering fellowship at the John Carter Brown Library and a Lapides Fellowship at the American Antiquarian Society provided an invaluable opportunity to deepen this investigation further and to embark on the generative and challenging terrain of juvenile literature addressing slavery. A Paul Oscar Kristeller Grant from the Renaissance Society of America allowed me to undertake invaluable archival research at the

Bodleian Library, as did a Visiting Scholarship at St. Johns College, Oxford, two years later. Summer Research Funding as well as a Faculty Research and Development Award from George Mason University supported work at the British Library, and I am deeply grateful to the American Philosophical Society for the Franklin Research Grant which enabled me to complete archival research at the National Archives (UK), the London Metropolitan Archives, and the Cambridge University Library. Finally, a Visiting Fellowship at the Gilder Lehrman Center for Slavery, Resistance, and Abolition at Yale University allowed me to explore the Special Collections of the Beinecke Library and provided an invaluable opportunity to place my work in conversation with longer histories of slavery. I am immeasurably grateful to the curators, archivists, and staff of these several institutions for their guidance through the collections, their help in accessing materials and more recently images, and their advice and feedback regarding various aspects of the project. My thanks are due in particular to Valerie Andrews, David Blight, Paul Erickson, Daniel Greene, Kimberly Nusco, Neil Safier, Thomas Thurston, Ken Ward, and Michelle Zacks.

Portions of this project were presented at the Stony Brook University Humanities Institute Symposium on "Beyond Equiano: Varieties of Blackness in the Atlantic, Pacific, and Indian Ocean Worlds, 1500–1833"; the Seventeenth-Century English Literature Colloquium at Georgetown University; George Washington University; the Early Modern Colloquium at Columbia University's English Department and the Columbia Shakespeare Seminar; the first RaceB4Race symposium at the Arizona Center for Medieval and Renaissance Studies; the Folger Symposium on "Political Personhood in the Early Modern British World Before 1800"; the Scholarly Sustenance series at the Huntington Library; and the Marshall Grossman Lecture Series at the University of Maryland. I am very grateful to the organizers of those events for inviting me to share my work, and to the audiences for their thoughtful feedback. Numerous seminar participants, co-panelists, and audience members at meetings of the Shakespeare Association of America, the Renaissance Society of America, the Modern Language Association, and the British Shakespeare Association provided a congenial and exciting environment for these ideas to grow and develop. An earlier version of Chapter 1 was published as "Livery, Liberty, and Legal Fictions" in *English Literary Renaissance* 42.3 (2012): 365–90, and a few pages in Chapters 2 and 3 first appeared in *Shakespeare Quarterly* 67.1 (2016): 14–29 in "'More Than Kin, Less Than Kind': Similitude, Strangeness, and Early Modern English Homonationalisms." I am grateful to the editors and publishers of these essays for permission to reproduce that work here. A few paragraphs from Chapter 3 appeared in earlier form in "'I Had Peopled Else': Shakespeare's Queer Natalities and the Reproduction of Race" in *Queering Childhood in Early Modern English Drama and Culture*, ed. Jennifer Higginbotham and Mark Albert Johnston (New York: Palgrave Macmillan, 2018); this material is reproduced by permission of Palgrave Macmillan. I am also grateful for the opportunity to share some earlier work on indentures on the Folger Shakespeare Library *Collation* blog, in "Bound to Serve: Apprenticeship Indentures at the Folger" (5 Jan. 2018).

I owe a debt of gratitude to colleagues and friends who have read portions of this work, thought with me about the questions at its center, and offered sterling guidance, wisdom, and support as we navigate the field together. In particular, I must thank Kim Coles, who has read the entire manuscript and offered invaluable suggestions and support; and Daniel Shore, who read and offered insightful comments on portions of this work and from whose conversation I learn so much (especially over dog walks). I am immensely grateful for the intellectual collaboration, feedback, and friendship of Marissa Greenberg, Ross Knecht, and Bénédicte Miyamoto. Jane Degenhardt, Marissa Greenberg, and Elizabeth Williamson's writing group and Wendy Beth Hyman's accountability group of early modernists have offered immeasurable support and much-needed wisdom, and I am also grateful to the members of the latter: Claire Bourne, Brooke Conti, Alice Dailey, Lara Dodds, Penelope Geng, Marissa Greenberg, Kim Hedlin, Jessie Hock, and Dianne Mitchell. I also want to thank Ronda Arab, Abdulhamit Arvas, Amanda Bailey, Piers Brown, Julie Crawford, Derek Dunne, Stephanie Elsky, Ari Friedlander, Colby Gordon, Musa Gurnis, Jennifer Higginbotham, Miriam Jacobson, Jeff Knight, Lucy Munro, Melissa Sanchez, Katie Vomero Santos, Debapriya Sarkar, Christine Varnado, and Thomas Ward for their vital insights and stimulating conversation over the years (in some cases, over several years). Two Folger seminars were central to this project and to ongoing work: a seminar on "Gender, Race, and Early Modern Studies," led by Ayanna Thompson and Kim Coles; and one on "Finance, Race, and Gender in the Early Modern Atlantic World," led by Jennifer Morgan. I am indebted to the organizers of both these yearlong seminars for the eye-opening and urgent conversations they created, and to the participants of the former seminar, in particular, for reading and offering comments on an earlier version of Chapter 5.

This book would not be possible without the astonishing, brilliant, and inspiring community of scholars working on premodern critical race studies and RaceB4Race, founded by Ayanna Thompson. My thanks must first go to Kim F. Hall and Ayanna Thompson, without whose mentorship and support this book—and this work—would not exist. Their scholarly work and professional efforts, along with those of Peter Erickson, Margo Hendricks, Imtiaz Habib, Arthur L. Little, Jr., Joyce MacDonald, and Ian Smith, have made this field itself possible. I also wish to register my deep debt of gratitude to colleagues and friends in PCRS and RaceB4Race, and on the RaceB4Race Board, including, in addition to those mentioned earlier, Dennis Britton, David Sterling Brown, Seeta Chaganti, Vanessa Corredera, Ambereen Dadabhoy, Ruben Espinosa, Jonathan Hsy, Mira Kafantaris, Farah Karim-Cooper, Dorothy Kim, Carol Meija LaPerle, Kirsten Mendoza, Leah Newsom, Elisa Oh, Shokoofeh Rajabzadeh, Scott Manning Stevens, Carla María Thomas, Emily Weissbourd, Geoff Way, and Cord Whitaker. I am especially grateful for the sustaining community and camaraderie of Brandi Adams, Patricia Akhimie, Miles Grier, Noémie Ndiaye, and Lehua Yim.

I can think of no better home for this book than Penn Press, and am honored that it appears in the RaceB4Race: Critical Race Studies of the Premodern Series. I am deeply grateful to Jerry Singerman for his faith in the project and for his expert stewardship of the book, and to the series editors, Geraldine Heng and Ayanna Thompson, for making this work possible. I am humbled by the care, attention, and generosity of the (no-longer-anonymous) reviewers of the book, Lynn Enterline and Rebecca Lemon. Their reading of the manuscript and thorough, and thoroughly *right*, suggestions for revision helped me refine my arguments and made this a much better book. I am also deeply grateful to Melanie Simoes Santos, Una Creedon-Carey, Puck Fletcher, and Amena Ahmed for their truly invaluable help in finalizing the manuscript, and to Zoe Kovacs, Noreen O'Connor-Abel, and all the editorial and production staff at Penn Press. In the very final stages of this work, Brandi Adams, Liza Blake (again!), and Katherine Schaap Williams each read part or all of the manuscript with care, generosity, and brilliance, and Caylen Heckel gave me the gift of turning it into a book. I cannot thank them enough.

This book is about genealogy, but it is also about family, its fictions and its fabrics—various, interbraided, sometimes surprising. Over the many years this book has taken shape, the support of my "aunt" Ranu Basu has meant the world, and I am very grateful to her, Anupam Basu, Alo Basu, and Siddhartan Govindaswamy; I also wish to thank my parents. My wonderful mother-in-law, Susan Lancaster, was a model of care and kindness, and she lit up every room. She is deeply missed. She, along with Johnny, Lauren, Ray, Geri,

Cynthia, Mike, Chester, Ferdinand, Gus, Captain, Sasha, and Bruce, and the entire extended family, provided a network of human, canine, and feline support I cherish. I shall always appreciate the warmth and kindness of Rick Hashagen and Barbara Thompson. I am also grateful for my sister Oormi, who—although we have always been separated by a decade and oceans—is always there, and for the memory of my late brother, Arnab Chakravarty. Dear friends have sustained me over many, many, many years, and I am very grateful to Flora Esterly, Leigh Goldstein, Lilith Mahmud, Sarah Mortimer, Aneeta Rattan, Jennifer Schneider, Aarthi Vadde, and Anri Yasuda.

My beloved dog Koli was with me as I read, wrote, or revised nearly every page of this book. She came into my life weeks after I submitted my dissertation, and she left it as this book was coming to a close. Her presence lingers in every word. The lessons she imparted—of joy, curiosity, exploration, love—are ones I shall strive to learn for the rest of my life. Amidst the grief of her death, we adopted our puppy Phineas, and he, too, is a wonder and a gift.

Finally, none of it would have been—none of it would *be*—possible without Jake Lancaster, who has crossed oceans and borders with me, and moved mountains. Words can't adequately convey the depth of my gratitude to him or for him, but suffice it to say: this book is for him.